O GOD OF PLAYERS

The Religion and American Culture series explores the interaction between religion and culture throughout American history. Titles examine such issues as how religion functions in particular urban contexts, how it interacts with popular culture, its role in social and political conflicts, and its impact on regional identity. Series Editor Randall Balmer is the Ann Whitney Olin Professor of American Religion and former chair of the Department of Religion at Barnard College, Columbia University.

Michael E. Staub
Torn at the Roots: The Crisis of Jewish Liberalism in Postwar America

Clyde R. Forsberg, Jr.
Equal Rites: The Book of Mormon, Masonry, Gender, and American Culture

Amy DeRogatis
Moral Geography: Maps, Missionaries, and the American Frontier

Arlene M. Sánchez Walsh
Latino Pentecostal Identity

O GOD
OF PLAYERS

THE STORY OF THE IMMACULATA MIGHTY MACS

Julie Byrne

Columbia University Press   New York

Columbia University Press
Publishers Since 1893
New York   Chichester, West Sussex

Library of Congress Cataloging-in-Publication Data
Byrne, Julie, 1968–
    O God of players : the story of the Immaculata Mighty Macs / Julie Byrne.
        p.   cm.—(Religion and American culture)
    Includes bibliographical references and index.
    ISBN 0–231–12748–0 (cloth)—ISBN 0–231–12749–9 (paper)
    1. Immaculata College—Basketball—History.   2. Immaculata Mighty Macs
(Basketball team)—History.   3. Basketball for women—Pennsylvania—
Philadelphia—History.   I. Title.   II. Religion and American culture
(New York, N.Y.)

GV885.43.I525B97 2003
796.323'63'0974811—dc

                                                                    2003043574

Columbia University Press books are printed on permanent and durable acid-free paper.
Printed in the United States of America
c 10 9 8 7 6 5 4 3 2 1
p 10 9 8 7 6 5 4 3 2 1

For
Donald Edward Byrne Jr.
and
Mary Anne Tietjen Byrne

Has it taken me this long to figure out again that the deepest, simplest subject of this hoop book is pleasure . . .

— John Edgar Wideman, *Hoop Roots*

CONTENTS

LIST OF ILLUSTRATIONS

LIST OF ABBREVIATIONS

AIAW   Association of Intercollegiate Athletics for Women

AAU   Amateur Athletic Union

CYO   Catholic Youth Organization

DGWS   Division of Girls' and Women's Sports

ICGLA   Immaculata College Gabriele Library Archives

MJBC   Monsignor John Bonner Collection

NBA   National Basketball Association

NCAA   National Collegiate Athletic Association

PAHRC   Philadelphia Archdiocese Historical Research Center

TI   *The Immaculatan*

NOTE ON NOTATION

For this book, I surveyed and interviewed more than 130 former Immaculata players and others associated with the program. I describe methodology and sources in the introduction. Here I explain my citation of these sources.

A full list of interviews, surveys, correspondence, and unpublished memoirs appears in appendix B. In the endnotes, I give the initials of the source, followed by (1) her year of graduation, (2) age, and (3) the type and date of the exchange. For the type, *int.* means I interviewed her, *ques.* means she returned my survey, *corr.* means she sent me a letter or an email, and *mem.* means she sent me an unpublished memoir. For example, when I cite *EAA46, age 72, int. 6.17.98*, it indicates that the source is EAA, identified in the text (or appendix B) as Eva Adams Atkinson. She was a member of the Immaculata Class of '46 and was seventy-two years old at the time I interviewed her on June 17, 1998.

When citing surveys, I also indicate the number of the survey question to which the player was responding. (Appendix A is a copy of the survey.) For example, *DGP56, age 62, ques. 7, 6.5.98* indicates that this source is a survey from DGP, identified in the text (or appendix B) as Dolores Giordano Prokapus. She was a member of the Immaculata Class of '56 and was sixty-two years old when I received her survey on June 5, 1998. In this citation, I am quoting from her answer to survey question 7.

For interviews with people who did not attend or graduate from Immaculata, I indicate their initials, ages, and dates.

A cross (+) after the initials indicates that this source is now a member of a religious community.

All sources quoted or cited are former Immaculata basketball players, unless otherwise indicated.

I conducted most interviews in person and some by telephone. All face-to-face interviews and several telephone interviews were tape-recorded, with permission.

Many sources allowed me to use their real names; some preferred to respond anonymously. All names used are real names, some with written permission granted to me and some as a matter of public record. Where I did not have permission to use a source's real name, I note instead her association with the team, for example, *Player '48, age 71, ques. 21, 7.10.98.* I distinguish among anonymous sources from the same year by designating them A, B, C, and so on. For example, *Player A '45, age 73, ques. 5, 5.18.98* is a different person from *Player B '45, age 74, ques. 6, 6.27.98,* but *Player B '45, age 74, ques. 6, 6.27.98* is the same person as *Player B '45, age 74, int. 7.24.98.* This applies to endnotes as well as appendix B. In a few cases where I quote what might be sensitive material, I make citations anonymous, noting simply *Player, 1950s,* for example.

PREFACE

On the last weekend in March 2000, teams from Tennessee, Penn State, Rutgers, and Connecticut arrived at Philadelphia's First Union Center to play three contests that would determine the NCAA Women's National Basketball Championship. More than just another national tournament, it was a homecoming for the women's collegiate game itself, birthed and nurtured in the city of Philadelphia. Articles and broadcasts celebrated visionary local mothers of college hoops—Pat Collins at Temple in the forties, Eleanor Snell at Ursinus in the fifties, Carol Eckman at West Chester State in the sixties, and C. Vivian Stringer at Cheyney in the seventies—whose players in turn populated the ranks of coaches throughout the country. In the First Union Center, Final Four spectators meandered in a lobby packed with photographs and memorabilia of women's game roots in Philly.

Soon after the game's invention in 1891, Philadelphia girls, both black and white, excelled in basketball. After World War II, local college programs contributed to early northeastern waves of women's basketball fever. On the white side, a great part of this regional enthusiasm originated in the intense rivalries of Philadelphia's Catholic girls' schools. And of the early college teams that benefited from the Catholic school feeders, none is more famous than the Immaculata "Mighty Macs." Winners of the first three national women's college basketball tournaments from 1972 to 1974, the Mighty Macs and coach Cathy Rush gave the U.S. game its first generation of female stars.

But long before the 1970s teams won championships, four decades of Immaculata women played basketball, day in and day out, winter and summer.

They played basketball because they were Catholic girls, and, in Philadelphia, Catholic girls could play basketball.

That is, Catholic girls were allowed to play. And Catholic girls sure enough could play.

They played basketball, they told me, because it felt good to run and jump, shoot and sweat. It made them happy to be part of the team, a select group of girls. It was fun to get on a team bus and go somewhere. It gave their prayers meaning and intensity. It thrilled them to play for raucous fans. And it was fun to win.

Remembering their playing days years later, former Immaculata team members told me stories about close games and hard practices, team masses and bus antics, losing streaks and national championships. And as they remembered stories of Immaculata basketball, they told other stories in between their words. About Catholic girls in Philadelphia. About mothers and fathers, nuns and priests who cheered them on. And about a local church whose favorite sport gave them hours and hours of their sweetest pleasure.

ACKNOWLEDGMENTS

*The spirit blows every which way, like wind: you hear the sound it
makes but you can't tell where it's coming from or where it's headed.*

—John 3:8a, Scholars Version translation

If this project conveys just a glimpse of God's hand in these
women's lives—and in my life—it fulfills its purpose.

I am grateful to the Charlotte W. Newcombe Foundation, whose generosity supported the final year of writing this project as a dissertation. I also benefited from grants from the Yale Pew Program in American Religious History, the Society for the Social Scientific Study of Religion, the Duke University Women's Studies Program, and the Duke University Graduate Program in Religion.

To the Immaculata College women whose stories gave life and breath to
this project, I owe gratitude and honor. Many basketball players and others
associated with the program filled out surveys, sent emails, and talked by
telephone. Others opened their homes to me for lengthy interviews. At Immaculata College, administrators and professors gave time, resources, and
company as I roomed and worked on campus. For the journey I took with
them—as a scholar but also as the daughter of a Catholic women's college
graduate—I keep the Immaculata community close in my heart and prayers.

My deep thanks go especially to Sister Loretta Maria Tenbusch, I.H.M.,
professor of English and archivist at Immaculata's Gabriele Library. Sister
Loretta Maria introduced me around campus, made research a pleasure, and
mailed items of interest long after I returned home. In her, the Immaculate
Heart charism of hospitality finds full expression. Other Immaculata staff
whose help made this book possible include Mag DiAngelis, Marie Moughan,
Lydia Szyjka, Carola Cifaldi, and Sister Marita David Kirsch, I.H.M.

I am also indebted to Shawn Weldon, Brent Stauffer, and the staff of the Philadelphia Archdiocese Historical Research Center at St. Charles Borromeo Seminary in Philadelphia for their cheerful assistance.

Members of the Texas Christian University Department of Religion have supported the writing of this book with readings, advice, and resources. More than that, they have welcomed and sustained me like family as I live and work far from kin.

I thank my adviser, Thomas Tweed, for embodying committed mentorship, daring scholarship, and vivid writing. His presence made graduate education a delight. In his class, I fell in love with American religion. Because he said he would use a book about Catholic women basketball players, I wrote it. And as I did, his vision and rigor changed every page. I cannot imagine having undertaken this process without him.

My committee co-chair, Elizabeth Clark, has bestowed on me her gracious and exacting support for the last fifteen years. When I took her graduate class on Augustine as a Duke sophomore in 1988, she gave me hope that someday I could do what she did. Since then, I have looked to her scholarship and leadership as my standard. I also thank dissertation readers Grant Wacker, Kenneth Surin, and Kathleen Joyce, whose intellectual commitment and personal attention shaped me and this project.

Robert Orsi and Paula Kane moderated a session entitled "Catholicism and the Body" at a 1995 Notre Dame Cushwa Center conference, the handouts for which included yearbook pictures of Catholic schoolgirl athletes. Obviously, the session stayed with me. I thank them for their example and encouragement in the study of U.S. Catholicism. Many other scholars, friends, relatives, and artists in Durham, in Chapel Hill, and across the country made their mark on these pages. I thank especially William Baker, Susan Cahn, Nahum Chandler, Roni Cohen, Katherine DuVal, Michael Eric Dyson, Thomas Ferraro, Michael Greene, Stanley Hauerwas, Paul Husbands, Willie Jennings, Robin Kelley, Laurie Maffly-Kipp, Lyn Malone, Mary McClintock-Fulkerson, Eleanor Mer, Thomas Robisheaux, Jon Rubenstein, Kathleen Rudy, Nicholas Salvatore, Christian Smith, Sister Pamela Smith, S.S.C.M., Jacqueline Spruill, Nilgün Uygun, Ross Watson Jr., John Edgar Wideman, and Ronald Witt.

I am also indebted to Wendy Lochner, my editor at Columbia, Randall Balmer, the series editor, Sarah St. Onge, the copyeditor, and Paula Durbin-Westby, the indexer, whose attention improved the book. Thank you to Wanda McGlinchey-Ryan and other journalists, from whose lively reports I gleaned information and quoted interviews.

I thank my families at St. Luke Community United Methodist Church in Dallas, Texas, and at Zion Temple United Church of Christ in Durham, especially its pastors, LaKeesha Walrond and Michael Walrond Jr. Mike Walrond is the best teacher I ever had. I know now that God kept me in Durham long enough to find my way to Sparella Street.

The scholar-friends in my writing group—Gillian Silverman, Ajantha Subramanian, Lisa Mulman, and Anne Blue-Wills—sustained me with their conversation, criticism, and enthusiasm. Meg Gandy kept me sane as we talked divine theory on long walks. Madeline McClenney-Sadler and Wilda Gafney, fellow teaching assistants at Duke Divinity School, posed to me the deepest questions about religion I ever heard. As my student assistant at TCU, Linda Moore tracked down bibliographic items. I wish to thank three who transcribed the interviews: Valena Peri Brown, Wanda Withers, and Mary Beth Conover. And I thank John Spann for a steady supply of prayers.

Best friend and sister, Michelle Morgan-Kelly was always my email lifeline to the outside world. With her husband, Andrew, she also gave me a home away from home and insider tips on Philadelphia throughout my research. When the Kellys said they liked the first chapter, my hopes for street legitimacy swelled. I thank Maimuna Mahdi, Daniel Wideman, and their daughter, Qasima, for their families' company and conversation. It was in their presence, watching ACC, WNBA, and Chicago Bulls games, that I first considered the relationship between religion and basketball.

The intellectual giants of my life are my mother, the late Mary Anne Tietjen Byrne, Trinity College Class of '63, and my father, Donald Byrne Jr. This book is dedicated to them. The intellectual companions of my life are my sisters, Clare Byrne, Mary Byrne, and Monica Byrne, and my brother, Donald Byrne III. Nothing engages me body and soul more wholly than a dinner conversation at home. No one could ask to be so blessed in this world.

Fort Worth, Texas

O GOD OF PLAYERS

PHILADELPHIA HOOP AND CATHOLIC FUN

T he big game of the 1946 season fell on a Tuesday evening, the fifth of March. As the dusky winter light faded and the hour of half past seven approached, buses and cars began to park in the vicinity of Broad Street and Montgomery Avenue in center city Philadelphia and empty toward Temple University's Conwell Hall on the corner. Bundled against the cold Pennsylvania air, Immaculata College students, nuns, priests, alumnae, brothers, sisters, parents, and miscellaneous fans pressed their way past the downtown row houses and sidewalk gawkers toward the brightly lit gym. Inside, the collective heat of a record-breaking thousand cheering bodies warmed them, and they peeled off scarves and hats.[1]

But beyond body heat, the atmosphere crackled with competitive excitement. A trio of senior guards on the Immaculata basketball team—captain Evie Adams, with Rita Haley and Pat Brennan—had waited all year for this rematch with the Temple University squad. Each season over the last three years, Temple had beaten them, but by smaller and smaller margins. This season, anticipated their campus newspaper, they were "out for blood."[2]

The underclass threesome of Betty Bissinger, her sister, Peggy, and Helen "Toddy" Kirsch played the offensive end of the court. The six starters had come from high schools all over the Archdiocese of Philadelphia to represent the "Mackies" of Immaculata, a tiny Catholic women's college about thirty miles west of the city, against their public and coeducational basketball rival Temple. All six knew the Temple Owlettes hadn't lost a game in four years,

Marianne Crawford '76 goes up in traffic at West Chester, February 1974.
ROBERT HALVEY COLLECTION OF THE PHILADELPHIA ARCHIVES AND HISTORICAL RESEARCH CENTER.

piling up thirty-one straight wins. They knew the eminent opposing coach, Pat Collins, had mentored their own young coach, Marie Schultes, who completed her physical education degree at Temple.

But the Mackies also knew they had a chance. Undefeated so far that season, they warmed up for an hour before tip-off, gathering confidence that tonight would cap their perfect season. There were no tournaments or championships for women's college basketball in 1946. An undefeated season was officially the highest achievement. But players themselves kept an unofficial tally for what they called the "Mythical City Championship." For years, the Temple sextet had been the champs. If Immaculata won tonight, they would usurp the invisible crown.[3]

Before tip-off, the two teams ran half-court drills at opposite ends of the court. Cheerleaders danced and pom-pommed in front of the bleachers. Referees conferred with scorers, shouting over the noise. Photographers readied their film and flashes. And reporters from all the city's major newspapers—the *Evening Bulletin*, the *Inquirer*, and the *Record*—settled in for a pleasant night's work. An *Inquirer* sportswriter, Dora Lurie, had already predicted in print that Immaculata's undefeated team threatened to end Temple's streak. Fans of both teams anticipated a great game.[4]

With tip-off seconds away, half the gym suddenly fell silent. Immaculata fans bowed their heads when they saw their team and coach praying together in a huddle: "O God of Players, hear our prayer," said the guards and forwards together, "to play this game and play it fair." In the stands, classmates whispered, "Please, God, please"; nuns gripped concealed rosary beads; fathers cleared their throats. In a moment, the prayers were over, the game was on, and the cheering surged.

Defense at first controlled the game, as the Temple guards broke up Immaculata's scoring plays and Immaculata's experienced senior defenders batted away Temple's shots. As both teams scored largely on free throws, the lead changed back and forth for the entire first half. In the third quarter, Betty Bissinger, Peggy Bissinger, and Toddy Kirsch found a scoring rhythm to put their squad six points ahead. But the Owlette forwards roared back, going over the heads of shorter Mackie guards to regain a one-point lead, 27–26, with five minutes to play. Then the two Bissingers scored three points with a foul shot and field goal. Temple answered with a layup. Again the Bissingers scored a free throw and field goal, and again Temple put up two. The score was 32–31, and the Owlettes had thirty seconds to make up a one-point deficit. But Immaculata had the ball and was freezing it in its backcourt. The stall almost backfired, when Temple guards chased Immaculata forwards toward the half-court line. They lost the ball. Temple grabbed it on the other side and put up four desperate attempts, the last one of which barely rimmed out of the basket. And then the final whistle blew.[5]

Immaculata players jumped in the air and collapsed on the floor. Their timekeeper, senior Betty Martin, could not stop screaming. Fans laughed, cried, and poured out of the bleachers. Toddy Kirsch—now Sister Marita David, I.H.M.—remembered her happy, stunned feeling at the bottom of a pile of bodies on Conwell's hardwood. "All I know is . . . the whole place came down on top of us on the floor, and I thought I would never get out of that crowd of people that piled on top of us," she said. "They were so excited, we were so excited." Toward midnight, when the team bus finally got back to campus, players found out that Immaculata College president Monsignor Francis Furey had declared a campuswide holiday from classes the next day to celebrate the victory.[6]

More than fifty years later, Immaculata team members remembered the first time they beat Temple as "probably the greatest game I can remember playing," as Sister Marita David put it. Even watching from the bench as a substitute player, Mary Mawhinney Puglielli '46 recalled it as "the most exciting basketball game I've seen in my life." "Little I.C. . . . played its heart out and did the impossible," she said. "It was an amazing feat."[7]

While capturing the Mythical City Championship over a storied Temple squad amazed the Immaculata players, what might be more amazing to us who hear the story more than a half-century later is that midcentury Philadelphia Catholic girls were playing basketball in the first place. In 1946, before most women ever heard they could play a sport? Catholic girls, whose church was infamous for regulating sexuality and gender roles? In Philadelphia, where Catholic leadership had the reputation of being more Roman than Rome? Giving surprising evidence in the affirmative, Immaculata's postwar city crown unearths a hidden layer of Philadelphia's Catholic community.

Looking at local phenomena and sidebar events as I am exploring Catholic women's basketball, scholars of U.S. religion have begun to nuance the conventional picture of midcentury U.S. Catholics, who purportedly lived in their own medieval world, building private schools and resisting American culture until their sudden assimilation after President John Kennedy's election and Second Vatican Council reforms. To be sure, urban working-class white Catholics lived and worshiped overwhelmingly with other white Catholics in neighborhoods centered around local parishes and schools. But as the twentieth century dawned, they also, like other urban Americans, increasingly labored, played, read, consumed, and politicked in contact and conversation with a variety of other citizens and mainstream U.S. culture. Like other Americans, Catholics both followed and disputed religious leaders who in turn spoke in multiple voices to interpret a common tradition. And like other U.S. faiths, Catholicism offered believers both mooring in the familiar and empowerment for change.[8]

Still, Catholicism was different from other U.S. faiths because of its populous numbers, diverse composition, institutional strength, separate schools, and antagonism against Protestant Christianity. And perhaps nowhere in the country was Catholic difference more striking than in Philadelphia. The Irish-dominated archdiocese inspired remark from Catholics and non-Catholics alike for its traditions of authoritarianism, conservatism, insularity, and uniformity. And for its school system. Educating 90 percent of the city's Catholic children through high school—that is, as much as 40 percent of *all* city students—the Catholic educational system bound believers one to another in mind and body, faith and practice across generations of church life.[9]

On the other hand, if Philadelphia's Catholic girls, accompanied by busloads of priests, nuns, and family members, were trooping all over the city to play basketball games in gyms full of "publics," perhaps local Catholics did venture outside neighborhood enclaves. If the Philadelphia Catholic school system nurtured the city's best female basketball players, perhaps archdiocese leadership was more progressive—or less pervasive—than we thought. If girls who played for Catholic schools suffered no censure and indeed got accolades for running, jumping, sweating, fouling, competing, and winning, maybe the faith's vision of femininity allowed for horizons previously invisible. And if some young women considered playing basketball a significant part of their Catholic upbringing, maybe midcentury Catholicism—even in Philadelphia—flowed in crosscurrents beneath surface homogeneity.

Finding Pleasure in Catholic Women's Basketball

When I first conceptualized this study, I expected to find a charged and oppositional relationship between Catholic women basketball players and their church. I was not altogether right. At a time when few women played sports, former Immaculata team members were not primarily basketball players. They were traditional Catholic young women from the working and new middle classes of Philadelphia's second- and third-generation immigrant families and grew up shaped by the social and spiritual rigors of Catholic schools and parishes. They played basketball alongside conventional obligations to family, church, and school. None of them got athletic scholarships. Their role model for femininity was the virginal and long-suffering Blessed Mother. Almost all expected to, and did, marry and rear children in the Catholic faith. Almost all remained lifelong practicing Catholics. And while in school they found reliable support in the Archdiocese of Philadelphia not only for their faith but for their game.

But if I expected basketball to disclose a site of friction between young Catholic women and their church, I was not altogether wrong, either. Listening to interviews and reading surveys, I found there was something more to Immaculata basketball than teen pastime and church approval. That "something more" was *pleasure*. At first it seemed so obvious that basketball was fun that I did not regard players' repeated enthusiasms as important. But finally it dawned on me that over the program's thirty-six years and dozens of stories, pleasure was the one common thread. I realized I had to take players' reports of fun seriously—or at least think about the deeper meanings of pleasure in Catholic women's lives. And when I started to ask players *why* basketball was so fun, I began to see athletic pleasure as a prism for the ways they both absorbed and contested their religious environment.

Basketball for girls thrived squarely within that religious environment. From at least the late twenties and thirties, some Philadelphia Catholic girls grew up on basketball. They played in their backyards with brothers and sisters and joined parochial school teams. They tried out for coveted spots on Catholic high school squads, played on playground courts, traveled with church teams, and joined city recreation center clubs. When Philadelphia priests organized chapters of the Catholic Youth Organization (CYO) in the late forties, they played for CYO teams. And if they continued their education at local Catholic women's colleges, they could play basketball there, too.

From the thirties through the seventies, Immaculata College, in rural Malvern, Pennsylvania, drew many highly skilled Philadelphia basketball players to its campus. Immaculata's nearly four hundred acres lay south of Route 30, better known as the "Main Line," the east-west path that paralleled the old Pennsylvania Railroad through Philadelphia's blue-blood neighborhoods. But near Immaculata the Main Line was just a country road cutting through villages and farmland. Situated on a hill in the middle of cow pastures and cornfields, the campus looked north over the Chester Valley. Regal oak and maple trees that changed colors and foliage with four full mid-Atlantic seasons loomed over a few granite and limestone campus buildings, all matching the Italian Renaissance style of the original Villa Maria Hall. High on top of Villa Maria's copper dome, a haloed statue of the campus patroness, the Virgin Mary, seemed to gather in her arms the whole campus and valley below. Town and traffic noises died far out in the cornfields, but leaves rustled, storms thundered, bells pealed, and students laughed.

By the time Immaculata captured the Mythical City Championship in 1946, the little college of three hundred students had already established a

Aerial view of campus in 1953 or 1954.
COURTESY OF IMMACULATA COLLEGE.

stellar basketball tradition, only a few short years after launching varsity competition in 1939. And a quarter-century after the first victory over Temple, in 1972, when the school enrolled just eight hundred students, the Immaculata team made sports history by winning the first national women's college basketball tournament ever played. Sponsored by the Association for Intercollegiate Athletics for Women (AIAW), this first national championship led to two repeat performances for the "Mighty Macs," who defended their title successfully in 1973 and 1974. Since then, the Immaculata championship teams and their coach Cathy Rush have been widely credited with revolutionizing the women's game and breaking early barriers to help make girls' hoops the wildly popular sport it is today.[10]

Immaculata players might have broken barriers for women athletes in the seventies, but they never said they were trying to change anything, much less make history. What players did say is that they had fun. Of course, different players remembered fun to different degrees. For about half the respondents, basketball was something on the side, a pleasant diversion from routine. "I looked at it as an extracurricular activity," said Epiphany Pantaleo Collins '64, "one that I would enjoy." But the other half said this fun was very important fun. A player who graduated in 1945 said she rearranged her extracurricular pursuits and changed her major twice to ensure she could make practice every afternoon. And when I asked Dolores "Dee" Cofer Cull '55 how significant basketball was in the scheme of her college life, she said, "It was the only thing. The *only* thing."[11]

Whether players got a little or a lot of enjoyment out of basketball, it was never merely fun. They talked about fun too much for it not to mean anything. "What was the driving force?" said Marian Collins Mullahy '54. "It was just fun. It was the most fun." Over and over, in interviews and on surveys, players described their participation using terms connected with pleasure: "fun," "enjoyment," "joy," "thrill," "good times," "happiness," and "excitement." "I played because I enjoyed playing," remembered a player who graduated in 1948. Similarly, a 1953 graduate recalled, "I remember it was just so much fun!" Marie Olivieri Russell '66 said the same thing. "It was fun for me," she said. "It was the one thing that I could do that I enjoyed." Often players began or concluded reminiscences with references to pleasure. Finishing a story, Dee Cofer Cull '55 summed up, "We just had a good time."[12]

Impatiently, I waved the evidence away. Of course basketball was fun, I thought to myself, but it's also analytically trivial. I pressed past them to ask questions I considered more serious. They would answer my questions and then say, as Pauline Callahan Earl '57 did, "I loved it, I loved it," or, like Lorrie Gable Finelli '78, "We just genuinely had a lot of fun, we had so much fun." After a while, I began to wonder if fun actually meant something. And then I realized that almost nobody—including me—assumed that midcentury Catholic women ever had much fun.[13]

Focusing on pleasure runs against the grain of Catholic women's history of subordination in ritual and theology, inscription in religious ideologies of gender and sexuality, implication in a Catholic "culture of suffering," and martyrdom to the patriarchal family. Focusing on pleasure also runs against the grain of other painful realities in these women's lives. Immaculata basketball players were not upper-class college girls leading charmed, pleasant lives in general. Certainly, they were more privileged than young women who wanted to go to college and could not. But many Immaculatans arrived on campus immersed in the difficulties of the working and new middle classes. Some were poor or had physical impairment. Others had caregiving responsibilities at home or struggled academically. And beyond class, there was life. Brothers and fiancés died in wars. Parents left. Sisters got pregnant. In short, former players dealt with full portions of human pain. But in that context they remembered basketball as pleasurable. I do not dispute the scope of overarching patterns in Catholic, class, and gender history. Rather, I propose that young women's experience of athletic pleasure provides a lens for noticing and exploring their everyday push and pull with their environment. Catholic women might have had little power at church, in politics, and in the marketplace. But perhaps their pleasure discloses the forms and flows of the attenuated power they did have.[14]

The term "pleasure" has been linked in the history of philosophy to notions of ultimate good and ultimate beauty, but I mean to invoke neither. For "pleasure," I use a commonsense definition: simply a person's sense of satisfying desire. Desire is also a complicated concept, but colloquially it indicates longing, whether it is socially sanctioned longing or not. In some recent philosophy, desire holds the place of human agency, that tangled assemblage of forces that constitute us, from the midst of which we move and are moved. As desiring agents, we do not necessarily resist the institutions that form us, and neither are we reducible to them. For just as we want to claim identity and belong to groups, we also long to change status and ruffle institutions. So we might experience pleasure when we harmonize with our social world, or when we thwart it, or both.

In any case, pleasure can signal an everyday politics of desire, pursued both *through* and *against* societies or organizations by ordinary people in their daily lives. Historians of subaltern groups have suggested numerous examples of pleasure as everyday politics, enacted mostly within and subtly against dominant structures: slaves singing work songs, domestic workers carrying home "leftovers," youth reinventing speech and fashion, colonials playing the empire's cricket, and drag queens forming alternative families. Understanding someone's pleasure, we are clued into both the continuity and struggle between that person and the institutions that shape her. And, as many historians of religion have shown, some of the most common structures *through* and *against* which ordinary people pursue pleasure and wield power are religious institutions. There is nothing inherently political or religious about basketball. Nor is it news to say that the sport was enjoyable for its early female devotees. But exploring the pleasures of female athletes at a Catholic college can deepen our understanding of the complex interactions between young women and their church culture.[15]

The Immaculata basketball players were certainly not unique in having fun in church-sanctioned activities. Though histories of lay Catholic women are still sparse, plenty of Philadelphia Catholic schoolgirls took delight in playing field hockey, singing in chorus, or taking yearbook photographs. Married or working, some enjoyed socializing at Tuesday night parish sodality meetings, or attending yearly retreats at Elkins Park, or making traditional holiday foods. Many loved their husbands and delighted in their children. In all these cases, fun sometimes meant the satisfaction of identity and affirmation within the Catholic community, and sometimes it meant the thrill of seeing how much mischief they could generate without attracting notice. There was nothing conflicted about such fun. Their lives, like all lives, mixed large chunks of community expectation with small fragments of personal desire in a kaleidoscope of overlapping and recombining pieces. Catholic women had fun and lived with the contradictions, more or less comfortably. But with more study, we can understand better the specific pleasures of these activities—and the intricacy of particular relationships between Catholic women and their church.[16]

In this book, I describe the consistent pleasures Immaculata basketball players over three decades said they experienced in their church-sponsored sport. Some players emphasized social pleasures, such as team identification or community enthusiasm. Some players remembered physical pleasures of the game: the exhilaration of jumping, passing, and scoring. Others recalled spiritual pleasures associated with basketball, like praying for victory in the huddle and wearing holy medals pinned to their uniforms. Still others enjoyed the new spaces and places basketball took them, both inside and outside the Catholic world. Recounting their stories, I argue that Immaculata basketball players loved the game because it offered particular social, physical, spiritual, and spatial pleasures through which they mostly accommodated and occasionally resisted the larger Catholic milieu.

Exploring Lived Religion

Scholars do not habitually analyze nonreligious activities to understand religion. We are not used to watching basketball games to shed light on Catholicism. In the last decades, scholars have increasingly turned to popular sources and lay subjects to tell the story of religion outside church walls. But we still tend to look for piety in traditionally religious phenomena, such as household devotions, missionary travels, or sacred artifacts. Even when this approach is embedded in social history, it implicitly isolates religion from the rest of life, bringing to light what people did when they practiced their faith but not the many everyday experiences that overlaid, surrounded, supported, and challenged formal observance. It is arguable that a Muslim is a Muslim not only when she prays five times a day but also when she shops for groceries. A Methodist is a Methodist not only when he works in a soup kitchen but also when he takes a cruise vacation. And a Catholic is a Catholic not only when she lights votive candles but also when she plays basketball. What—if anything—do shopping, vacations, and basketball tell scholars about religion? We don't know yet. But we know religious people do those things. Exploring everyday piety calls for attention to whole lives of faith and broad religious cultures, putting us more in touch with what has been called "lived religion": the fluid piety that always overflows official vessels.[17]

If we don't study lived religion, we risk an incomplete and inaccurate picture of American faiths, described apart from the complex and creative ways that ordinary people, deeply formed by religious institutions, also recreate and compromise their traditions. If religion changes people, so people change religion. The way people change religion seems obvious in cases of new religious movements or free-spirited seekers. But it is more difficult— and therefore particularly important—to see how people change religion in the case of traditions with highly articulated institutional structures, such as Roman Catholicism.

Thinking Subjectivity in Religious Organizations

For much of the history of Catholicism in America, the arcane Roman ecclesiology cementing and separating church and world both estranged the Protestant mainstream and sheltered U.S. Catholics. Especially in the first half of the twentieth century, American bishops, priests, and sisters worked to build a network of Catholic institutions, from churches and schools to athletic clubs and relief agencies. They hoped this church-affiliated network would help settle and insulate the millions of immigrant Catholics who arrived in northern U.S. cities from the mid-nineteenth through early twentieth century. In Philadelphia, "among the most carapaced and separatist" of U.S. Catholic urban subcultures, they succeeded spectacularly.[18]

In large part, their success was due to "the Cardinal," archdiocese leader Dennis Cardinal Dougherty, who pursued his vision of a parallel Catholic universe within the city of Philadelphia for thirty-three years, from 1918 to 1951. A genius of organization, Dougherty was also "authoritarian to a degree that can hardly be understood in the post-Vatican II Church," wrote historian Hugh Nolan. The Cardinal shortly turned his realm into a tightly centralized hierarchy in which he personally set policy and briskly commanded a fleet of priests. Philadelphia Catholics "found it difficult to ascribe pastoral character to their vigorous leader," as historian Thomas Donaghy delicately put it, but roundly supported Dougherty's vision with their feet, their children, and their money. The Cardinal and his flock—which at the time of his death made up more than 40 percent of the total Philadelphia population—got things done.[19]

In particular, Dougherty nursed "a holy, almost ruthless determination to permanently establish a complete system of Catholic education," from grammar school to college. Under his guidance, Philadelphia Catholics built and maintained a Catholic school system without parallel in the United States. When Dougherty died in 1951, each and every parish supported a school that collectively served almost 100 percent of Catholic grade-schoolers in Philadelphia—at least a third of all the city's children—funded entirely by parish donations. Some parishes supported parochial high schools as well.[20]

Also building a system of diocesan high schools "unique in the entire country," Philadelphia offered tuition-free secondary education to all Catholic youth as well. Sisters of several different orders working for the proverbial "dollar a day" made it all financially possible. These high schools were complemented by several historic and prestigious private academies staffed by religious orders. About two-thirds of Catholic secondary students attended these diocesan, parochial, and private schools. While the archdiocese's comprehensive school system awed Catholic leaders across the country, locally it gave the religion credibility even among its detractors. "Philadelphia is a different place as far as Catholic schools are concerned," recalled Sister Mary of Lourdes McDevitt '36, who served as Immaculata's president from 1954 to 1972. "There's no place like it, really."[21]

The high schools in turn channeled students toward a number of moderately priced local Catholic colleges, from Villanova University and LaSalle University for men to Immaculata and Chestnut Hill College for women. In Philadelphia, "filthy with Catholic colleges," many Catholic youth who in other cities would not have attended college at all received their degrees from these institutions.[22]

Archdiocese leaders and laypeople also established hundreds of confraternities, hospitals, businesses, savings and loan associations, charitable homes, and other institutions to address every aspect of believers' lives. After Catholic Philadelphians graduated from high school or college, a full array of parareligious institutions continued to support traditional faith. To casual observation, this Catholic world looked like some real-life neo-Thomistic flowchart in which doctrine determined culture. Catholics attended Mass, memorized the Baltimore Catechism, and studied scholastic theology; they also lived in the same neighborhoods, patronized each others' businesses, and married within the faith. Within this massive parallel universe, it was possible and probable for Philadelphia Catholics not to interact personally with non-Catholics for large portions of their lives. Many of the basketball players affirmed that their urban experience was not just religiously Catholic but also socially and culturally Catholic. "Basically the rules of the church were the rules of everything," recalled Gloria Rook Schmidt '64. Every aspect of life, she said, "was just a part of it." Margaret Klopfle Devinney '62 agreed. "It was *all* Catholic," she remembered.[23]

If "it was *all* Catholic," what of the supposed complex and creative ways religious people adapted their faith? Did Philadelphia Catholics, formed since birth within Catholic homes, schools, and extracurricular institutions, change Catholicism? Or when Philadelphia laity supported a hierarchy whose reach extended from the Cardinal's desk to every corner of their lives, must we picture an uncurious people fully content to follow their religious superiors—or incapable of doing otherwise? Was the Catholic Church in Philadelphia the perfect modern institution, a "state-within-a-state" that disciplined bodies until individual desire accorded with institutional interest in all things?[24]

The model of the disciplining institution that creates subjects is to some extent useful for understanding the Philadelphia Catholic Church, which was more successful than many American religious groups, and most other Catholic dioceses, in forming bodies and constructing selfhood. But this model generally falls short by implying that subject-creating institutions efface agency altogether, leaving us to wonder how people and institutions change. Certainly, agency cannot mean some Enlightenment ideal of self-determination, because people are always fundamentally constituted by, and radically dependent on, institutions that form them. But, on the other hand, institutions are comprised of people and therefore are in turn radically dependent on the subjects they form for their embodiment and reproduction. For the most part, disciplined bodies replicate the interests of the institution, which, after all, usually coincide with their own desires. But every time the institution depends on a person to reproduce it, it also submits to slight failures of exact replication. In other words, historical subjects fashion tools of transformation specific to the contexts that produce them. It is with this insight into the relationship between the institution and the individual that I ask how basketball players at Immaculata became subjects for whom sports could provide a resource and strategy within Catholicism.[25]

For no matter how thoroughly the church formed a young Philadelphia Catholic girl, the particular desires and satisfactions of her daily life still modified and re-created Catholicism in her image. She might have worn the school uniform but safety-pinned its modest hem up two extra inches. She might have memorized the catechism but wondered why it was wrong to like the Jewish baker who gave her free doughnuts along the walk home. She might have played basketball for the school team but secretly loved to push and pummel other girls' bodies. In short, she "lived religion," negotiating the institution in her own interests dozens of times a day. At the very moment she embodied Catholicism, she changed it. Precisely because the Catholic Church created her, its power was at risk in her body.

One might say these are small changes, by an insignificant actor, carrying little risk for the institution. True. Our imaginary little girl might never have consciously questioned her church, much less later reformed it or left it. But sometimes in the back-and-forth between the institution speaking the subject and the subject speaking the institution, a person changes. And if that is how people change—and how seemingly impervious organizations change—it is all the more important for us to notice fractional individual mutations and trifling institutional forfeits. Because the Roman Church enfolded Philadelphia Catholics' lives so intimately, even slight discontinuities between church and believer become significant.

Even if lasting organizational change rarely resulted, we need to understand better the complicated and creative ways ordinary people in American religion embodied and reinterpreted the institutions that shaped them. That is why we enrich our accounts by looking for religion apart from specifically religious activities. To understand religion in the United States, we have to know what Catholic schoolgirls in Philadelphia wore, where they walked on the way home, and what they did after school.

What some Philadelphia Catholic girls did after school was play basketball. "It was just like a way of life," said Eva "Evie" Adams Atkinson '46. "It was like going to class. You just knew automatically after school you were off to basketball practice." To discover more about the relationship between basketball and Catholicism in these girls' lives, I talked to them.[26]

Methods and Sources

My approach to understanding the meaning of basketball for Catholic women at Immaculata College started with the former players themselves. After framing the project between 1939, when Immaculata launched its varsity program, and 1975, the year after its third and final championship, I culled lists of team members from rosters published in the college newspaper, *The Immaculatan*, and other sources. To more than three hundred women who had played, cheered, managed, or coached Immaculata basketball during those years, I mailed detailed, four-page surveys (see appendix A). I received back sixty-five surveys (about 21 percent). All but fifteen respondents were former players. I also interviewed in person and by telephone fifty-seven team members and others associated with Immaculata basketball. Additionally, players sent me letters, electronic mail, memoirs, photographs, and mementos of their basketball experiences. The surveys, interviews, and other correspondence comprise my chief primary sources.[27]

I wrestled with the question of whether to use real names. Almost all to whom I spoke were enthusiastic about their basketball glory days and said they did not care about protecting their identity. And I wished to give players' accomplishments long-overdue publicity. On the other hand, I wanted to provide for their memories a safe space—safe for them to speak and safe from my published interpretation. I ended up doing both. Players who granted me written permission are cited by their real names. Those who didn't are listed anonymously, identified just by their graduation years.

I found other primary sources at Immaculata College, in the Gabriele Library Archives and in the Office of Public Relations. These included issues of *The Immaculatan*, college yearbooks, course catalogs, video and television footage, photographs, mementos, pamphlets, trophies, letters, and media guides. An especially helpful source for the early basketball years was a scrapbook of programs, keepsakes, and newspaper articles collected by Immaculata's president from 1936 to 1946, Monsignor Francis Furey, who later became an archbishop. The Gabriele Library staff recently reorganized and microfilmed this collection, the Archbishop Furey Scrapbook, along with a rich clippings file spanning the history of Immaculata and the basketball program. Still other primary sources included Catholic prescriptive literature, papal encyclicals, and women's basketball manuals.[28]

Combining all these sources, I wanted to understand Immaculata basketball from many different perspectives and tell a textured story. But primarily I aimed to convey the meaning of basketball in former players' lives, not to give facts about the Immaculata program. I regarded all the sources that made up this story, from memories and articles to mementos and photographs, not as data so much as interpretations of reality. But all were important as windows onto distinctive experience and located meaning making.[29]

Just as my sources interpreted experience to make meaning, so did I. Privileging oral history, I hoped to foreground former players' voices and not my own. I based my conclusions on patterns of voices, not singular opinions. I tried not to favor some voices over others and to respect the integrity of their words. But, of course, I also have interpreted their interpretations. From arranging the chapters, to cutting the quotes, to framing the argument, I have put my imprint on their story.

Sometimes my ideas corresponded to what former players said about their experiences and at other times they did not. For example, while numerous former Immaculata team members said they had fun playing basketball and gave detailed reasons why, very few would say they were exercising a small-scale politics of pleasure within Catholicism. "I enjoyed it. I liked it. So, I think that's basically why I did it," said Pauline Callahan Earl '57. "Other than that, I don't think there's any deep psychological reasons . . . you know, I wasn't proving anything." In the face of this and many alternative interpretations, I have chosen simply to let the differences stand and acknowledge them as I go.[30]

Women's Basketball in the Philadelphia Archdiocese

The story of Immaculata basketball starts with the story of Philadelphia Catholic girls' basketball. Within months of James Naismith's December 1891 invention of the game at a Springfield, Massachusetts, Young Men's Christian Association (YMCA) training college, his students were teaching the game at YMCAs throughout the Northeast. Introduced to Smith College women a year later by Senda Berenson Abbott, the game was an instant hit with girls as well as boys. By late fall 1903, a studious and sports-crazed Irish kid named John Bonner was bouncing a round leather ball in a gymnasium at Broad and Vine Streets, killing time before football practice at Roman Catholic High, the archdiocese's flagship boys' secondary school. Celebrated later as "one of the greatest athletes who ever performed for the Purple and Gold," Bonner graduated to study for the priesthood in Philadelphia and Rome.[31]

Monsignor John Bonner and the Catholic League

When he returned to the archdiocese to teach students at Roman Catholic and later at Immaculata, Bonner was confirmed in his own experience that sports gave young people "something from . . . school life that comes in no other way." As vice-rector of Roman Catholic, he convened a meeting of like-minded priests and laymen in the fall of 1919 to organize the Catholic League, which quickly raised the quality of schools' football, basketball, and track programs. Bonner served as Roman Catholic football coach and the league's first president, proselytizing its ideals of sportsmanship and competition but also of community and fun. "Slip quietly amongst the excited, enthusiastic throng at one of our big foot-ball games; crowd into the hall at a League basket-ball match; or watch with bated breath the thrilling finish at the annual track meet," he told an anniversary gathering of Catholic League supporters, "and you will understand something of what the League has ac-

complished." In 1926, when Dougherty appointed Bonner his superintendent of schools, Bonner committed himself to the development of sports programs as one of several progressive initiatives in the archdiocesan system.[32]

Even before Bonner's appointment, Philadelphia Catholic girls played
basketball at informal to varsity levels. It was a cheap, urban sport, requiring
minimal gear and space. In city neighborhoods, Catholic girls learned the
game from brothers and friends at local playgrounds and recreation centers.
In outlying areas, big Catholic families of siblings "could go out the back
door and [have] a three-on-three," said Jenepher Shillingford, who coached
the Mackies from 1962 to 1970. With numbers and sibling rivalry, the games
were intense. "If you play your brother or your sister in the backyard, it is
tough," Shillingford said. When a new parochial school opened, basketball
was always the first—and often the only—sport the parish could afford. "You
don't need a swimming pool, you don't need a field, you don't need all the
equipment, and [there was] not much money around," explained former
Immaculata president Sister Mary of Lourdes McDevitt. "So that's why basketball." Likewise in the diocesan girls' high schools, basketball was often the
only varsity sport offered. Around the time Bonner became superintendent,
the flagship girls' secondary school, John W. Hallahan, played its first varsity
schedule, including games with other private and public schools in Pennsylvania and New Jersey. And in the high schools basketball wasn't a class thing.
All the private Catholic academies had teams, too, and daughters of bankers
played against daughters of butchers. Several Mackies specifically mentioned
playing against Liz Ann Kelly—sister of famous actress Grace Kelly and
daughter of Philadelphia Catholic scion Jack Kelly—who was Penn's dominant center in the midfifties.[33]

This early basketball opportunity for girls owed in part to Dougherty's in-
sistence on single-sex education. Whereas many dioceses and public schools
saved on cost by educating girls and boys together, Dougherty usually built
two separate buildings and paid two different faculties to run nearly identi-
cal curricula. He bought acres of land to accommodate twice the schools,
often previewing sites and planning purchases with his best friend, Jewish
leader and real estate magnate Albert Greenfield. Whatever the pros and cons
of this separate-but-equal policy, it meant that most Philadelphia Catholic
all-girls' schools fielded basketball squads long before their coeducational
counterparts, public or Catholic.[34]

But it is not clear that varsity sports would have flourished in the archdiocese without Bonner, who used Dougherty's system to promote interscholastic play through his beloved Catholic League. Temperamental opposites,

Dougherty and Bonner clashed on numerous occasions. The Cardinal was "shy and private and hated speaking or preaching in public," while Bonner's "spirit and vitality [were] outstanding in any gathering." Dougherty was a squat and red-faced scholar whom his own priests avoided, while Bonner, the gracious and handsome former athlete, inspired gushing admiration, especially from women. The Cardinal appointed Bonner superintendent and from then on seemed to relish overworking the popular priest. For most of the appointment, Dougherty charged Bonner to visit personally over three hundred schools every year. Bonner did the job but repeatedly asked for assistants. The Cardinal brusquely turned down such requests, relenting only after Bonner was hospitalized several times with exhaustion and heart attacks. While it is not evident that the two ever specifically disagreed over school athletics, Bonner did not wave his enthusiasm for sports in Dougherty's face. In his annual reports to the Cardinal, he never mentioned athletics, though he did mention Dougherty's favorite extracurricular program, music. For his part, Dougherty's strange disregard for the younger man's health could suggest cool unsympathy for the star ex-athlete's failing body.[35]

But in the schools Bonner's charisma and dedication inspired loyalty, and he was able to set an unquestioned tone of support for boys' and girls' varsity play. On the girls' side, this created quite an anomalous situation for the time. Certainly, the 1920s had witnessed growth in women's athletics, and women's colleges led the expansion. But support for women's varsities—that is, for interscholastic competition—was rare. In other diocesan and public school systems, if girls had basketball programs at all, they generally played noncompetitive intramural games, not interscholastic contests. This was because reigning opinion among national physical educators held that competitive sports debased feminine nature and therefore girls' athletic activity should involve only cooperative games of mild exertion. In the late twenties—years when a formidable Catholic League rivalry developed between the Hallahan and West Catholic girls' teams—most physical educators, women and men, considered girls' competitive play, particularly in basketball, "an acute problem of national significance." In the late twenties and early thirties, they even campaigned to keep basketball, as well as other women's events, out of the Olympics. To address the problem, the Division of Girls' and Women's Sports (DGWS)—the oversight organization influencing much of the Northeast—appointed various committees of female physical educators. DGWS committees continually modified the rules of the game, decreasing the contact and stamina exacted from women's delicate bodies, until the refashioned half-court, six-player, limited-dribble game was nearly unrecognizable as basketball. As late as 1956, the DGWS reaffirmed the view that sports for women should deemphasize competition. Along similar lines, for the first five decades of women's basketball history, most state public schools explicitly banned interscholastic play.[36]

Yet it seems never to have occurred to Bonner to downplay or justify Catholic girls' teams. He proudly spoke of girls' and boys' sports participation in addresses on Catholic education he delivered locally and nationally. In an address defending Catholic schools to the American public that he prepared around 1941, Bonner boasted that "in athletics, both our girls and boys boast championship teams." A year later, he spoke at the dedication of a new gymnasium, christened Knute Rockne Memorial after the revered Notre Dame football coach, at Sacred Heart parish in Allentown, Pennsylvania. With his own heart physically failing, Bonner celebrated the "strong heart" of the "boy or girl who stands little chance and then goes out and wins." And he showed up at girls' games all the time. Sister Mary of Lourdes McDevitt '36 remembered Bonner standing under the basket, glaring dubious encouragement as she prepared to take two foul shots to win the game for Hallahan. "He was for Hallahan" over West Catholic, she said. "He shouldn't have been, but he was." Whatever Bonner's favorite girls' school, however, participation in competitive sports was a nonissue.[37]

Apart from the structural fact of single-sex schools and his own love of sports, how and why Bonner arrived at promoting interscholastic play for girls as well as boys—and how and why leaders and parents of the archdiocese seemed by and large to accept it—is not altogether clear. Perhaps it never occurred to them that it should be an issue. Perhaps it was plain common sense that sports kept kids—not just boys—out of trouble. "You said girls," Immaculata player Dee Cofer Cull '55 said to me in an interview. "Now, athletics were good for anybody, boy or girl. To keep them out of trouble."[38]

But it is clear that Bonner saw sports as part of education and considered it to be part of his job as superintendent to cheerlead school teams. Bonner's extant speeches suggest he gave more thought to why athletics had a place in *boys'* education; for example, he titled one essay "The Value of Athletics for Boys" and listed a few gender-specific reasons for school sports, such as the development of gentlemanliness. But, even in this essay, most of his reasons could apply to girls just as well, such as physical, intellectual, and moral development. If Bonner thought sports gave solely boys tools for life, he had a perfect occasion to say so during World War II, when he, like most American educators, added civic preparation to his list of physical education benefits. But in his mind, as he said at the Knute Rockne gym dedication, the national crisis called for *both* girls and boys to be physically prepared.[39]

For Bonner, athletics were self-evidently part of education—that is, part of *Catholic* education. To him, his Catholic League was Catholic because it integrated moral lessons with play. Time in the gym, he told the parishioners at Sacred Heart, "makes play of work." The virtues he said sports instilled, such as discipline, courage, perseverance, teamwork, and leadership, were not distinctively Catholic, of course, but participated in a national ethic of sportsmanship, in turn deeply tied to American identity. But Bonner and his community considered them Catholic virtues. They were not self-conscious about the sociological commonplace that through sports Catholics became more American—even though they cheered when Catholics carried the struggle for Americanness onto the playing field, as when Notre Dame battled Protestants on the gridiron. And, certainly, Catholic *girls* playing *basketball* did not function to stake claims to national identity the way boys playing football did, because girls playing basketball was not very American in the first place. Instead, for Philadelphia Catholics, sports in a Catholic context taught Catholic values, not American ones. Furthermore, outside a Catholic context, games did not necessarily teach anything and were subject to corruptions and scandals abounding in the sports world. Accordingly, Bonner worked to put athletics in its place in a holistic Catholic education envisioned by leading pedagogues of his day. Such an education would encompass sports, as well as other extracurricular pursuits, alongside school, church, and family life. In Philadelphia, working in Cardinal Dougherty's "System," Bonner had a better chance than many superintendents of realizing that vision.[40]

Perhaps ultimately it was the archdiocese's self-sufficiency in educational matters that sheltered Bonner and his coreligionists from the raging public debate about women's basketball. Structurally, the Philadelphia schools answered to no one but the Cardinal. Philosophically, its Thomistic outlook described the student's development toward wholeness in God, unlike public education discourses that increasingly leaned on social and natural sciences, including supposed evidence of female physical frailty. For whatever reason, most Immaculata players to whom I spoke shared Bonner's assumption that basketball was not just a boys' sport. "I just [thought] everybody played it," remembered Margaret Guinan Delaney '62. "All my friends did."[41]

Or perhaps Catholic girls' basketball enthusiasts made unwitting alliance with some like-minded "publics" in Philadelphia. Unique in the Northeast, a vanguard core of women physical educators in local non-Catholic universities questioned bans on basketball competition and coached cutting-edge programs. While Bonner and these physical educators might never have exchanged words, for different reasons they both nurtured a local environment favorable to competition in women's basketball.

Philadelphia's Women Physical Educators

Bonner's early support for girls' varsities was unusual in the national anti-competition climate. Even in 1950 two-thirds of all eastern women's college teams still played only intramural games. But, in Philadelphia, visionary physical educators pushed for advances in women's sports that eased local conditions and created further opportunity for Catholic League girls. Drawing some Catholic players to Bryn Mawr, Temple, Ursinus, and West Chester State, these women coached precocious teams and spearheaded illustrious programs at the city's public and private institutions. In turn, the Catholic League and Catholic colleges, including Immaculata, drew on graduates of these programs for their coaches and referees. From the early sixties, Immaculata regularly filled athletic department positions with non-Catholics from local schools. To get an Immaculata basketball job, training in the Philly sports mindset was at least as important as religious affiliation.[42]

From the beginning of the wars over the appropriateness of basketball for women, some Philadelphia physical educators took the progressive side of the fight. For example, in 1897 Alice Bertha Foster of Bryn Mawr College, chair of the first National Women's Basketball Committee, protested medical naysayers who would question the physical good of basketball for thousands of young women on account of a few instances of injury, a fact that did not lead anyone to suggest eliminating football for men, Foster pointed out. This stance favoring the competitive flavor of the game gained ground in Philadelphia, as physical educators trained coaches and players who later coached others. In the forties Pat Collins built the first women's college basketball dynasty at Temple. In the fifties, at Ursinus in Bethlehem, Pennsylvania, northwest of the city, Eleanor Snell taught basketball with a mind toward the men's rules game, which she had played on Amateur Athletic Union (AAU) teams in the Midwest. In the sixties Lucille Kyvallos and Carol Eckman ran full-court practices at West Chester State, and in the seventies C. Vivian Stringer at historically black Cheyney developed an advanced program by running joint practices with Temple men's coach John Chaney.[43]

One of Kyvallos's players was a young woman named Cathy Rush, future coach of the Immaculata championship teams. Later, Kyvallos would coach her Queens (N.Y.) College team against Rush's Immaculata squad in the first women's basketball contest ever played in Madison Square Garden. But in 1966 Kyvallos lost her job at West Chester for flouting regulations to take her team to an AAU tournament. Her successor, Carol Eckman, was no shrinking violet, however, agitating for tournament play and the adoption of men's rules. Already in 1961, the DGWS had instituted an experimental partial-full-court game, largely because AAU and Olympic rules still approximated the men's game. In this experiment, one player, a roving guard or "rover," could cross the center line. After ten years, "nobody had died on the court," remembered Immaculata coach Jenepher Shillingford, who studied under Snell at Ursinus. The DGWS finally permitted the full-court, five-player men's rules in 1971.[44]

Now known as the mother of women's collegiate postseason play, Eckman organized and hosted the first national invitational tournament in 1969; her West Chester team won. Only a few years later, West Chester and Immaculata faced off in the finals of the first truly national tournament, in Normal, Illinois. There, Cathy Rush's fifteenth-seeded Immaculata players pulled off the upset of their Philadelphia neighbors for the title, largely by importing traps, screens, and presses from the men's game, considered radical for women at the time. But it did not escape notice that both teams in the national finals came from the same hometown. "You just had a lot of extraordinary women in [Philadelphia] who pushed," said Shillingford.[45]

Working in the same city with overlapping constituencies, the Catholic League and local physical education programs reinforced each other and together put Philadelphia on the map as a girls' basketball hotspot. Physical educators used the numerous Catholic League games as a training ground; Shillingford remembered her mentor Snell "would send us out to officiate some of [the Catholic League] games to get experience." In turn, schools like West Chester and Ursinus could marshal exceptional players for their programs, she said, "partly because [of] the large Catholic influence on basketball."[46]

Catholic League Girls' Basketball

In the twenties and thirties, however, before collegiate programs really prospered, Catholic high school girls played the best women's game in town. From the forties through the sixties, Catholic League girls boasted the premier high school teams in the nation, rivaled only by Iowa schoolgirls' programs. Even in the seventies, national-caliber Immaculata honed its game by scrimmaging against the best Catholic League squads.[47]

Catholic girl athletes often learned the game on city playgrounds, so they were experienced, and since their schools often offered no other sports, they focused exclusively on basketball. The diocesan high schools were large, routinely graduating classes of four or five hundred, so each Catholic League team comprised the absolute cream of players chosen from skilled multitudes trying out for a few spots every year. Fierce rivalries developed among the diocesan and private high schools that made up the league, like Little

Flower versus Archbishop Prendergast or Sacred Heart versus Villa Maria. Not just the girls but parents and coaches took games extremely seriously. As a Villa Maria forward in the late forties, Marian Collins Mullahy '54 said she once missed two foul shots that would have won the game by one. "The next Monday, Sister Lucina . . . made me go and take fifty foul shots every day for a solid week—at lunch time!" Marian said. "And I did it . . . I got a lot better at foul shots. I never wanted that to happen again."[48]

By the 1950s basketball was the also the cornerstone of parish-based CYO athletics, which disciplined Philadelphia Catholic girls' bodies in the game at even earlier ages. In other northeastern cities, such as New York and Boston, the CYO and its array of athletic and cultural activities arrived shortly after its 1930 founding. But in Philadelphia, the thriving school system and Catholic League already addressed many CYO functions. Only after about fifteen years, in the late 1940s, did archdiocesan priests begin starting chapters for their parish grade-schoolers. When the first waves of girls familiar with competitive basketball since sixth or seventh grade started to hit the Catholic high schools in the midfifties, the intensity and quality of play rose even higher.[49]

To be sure, girls' school ball did not exist in a vacuum. The Philadelphia Catholic community was thick with sports teams for both genders and all ages, sponsored by parishes, like the Ascension baseball team, or confraternities, whose teams included the Hibernian League clubs. Catholic Young Men's and Catholic Young Women's clubs provided space to play, too. Catholic boys' high school basketball programs were also competitive; each year, the top Catholic League team played the public league winners for an official city championship. And by the fifties Philadelphia's "Big Five" college men's rivalries, among St. Joseph's College, Villanova, LaSalle, Temple, and the University of Pennsylvania, routinely played to boisterous crowds at Penn's Palestra. For archdiocesan faithful, the three Catholic Big Five teams inspired fanatical loyalty, and whole families attended games together for cheap entertainment during the long winter months.

The other Catholic teams that consistently sold out city venues, however, were the high school *girls*. Catholic League girls did not play for a Philadelphia high school championship, because the public schools did not have squads that could even come close to measuring up. Instead, starting in the forties, crowds of Catholic folk packed Convention Hall for Friday night all-girls doubleheaders for the entire regular season. As the years went on, tickets for the girls' Catholic League championship, played at the Palestra, and even tickets for big duel matches sold out weeks in advance. "We'd be four thousand girls in that building screaming [our] heads off," remembered

Mary Frank McCormick '50, who played at Convention Hall with her team from Notre Dame Academy in suburban Moylan. Fans "got to know your name . . . [and] identified [you as] a player from Notre Dame." Playing for a league girls' team was incredibly prestigious. "We were it, we were the show in town, we had pep rallies," said Mimi McNamee, who played for Sacred Heart Academy in the sixties. "It was [all] for us." And the competition got hot. Officiating Catholic League games early in her career, Jenepher Shillingford remembered fearing for her safety during some of the fiercer rivalries. "You sometimes had an escort to get out of the gym as the official," she said. "Usually a nun. Nobody would mess with a nun."[50]

Catholic girls' basketball was "the big, big thing" in Philadelphia because of large families, single-sex schools, limited budgets, John Bonner, the Catholic League, progressive physical educators, neighborhood playgrounds, and the CYO. But none of these explained the sheer momentum and spirited tradition established by the teams. The girls loved playing basketball. By the mid-forties, their mothers had loved playing basketball before them—along with their aunts, sisters, and favorite nuns. And, after one generation, Catholics in Philadelphia, from bishops to teachers to parents, apparently saw nothing strange about daughters of the diocese devoting a lot of time and energy to intense basketball competition. Many city-born players affirmed that basketball "was deeply associated with [the] Catholic schools" they attended. "In my neighborhood [and] parish especially, basketball was an important part of Catholicism," wrote Margaret Klopfle Devinney '62. As Catholic clubs playing city recreation center teams, she said, "God *was* on our side in CYO." Not just a sport, girls' basketball became a cultural touchstone in the network of parareligious institutions that made up the Philadelphia Catholic world.[51]

Few colleges benefited from this basketball breeding ground more than Immaculata. With a local reputation for educating working-class girls at low cost, Immaculata drew to its nearby campus many Catholic League players, who lived in dormitories or commuted. On the 1946 team that defeated Temple, all six starters had been captains of their Catholic high school clubs, at St. Katharine's, Mater Misericordiae, Mercy, Notre Dame Moylan, and Villa Maria. Twenty-six years later, of eleven players who made up the 1972 national championship squad, five came from one high school, Catholic League powerhouse Archbishop Prendergast, where former Immaculata player Barbara Mooney '65 coached the team. Throughout the years, the tradition of girls' basketball in the Archdiocese of Philadelphia largely explained the success of the Immaculata program.

View of back campus with Villa Maria Hall and Lourdes Hall, October 1957.
ROBERT HALVEY COLLECTION OF THE PHILADELPHIA ARCHIVES AND HISTORICAL RESEARCH CENTER.

Basketball at Immaculata College

While Catholic Leaguers made up some of the best high school teams in the country, hampered as they were by DGWS "women's rules," they couldn't have competed with the best women cagers, who already ran full-court in the twenties and thirties. One such team hailed from West Philly, the Philadelphia Tribune Girls. A semiprofessional team sponsored by the local black newspaper, the Tribune Girls dominated nationwide—at least, wherever they were allowed to play. In the thirties, white teams looking to legitimate their titles had to beat the Tribuners. Other early top teams included the Texas-based semipro Wayland Baptist Flying Queens, associated with Wayland Baptist College since 1911 and sponsored by a local oilman since 1951, and the professional All-American Redheads, a 1930s traveling band of working-class women who all had red hair and sometimes played men's teams.[52]

For a long time, Immaculata College fielded teams quite inferior to those of its Catholic League feeder schools. Growing from an enrollment of three hundred to eight hundred between 1949 and 1972, Immaculata's total student body barely matched the numbers of one class in the thousands-plus diocesan high schools. So competition for team spots was far lighter. League players showed up for Immaculata tryouts thinking it would be "a cinch [to make] this dinky college team," said Maureen Callahan Bigham '63. But, over the years, the school developed a reputation for good basketball, and former league players began to have to compete for college team spots as well. By the fifties, a good Catholic League player could find herself "out of [her] league" at Immaculata. In the sixties and seventies, even junior and senior Mackie starters could suddenly find themselves displaced by younger, more skilled CYO-trained players materializing as freshmen. Alone among area Catholic schools, Immaculata consistently challenged teams from local physical education programs, which enrolled both non-Catholic and Catholic players. In certain years—the midforties, the early fifties, the early sixties—Immaculata stirred citywide attention comparable to the Catholic League girls. And, by the midseventies, the national championship team had become a bona fide phenomenon of Philadelphia sports history.[53]

When the first Immaculata varsity team assembled in 1927, there was little hint of future glory. That year—the winter after Bonner left his Immaculata job for his new post as superintendent and around the same time that Hallahan high school played its first interscholastic games—Immaculata's basketball players also contested other colleges for the first time. However, for unclear reasons—probably having to do partly with finances and partly with lack of administrative zeal—the initiative did not last. For eight years after that, Immaculata cagers again played only intramural games or gathered with other schools for "Play Days," a widespread women's college movement that promoted noncompetitive athletics. Not until student athletes began agitating for intercollegiate play in 1935 did other Immaculata varsities assemble, only to sputter again. Then, in 1938, college president Monsignor Furey hired a new physical education teacher, Temple- and New York University–trained Alma Jackson, who promptly scheduled six games with local schools. Playing in the winter of 1939, the team won some, lost some, and had a lot of fun. "I love[d] it," said team captain Josephine McFarland '42. This time, the program stuck. Even during World War II, when physical educators were scarce, Furey secured as coach a Temple-educated Catholic, Marie Schultes, who proceeded to guide Immaculata to the Mythical City Championship in 1946. The Immaculata basketball tradition had arrived.[54]

Eighteen years before the real start of the varsity, in 1921, the Sisters, Servants of the Immaculate Heart of Mary, known as the I.H.M.s, had welcomed a charter class of collegians to their rural Villa Maria campus, and in 1928 they changed the name of the new college to Immaculata. The school became the apex of a vast network of Immaculate Heart sisters already working in education in the Archdiocese of Philadelphia, from grade schools to high schools. Since 1858, when John Cardinal Neumann first invited the order to Philadelphia from its Monroe, Michigan, founding site, the sisters had become one of several major religious orders educating the archdiocese's children.[55]

The Philadelphia I.H.M. community largely stepped in time with the conservative archdiocese. The sisters enjoyed a close working relationship with Dougherty, who used to visit Immaculata on afternoon drives, and Bonner, who called the campus "home." Centered in the liberal arts and sciences, Immaculata also offered strong home economics and education degrees. Charged to keep and mold Philadelphia Catholic daughters, the sisters vigorously regulated campus life, from religious duties to dress code.[56]

But internal I.H.M. discipline and vision also fashioned a community of teaching sisters progressive for its time in several respects. From at least the 1910s, the sisters took certain courses and degrees at non-Catholic institutions, making them more "diversified" than many of the archdiocese's seminary- and Rome-educated priests. Used to infusing secular classes with Catholic faith, the sisters taught their subjects, from chemistry to English, as parts of the totality of God's world, inserting into each "something of the spiritual." They accepted a charge from Dougherty to establish missions in South America, pushed for community governance of Immaculata, and maintained liberal policies on matters such as leisure time and home visits. Students remembered being impressed with the sisters' leadership and worldliness. They were "forward-thinking, independent-minded" women who "w[ore] the conservative dress and all, but they [were] feminists at heart," said student Kathy Clark '70.[57]

Both the sisters' harmony with archdiocesan leadership and their progressive tendencies might have helped establish a supportive environment for extracurricular activities such as basketball. But even more crucially, the I.H.M. profile attracted many Philadelphia postulants, so that by 1951 almost all 1,800 of the local community's numbers came from the archdiocese. This meant that I.H.M. sisters who taught at Immaculata were often city-born-and-bred basketball players and fans themselves. In fact, the I.H.M. novitiate center, at the motherhouse just across King Road from the college, provided a basketball court for postulants' free hours. Sisters filled buses and stands for every game, seeming "to enjoy basketball as much as the students," said Evie Adams Atkinson '46, one of the 1946 champion guards. Campus priests, who served as presidents, chaplains, and professors, followed the more populous sisters' model of support, sometimes personally supplementing minuscule basketball budgets.[58]

In 1954 a former Hallahan basketball star and 1936 Immaculata graduate, Sister Mary of Lourdes McDevitt, was appointed the first I.H.M. president of Immaculata since 1930. Sister Mary of Lourdes's open-door office policy built extraordinary rapport with students, and board members and alumnae adored her, too. During the course of her eighteen-year tenure, Immaculata doubled enrollment, constructed eight new buildings, and graduated seniors to the top law and medical schools in the country. The new leader also made little effort to disguise her partiality toward sports in general and basketball in particular. She often stopped by basketball practice to scrimmage with the team. Easing resistance among some fellow nuns, she mediated for players when games conflicted with classes. The college sports budget was tiny, but Sister Mary of Lourdes made sure the team had the basketballs, buses, uniforms, warm-up jackets, and snacks they needed.[59]

Sister Mary of Lourdes departed from Catholic and Immaculata custom by looking for the best coaches from local programs she could afford, whether they were Catholic or not. In 1962, she hired Jenepher Shillingford, a Methodist, to coach the basketball team. Eight years later, Shillingford became athletic director, and Sister Mary of Lourdes signed on a Baptist, Cathy Rush, who coached the team to three consecutive national championships, from 1972 to 1974. There were Catholics with physical education degrees, but Sister Mary of Lourdes said religion "didn't have a thing to do with it." "I don't think it entered my mind; I was looking for a good coach," she said. Throughout the years, I. H. M. enthusiasm for basketball, embodied to the fullest in Sister Mary of Lourdes for the nearly two decades of her presidency, kept attracting Catholic League players to Immaculata.[60]

Students who came from beyond the archdiocese's basketball-nurturing boundaries found the Immaculata sports environment astonishing. At her upstate Catholic high school, "I never heard of girls playing basketball [and] never had a chance to do a single athletic thing," recalled Josephine Valentine '38. Cheerleader Geraldine Ferrari Burton '57, attending Catholic school in South Jersey, also said sports at Immaculata surpassed her experience. "I never played sports because in the schools that I went to we didn't have [girls' teams]," she said. "All the emphasis was on the boys' sports. So the only thing left for girls was cheerleading, and that's what both my sister and I did." Another cheerleader, from the class of '63, said the same thing. Having rooted for boys' basketball at a north Jersey public high school with no girls' sports, she wrote, "To find such widespread acceptance for girl athletes was quite a pleasant surprise!" Young women from Philadelphia, on the other hand, came expecting nothing less than the continued fun of playing and watching grand, thrilling basketball games.[61]

In the pages that follow, I tell the story of Immaculata basketball as an account of particular pleasures young Catholic women said they found in the game. The six chapters proceed through six sites or moments of Immaculata basketball players' experiences during the course of a season: tryouts, practices, games, chapel, road trips, and postseasons. The last chapter caps the story chronologically as well as thematically, dealing mostly with the early seventies championship years. As the chapters follow the experience of basketball from the beginning to the end of a season, they also describe different pleasures of playing the game, as players negotiated various dimensions of their Catholic world.

In chapter 1, I describe young women's pleasure in *identity* as basketball players within the Catholic community, and, in chapter 5, I narrate more identity making in contrast with other Catholics and non-Catholics the players met on road trips. In chapter 2, I tell of the Immaculatans' satisfactions reworking *class* status in the space of the basketball court. In chapter 3, I explore the sport's physical pleasures, reporting how players dealt with their church's *gender* norms. In chapter 4, I show how basketball offered young Catholic women new opportunities to express *faith*, and, in chapter 6, I examine *communities* in contact with the basketball team, both at Immaculata and in the wider world.

The story ranges across three and a half decades of the twentieth century, years that saw tremendous change in the Catholic Church, women's status, and American life. I have noted throughout the chapters how these changes inflect the story and contextualize the argument. Especially from 1962–75, U.S. social upheaval and the Second Vatican Council conspired to unsettle many old familiarities of American Catholic life. I address this cultural and religious revolution in chapter 6.

For the overall argument, however, I chose a thematic rather than chronological arrangement. This choice inevitably slights subtleties of change over time. But for two reasons I decided the project warranted thematic treatment. First, in the Archdiocese of Philadelphia, one of the most conservative and tightly knit Catholic communities in the country throughout these years, believers saw relatively little institutional change over time. Already given to guarding their neighborhoods, parishes, and schools from social and religious change, Philadelphia faithful greeted Vatican II with caution, if not hostility. Their leader until 1960, John Cardinal O'Hara, "the last of the old order," pointedly resisted the council-prescribed vernacular Mass and lay-centered ecclesiology. His similarly disposed successor, John Cardinal Krol, was the last of all U.S. prelates to allow Saturday night Mass and approached social justice issues coolly. Well into the seventies, most Philadelphia parishes, except for those headed by the rare liberal priest, operated socially, liturgically, and theologically much as they had in the fifties, except for celebrating Mass in English.[62]

Second, I intended to highlight players' experiences in this story, and the thematic structure allowed me to trace commonalities in their narratives over many years. Immaculata team members from 1939 *and* 1972, for example, played in the same skirted uniforms, enjoyed the same locker room adventures, attended the same pregame masses, and recalled the same physical freedoms. In a chronological narrative, these striking continuities would fade. So would the possibility that, from many ordinary Catholics' perspectives, there were throughout these years more constancy and less disruption than the standard "before and after Vatican II" periodization suggests.

Throughout these decades, Immaculata basketball devotees found a city and a college that let them play. And as they played, they both reaffirmed and re-created what it meant to be young Catholic women. For them, adjusting Catholic female identity started at basketball team tryouts. They might have played on high school teams or just watched other Immaculatans practice. Now they wanted to join the team themselves. At tryouts, hopefuls looked forward to a basketball season full of excitement and ambition. But they also looked forward to months of making their marks as young female athletes within the wider Catholic community.

CHAPTER 1

MAKING THE TEAM, MAKING IDENTITY

For the 1940 season, team tryouts were scheduled for a December afternoon shortly before the Christmas holidays. As late classes ended and stragglers hurried to the gymnasium in Villa Maria Hall's basement, they were surprised to find more than fifty other girls—about a quarter of the entire student body—already bouncing heavy leather balls and practicing favorite shots. Only in its second season, the team attracted a multitude of Immaculatans enamored of basketball. Many of them came from local Catholic high school squads and wanted to keep playing. Some had missed making their high school teams and saw the fledgling college varsity as a second chance. Still others, Catholic girls from New Jersey, northern Pennsylvania, and other states, had never touched a basketball in their lives. But they found themselves trying out anyway, drawn by buzz and curiosity and hope.[1]

Most Immaculatans in the gym, however, had already decided there was something special and wonderful about basketball. Most had already spent countless hours honing their games. There were lots of fun things about the sport. You ran the court, goofed around with teammates, went on road trips, and played to crowds. But at tryouts girls were expressing a more fundamental desire: simply to make the team. To earn the right to be called a basketball player. To *be* a basketball player.

Sister Marita David "Toddy" Kirsch, who made the Immaculata team at 1944 tryouts, liked being a basketball player. "I was thrilled, to say the least," she said. A strong wiry forward from Wayne, Pennsylvania, a few miles from

Immaculata, Toddy was typical of Immaculata players who arrived on campus already deeply in love with the game. Basketball was her identity, the core of her being, the time of day she felt most fully herself. Fifty-four years later, Sister Marita David told me about her playing days as we sat in a seminar room of Immaculata's Gabriele Library. A college librarian, she was still small and tough, and her blue eyes darted as she talked, as if looking for the open shooter. She told me she had had "eyes for basketball" ever since sixth grade, when her parents gave her a basketball for Christmas—instead of the football equipment she requested. "After that, I was gone," she said. "Out. Wherever the basket was, that's where I was."

Then she said, "I mean as much as within reason, regarding other things I had to do at home." Basketball was Toddy's identity, but her identity was, of course, relative to parents, siblings, friends, and the wider community. As the middle child in a Catholic family of seven siblings, she helped her mother with childcare, cooking, and cleaning. Such chores were routinely expected of daughters, and Sister Marita David said she didn't mind. But she did discover that basketball got her out of the house a little bit more. Furthermore, sports meant time with her father. The brothers did chores with their dad, but the girls' hours with him consisted mostly of fun and games. Mr. Kirsch had played basketball and football at Villanova, and with him she and her siblings "did . . . most everything sportswise that you could do," from basketball and ice-skating to tennis and baseball. "We always had a basket in the backyard so we did do that together, played H-O-R-S-E," she remembered. "Dad would play with us."

Basketball was a source of identification with her dad, and also with boys. If her father was at work, Toddy shot around or picked up games with siblings and friends. Usually, girls outside her family did not play. "The girls that were in my neighborhood didn't seem to really want to get into the sports that much," she remembered. Athletic interest marked a difference between Toddy and other, mostly Catholic neighborhood girls. "I don't know for sure what some of them did when they were at home in the house, whether they just did house things," Sister Marita David said. "There were some things that we could do together, but . . . I couldn't find them to do any of the sports that I wanted to do, so I just went and did them."

Basketball anchored her college experience, too. By that time, she said, it was the most important thing in her life. "There was no way I was not going to go out for the team," she said. "I was going to give this a shot because I really wanted to do it." Sister Marita David told me proudly that she "made the first team, the first year." Looking forward all day to practices, she could barely contain her excitement before games. As a sophomore, Toddy helped the

Mackies steal the Mythical City Championship from Temple. Eventually, the grade-schooler who had found she'd rather shoot hoops than play house discovered she liked playing basketball more than taking classes. To spare her parents wasted expense, Toddy dropped out after her sophomore year. But she remained a basketball player long after she stopped being a student, joining a team sponsored by her parish and coaching Catholic school teams. Even when she felt called to join the Immaculate Heart order, basketball stayed with her. Sister Marita David said she endured the grunt work of the novitiate by remembering excruciating hours devoted to dribbling, jumping, and shooting. "Well, if I can play basketball that hard, then I can scrub this floor," she told herself. Proving herself to a new community, Sister Marita David thought of herself as a dedicated basketball player so she could become a faithful nun.[2]

Among Immaculatans assembled for basketball tryouts any given year, Toddy was not unusual in putting the game at the head of life. For most former players to whom I spoke, being a basketball player was not just another extracurricular pastime, not just another identity among many. It was a central activity by which, at least for a period in their lives, they identified to themselves and others who they were. Of course, Immaculata players were also Catholics, daughters, sisters, students, friends, and girlfriends, and they did not feel the need to separate out different strands of their composite identities. Certainly, most of them heard more at home about chores, more at church about God, and more at school about studies than about basketball. But in their own minds, they said, basketball had a way of pushing itself to top priority.

How did basketball get so important? Surely, some hopefuls had developed a taste for fame, fresh from high school games played in packed gyms. But most Immaculatans didn't try out for glory. Through the sixties, women's college basketball played second fiddle to the high school girls', and only in the seventies did Immaculata's teams command huge venues full of spectators. Some years, the Mackies barely pulled off a winning season. Some team members didn't get much playing time. So making the team mostly involved going to practice day after day, stealing time from studies and social life, and getting to bed late. But Immaculata players didn't seem to care. They just wanted to make the team. They just wanted to be basketball players.

If it wasn't about fame and glory, then why? I asked former players that question and got many different explanations. That *why* goes to the heart of basketball's pleasures for traditional Philadelphia Catholic girls. And as I tell their story, I pursue their answers—answers about class and community, spirituality and physicality. But before Immaculata players explained the *whys*, they took for granted that just being a team member was a pleasure in itself. It was a pleasurable identity. Basketball was fun, Marian Collins Mullahy '54 said, "but, you know what, it was also my identity . . . Marian Collins played basketball." It made them special with regard to fellow Catholics, other girls, and new possibilities. It marked them within the Philadelphia Catholic world, a subculture devoted to the girls' game but also vigilant of overall gender formation. It got them affirmation from Catholics who supported girls' basketball and negative attention from those who didn't. Before any other reason, Immaculata team members liked the game because as basketball players they identified who they wanted to be—and who they did not want to be—as young Catholic women. For Immaculata hopefuls, making the team also meant making identity.[3]

Making the Team

It was because identity was at stake that basketball tryouts became an occasion of paramount importance. Of course, Immaculata basketball players had the chance to "make identity" only to a limited degree. The identity of young Catholic women, as with all social identity, was largely given. For the most part, young women who tried out for Immaculata basketball were traditional Catholic girls who conformed to the expectations of parents, teachers, and religious authorities. But basketball was a specialized activity. Though overwhelmingly endorsed in Catholic Philadelphia, it still fell outside the scope of given identity for Catholic girls. And while almost every parish and school eventually sponsored a girls' basketball team, only a lucky few made the roster each season. As such, basketball opened possibilities for new relations with self and others—and for new, even if partial or temporary, identities within Catholicism. For Immaculatans, the chance to be basketball players offered an opportunity to fashion, in some small way, fresh senses of Catholic girlhood. And the fresh girlhood that basketball seemed to promise could be heady. For many Immaculata players, it was as if basketball became the yardstick by which they gauged themselves, as much as by traditional standards of family, school, and church. At tryouts, they gambled a chunk of self-esteem in hopes of measuring up. Whatever the substance of the new identities players imagined for themselves, they felt team membership could help give it to them.

At Immaculata, tryouts perennially drew more basketball devotees than coaches needed for two squads, varsity and junior varsity. To some extent, though, the popularity of the sport at Immaculata fluctuated with its success. In the late sixties, during the college's only losing seasons, tryouts drew the fewest aspirants, just thirty or so girls out of a student body of nearly eight hundred. In those years, "anyone who went to practice . . . was on the team and got to play," recalled Patricia LaRocco '71. But in the fall of 1974, after three championships, over 350 girls—a little less than half the student body—showed up for the first practice, including dozens of national-caliber players from all parts of the country.[4]

Still, whether the hopefuls numbered thirty or three hundred, they all came to tryouts for the same reason—the chance to be part of the team. Years later, regardless of season records or personal accomplishments, some players said their happiest memory of basketball was "joy at being part of a wonderful group" or just simply "being part of the team." For that reason, they said over and over, tryouts were gravely important. After playing high school ball, said Ann McSorley Lukens '53, she "desperately wanted to be picked for the team." If players worried about their chances, tryouts definitely merited prayer. "I prayed hard to make the varsity team," recalled a player from the class of '52. And when Margaret Klopfle Devinney '62 tried out, she planted her own special cheering section in the bleachers. "I was an experienced player, but others were much better than I," she wrote. "But I had fine friends who cheered very loudly whenever I did the least positive thing (especially when the coach was not paying particular attention to me) . . . so the coach was at least subconsciously influenced with the sound of my name shouted so often." After tryouts, players waited with hearts pounding to hear who had made the cut. If their gamble had paid off, wracked nerves gave way to relief and happiness. Ann remembered feeling "elated that I was part of this group."[5]

When a young woman made the Immaculata team, she had already decided that the kind of girl she wanted to be and the kinds of girls she wanted as friends played basketball. "You made friends, . . . almost for life," said a class of 1945 player. "Because they were the same way as you—they understood, you know?" Often, friends had introduced them to the sport. A 1950s player made her high school basketball team after trying out on a girlfriend's whim. "She said, 'Come on, we're both tall, let's go,'" she remembered. Basketball and the friends who played it reinforced each other. When it was time to choose a college, players said, they often heard about Immaculata by word of mouth from former teammates and other hoop acquaintances. They would visit a friend who played at Immaculata, attend a basketball practice, and like what they saw. Margaret Mary "Meg" Kenny Kean '58 enrolled at Immaculata because she was "so impressed with the team members." Mary Frank McCormick '50 chose Immaculata because former players on her parish team already went there.[6]

Trying out for the team as freshmen, players found some welcome familiarity in the scary new world of college. "We had known one another from playing locally in the area," recalled Evie Adams Atkinson '46. "So, we sort of felt as though we knew somebody. Even though we were in a strange college, there were other people that we knew. And we had a common bond." From there, she said, the new teammates only got more tightly attached. They had played against each other, she said, "but it was different when you played together. . . . Oh, it was fun." Many years later, Janet Young Eline '74 also felt reassured to meet others like her in the gym. "At tryouts I met other players who were also captains or outstanding players at their high schools."[7]

Throughout the years, Immaculatans remembered teammates as "special friends," "best friends," and "my best friends in the whole world." Spending time together, enduring hard practices, pulling together to win, and sharing common interests, Immaculata basketball players built "unmatched" relationships. "You never thought, like, oh, another day at practice," said Helen Frank Dunigan '56. "You went because it was a great time, [you] had fun." Those relationships extended off the court, too. Teammates grew to know each others' families, interests, and love lives. These friendships were half the fun of the sport. "You'd relive the basketball game to begin with, if you played that night," said Evie Adams Atkinson '46. "Then, of course, you talk about studies and you talk about who you were dating and who was going to go to the prom. You know, it was not all basketball, nor was it all studies. It kind of all intermeshed."[8]

If players did not have full-fledged friendships with each teammate, still the bonds of basketball could surpass many friendships, forged not only during long hours on the court but also in the "sense of importance of being a select few." They were the ones who got to wear what their campus newspaper called "the coveted blue and white uniforms." They got perks. "All the perks," said Marian Collins Mullahy '54. "You couldn't beat 'em. First of all, you missed about half a day at school, so you didn't even have to prepare for those classes. . . . It doesn't sound like anything now, but at my time, it was extraordinary." Out of class early, players took "pride" in walking with teammates and "wearing the I.C. jacket"—for most years, a thin blue satin coat with the white letters _I_ and _C_ intertwined on the front left. "People . . . had a lot of respect when you wore your jacket," said a player who graduated in 1945. "We wore them everywhere we went." Strolling together, wearing the gear, or just hanging out after practice, players felt a "sense of belonging" with this "wonderful group of girl athletes." Altogether, team members felt they were "different" and liked it. What exactly was different? Maybe they got to run outdoors and skimp house duties, as Sister Marita David said. Maybe they were more dynamic or more confident than other girls, others suggested. "My friends that were on teams never stopped," Marian said. "We liked who we were and what we were doing." However they defined it, the team was a pleasure, a small collective of female élan, a tight crew whose pride competed with that of school, family, and church.[9]

Of course, tryouts meant that some made the team and some did not. The competitive preseason conferred on new team members not only the prize of being basketball players but also the affirmation of beating out other hopefuls. Immediately after tryouts, the game marked both commonality with new teammates and distinction from unluckier attendees. And throughout the season, the elite crew of Immaculata players also used basketball to identify with—or distinguish themselves from—others in their Catholic world. For them, the community's significant categories included not only women and men, priests and parents, students and teachers but also—according to their take on basketball—fans and foes.

Girls' Basketball Fans

The Catholic community's basketball fans gathered from all constituencies to support players in their "different" venture. Fans' enthusiasm made the sport, of course, not so different after all. As players gave fans the thrill of vicarious participation and fans buoyed players with energy and affirmation, together they made the figure of a Catholic girl basketball player acceptable, if still exceptional.

Mothers, Sisters, Coaches

A number of former Immaculata players grew up hearing about their own mothers' basketball glory days and learned from them to play and love the game. Margaret Guinan Delaney '62's mother had "played basketball as a kid" in the thirties. "My mother was the competitor in the family," she said. Because of her mom, Margaret said, her and her siblings' lives "revolved around competitive sports." Similarly, Elizabeth Hoffman Quinn '73—also known as Betty Ann—said basketball was a family thing, because her mother had played ball first in college and afterward in industrial leagues. And at least one mother-daughter tandem graced the history of Immaculata teams. In the fall of 1966, Izanne Leonard Haak '70 made the team; her mother was star forward Isabel Flannery '43, the first Immaculatan ever named to the city's All-Philadelphia first team.[10]

While some followed in their mothers' footsteps, Immaculata cagers also often identified sisters from whom they learned the game. Helen Frank Dunigan '56 remembered tagging along with her older sister, Mary Frank McCormick '50, when Mary would join their brothers and neighborhood boys for backyard games. Helen was so little, she would normally have been chased away, but the guys' acceptance of big sister Mary eased Helen into the contests. When Helen was just twelve, Mary took her out for a prominent parish girls' team, Our Lady of Peace, which played both softball and basketball. But first Mary had to persuade the doubtful coach, parish priest Father Walter Nall, that her spindly sister could really play. Both women told the story of tiny Helen in the outfield for her first softball game, where she ran for a hard low liner over second base, caught it with one hand, and promptly fell into a hole—but still came up with the ball in her glove. Father Nall was deeply impressed, and Mary told him, "See, I told you she could catch a ball!" The next year, Mary enrolled at Immaculata and played four spectacular years of college basketball. Two years after graduation, when she returned to campus to coach the team, she mentored sister and star player Helen for another four.[11]

Other players also felt proud of their sisters' talents. Former coach Marie Schultes McGuinness bragged about her sister, Irene Schultes Jordan '45, whom she mentored as a "star" at Immaculata. Mary Murphy Schmelzer '62 praised younger sister Therese "Terri" Murphy McNally '63's skills even when she and four other freshmen bumped her off the starting lineup. At least three other pairs of sisters also played at Immaculata over these three and a half decades.[12]

Other key women in players' lives were basketball coaches—at Immaculata, always female. Beyond what mothers and sisters could offer, coaches had experience and education. As players, they had worked to become stars on their teams; later they had completed physical education degrees. Immaculatans credited these mentors, from Marie Schultes in the forties to Cathy Rush in the seventies, with inspiring them to reach the top of their game. More than that, they identified with coaches, who, like them, remembered what it was like to run playground courts with the guys or beg reluctant parents for new Chuck Taylor high-tops. With very few exceptions, Immaculata players adored their coaches. A player from the class of '56 said her happiest memory of basketball was just "hanging out" with a coach she admired. A few players even felt that their coaches, among all others in the Catholic world, really knew and loved them. "I loved my coaches because I felt [if] anyone cared about me in those days it would be my coaches," said Christine Lammer DiCiocchio '70.[13]

Even more, coaches were women who had turned their love of basketball into careers. Young basketball players saw in their coaches a new professional option. Not only that, it was a career that, like teaching or joining a religious order, served the church. The vast Philadelphia system always needed more women for coaching positions that the nuns, already stretched too thin in the classrooms, could never fill. For most of these years, then, coaching at Catholic girls' schools was one of the few church leadership positions, much less paid jobs, open to laywomen.

In the sixties and seventies, as young Catholic women faced new pressures to combine career and family, several Immaculata coaches tried to balance coaching with responsibilities as wives and mothers. By chance, these coaches were Protestants. In the forties and fifties, when the whole Immaculata physical education staff was Catholic, Immaculata basketball coaches usually quit when they got married. But in later decades Jenepher Shillingford, a Methodist, and Cathy Rush, a Baptist, gave players what they considered "a good role model as a working mom," coaching through pregnancies and toting toddlers and portable cribs to practice. The kids were "not terribly supervised, but they never got into that much trouble," remembered Marie Olivieri Russell '66. "And we all kind of looked out for them." Career or no, almost all Immaculata players said they assumed they would marry and have children, and most did. But very few gave up loving basketball. For Immaculata players in the sixties and seventies, Protestant coaches modeled the possibility that their lives as wives and mothers could still allow room for basketball.[14]

Throughout the years, dozens of Immaculata players graduated to land jobs coaching basketball with CYO, grade school, high school, and city recreation center teams. Others refereed local girls' games, initially getting certified to make some pocket cash for school and later officiating as a flexible career. A few players used sports savvy to invent other work options. Kathryn Peterson '28, who captained the first protovarsity team Immaculata ever fielded, went to work for the Philadelphia Department of Recreation and worked her way up to general program director, introducing thousands of Philadelphia kids to sports along the way. One player founded a summer basketball league on Sea Isle, New Jersey; another 1963 graduate worked at a Catholic mission for Native Americans in Nebraska, teaching gym and starting youth clubs. Barbara Mooney '65 headed the "Malvern Project," a program that enlisted Immaculata volunteers to teach physical education to grade-schoolers at St. Patrick's in Malvern.[15]

Especially from Cathy Rush's years, Immaculata players went on to coach other college programs: at LaSalle, St. Joe's, Colorado, San Jose State, and Gettysburg. At least three team members quickly broke into NCAA Division I schools and led teams to Final Fours and national titles. Rene Muth Portland '75 took the head coaching job at Penn State after years at St. Joe's. Theresa Shank Grentz '74 coached briefly at St. Joe's before taking the helm at Rutgers, coaching the U.S. Olympic team, and then moving to the University of Illinois. And Marianne Crawford Stanley '76, in her first job after graduation, won three national championships as coach of Old Dominion University. Later, Marianne moved to Penn, Southern Cal, Stanford, and Berkeley, before taking a job in the pros, as head coach of the Washington Mystics club of the Women's National Basketball Association. The legacy of Cathy Rush, who resigned from coaching after her six-year Immaculata stint, is "not just three AIAW titles but the people that worked with her," said Jenepher Shillingford. "Her players . . . went on to lead very, very fine programs."[16]

Sister-Fans and Patron-Priests

Immaculata players also found deep wells of support among religious sisters who were basketball fans and sometimes former cagers themselves. Several players said nuns had introduced them to the game. Growing up in center city Philadelphia in the late thirties, Evie Adams Atkinson '46 described transferring from public school to Catholic school and feeling "a little shaky." But after meeting her new seventh-grade teacher, she recovered. "She was a nun by the name of Sister Jane Frances who was quite a sports lady," she remembered. "And she introduced me [to] basketball. . . . We had gym class, and from there on in, it was a love." At Immaculata, players thrived among Immaculate Heart nuns who formally sponsored and personally befriended the basketball team.[17]

To some extent, the college's institutional support can be explained as a by-product of single-sex schooling, traditional in the Philadelphia archdiocese. At Immaculata, women played basketball partly because women-only environments could function to open traditionally male gender roles, not only in sports but also in leadership and intellectual areas. "Generally it was like, sports is for guys, girls aren't supposed to play sports," Mary Lou McCahon Noone '65 said she sometimes heard. "But at Immaculata, being an all-girls' school, you never heard it." Young women led the debate team and ran for the Student Association during the day; they filled the stands for school basketball games at night.[18]

But beyond the women's college environment, many players credited the popularity of basketball at Immaculata to the Immaculate Heart sisters, themselves well schooled by the Philadelphia Catholic subculture of girls' hoops. Some of the nuns were basketball fans so loyal to their high school alma maters that they were known to hatch elaborate schemes to get free of community duties and attend big games in town, chauffeured by some collaborating priest. And among otherwise indifferent sisters, the Immaculata basketball environment cultivated interest. According to players, basketball

Theresa Shank '74, Rene Muth '75, and Marianne Crawford
'76, on the sidelines in 1974. By 2002 these three coached the
University of Illinois, Penn State, and the WNBA Washington
Mystics, respectively. COURTESY OF IMMACULATA COLLEGE.

was "the favorite sport of the nuns," whom they sensed found the games a
pleasurable "outlet" in their demanding lives.[19]

Many players singled out Sister Mary of Lourdes McDevitt '36, president of
Immaculata from 1954 to 1972, as their "top supporter by far." "Almost all the
sisters were supportive," wrote Margaret Monahan Hogan '63, "but none had
the understanding of the game that Sister Mary of Lourdes had." Born in 1915,
the youngest in a North Philadelphia family of seven, Sister Mary of Lourdes
said she "played basketball all the time." "My sisters ignored me to a point because I wasn't interested in all the things I was supposed to be interested in,"
she remembered. "I hate to say it, but I was never very ladylike. I was always
out playing basketball or baseball or football with my brothers." Attending
Hallahan, she played on a school team that won the Catholic League championship. After that, even as chemistry professor and college president, she never
lived down a reputation as "a fantastic athlete" and always gravitated to the
basketball court. Habitually stopping by practice, Sister Mary of Lourdes
would find herself catching a pass, running a play. "We wouldn't let her leave
until she had shot a few goals," remembered Fruff Fauerbach Timby '50. Sister
Mary of Lourdes and her roommate, college treasurer Sister Cor Immaculata
Connors, always led the procession of nuns who filed into gymnasiums across

Philadelphia wherever the Mackies were playing. "The whole time I was at Immaculata," she said, "I never missed a game."[20]

While Immaculata could never afford to give athletic scholarships, Sister Mary of Lourdes's tenure implicitly authorized perks for members of the basketball team, even academic perks. "Technically, we were never to miss a class for a sports activity," recalled Mary Murphy Schmelzer '62. But some sisters "gave some flexibility for practice [and] travel time" and sometimes even "rearrang[ed] test schedules." After the first championship, players stayed up far past midnight celebrating the victory with the whole student body in the rotunda of Villa Maria Hall. "I was supposed to have a big test the next day," recalled team manager Jean Brashears Vause '74. "Sister Bernadette whispered in my ear—'No test tomorrow, get some rest!'"[21]

Not only nuns but also priests became crucial supporters for many Immaculatans' athletic endeavors. In all the Catholic United States, priests garnered respect as religious authorities and community figures, but in the Philadelphia archdiocese, populated by the notably proclerical Irish, the "accepted priestly image," wrote one historian, "was almost wholly positive, at once wise, hypermasculine, warm, athletic, [and] jovial." In such a climate, attention from priests could feel more special than attention from other grown-ups, even from other adult men. When priests coached basketball, attended games, or invited the team over for dinner, Catholic girls experienced the pleasure of unusual access to centers of community power. They also found support for girls' basketball in the ranks of the faith's acknowledged leadership.[22]

Although the Immaculata teams never had male coaches or even team chaplains, many players' CYO coaches had been priests, whom they counted among their earliest advocates. And long before the CYO, there was Father Walter Nall, pastor of Our Lady of Peace in Belmont Park, who organized and coached basketball and softball girls' teams associated with the church throughout the forties and fifties. Since CYO leagues were in their infancy in Philadelphia and could not compete with Our Lady of Peace, Father Nall scheduled "his girls," ranging from twelve years old to college age, against local teams in industrial, recreational, church, and neighborhood leagues. Technically, the team represented Our Lady of Peace; two of his star players, the Bissinger sisters, were parishioners, and their mother served as Nall's rectory housekeeper. But when the Bissingers recruited players from outside the parish, Father Nall didn't care, as long as the new girls could hold their own. The Bissingers and several other stars from Our Lady of Peace later attended Immaculata, because Father Nall, whose sister was an Immaculate Heart nun, steered them toward the college. At Immaculata, he quickly became a familiar figure to everyone associated with the basketball program.[23]

Father Nall committed himself to female athletes, coaching them to superior play, driving them to games, and lavishing time and money on them. "He loved [us], he couldn't do enough for his girls' team. He'd pop you in a school bus and drive," remembered Mary Frank McCormick '50. "We'd go to Pottstown from Belmont Park on Sunday, play two softball games, and drive home. And somewhere on the way home, he'd stop and buy us all dinner. I mean like at a restaurant, it wasn't a McDonald's." Other players remembered longer trips, to New Jersey and New York, anywhere Father Nall could get a good game. Mary's younger sister, Helen Frank Dunigan '56, said Father Nall's support of girls' sports "was way ahead of his time." His players credited him with the confidence and talent they developed as athletes. "He [had] an understanding that the girls needed something, too," Helen said.[24]

Former players described Father Nall as a congenial, soft-hearted priest. "When he walked into a room, children gathered around him like he was Hans Christian Andersen," remembered Helen. But as a coach, he demanded the best. And the best meant they "didn't play like girls," said Mary. "That was his criteria. . . . He figured we were all good athletes and we were playing more like boys. So that was the bottom line, for him." Father Nall's "girls" didn't seem to mind being "more like boys," because they knew it was his highest compliment. Besides, his exacting standards paid off. Once going undefeated for nine straight years, his teams "never lost," Mary remembered.[25]

A unique person in many ways, Father Nall also just took to another level the support many parish priests afforded girls' teams, even if they didn't actually coach. In her parochial grade school in the early fifties, recalled Maureen Callahan Bigham '63, "girls' sports were on a par with the boys." A few parishes even supported adult women's teams as well as school sports. Priests reserved them gym time and allocated funds for uniforms, equipment, and transportation in parish budgets. Many Immaculata players remembered priests, and the archdiocese they represented, as advocates who believed athletics forecast "a new and exciting era women were moving into," as Mary Jane Renshaw Lewandowski '64 said. Similarly, Alvina DeLazzari Long '57 wrote, "My entire experience was that the Catholic Church supported and promoted women's basketball."[26]

At Immaculata, players remembered Nall and other priests for their particular support. Assigned as professors or chaplains, priests usually "[attended] all games possible," while college president Monsignor Francis Furey (1936–46) "was a great supporter of women in sports," said Evie Adams Atkinson '46, "and wanting women in any way to get ahead." But a few priests contributed much more than general support. Immaculata sociology professor Father Charles Gorman stood out. From the early forties, Father

Gorman was "an avid admirer of the basketball team." After each season, he invited the team to a dinner at his mother's house, to the exclusion of other teams, such as field hockey and swimming. "Basketball was his pet team, I think," said Evie. Inviting Monsignor Furey, Father Nall, and team alumnae to the postseason dinners as well, Father Gorman capped the evening's festivities by showing his home movies of the season's games. He wasn't the most reliable cameraman: Eva said she and her teammates teased him for failing to record their big Temple victory in 1946. "He got so excited he forgot to put the film in the camera. . . . We said, 'Well, you were supposed to be recording this!'" Perhaps to make up for his oversight, he took the whole team out for steak dinners to the newly opened Mansion House Hotel in West Chester.[27]

In support of women's basketball, Father Gorman put his money where his mouth was. It was widely known on campus that the priest, who also taught at LaSalle, reinvested the entire salary he drew from Immaculata into the athletic department, personally financing basketball backboards and later an electronic scoreboard. He also sponsored at least one under-the-table athletic scholarship. "I don't know if I should be telling this, but I'm going to tell," said Dee Cofer Cull '55. The daughter of a widowed mother, Dee faced the prospect of leaving Immaculata after her sophomore year. "'Cause I could have gone to Temple for no money," she said. But Father Gorman "liked the way I played basketball . . . so [he] said, 'I'll pay half if you keep playing like you're playing.'" For her remaining two years, Dee was able to stay at Immaculata because of Father Gorman's help. Other basketball players and the priest developed close relationships, too. After college, he would officiate at their weddings and baptize their babies. In all these ways, Gorman and priests like him put individual male faces on the archdiocese's official sponsorship of women's basketball.[28]

Fathers and Brothers

Other men also made appearances on the basketball scene. Some players identified with their fathers as comrades in sport and basketball fans. Going to games or talking stats with their dads, Immaculata team members played basketball with paternal affirmation. Monica Burns Atkinson '51 said her dad took her to baseball games. "He was a big influence and very proud that . . . I was real coordinated," she said. Pauline Callahan Earl '57 remembered the thrill of going to a Penn football game or watching a televised fight with her dad. Even though she didn't particularly like boxing, she said, "I was my father's daughter, so I watched it with him." Barbara Flanigan '68 said her dad began taking her to St. Joe's games and any other men's college game around when she was eight years old. Epiphany Pantaleo Collins '64 went to men's professional games with her father when Philadelphia's National Basketball Association (NBA) team was the Warriors.[29]

Watching sports with their dads, they also played sports like their dads, many of whom had been athletes. "My father was my biggest supporter," remembered Pauline Callahan Earl '57. An all-Catholic football player, her father was the reason sports were "a part of my life," she said. Betty Ann Hoffman Quinn '73 also attributed her athletic interests to her dad. "He played football in college," she said. "And that's how I was brought up." Fathers could take advocacy for their daughters' athleticism quite far. When one player's father found out she was barred, being a girl, from his tennis club, he switched clubs.[30]

Several players hypothesized that their fathers supported athletic daughters in the absence of sons. During World War II, Mary and Helen Frank's four older brothers went overseas. Helen helped her dad at home, and he attended her basketball games. "I was the one that helped my father paint and dig gardens and do everything that you had to do outside the house . . . which my brothers would have done," she said. "I seemed to get in the direction of doing things with my dad." Single daughters sensed that regarding sports they filled the role of "daughter and son" for their dads. As an only child, Pauline Callahan Earl '57 recalled that since her father "was very athletic-minded . . . I wanted to be able to do something as good as [a son]." She went on, "I'm sure there was some of that in my life." Similarly, only child Epiphany Pantaleo Collins '64 reported her basketball activities "made my father very happy." He would wait up at home after every game "to hear how I did and how many points I scored and so forth."[31]

Often less occupied during evenings and weekends than mothers, some fathers attended daughters' games religiously. "My father got so caught up in our team . . . he would arrange to come to as many games as he could," remembered Maureen Callahan Bigham '63. In the early seventies' championship years, fathers played key roles in orchestrating the cheering section. "My father and Rene [Muth Portland]'s father are responsible for the signs at our games," Marianne Crawford Stanley '76 told local reporter Herm Rogul in 1974. Rene's father, a hardware store owner, also supplied the metal buckets that Immaculata fans became infamous for banging during games. During the 1974 national tournament, when officials banned the buckets, the Immaculata dads protested for hours. "The fathers went hysterical," Rene said. In turn, daughters were moved that their dads showed so much care. "My father is proud of me," Marianne told Rogul. "I work hard to make him proud of me." Rene was exhilarated that her father even closed the hardware store for her sake. "We didn't even close for my brother's wedding," she said. "But we've closed four times for my basketball games."[32]

Immaculata players also got respect for athletic endeavors from brothers, who were often their first basketball teammates. Growing up with four older brothers in rural Springfield, Mary Frank McCormick '50 said, "I played the whole time with my brothers. . . . We played football and baseball and anything. So I sort of learned athletics from the boys." Throughout the years, players credited their skills to playing with brothers. "I was a strong player because of my brothers," said Mary Lou McCahon Noone '65. Janet Young Eline '74 also "spent a lot of time with my older brother," the one who "taught me how to throw a ball." Judging from their sisters' impressions, these Catholic brothers took for granted girls' participation in sports and just appreciated having more bodies for teams. Margaret Guinan Delaney '62 said she never heard from her father or four brothers that girls should not play basketball. "Absolutely not. Oh, no. Everybody was most enthusiastic for the team." Mary Lou said she knew some people disparaged girls' athletics, but "it didn't bother me," because "my siblings never said that. I never heard anything from my siblings or family."[33]

Boy Friends and Boyfriends

For Catholic girls, basketball gave occasions for close contact not just with priests, fathers, and brothers but also with boys outside their families. Attending single-sex schools, Catholic young women and men in Philadelphia lived in virtual segregation, except for supervised dances or the occasional mixed glee club. But outside official parameters, on playgrounds and in the neighborhoods, Immaculata players remembered male teammates as friends. Dee Cofer Cull '55 grew up in the forties running with a gang of eight boys, "and I could beat any of them," she said. "I'm not bragging. . . . In fact, when they picked a team, I was the first one picked. And they weren't puny-looking boys." A decade later, Gloria Rook Schmidt '64 played in her southwest Philadelphia neighborhood with one brother, male cousins, and a neighborhood full of boys. "I grew up basically in a boy-dominated area," she said. "So I played basketball and baseball and football, anything that was going on." Playing sports with her male friends was "normal," she said. "Completely . . . because [I] could play. I could hold my own. I mean, it wasn't something that was handed to me. You had to prove your own." In the sixties, Janet Young Eline '74 learned to play basketball with boys, mostly African American, growing up in a housing project in York, Pennsylvania. "I didn't think anything of it," she recalled.[34]

At least two Immaculatans even played on organized boys' teams before going to college. From seventh grade through high school, Evie Adams

Atkinson '46 said, she played on a boys' team associated with St. Francis Xavier, a Catholic parish and school. "One of the gals that I played with . . . lived at Twenty-third and Spring Garden. And they had this boys' basketball team and they would play . . . once a week," she remembered. "And we were asked [to play]. We liked to play. She was a forward, I was a guard, but we both liked basketball very much. So we figured we could get a few tips from playing with the boys. So we used to play full court with the boys." There was no separate girls' team. "Whoever could come would come and play," Evie said. "And any of the girls who were available would come and play." When I asked Evie if any parents or teachers questioned girls playing on the team, she said, "No. Just so long as you could handle that ball, they didn't care whether you were male or female. Didn't make much difference." While this arrangement might have been unusual even for the Philadelphia archdiocese, it was not anomalous. Anne Carroll Camp '51 also said she played on a Catholic grade school boys' team in her Germantown neighborhood.[35]

Later, at all-girls Immaculata, playing basketball continued to afford young Catholic women unusual contact with young men. On at least one occasion, in 1950, Immaculata's student-run athletic association invited the Villanova University football team to campus to play the girls' varsity in basketball. The football players adopted the women's rules format, but Fruff Fauerbach Timby '50 did not say who won. "Half-court, one bounce—It was a hoot!" she wrote. "We all had a good laugh and a good time."[36]

Even if they didn't usually play basketball with guys, Immaculatans said basketball invited them to identify with male basketball stars, both local and national. Going to Big Five or Philadelphia Warriors games or, later, watching televised NBA matchups, Immaculata players spectated differently from non-basketball-playing girls. They watched for fun but also looked for new moves. They liked the guys, but they also wanted to be *like* the guys. Regarding men as fellow athletes as well as members of the opposite sex, Immaculata team members said basketball somehow relaxed pressure about dating. "Like some [girls] would go nuts to have a date," remembered Mary Frank McCormick '50. "Well, if I had a date, you know, it had to be somebody I liked. Because . . . to go out with a boy just because, just to go out, was no treat for me."[37]

But certainly some Immaculata players wanted to date the guys as well as study their moves. And with some guys, especially a lot of Catholic college men in Philadelphia, basketball could help with getting dates. Having grown up in the same basketball-crazed culture as the girls, many Catholic young men "were kind of glad that you played in sports and could talk to them about sports," said Evie Adams Atkinson '46. Attending local powerhouses St. Joe's, Villanova, and LaSalle, young men lived on campuses where basketball had huge cachet. "Most of us dated boys from those schools," remembered a player from the Class of '53. "And so . . . if you played and you were lucky enough to get on the team, then it was great."[38]

Boys came to watch the Immaculata games, perhaps accompanying a player's brother and bringing a few more friends. "Boys. Not just boyfriends. Boys from Villanova and St. Joe's would come to watch Immaculata play," recalled Dee Cofer Cull '55. "And not necessarily dating a girl. Just liked the way we played." Afterward, recalled Mary Lou McCahon Noone '65, "everybody kind of went out in groups, the guys and the girls." But if it was an Immaculata home game, way out in the cornfields of Malvern, young men had already gone quite out of their way to attend, a good sign they were amorously invested. "Might be a guy that's dating some girl and brought a guy with [him] or something like that," said Helen Frank Dunigan '56. Her husband, Tim, who went to Villanova, explained. "If you wanted to visit a girls' college, you went to Rosemont; it was convenient," he said. Otherwise, "why would I go out [to Immaculata]? You almost needed a road map in those days." Despite the trip, several players affirmed there were suitors in attendance for most games. Suitors who became boyfriends and fiancés turned into audience regulars and team groupies.[39]

Many young men never got past the suitor stage, but Immaculata players enjoyed the attention anyway. "I had lots of phone calls and things like that," remembered Mary Frank McCormick '50. "Candy would show up one time, flowers on Valentine's Day, that kind of stuff." Later, during the championship years in the seventies, Janet Young Eline '74 recalled, "we all got letters from guys that would watch the games." Sister Marian William Hoben '44, former Immaculata president (1982–92) and team fan, also told the story of a reporter who requested an interview with one Mighty Mac but, when she agreed, took her out to dinner instead.[40]

Players said there was "most definitely" a type of young man who liked girls who played basketball, which Christine Lammer DiCiocchio '70 described as "very easy-going, unpretentious, friendly." Different players might have ascribed to this type a variety of characteristics, but at least it included being comfortable with women playing basketball. If they weren't, "they wouldn't come around," said Mary Frank McCormick '50. It was clear to players that not all guys could handle a girlfriend who could take them one-on-one. "I didn't run around telling everybody that I was a fullback at Immaculata," said Marian Collins Mullahy '54, who also played field hockey. "Because some of these guys could not have kept up with something like that." From their end, players liked young men who admired their athleticism, who didn't seem intimidated by girls playing basketball or "didn't express it if they were," said Mary. Whether or not they were athletes themselves, these guys, players felt, liked and respected their way of being women. "[I was] still independent when I got married," said Mary. "[My husband] knew what kind of girl I was." Marie Olivieri Russell '66 even said her husband "married me because I was on the basketball court." In medical school in Philly, she and her roommate took a study break. "We went out and were just running around shooting some baskets and next thing you know I was going out with him," she recalled. "So I guess [basketball] got me my husband." Marianne Crawford Stanley '76 also met her husband through sports. According to reporter Ann Killion, future Villanova basketball player Rich Stanley asked Marianne to his high school senior prom after seeing her outrun a softball by sliding headfirst into home plate. Soon they formed a partnership on Upper Darby playground courts, regularly besting all comers in games of two-on-two. After they beat everybody else, they played each other.[41]

Room for Women

As much as men supported women playing basketball, they were never formally involved in it at Immaculata. More subtle than other kinds of affirmation for Catholic girl hoopsters, the female-dominated nature of the sport at Immaculata afforded a chance for leadership and self-sufficiency slightly removed from men, particularly the male-ordered hierarchy. To be sure, female-only activities were not unusual at a women's college. After the last priest who served as college president finished his term in 1954, I.H.M.s ruled the school from top to bottom, while just a few campus priests taught classes, celebrated Mass, and heard confessions. In school assemblies, club meetings, and cafeteria lines, very few men were present, and walking across campus between classes the Catholic hierarchy was barely visible, while sisters floating in dark blue habits dominated the landscape. Immaculata's entire environment of single-sex education could cultivate students' independence and initiative.

But Immaculata sisters and students were still women in a Catholic community that symbolically and structurally ranked men above women. Laywomen filled the pews, but men sat on parish councils. Nuns ran the schools, but bishops decided policy. Sisters taught chemistry, but priests taught theology and philosophy. And the Roman Church's exclusive ordination of men required their presence at every mass and most public events. So even at Immaculata, priests presided at defining moments. Chaplains officiated ceremonies. Clerics spoke at commencements. The I.H.M.s, like all women's orders, opened their Gillet Hall private chapel to priests, who alone could consecrate the Eucharist and read the gospel. In the Catholic Church, even

A typical Mighty Macs audience, at West Chester, February 1974.
ROBERT HALVEY COLLECTION OF THE PHILADELPHIA ARCHIVES AND HISTORICAL RESEARCH CENTER.

when sisters headed colleges, they remained structurally subordinate—*and* signally represented the institution that subordinated them. In a sense, sisters signified the presence of priests, even when priests were physically absent.[42]

But Immaculatans played basketball entirely without priestly mediation. Because basketball was not thought central to religious life, it put players at a temporary remove from clerical oversight. At Immaculata, there was never even a team chaplain, unlike local men's colleges, where during games a priest was always sitting at the end of the bench. When players reported for practice, only laywomen—team members, coaches, and student managers—usually attended. At the beginning of practice, they got out equipment and swept the court; at the end of practice, they parceled out duties of copying game programs or calling in scores to the papers. Everything that a basketball program demanded, women did it. Games were similarly self-sufficient. Referees, scorers, and timekeepers were women. Certainly, fathers, brothers, boyfriends, and the occasional priest cheered in the stands, "but not in any great numbers," said Helen Frank Dunigan '56. "It was mostly the girls and the nuns." Playing basketball, Immaculata young women contributed, at the very least, to a prominent public activity conducted without the leadership of priests. At most, they enjoyed an extracurricular project that blunted or temporarily neutralized the usual gender hierarchies of their community. Whether or not they realized it, basketball players practiced long shots and zone defense in one of few Catholic arenas where the authority of the "Fathers" was irrelevant—and where bodies that happened to be women's bodies had a little more room to run.[43]

Immaculata cagers loved being basketball players, an identity supported and affirmed by fellow Catholics. Foremothers in the game embodied how to be women and athletes at the same time. Fathers and priests embraced basketball and the young women who played it. The support of both women and men told players that basketball was one route to becoming a well-regarded Catholic daughter, sister, or girlfriend. In turn, Immaculata players used basketball as a measure of whom they held in high regard.

Girls' Basketball Foes

In a general culture of support, Immaculata players occasionally encountered critics. In the earliest years, the sport was so new that Catholics as well as others questioned whether it was appropriate for girls. Sister Mary of Lourdes McDevitt '36, who played high school ball at Hallahan, said there were definitely Catholics "who thought we shouldn't be playing." But in Bonner's era, the tradition caught on. World War II also helped. The draft decimated ranks of male teams, so girls played with new attention from fans and even newspapers, which sent out their first few female sportswriters, such as Helen Mankin and Dora Lurie, who wrote up the 1946 Immaculata-Temple game. But after the war national rhetoric that aimed to resettle white women in their traditional roles also renewed debates about girls' athletics, especially concerns about reproductive health and middle-class femininity. In the national mainstream, a climate of opposition to women's sports persisted for three decades. Throughout these years, Philadelphia Catholics strongly supported girls' basketball, but they weren't completely isolated from conventional sentiments. For all its cachet, basketball still marked young women as different and sometimes strange. And Immaculata basketball players remembered occasional disapproval and antagonism from coreligionists.[44]

Unlike Immaculatans who followed mothers' and sisters' footsteps onto the court, a few said their love of athletics set them apart from Catholic women and girls who walked more traditional paths. Some players pointedly left the kitchen for the playing field. "One day when I was 15 or 16, I made a dash out the kitchen because the 'guys' needed one more for touch football," remembered Fruff Fauerbach Timby '50. Theresa Shank Grentz '74 also said basketball offered a way out of housework. "I could either play with the boys on the block or help my mother clean," she told a reporter in 1973. If former players suggested they were different from mothers who cooked and cleaned, they were also different from sports-averse sisters who were too "girly"—that is, overly invested, for athletes' tastes, in things stereotypically feminine, from dresses and dolls to marriage and kids. "My youngest sister . . . is the most girly girl that you ever saw in your life," recalled a player from the late forties. "She wanted to get out [of high school], she wanted to get married . . . she had a boyfriend, and I mean she did all the girl things." Not only sisters but also girlfriends could seem caught up in activities they "were supposed to do," for example, watching basketball instead of playing it. Janet Young Eline '74 said she was always puzzled by friends who would accompany her to the court only to sit on the sidelines. They wanted to "watch me shoot, actually, because they weren't interested [in playing]," she said. Nonathletic peers could become friends, players said, but not friends who knew the basketball-loving side of them. "It did separate me from my close friends, for none of my friends liked sports," said a player who graduated in 1953. Even at basketball-happy Immaculata, some players sensed a gap between girls who were athletes and those who weren't. About a third of survey respondents said they felt fellow students seemed not to care for the team all that much.[45]

Another set of women in basketball players' lives, the Immaculate Heart sisters, included a few who disparaged their involvement in sport. Some players who ran into nuns' disapproval blamed the difference on a generational gap. "I had a lot of very, very old nuns. . . . All they did was teach their own way and did their own thing," said Mary Lou McCahon Noone '65. "I mean, [they] didn't find out, 'Oh, what are you doing, how's the basketball team,' none of that." As late as the seventies, a few players sensed some nuns' resistance to basketball—until the team started winning. "When we got good is different . . . because a lot of the nuns, you know, they were from a different generation and . . . sports weren't their thing," said Betty Ann Hoffman Quinn '73. "It was kind of like they tolerated it. They didn't necessarily see the value of it." Other teachers resented giving quarter to extracurricular activities. Helen McElroy '44 recalled a sister who prevented her from leaving a biology lab for an away game until the coach came for her. Throughout the years, team members would exchange intelligence to avoid taking the classes of sisters who "wouldn't be caught dead in the gym" and gave basketball players a hard time. But, players said, I.H.M. nuns who objected to girls' basketball on principle were few and far between. Usually dissenting sisters seemed most worried that players spent time on the court at the expense of studies. Fruff Fauerbach Timby '50 said a sister stopped her on campus one day to suggest she drop sports so she could concentrate on school. When Fruff told her how much she loved basketball, the nun "seemed to appreciate this and never mentioned it again."[46]

Men as well as women of the Catholic community also occasionally questioned girls' athletic interests, Immaculata players remembered. For men, concern seemed to center on how playing basketball affected femininity. Even the most supportive dads sometimes attempted to rein in daughters' athletic versions of the feminine gender. "Every once in a while, [my father] would get on my case," recalled Mary Frank McCormick '50. "He'd make me help Mother do a cake or something. And I'd think, this is crazy." Brothers, too, could put down sisters' athletic pursuits. Monica Burns Atkinson '51 said her brothers tried to curtail her athleticism as she hit puberty by saying, "Cut that out! How can you expect anybody to be interested in you if they see you doing things like that?" Fruff Fauerbach Timby '50, on her way out to play football one day, remembered her brother calling after her, "When are you going to realize you're a *girl*?" "Never," she wrote in answer. "I was petite and little, but I loved sports." Players could also face the opposite insinuation from men: that their game—the attenuated DGWS format with strict regulation of rough play—was *too* feminine, hardly even real basketball. "My brother always laughed at the feeble [officiating] calls as compared to boys' basketball," said a player from the class of '53. Others reported that this or that boyfriend trivialized their participation in sports. Immaculata players would attend boyfriends' basketball games, said a 1957 graduate, "but they didn't come to ours. . . . I don't think it even mattered to them if we played basketball or not at all." Even when the Mighty Macs won their first national championship, "I think the guys maybe [did not see it] as serious as it turned out to be," said Janet Young Eline '74. "They were, like, 'Oh, they're so cute. They're so dainty-looking with their bows and their jewelry.'"[47]

Finally, a few priests were known to disapprove of girls' basketball, as much as most supported it. Always signifying religious authority, priests' objections seemed to weave gender concerns with moral ones. "I think the archdiocese [leadership] felt sports were 'unfeminine' for girls," said a 1953 graduate. Mary Jane Renshaw Lewandowski '64 also sensed that some priests "believed women should not be running around the court in shorts." Most, however, conveyed that a few naysayers didn't spoil their impression of general clerical support and excused them as older men, "unaware, and unfamiliar" with changes in women's roles in the world.[48]

When Immaculata players found affirmation of being basketball players in the Catholic community, it is easy to see why making the team was a source of pleasure. But what about when they encountered opposition from people they loved and respected? Wouldn't that be more painful than pleasurable? Certainly, some players remembered feeling hurt when they caught wind of disapproval, anger when others dismissed a beloved activity. But only sometimes does pleasure come from fitting the mold; other times, it's fun to break it. And for the most part, when Immaculata players remembered disapproval, they relished it. The weight of Catholic culture was on their side, and when a few curmudgeons disapproved, it made things spicy, not difficult. They liked how basketball set them apart—among those who liked it and among those who didn't.

. . .

Making the team meant more to Immaculata players than the chance of athletic participation. It also meant making their identities as Catholic young women. As traditional girls attending a Catholic college, they largely upheld community norms. But, as team members, they used basketball as an additional measurement of themselves and others in the Catholic community. Basketball in part decided whom they respected or befriended, from relatives and teachers to boyfriends and religious authorities. It helped decide which gender roles and stereotypes to question, among those they accepted. It influenced where they went and what they did with their time, even if it urged giving short shrift to homework to finish a pickup game with the guys. Perhaps basketball meant they saw their religion's given rules for women and men in slightly fuzzier contrast, as they sometimes viewed members of both sexes, lay and religious, as fans or foes. Even when community members opposed basketball, Immaculata players took it as veritable confirmation of a new athletic feminine identity. This new identity started with making the team. And it remained busily under construction throughout the seasons, in collaboration with teammates and foremothers, in full sight of the whole Catholic community.

Both enfolding themselves into and setting themselves apart from the Catholic world, Immaculata players took for granted the identity-making powers of basketball. They were just glad to make the team. But beating out other hopefuls at tryouts didn't always end competition and conflict among fellow team members. Gathered together every day on the court, Immaculata players stumbled on deeper community fault lines than the division between basketball fans and foes. In the confined, regulated space of the basketball court, the team practiced and played out a microcosm of Catholic class tensions.

CHAPTER 2

PRACTICING BASKETBALL, PRACTICING CLASS

When the fire started, dozens of Immaculata sophomores were decorating the Field House gymnasium for their class cotillion. It was Friday, November 17, 1967, a brisk late fall day of last leaves swirling off huge campus oaks and maples. All afternoon, girls twirled streamers, inflated balloons, and hung banners for their big Saturday dance, adorning the interior stage and floor of the granite Field House. Talking about ballgowns and boys, they looked forward to the next evening's dates with young men from local Catholic colleges. As four o'-clock approached, Immaculata gym teacher and basketball coach Jenepher Shillingford said good-bye to the decorators, got in her car, and headed home at the end of a long workweek. Gym classes had finished for the day. The field hockey season was over. Basketball had not yet started, but Shillingford was anticipating a solid turnout for tryouts scheduled after Thanksgiving. Just as she departed, what firefighters later determined was faulty electrical wiring sparked and ignited stage curtains at the back of the gym.[1]

Driving home, Shillingford turned on the radio and heard reports of a blaze at the Field House at Immaculata College. She turned the car around. "I got there just [in time] to see the doors blow off," she said. After the curtains caught fire, flames spread rapidly to paper decorations, wooden beams, and especially the gym floor, perpetually "varnished . . . to within an inch of its life," said Shillingford. "And the fire just roared down the length of the gym and blew the doors off." Students had called the fire department, cleared the building, and run to get college president, Sister Mary of Lourdes, who was in her Villa Maria office finishing the week's paperwork. Within minutes the sister arrived on the scene of a fire already jumping through the Field House roof. She could hardly believe all the girls had escaped and kept asking, "Is every kid out of there?" For four hours, five fire companies, a hundred and fifty men, and eighteen vehicles battled the blaze. At eight o'clock, when the fire finally died, nothing was left but charred ruins and stone walls.[2]

Shaken and "petrified," Sister Mary of Lourdes, Jen Shillingford, and athletic director Marge Spencer walked among the smoldering ashes that very night to survey what the fire chief had declared a total loss. Nobody had been hurt, but for the whole Immaculata community, losing the Field House was "a real blow." It was the school's first genuine gymnasium and auditorium, built seventeen years before and used constantly for classes, games, dances, and assemblies. At a cost of three-quarters of a million dollars, it could not be easily replaced by a tiny, underfunded Catholic women's college whose accounts were always only dollars out of the red. All the gym equipment that burned, from balls to scoreboards, would take time to replace as well. Basketball player Fruff Fauerbach Timby '50, who played her senior season in the Field House when it was brand-new, recalled that as an alumna she was "horrified to hear it burned down, so precious as it was to at last have [a gym]."[3]

As many former players recalled, the Field House fire was only the most dramatic moment in a long history of dislocation and itinerancy for the Immaculata basketball program. As successful as some of the squads became, for only half of these thirty-six years did the team ever play games on its own court. Before 1950, Immaculata practiced in a makeshift gym in the basement of Villa Maria and played home games on borrowed courts. Then, for seventeen years, school teams enjoyed use of the Field House. But after the 1967 fire, Immaculata again played every match on the road. As much as the college supported girls playing basketball, it could not always afford to give them a court of their own.

Immaculata's meager financial resources, reflected in its frequent lack of adequate athletic facilities, corresponded to the social location of most of its students, who hailed from the poor, working, and recent middle classes of immigrant and postimmigrant Catholic Philadelphia. The Immaculata sisters, in tune with the wider Catholic educational program, sought social uplift for the immigrants' children entrusted to them. On campus, class divisions between richer and poorer students played out within a social hierarchy that placed those who lived on campus over those who commuted. When you commuted, everyone assumed, you probably could not afford to board. And throughout the years covered in this study a higher percentage of basketball players commuted than of the student body as a whole.

While commuters were in the minority on campus, on the basketball court they accounted for two-thirds and sometimes three-quarters of the team. The campus hierarchy of boarders over commuters followed players to practice sessions. At two levels, then, Immaculata team members negotiated class and Catholicism on the basketball court. Because their school was underfunded, they found themselves playing for a disorientingly nomadic team. And because Immaculata trained Catholic girls for upward mobility, players who boarded and players who commuted labored to make one team out of two classes of students.[4]

But team dislocation and class differences somehow mattered less on the basketball court. At practice and at games, Immaculata players all had one thing in common: the space of the court. On the surface of things, the typical indoor basketball court was nothing special, just two ten-foot-high iron rims with nets and a rectangular wooden floor with four white boundary lines. A few other colored lines marked half-court, foul line, lane, and arc. But for basketball players, the standard space of the court was a space like no other space. It called forth in players' bodies and imaginations a game: a game played in this simple space with its baskets and boundaries, governed by a clock and rules different from those that legislated life in other spaces, at home, school, or church. Gathering in a gym for practice or jogging onto the court before games, Immaculata players temporarily inhabited a separate space where only a few specialized rules applied. Those rules didn't say anything about who your people were or where you lived. They didn't ask where you bought your clothes or whom you were marrying. The space just suggested a game and invited you to play it: take time out, enter this space, test your limits, find some freedom. Year after year, like so many basketball lovers before and after them, Immaculata cagers accepted the invitation of that space and reveled in the eddies and flows of the game. They did not always assemble on the same court, but it was the white-lined space, not the physical place, that mattered. Nor did players all hail from the same background, but when they played together, they stepped into the rules of the game and checked other standards at the gym door. On the basketball court, commuters and boarders remembered, they became teammates. "No matter where you came from, no matter what your background was, you were now together as one group, one unit," said boarder Mary Scharff '77.[5]

The space of the court was not a utopia, to be sure. Only a couple square yards of hardwood and a few hours a day in the midst of a whole Catholic world and complex young lives, the court did not make players' campus identities suddenly invisible to one another. The space of the court took shape fully within an upwardly mobile Catholicism with all its class tensions.

Still, the basketball court was a space apart, where time, rules, and—it could seem—possibility itself changed. On the court, middle-class players could find their privileges suspended, while lower-class players could find their fortunes reversed. As they ran drills, planned strategies, and played scrimmages day after day, Immaculata players mediated perduring tensions and crossed social lines. Over and over, they told me, they loved the game because on the basketball court they felt bonded with other girls—often girls they never would have met in more classified spaces of the Immaculata campus and Catholic Philadelphia.

For one thing, both boarding and commuting basketball players had to deal with the dislocation of the Immaculata program. From 1939 to 1949 and then again from 1967 to 1971, part of team bonding derived from the shared experience of not having a gym to call home.

A Court of Their Own

When the first ten Immaculata varsity teams gathered for practice, from 1939 to 1949, they made their way to a primitive basketball court cobbled together in the basement of Villa Maria Hall. In honor of their hoops-loving sociology professor, they called it Gorman Hall. When I first visited the campus in 1997, Gorman Hall was storage room full of discarded furniture, difficult to imagine as a playable space. The backboards and hoops were long gone, but marks from other fitness equipment fixtures remained on the walls. Only a few low-watt bulbs dimly lit the painted brick walls and cement floor. Far smaller than a regulation-size court, Gorman Hall also featured a twelve-foot ceiling, only two feet higher than ten-foot hoop rims. But what made practicing basketball there even more improbable were the two enormous support pillars standing squarely in the middle of the floor.

Immaculata players knew they practiced in the basement hall to their "great handicap," as their campus newspaper put it. "We always used to say, if we only had a good gym we could be so much better," recalled Evie Adams Atkinson '46. But if they wanted to play at all, they played in the basement. For a long time, the school simply could not afford to build a real gymnasium. "We had no other options," said Evie. "It was either play there, or there was nowhere to play."[6]

Still, many players recalled the "feat" of practicing in this inadequate space. Sister Marita David Kirsch said the low ceiling and pillars made certain skills "difficult to perfect." "As far as any long shooting," with the net positioned only a few feet below the ceiling, "there was no such thing," she recalled. And to pass to teammates, players had to peer "around these pillars

Seniors and fathers gather at the field house, May 1949.
PHOTOGRAPH BY HAGAN-HALVEY/COURTESY OF IMMACULATA COLLEGE.

for somebody on the other side of the court to throw the ball to," Sister Marita David recalled. To practice long shots and effective passing, Immaculata teams borrowed local Catholic high school gyms. Once or twice a week, they crammed themselves and their equipment in the back of a seatless Immaculata van that bumped them to workouts off campus.[7]

But for most practices, still held at Gorman Hall, "it was hard playing around those pillars," remembered Evie Adams Atkinson '46. "And it was down in the basement, and it was not well lit. So it was a real obstacle." After a while it became apparent that sessions in Gorman Hall were not just difficult but dangerous. "You'd be afraid that you'd bump into [the pillars]," Evie said. One day, reported Fruff Fauerbach Timby '50, the basement practices ended for good. "In a quick pivot and dribble, my friend slammed into the pillar and was knocked out. We didn't practice there after that," she wrote. Instead, Immaculata players boarded the van for every practice, for example, at nearby Villa Maria Academy, also staffed by the I.H.M. order.[8]

Without a standard basketball court to call home, the Immaculata team in the Gorman Hall years played all their games on the road. For seven years, student basketball managers simply never scheduled any home games. Then, for the 1946 season, managers got permission to rent Turners Hall at the corner of Broad and Columbia Streets in downtown Philadelphia as the Mackies' "home" court. Other years, Immaculata borrowed or rented high school courts to host games, such as the West Catholic girls' gym. Still, home games were not really at home. Unfamiliar with constantly changing venues, the team played on home-away-from-home courts at odd hours before opposing crowds and whatever handfuls of fellow students and sisters could scrabble transportation to the off-campus site. In other words, there was no home court advantage on those home courts.[9]

Still, Immaculata had few means to do better by its team. With a community mission to educate all comers, the I.H.M. nuns ran the college on a paltry budget. Sisters in the treasury constantly finagled accounts to make the school "look great on the books," and at least one president forked over her salary of a couple thousand dollars for basic school expenses and supplies. Spending money on sports was an afterthought, and spending money on athletic scholarships was out of the question. The school "hardly had enough money to give scholarships for academics," said Sister Virginia Assumpta McNabb, who worked in college financial aid in the late sixties.[10]

Loyal alumnae steadily contributed small donations for extras. As early as 1936, the class of 1937 inaugurated the Gymnasium and Auditorium Fund with a gift of two hundred dollars. But additional contributions accrued slowly. Three years later, as the varsity finished playing its first season, Immaculata president Monsignor Francis Furey rejuvenated the fund by announcing a campaign for a gymnasium he hoped would make the school "a leader in the field of college sports," according to *The Immaculatan*. But the Second World War slowed all fund drives and building plans. Only in the fall of 1948 did Immaculata request Cardinal Dougherty's permission to construct the "long-awaited" Field House. Finally, in October 1949, Dougherty laid the building's cornerstone, and on the third of February in 1950, the basketball team inaugurated its first season in a real home gym, playing an exhibition game against Mackie alumnae.[11]

Gloriously "home" from 1950 to 1967, Immaculata teams played seventeen seasons in the Field House, a hardy structure framed with concrete and steel and finished with granite and limestone. Designed to fit Immaculata's small budget, however, the Field House was outdated almost as soon as it was built. It had no locker rooms or showers, only a bathroom in which the visiting team changed. It had no bleachers, so spectators sat in two rows of folding chairs

Izanne Leonard '70 shooting foul shots at the field house.
COURTESY OF IMMACULATA COLLEGE.

around the court. The lack of adequate seating meant the college still had to rent or borrow local high school gyms for big home games. Still, for Immaculata, just having a gymnasium counted as luxurious. With a stage, equipment rooms, and a court you could convert into an auditorium, it afforded space for activities from assemblies to dances, as well as assorted gym classes. And even if the basketball team played some home games away, for everyday practices the Mackies had a court—a bright, high-ceilinged, regulation-size, pillarless court—to which they could easily walk after classes. Bunny Naughton DeArmond '66 located her happiest memory of basketball at those Field House practices, recalling the "fun of playing indoor basketball," with the feel of "wood floors" and the smell of "leather balls." "When we finally had a field house, it was joyous!" wrote Fruff Fauerbach Timby '50.[12]

After the 1967 blaze burned the treasured building to the ground, members of the basketball team, along with the entire college community, felt the setback deeply. From Sister Mary of Lourdes, who raised money for eight buildings during her tenure as president, "there was almost an immediate promise to build a new field house," recalled Jenepher Shillingford. But everyone knew money at Immaculata did not materialize overnight. Once again, Shillingford said, "there they were, without a gym." Again the team played all games on opponents' home courts, while for practices they trooped a fifteen-minute walk, equipment in tow, to the I.H.M. novitiate center gym, across King Road adjacent to campus. Meanwhile, true to her word, Sister Mary of Lourdes raised money at a furious pace, nabbing a half-million-dollar federal grant. She broke ground for the new gymnasium just a year after the fire, in November 1968. Opened for use during the 1971 basketball season, the new Alumnae Hall was big and modern, with an auditorium and theater. But again, the basketball court featured no permanent seating. "We didn't have enough money to make it that spacious," Sister Mary of Lourdes said. The poverty of spectator space in Alumnae Hall took on rueful irony over the next several seasons. Within three years, the Immaculata basketball teams had won three national championships and began attracting hundreds and sometimes thousands of fans for every game. For home contests, athletic department staff, players, and volunteers set up five or six hundred folding chairs on the perimeter of the Alumnae Hall court. When crowds surpassed a couple hundred, Immaculata again borrowed or rented gym spaces at Villanova and other larger venues, unable to offer its basketball champions a true home court.[13]

Despite the well-known inadequacy of Immaculata's sports facilities, the school retained its reputation for good basketball, and skilled players kept enrolling. It is possible that playing home games at local high school gyms actually helped recruit players. "Immaculata just seemed to be able to draw that person from the Catholic League, to keep the supply going," said Mary Frank McCormick '50. In the early years, those trying out for the reputable Mackies were "amazed" to walk down the steps into Gorman Hall for the first time, "comparing I.C.'s champion record with I.C.'s gym with poles," wrote a columnist for *The Immaculatan.* "Just think what a disappointment the new [Field House] will be to future students," she joked.[14]

Certainly, seventeen years of play in the Field House stabilized Immaculata's basketball program. But the 1967 fire did not seem to scare away the best local talent. "The Field House burned down . . . before I got there," said Betty Ann Hoffman Quinn '73, who with four others earned a starting spot on the homeless Immaculata team in the fall of 1969. Betty Ann and her teammates graduated four years later as two-time national champions. From the beginning of the varsity to the championship years, the adverse logistics of the program "seemingly . . . never caused too great hardship to the Blue and White basketball teams, who enjoy unusually successful seasons," as an *Immaculatan* writer put it in 1945.[15]

Why did the displaced teams find such success? On the one hand, dislocation probably did hurt the program: Immaculata teams might have won even more with better facilities. But, on the other hand, adversity had its advantages. First, Immaculata teams developed "solidarity" when they had to play "hide-and-seek among the pillars" or had no court at all. Also, enrollees at Immaculata knew the small Catholic women's school did not prioritize sports funding, unlike nearby public universities Temple or West Chester, where students could get scholarships and degrees in physical education. Financially disadvantaged, Immaculata teams could always see themselves as impoverished underdogs going up against moneyed powerhouses—no matter how good they got. "We regularly trumped people that were supposed to be good," said a player from the class of '57. Even more, players translated financial disadvantage into moral advantage, considering opponents hired guns whose grades and scholarships depended on court success, while they themselves were purists who played the game merely for pleasure. It was a point of pride, said Anna Maria Reilly '43, to have a great team while "not being an athletic college." Without financial pressures goading their play, Immaculatans assumed they had more fun on the basketball court than phys-ed major adversaries. It is questionable, of course, whether they actually found more pleasure in the game than competitors did. But structurally it was true that they played with few academic or financial incentives, which might indeed have kept their moves free-wheeling and their attitudes cocky. Finally, it is possible that Immaculata teams actually sharpened game skills by practicing with physical obstacles. Other teams seemed to think so, reported a player who graduated in 1952. "Oh, the jokes," she said. "'No wonder [Immaculata] won so much. When they played away from those [pillars] they were unbeatable.'"[16]

Whatever the reasons, it was undeniable that the teams' success regularly outstripped college resources. This angle rarely passed without comment in media coverage during the championship years, when Immaculata's trophies ranked "in the super-stunning category because there isn't a [physical education] major on the squad," wrote reporter Steve Hochman for the *Philadelphia Daily News*. "Win a national title with French and economics majors, that's like Tufts winning the NCAA basketball crown." Using team dislocation to their advantage, Immaculata players did not remember gymless years as a problem. Instead, they regarded the lack of facilities as part of team tradition, at best noble and at worst humorous. Gorman Hall pillars, the Field House fire, and bleacherless Alumnae Hall helped constitute a mythology of success in deprivation. It was a mythology that embraced the working-class roots of the Catholic community as well as its middle-class aspirations, so often carried in part by sports teams representing the faith against more entitled neighbors.[17]

If the physical dislocation of the Immaculata squad somehow bonded them tighter, so the space of the court mediated internal class tensions. College players, almost all Catholic, nevertheless came from different economic and social backgrounds. Departing from the gym in different directions, commuters ran to catch buses back to the city, while boarders lingered before retiring to nearby dorms. But together at practice all players contracted themselves to a different space that, while always partial and temporary, held at bay—and put in play—divisions of the outside world.

Catholics and Class at Immaculata

From the early prewar years of the Immaculata varsity to its national visibility in the early seventies, the economic life of Catholics in the United States changed dramatically. Coming out of the Depression before the Second World War, most Catholics were first- or second-generation immigrants of the country's poor and working classes. As the immigrants' sons and daughters grew up in the postwar economic boom, more Catholics of the third generation finished high school, earned middle-class incomes, and moved to the suburbs. Many Catholic sons returning from military service enrolled in college on the G.I. Bill, and some Catholic daughters sought higher degrees, too. By the midfifties and early sixties, numbers of Catholics had begun to arrive in the middle classes. Still, throughout these years, most Immaculata students were the first generation of women to seek higher degrees. And for every Immaculatan whose family encouraged her continued education, another confronted questions or ridicule from kin and neighbors. From her background, "you educated boys and not necessarily girls," said cheerleader Geraldine Ferrari Burton '57. "That was a fringe, and if you didn't have any money you certainly didn't do that. And so [my father] was often asked, 'Why are you making such a fuss about sending your daughters to college?'" In Gloria Rook Schmidt '64's southwest Philadelphia neighborhood, "my brother and I were the oddballs . . . because we were headed for college," she said. "I got a degree in mathematics and people thought I had things growing out of my head."[18]

Class and educational status remained uneven within specific Catholic communities and neighborhoods, despite a national postwar trend of upward mobility. In addition, across the Catholic United States, the very category of class was complicated in dioceses with extensive networks of schools and ready access to colleges. Catholics' education levels regularly outstripped their capital, partly because they funded religious schools. "We all went to private school, but we were poor because of it," said Christine Lammer Di-Ciocchio '70. In the Philadelphia archdiocese especially, where leaders' obsession with education generated a number of low-cost higher-learning choices, Catholic girls attended college before many of the same faith or economic level across the country.[19]

Immaculata drew students from across the class spectrum, just as other religiously affiliated and public universities did. But even among Catholic colleges, Immaculata's student population included a significant proportion on the lower end of the economic scale, because the Immaculate Heart sisters commissioned themselves to educate Philadelphia's poor and working-class Catholic daughters. In 1948–49 Immaculata set tuition at $350 per year; room and board cost an additional $500. Ten years later, at the end of the fifties, tuition was $650 and board was $800. By comparison, Immaculata's crosstown rival, Rosemont College, nicknamed the "Catholic Bryn Mawr," cost several hundred dollars more at each end of the same decade. Staffed by the Holy Child order and located on the blue-blood Main Line, Rosemont drew many of the city's academy-educated, upper-class Catholic girls. Good out-of-state Catholic schools, such as Trinity in Washington, D.C., also priced themselves beyond the budgets of most Philadelphia Catholics. At Immaculata, however, as historian Sister Mary Hayes, S.N.D., put it, students could get "a practical education . . . to help the daughter of the immigrant poor get a leg up." Consistent with the flavor of Catholic higher learning nationwide, at Immaculata, "liberal arts ruled," said college music professor Sister Cecile Marie Phelan, both in curricular requirements and intellectual prestige. But alongside arts and sciences, the college offered professional courses for women immediately marrying or entering the workforce, including home economics, education, business, and music. The home economics program, for example—whose dozens of majors took pre-med science classes, lived in a campus "practice house," and cared for its foster baby-in-residence—was dropped only in 1974.[20]

The combined liberal arts and practical offerings gave Immaculata a reputation among Catholic elites as a second-tier school and among Catholic workaday families as a good, affordable institution. In 1948 a class of '53 player started coursework at Immaculata, just up the road from her working-class family's home in Malvern. In her mind, Immaculata drew Catholics like her, whose parents "somehow or other [would] scrape enough money together," she said. "It wasn't a snobby school at all . . . you always felt very much at home there." Twenty-five years later, Immaculata still drew numbers of first-generation college attendees. In 1973 Mary Scharff '77, from a working-class

New Jersey family, enrolled at the college she had found unexpectedly warm and welcoming. "The people [at Immaculata] were just extremely outgoing and friendly toward you," she said, "and wouldn't treat you like you were something below them."[21]

Immaculata had a portion of aristocrats but rarely from Philadelphia Catholic families: the locally eminent Kellys, Drexels, Cahills, and Fitzgeralds sent their daughters to Rosemont or even the University of Pennsylvania. Instead, Immaculata's high-society students came from wealthy families in Peru or Chile, directed to the college by I.H.M. sisters teaching in the order's South American mission schools. The daughters of Latin nobility were conspicuous but few. Most Immaculata students came from the new middle and working classes; a few came from debilitating poverty. Most were ethnically Irish or German from Philadelphia, with proportions from other parts of Pennsylvania and New Jersey. For some non-Irish Immaculatans, English was a second language. Epiphany Pantaleo Collins '64 came from a poor Italian family on the "wrong side of the tracks" in South Philadelphia where whole neighborhoods spoke the mother tongue. Epiphany considered herself "lucky to have gone to Immaculata." She was the first woman in her extended family to get a college degree—and, for more than twenty years afterward, also the last.[22]

Because of the Philadelphia girls' hoops tradition, Immaculata basketball players hailed from local families at a greater rate than did the general student population, and on the whole Immaculata's local families were less wealthy than other tristate families who could subsidize far-off daughters' extra housing and transportation costs. Basketball players also tended to be less wealthy because by the 1920s the sport was quickly becoming the quintessential urban, working-class, and poor people's athletic outlet of choice. On a small rectangular space, equipped with only your own body and someone else's ball, anyone could play hoops, indoors or outdoors, winter or summer, without money or land or even much time. Attractive to all classes, basketball was historically often the only sport—and a rare free leisure activity—accessible to urban or poor people, both black and white, who therefore played it more exclusively, intensely, and skillfully.[23]

So Immaculata's enrollment from the local working classes goes further to explain the success of its basketball program. Catholic League players went to Immaculata because it was "affordable as opposed to, say, Rosemont, which was probably a lot more money," said a player from the class of '57. To make ends meet, many basketball players sought financial aid, won academic scholarships, or worked part-time jobs. And even combining aid, scholarships, and paychecks, some basketball players ran out of money and had to drop out of school. "We wanted to get them here and change their lives, but that didn't always work out," said Sister Virginia Assumpta. A third of each Immaculata entering class dropped out before graduation, some for financial reasons; so did a third of basketball players. For example, one player who made the team in 1955 dropped out after freshman year. That one year "was a wonderful experience," she said. But after her father died and family finances tightened, she believed it was more important for her six brothers to go to college. "So I dropped out," she said. "Nobody told me to, but that's what I did."[24]

Not all Immaculata players had to watch their pennies. Some players came from comfortably middle-class and upper-middle-class homes, because in Philadelphia basketball among whites was a Catholic phenomenon even more than an urban one, having spread quickly from Catholic city schools to the suburban schools and academies. And as some students' families moved out of immigrant neighborhoods, so Immaculata as a school reflected the wider Catholic impulse to social uplift. While the sisters viewed their mission as educating blue-collar Catholic daughters, they also meant to usher them toward better economic lives, acquiring class refinements and earning social respectability along the way. They were taught to be "ladies." "Girls will be girls, but Immaculata girls will be ladies," recalled Epiphany Pantaleo Collins '64. "We were ladies at all times." Like many other Catholic school policies, Immaculata rules upheld a rigorous dress code; they disallowed "sleeveless dresses," which "are in bad taste," and required hats and gloves for students' travel "in trains, buses or other public conveyances in going to and from Immaculata." Monitoring private as well as public campus life, the I.H.M.s lived in pairs on each floor of the dorms, regulating noise levels and fining students for messy rooms. The 1950 college handbook drew other parameters to prohibit anticipated Catholic ghetto behavior. "Everyone resents being thought rude, vulgar, or cheap," the handbook read, "yet this is the impression students make when they indulge in loud talking, boisterous laughter, gum-chewing, and whistling." Introducing the dress code, it continued, "extremes of style, flashy hair-do, [and] gaudy make-up are indications of poor taste and are out of keeping with the dignity and refinement that are characteristic of Immaculata." Through the sixties, sisters also frowned on smoking and earrings, other markers of the lower classes, while in 1945 they brought to campus a beauty expert who championed "the natural look"—making up to look artless rather than painted. All these measures aimed to transform the appearances and tastes of immigrant girls into middle-class versions of themselves.[25]

When the basketball team traveled off campus, players knew the sisters expected them to exude respectability for the sake of their school and their

religion. Being ladies meant they should never stoop to unseemly tempta-
tions of the game such as chewing gum, throwing elbows, or swearing. "I
don't ever remember a cuss word," said Epiphany Pantaleo Collins '64. "I
don't remember anything that could be considered dirty play." Though they
bristled at some restrictions, players mostly prided themselves on the ladylike demeanor of their team. Going out to dinner after games, "we didn't go
out as bums," Gloria Rook Schmidt '64 said. "Everyone brought clothes and
you dressed and went out the right way . . . according to where we were
going." In general, Margaret Klopfle Devinney '62 recalled Immaculata as "a
wonderful place for a city girl to develop social and professional skills."[26]

Philadelphia homegirls and hoops fans themselves, the Immaculate Heart
sisters' investment in social uplift nevertheless equivocated their support of
basketball in several ways. They loved the sport, but only if Immaculata girls
played it with no offensive lower-class styles and mannerisms. The college
sponsored several professional programs, but administrators drew the line at
offering a physical education degree, considered beneath Immaculata standards. Most significantly, campus culture privileged resident students over
commuters. And everyone knew the basketball team pulled a rare majority
of commuters.

Boarders and Commuters

Apart from the South American students, few players said they remembered class distinctions as such on campus. But players did note the
salience of the difference between boarders and dayhops. While there were exceptions, a pattern the Immaculata community took for granted was that
boarders had more money and commuters had less and that there was a higher percentage of commuters on the basketball team than at the school as a
whole. Throughout these years, the college population of commuters hovered
at about 40 percent. On the basketball team, however, at least 60 percent of
players commuted, and on some teams the proportion of commuters reached
70 or 80 percent. In 1972, on the first championship team, all five starters
commuted. Immaculata was an institution proud of its basketball team, but
campus tenor nevertheless tended to set resident student life as the norm and
"ideal," as an Immaculata graduate opined in the archdiocese newspaper in
1936. Boarding was considered "part of the experience" of going to college. In
turn, the experience of college privileged boarders, in both resident and commuting students' memories. Separated first by campus status, boarders and
commuters also were separated in campus space. Some campus activities formally separated the two groups, such as fund drives and intramural teams.

Beyond that, whether a student boarded or commuted determined where and with whom she studied, ate, socialized, traveled, and even prayed.[27]

As a boarder, said Josephine Valentine '38, "you owned the college." Residents had full-time access to the dining room, library, chapels, professors, and study groups; they could participate freely in campus extracurricular activities and attend special evening or weekend events. Living at school, said one team member who boarded for her last two years, was "more fun." Residents traveled in packs on campus, usually interacting with the dayhops only superficially. "Your friends were those [like you]," said boarder Margaret Guinan Delaney '62. "I mean, you certainly talked with the [commuters] and mingled and shared . . . but I wasn't that friendly with them." Privileged as the ideal, however, boarders tended not to notice the hierarchy so acutely. Resident Eva Adams Atkinson '46 said there was "never" any tension between the two groups. "None of [my] friends . . . ever felt any resentment between boarders and commuters."[28]

In contrast, commuters smarted at what they perceived as a breach between two classes of students. "There was a definite separation," said Epiphany Pantaleo Collins '64, who took the Broad Street subway from her South Philadelphia neighborhood to Hunting Park, where a school bus picked her up and took her to Immaculata. "It was difficult," she said. "I never 'went off to college' . . . I had no college life per se." The hierarchy of residents over dayhops was partly structural. Going home afternoons, commuters "missed out on a lot" of campus life: evenings in the library, mischief in the dorms, and co-ed mixers. They also missed many Immaculata chapel services and after-dinner walks to the campus grotto, modeled on the famous shrine at Lourdes, France. "That's only natural," said commuter Pauline Callahan Earl '57. "We just were not able to be a part of things. . . . We had to make a special effort . . . to be doing whatever was done, socially." Structural or not, some commuters longed for the campus experience. "The sad part about being a commuter was I always felt I missed something by not being on campus," said a dayhop who graduated in '53.[29]

Beneath logistical differences between the two groups, however, lay widespread imputations about class. Commuters not only missed the full collegiate experience; they were also social inferiors who "could not afford to board." Some commuters felt keenly the stigma of not being a boarder. "I look back now and I almost feel we were discriminated against," said Epiphany Pantaleo Collins '64. But, for most commuters, it was true that they could not pay to room on campus, so they lived with the slights. "It was hard to be a commuter, but that's how I was going to get an education," said Helen Frank Dunigan '56.[30]

In compensation, commuters created spaces of their own and inventoried the advantages of greater mobility. For example, resident students had to abide by early curfews and constant supervision, as I.H.M. monitors signed them on and off campus and restricted boyfriends' visiting hours. Through the early seventies, there were religious requirements to attend Mass at 8 A.M. on Sundays and holy days of obligation, as well as on Friday afternoons, fully outfitted in cap and gown. And Immaculata was "isolated," "way out" in the country. In commuter Helen Frank Dunigan '56's opinion, "boarders had no life," stuck on campus. "If you didn't have wheels," she said, "you were dead." In contrast, commuters could come and go from campus at will and had the whole city for their playground. Basketball-playing commuters sometimes took advantage of living in Philly by gathering on weekends for extra pickup games at different venues. Always carpooling or riding buses, commuters bonded and cavorted. "When you got on the bus in the morning, it was like a picnic," said a class of '45 player. "In the spring everybody [was] putting this stuff which was tan on their legs, which turned orange, and we would sing." On campus, they gathered at the commuters' lockers or at a certain "cafeteria table which was the focus of great friendships," recalled Marie Olivieri Russell '66. And despite the travel, there could be good sides to living at home, from familiarity to home-cooked dinners. Unlike some residents, commuters never had to spend holidays stuck at school.[31]

Still, residents' lives were practically easier, accommodating multiple extracurricular activities, including playing basketball. Resident team members changed into workout clothes in their rooms and after practice showered in dormitories. For daily sessions, they popped over to the gym in five minutes; after late away games, they stumbled straight to their beds. For pregame masses, they gathered as a team in the campus chapel. In contrast, commuters changed in campus lavatories and after practice rode home on public transportation wet and sweaty. Often they missed Mass with the team and went alone to their separate parish churches to petition for big games.[32]

For commuters, both the financial constraints of paying for school and the time constraints of daily travel pinched. Often holding part-time jobs, commuting players rarely participated in any extracurricular besides basketball. Even then, practices and games could turn into "a great sacrifice," said Barbara Flanigan '68, "in terms of getting rides and transportation." Dropped off on campus after late games, they still faced a wearying trip home. Traveling between Immaculata and the city or suburbs rarely took less than an hour, even if one just rode the Paoli local to nearby Wayne.

After the field house fire, November 1967.
PHOTOGRAPH BY JOSEPH H. THOMPSON/COURTESY OF IMMACULATA COLLEGE.

Some commuters reported round trips that took over three hours, plus waiting for school or public buses that ran at fixed, infrequent times. On nonpractice days, "you had to wait for the bus to leave at four o'clock, done classes at one," said Pauline Callahan Earl '57. On practice days, a critical bus often left too early. "It was always a rush," recalled another player, class of '53. "We practiced from 3:30 to 4:30 . . . then we would run to make the 4:30 bus to 69th Street." In short, transportation was a major headache. "One of my friends and I decided that our picture of hell was riding down West Chester Pike for eternity," said Marian Collins Mullahy '54.[33]

But some commuting players indicated it was hardly buses that they missed most. They especially missed down time with teammates, lingering after practice or hanging out in the dorms. "After I left [campus] in the afternoon I wouldn't see them until practice the next day," said Sister Marita David Kirsch. That was the real reason, she said, being a commuter "was a little bit more of a sacrifice."[34]

The Space of the Court

Arriving at practice, boarders and commuters left the space of a community and college that demarcated class and crossed into the different space of the basketball court. Unlike the campus classrooms, cafeteria, library, dormitories, and chapel, the basketball court was, in terms of class, a space as close to a level playing field as Immaculata offered. Commuters arrived from across the city, while residents left their dorm rooms. Some were well-off; some were poor. But from all corners of Catholic Philadelphia, women who played basketball for Immaculata College converged to practice in the same space. It wasn't always the best gym, and neither was it the same court every time. But it was the same space: the same rectangle of white lines and the same two bookends of ten-foot-high hoops that designated a temporary space apart. There, on the basketball court, boarding and commuting Immaculata players looked a little different to each other. Distinctions of the outside world faded or even reversed. And both sets of players said they enjoyed this equalized space—and enjoyed interactions with young women with whom they otherwise would not have crossed paths.

For one thing, the proportion of commuters and boarders changed, so that while boarders owned the college, commuters owned the basketball court. And not only did the proportion change, but also the cachet attached to each group reversed. On campus, residents basked in privilege, but on the court, commuters held automatic prestige. Partly it was because commuters had numbers and set the tone. But it was also because commuters were from Philadelphia, and basketball players from Philadelphia were legendary. City players were assumed to be better players, whether they boarded or not, and the small number of non-Philadelphia girls who made the team at all were awed by their local counterparts. Hailing from Maryland, Joanne Seemans Kolen '58 said Philadelphia players had a very serious, "different perspective" on the game. New Jersey native Marianne Specht Siecko '66 said she found it "interesting to see so many girls, especially from Philadelphia, . . . that really knew how to play." A fellow student from Harrisburg, Pennsylvania, Barbara Glunz Miller '71, characterized the city players as "real tough girls." "They all played in the streets of Philly," she said. "Real nice girls but yeah, tough cookies . . . they had played with the boys." In her mind, Philadelphia players and commuting went hand in hand. "They didn't even live at Immaculata," she concluded. The "names"—team stars—were often commuters, and so were many elected team captains, one of the few campus leadership positions dayhops regularly enjoyed.[35]

This on-court reversal of status gave basketball-playing commuters a source of unadulterated affirmation, a space where they really belonged and excelled. Perhaps it even gave some of them a venue for imagining that fortunes, even their own futures, could change. And residents, relegated on the court to the level of their skills, nevertheless seemed to care more about learning moves and winning games than preserving superiority. Many found it unabashedly intoxicating to play side by side with stars they admired. It is possible boarders' admiration for fellow players challenged stereotypes of commuters. It is also possible that residents who experienced being a minority at basketball practice discovered avenues of sympathy for commuters' marginality in campus life. But whatever the possible imaginative spaces opened by playing basketball, the space of the court did reverse a pattern of privilege. On campus, residents had nicer homes and wore better clothes. But on the basketball court, commuters started games while residents warmed the bench.

While some Immaculata players remembered a reversal of status of commuters and boarders, others said the distinction simply withered on the court, because in that space, as nowhere else on campus, the two groups of students met and interacted. For one thing, on the court, the two groups made up one team, and team mythology held they were all underdogs, collectively handicapped by their school's lack of appropriate facilities. So common hardship on the court muted off-court class differences. For another thing, from getting to know each other at practice, commuters and boarders became friends. Boarders like Marianne Specht Siecko '66 said they treasured "more association with commuters." And greater association on the court led to more mixing off the court. "There seemed to be a separation" between the two groups, said boarder Mary Lou McCahon Noone '65, but as a basketball player she hung out with commuting teammates at the dayhops' lunch table. "I [had] friends that were boarders and commuters. I enjoyed that, the mix." As for commuters, they liked getting to know teammates who boarded, whom they liked and sometimes envied. Also, relationships with residents made the campus friendlier. Boarders eased the logistics of commuters' lives, lending their dorm rooms for study, changing, showering, napping, and even a night's sleep after practices or games. Evie Adams Atkinson '46 recalled a commuting basketball player who "would come up to our room and change up there," she said. To commuters, the boarding life could be more than a convenience; it was a delicious treat of status and inclusion. Commuter Anne Carroll Camp '51 recalled that when "there was an away game, I usually got to stay at school overnight. . . . Enjoyed it." Commuter Patricia Furey McDonnell '53 singled out one sleepover at school as her happiest basketball memory: "Being a boarder, that one night." Through team relationships, commuters gained access to comfortable and privileged campus spaces off the court.[36]

Occasionally the off-court partnerships between commuting and boarding players not only melded two groups in the same spaces but also skirted campus rules. When the commuting life became especially taxing during the frenzy of the championship years, several teammates "lived in my room," said Janet Young Eline '74. "It got to the point where we were at basketball [practice] so much and then it was like first thing in the morning we're going to have a magazine come in and do pictures," she said. "The travel back and forth, I think, was getting to be too much [for them]." Resident players sacrificed privacy but loved the company and didn't mind that their parents or financial aid packages were paying for someone else's room and board. "It was fun," Janet said. Friends were "there all the time. . . . I'd come back and one of them would be laying in bed, 'I'm just snoozing.'" While commuting players liked the convenience of a bed on campus, Janet said she profited from the contraband commuters could import past monitoring nuns. "I'd get the commuters to bring beer onto the campus in their little suitcase," she said. The sisters let the celebrity basketball players past their sensors. "'They're staying the night,'" Janet would tell the nuns. "'Oh, God bless you, dear,'" she said the sisters replied. "And they came walking up with a case of beer."[37]

Off the court, tensions between commuters and boarders were undeniable, and the space of the court did not magically dissolve them. Both groups still noticed it took some effort to relate to each other as teammates. Commuter Sister Marita David Kirsch said at practice the boarders acted "friendly," and since commuters dominated, "there was enough of a mix and match that it melded all right." Even if there was "a definite division between boarders and commuters," said boarder Margaret Guinan Delaney '62, it "didn't play out on the teams at all, because there you were really friendly." And resident Mary Scharff '77 said, "You just needed to get along both on and off the court."[38]

• • •

Despite tensions, the space of the basketball court—where commuters had cachet and residents cherished their association—inverted and diffused the hierarchy of class Immaculata players negotiated every day. And they liked the feel of that change, even if it only lasted a couple of hours a day. "We all got along real well and had a good time," said Izanne Leonard Haak '70. The teams' interaction on the court as boarders and commuters didn't noticeably change the Immaculata community or the Philadelphia Catholic world. But perhaps precisely because its effects evaporated so quickly, Immaculata players returned to the gym again and again to partake in a space apart. They returned to it with eagerness, investing that space with meaning, sometimes more meaning than other supposedly more important community spaces, such as the classroom, chapel, or home. The space of the court could soothe—if not heal—social fissures and wounds. At least until the end of practice that day, Immaculata players could live out some equality of status and the possibility of reversal, experiences more elusive in the outside world.[39]

Walking into the gym, Immaculata players entered a space where usual community boundaries were loosened and tested. But basketball not only pressed lines of class; it also jumbled distinctions of gender. When team members played the game, they engaged in a traditionally male activity that demanded intense physicality. More than anything, it was the physical feel of the game that attracted young Catholic women to basketball.

CHAPTER 3

BODIES IN BASKETBALL

I t was fun to be a big-shot basketball player, Immaculatans told me. It was also fun going to practice, taking a break from the everyday world for a couple of hours. But more than anything, players said, it was fun to play the game of basketball. After all, basketball was fundamentally a game about bodies. And it was nothing if not a physical high.

When Evie Adams Atkinson '46 talked about her years playing guard for the Mackies, she focused—as so many did—on the physical pleasures of the game. When Evie met me at the door of her elegant Bryn Mawr home, I saw a blonde, slender, and proper grandmother who graciously offered a guest wine and cheese. But as Evie began to talk about basketball, the fashionable suburban widow seemed to retreat as the fierce Immaculata guard emerged. I forgot I was talking to someone seventy-two years old when her eyes flashed as she remembered pickup games against all comers on inner-city courts. I forgot I was sitting in a living room with a white carpet and silk flowers and could almost see Evie dribbling at half-court, sweat dampening her hair, knees bent, body low to ground, eyes searching for the open teammate. "It just gave you a euphoric feeling," she said. "I don't know how to explain it other than that. I've never had marijuana, but when I played basketball I felt like I was at a real high. You just felt as though you were elevated."[1]

Other players echoed Evie's recollection of the physical pleasures of the game. Basketball meant being "physically involved in something challenging, something pleasurable," said Sister Marita David "Toddy" Kirsch. They recalled games as "absolute joy, energy," and "fun." Over and over, Immaculatans said they "loved to play basketball." They ran fast breaks, played tough defense, performed for the crowds, and pulled off new moves under pressure. And, players recalled, they struggled at the limits of physical pleasures, whether those limits were defined by school authorities, community standards, or their own bodies.[2]

The physical dimensions of basketball might have stood out in former players' minds because of the corporal nature of the game, which, even more than most sports, engages and taxes the whole body. Within a structure of almost constant motion, basketball calls for both big movements like running and jumping and fine skills like dribbling and shooting. It also features frequent contact with no protective padding. As writer and philosopher of basketball John Edgar Wideman put it, "In no other game is your just-about-naked body so constantly, helplessly, acutely vulnerable to a cheap shot." To many of its fans and participants, basketball takes bodies to the heights of graceful skills and unenhanced athleticism. "I was very physical," said forward Betty Ann Hoffman Quinn '73. For her, basketball was an opportunity "to be physical . . . to push yourself maybe farther than you've ever done before," she said. "To sweat, to breathe hard."[3]

Or the sport's physical dimensions could have stood out in players' minds because in the Catholic community it was unusual for women to be physical at all, much less physical with each other in front of audiences. Only on intramural and varsity teams did Philadelphia Catholic girls find outlets for full-body physicality; among field hockey, swimming, volleyball, and tennis, basketball by far involved the most bodily contact and the most fans. Similarly, though there were many opportunities to enjoy the company of women in Catholic culture, basketball compared with few other activities. Altar guild members tidied church sanctuaries on Saturdays, but you didn't sweat there. Female family members congregated in holiday-time kitchens, but you didn't bump and bang there. Other sports, such as field hockey, didn't draw crowds. Basketball alone put your body in the mix of other bodies in front of cheering fans, and for many Catholic girls, that was heady enough reason to play.

Finally, players could have relished the physicality of basketball because the sport tended to affirm young Catholic women as *women*. On the Immaculata team, basketball was a single-sex activity that invigorated bodies, which happened to be *women's* bodies. If basketball fundamentally involved bodies, and bodies are always gendered bodies, understanding what Catholic girls found physically pleasurable about the game lies close to the center of its import in their lives—and at the core of what it meant to them to be Catholic young women. Immaculata team members who loved feeling basketball in their muscles also got the message that girls had strength, girls could run, girls could pile on for loose balls. Basketball meant something new about what it meant to be young women. Often players had different ideas about the content of that new something. But as they pivoted, passed, and fouled, they also revised the meaning of womanhood—whether or not their new versions synchronized with prevailing views of appropriate Catholic femininity.[4]

If Catholic women had room to run on the basketball court, what are the implications for understanding twentieth-century Catholicism? While basketball has been understood as a game particularly about bodies, so Catholicism has been understood as a faith particularly about bodies, especially women's bodies. Catholic girls grew up, so assumptions go, in a church particularly concerned with their sex and gender regulation. Well, not really. Almost all religions give great attention to the regulation of bodies. American Presbyterian or Jewish leaders sought no less than Catholics to *embody* faith. More accurately, U.S. Catholic leaders happened to be highly successful in their efforts, forming both girls and boys holistically in church, school, and community from an early age.

It remains, however, that if many Catholic communities, including Catholic Philadelphia, constituted a "thick physical and psychological web," as historian Charles Morris put it, then we need to explore the disciplines that formed children's bodies into young Catholic women and men. But, to push the metaphor, if the community was a web, it was an assemblage of loose, torn, and improvised strands hanging across central threads and gaping holes, not a seamless fabric machinated in straight lines. Perhaps central disciplines shaped bodies one way, while minor disciplines worked them at occasional cross-purposes. If we aim to understand how the Catholic community disciplined bodies, we should look at *all* the disciplines, including supposedly peripheral activities like basketball. Young Catholic women certainly prayed to Mary, guarded their modesty, fed the family, and watched the children. But some Catholic girls also played a mean game of hoops.[5]

And they played because they loved to play. In a religious culture that thoroughly regulated bodies, basketball players remembered physical euphoria. In this chapter, I show how players who loved basketball because it "just felt good" also liked the twists it gave to Catholic femininity. And I explore how Philadelphia Catholicism, heartily endorsing the women's game, nevertheless policed its potential dangers to Catholic gender norms.[6]

Bodies and Basketball in Catholic Philadelphia

Women's basketball flourished in a Philadelphia Catholic community largely indifferent to widespread stigmas against females on the court. The community's insularity, leaders' advocacy, and manifest tradition, among other factors, contributed to that environment. Still, Immaculata basketball players received mixed messages about athletics and gender. On the one hand, Catholic thought promoted the physical education of girls' bodies. On the other hand, teachings on Catholic womanliness emphasized gentle carriage and modest comportment, qualities not useful on the basketball court.

Physical Education in U.S. Catholic and Protestant Thought

Catholic leaders interpreted the reigning church theology of Thomas Aquinas to support physical education for women, even while they also used it to underwrite traditional gender roles. If the Catholic church often accomplished what all educational systems attempt—forming bodies and minds—it succeeded in part because it combined physical disciplines with philosophical explanations from an early age. And in the Philadelphia archdiocese, no less than in the rest of Catholic America, Thomism was the official Catholic philosophy. From Pope Leo XIII's 1879 encyclical hailing Aquinas as a bulwark against modernism to the post–World War I neo-Thomist Catholic Renaissance, its codifying and distinguishing role in mid-twentieth-century U.S. Catholicism would be hard to overestimate. Presenting a world marred by sin but restored by grace to the hope of its natural end in God's order, Thomism posited that everything in creation also had separate natural ends that, with a little reasoning, one could discern. Firmly in place by the twenties as the philosophy of choice, Thomism offered Catholics, through turbulent American decades to follow, a worldview at once rigorous and hopeful, both setting Catholics apart from mainstream America and enhancing internal morale and coherence.[7]

Thomism informed the everyday world of Catholic grade-schoolers no less than it underlay seminary curricula. Even the famous opening questions of the Baltimore Catechism—memorized by Philadelphia Catholic school-children as they progressed through years of religion classes—used Thomist idiom to teach the natural end of humanity: "Why did God make us?" it asked and then answered, "God made us to show forth His goodness and to share with us His everlasting Happiness in heaven." Students had to learn this, because while trees and dogs instinctively followed their ends toward full treeness and dogness, humans, whose natural end was reunion with God, had a choice about being fully human. And it was the job of Catholic moral theology to teach right choices in matters large and small, from social polity and family life to movies and clothes. Thomism provided "the intellectual cement that could bind religion and culture together," historian Jay Dolan wrote. It justified Catholics as they "not only sought to write the Catholic novel, but . . . also celebrated Catholic all-Americans in basketball." After all, sports had natural ends, too. If we were destined to rejoin God in heaven, care for the mortal body made sense. The body was the vehicle of the immortal soul as well as the object of physical resurrection at the end of time. Exercise kept our bodies healthy. It also distracted us from other pursuits—vulgar books, wayward friends, or immoral habits, for example—that frustrated our natural celestial telos.[8]

From the perspective of our heaven-bound journeys, the sex of human bodies made no difference, as Catholic leaders read it. In the Thomistic view, sex was an accidental or peripheral feature of bodies rather than an essential one. For that reason, most twentieth-century U.S. Catholic educators saw no reason not to advocate physical education curricula for girls as well as boys. In Philadelphia, Monsignor John Bonner was able to implement varsities for both sexes to an unusual extent, but his tone of celebration for physical education stepped in time with Catholic contemporaries. He believed sports taught the body virtuous habits such as discipline and hard work and also offered "wholesome activities" to siphon the overflow of youthful hormones. "Athletics help a boy morally," he wrote, by "suppl[ying] that necessary outlet for his excess energies." Training the body to protect the soul, sports figured crucially in Catholic education. "Our educational system calls for a sound mind in a sound body," he said, adopting the well-worn Lockean phrase as he christened the Knute Rockne Gymnasium in Allentown, Pennsylvania. In turn, Bonner and other Catholic supporters of physical education followed the popes of the time, especially Pius XI and Pius XII, who had pondered the new trend of physical education and approved it for both boys and girls, as long as, in Thomistic terminology, it "in its proper place helps in the attainment of ends." Melding with other local inclinations in Philadelphia, Catholic educational thought helped normalize sports for girls.[9]

Basketball for women in Catholic Philadelphia was therefore to a large extent just plain, ungendered basketball: a great spectator sport of bodies, skills, and competition. Throughout these years, reports of games in the college newspaper, *The Immaculatan*, read like any other in-house sports journalism, describing "our" team's strategies and statistics. Reading reports, fans could get a taste of the action they might have missed: Mackie guards who "'sat on' their forwards"; defensive switches between zone and man-to-man; trying the press for "harder play and more action"; launching a new fast-break offense. The games were always physical, "good [and] fast," as one spectator said, with "speedy" and "flashing" guards complementing sharpshooters and hook specialists. Games were also occasionally ugly. One *Immaculatan* reporter said that two players who habitually sported cheekbone bruises were starting a tongue-in-cheek "Shiner Club"; star Henri Dunlap's rough-and-tumble play against Penn landed her with a bloodied and broken nose. At Immaculata, basketball was a sport, not a girls' sport. And, like any sport, its substance and satisfactions were self-evidently physical.[10]

Key national figures in athletics, however, took exception to more physical aspects of the women's game. Within Philadelphia, progressive public educators synchronized with Catholic support for girls' athletics. But neither Catholics nor Philadelphians held sway in the northeast-based Division of Girls' and Women's Sports (DGWS), the organization governing most East Coast collegiate women's athletics for these years. Comprised largely of mainline Protestant women from elite institutions such as Wellesley, Smith, and Vassar, DGWS physical educators argued for women's sports not on the basis of natural ends but, like other Protestant women's rights advocates, on the basis of female difference. To counter women's inferior status, they argued that women were not lesser versions of men but different beings, whose activities required a "separate sphere" geared to cultivate women's natural gifts of grace, relationality, and nurture. Agitating along these lines, DGWS physical educators successfully legitimized women's sports in elite institutions.[11]

On the other hand, the DGWS considered contact and competition in women's sports a threat because they contravened feminine nature. Basketball presented a particularly nettlesome problem. Founded in 1891 as a noncontact game for boys, the sport quickly became a speedy, aggressive, high-contact game, played with no protective gear by both boys and girls. Acting in what it considered women's interest, the DGWS Rules Committee of 1899—which included Senda Berenson Abbott, who first taught the game to women at Smith—held the first of endless meetings introducing game modifications, all designed accord the girls' game with mild, noncompetitive feminine nature. "The Basket Ball Rules Committee recognizes and wishes to emphasize that as 'woman is not undeveloped man, but diverse,' so is Basket Ball for Women not a modified, expurgated imitation of Basket Ball for men, but a different game," they wrote. Until the late sixties, collegiate women in the Northeast and most of the Southeast played a game in which teams fielded six players, three on offense and three on defense, who could not cross the half-court line and were allowed a limited number of dribbles each time they touched the ball. These modifications were specifically intended to cut down on running, speed, contact, and competition—and, of course, the excessive excitement that went with them. Publishing their rules in the influential *Spalding Women's Basketball Guide*, the DGWS regulated the sport in the collegiate protoleagues in which Immaculata and other local schools played.[12]

For their part, Catholic women's colleges played by DGWS rules not because of theoretical agreement that the girls' game should be different; on the contrary, Thomistic understandings of physical education legitimized archdiocesan girls often accustomed to playing the boys' game. But, for practical reasons, Catholic schools adopted women's rules. If girls were going to play organized ball, this was how girls played it. If Immaculata wanted to schedule games with other colleges, the DGWS wrote the rule book.

Catholic Girls and Future Mothers

To be sure, not only DGWS rules but also other prescriptions about women internal to the Catholic community stood in tension with local affirmation of girls' competitive sports. On the one hand, Immaculata players enjoyed church support for hoops, but, on the other, they took for granted that its particular pleasures would end when they got married and had children. Girls could be girls, the church seemed to say, but only until they became women. For while Catholic leaders read Aquinas for support of girls' physical education, they also read it for the natural ends of the sexes. And while biological sex had no relevance in heaven, it mattered deeply on earth, where the natural end of femaleness was to bear fruit, physically for married women and spiritually for nuns. "Every woman is destined to be a mother," wrote Pius XII in 1945, "a mother in the physical sense of the word, or in a more spiritual and higher but no less real meaning." And before the late sixties, when more Catholic couples followed church teaching against birth control, marriage automatically implied children. "That was always the underlying thing," remembered a player who graduated in 1953. "If you get married you have to have your children . . . that's part of the deal." Marian Collins Mullahy '54 agreed. "The worst thing you could do in my time was use contraceptives," she said. "If you knew someone that was doing it, it was an absolute shocker."[13]

Idealizing a sort of Catholic "separate sphere" for *married* women, the popes and most American bishops had much in common with the DGWS philosophy. Women's difference "in organism, in temperament, and in abilities" demanded that married women's primary work should involve making a home and caring for children. Nuns' work also most properly involved caretaking and children, such as nursing and teaching. While at Immaculata, most basketball players said they agreed. Not all ceased out-of-home work after marriage, continuing to work as teachers, coaches, and referees. But very few worked after they had children. Married, Rosemary Duddy McFadden '46 taught physical education and coached before she delivered the first of her twelve children. After that, "you stay[ed] at home and raised your family," she said. Only among players who graduated in the seventies was there a shift toward working out of the home during child-rearing years.[14]

Despite considerable gender equity in the curricula and activities of Philadelphia schools, this future sexual division of labor refracted back into Catholic young women's educational years. The Immaculata sisters trained them for careers, but "they were also preparing us for marriage," said a cheerleader from the class of '64. At Immaculata, said Margaret Guinan Delaney '62, "we were supposed to be perfect young ladies, future mothers, moral, well-educated." Immersed in an entire Catholic world, sports-minded girls at Immaculata played basketball a couple hours a week but got schooled in Catholic homes, classrooms, and churches all day, every day.[15]

Sisters and priests often illustrated ideal Catholic womanhood by pointing to the Virgin Mary, the church's preeminent devotional personage. In a conservative archdiocese already devoted to Mary, a Catholic girl could hardly have chosen a place more steeped in the Virgin's presence than Immaculata College. The campus community celebrated Mary's numerous feast days with novenas, rosaries, and forty-hour observances. It dedicated three full months to the Blessed Mother: December, May, and especially October, when "Immaculatans fairly live the Rosary," according to a freshman guidebook. Every single sister of the I.H.M. order—itself named for devotion to the Immaculate Heart of Mary—bore some version of Mary's names or titles as part of her own name: Sister Mary of Lourdes, Sister Marita David, Sister Marian William, Sister Loretta Maria. Campus rituals started and ended with Mary. An incoming student was initiated as "a child of the collegiate family of which Mary is the Mother" by a walk down a woodsy path called Rosary Lane to a shrine modeled on the grotto of Our Lady of Lourdes in France. Four years later, graduating seniors knelt in the Chapel of the Immaculate Conception to say "'The Farewell Prayer' of the Children of Mary to their Heavenly Mother." Campus landscape, architecture, and art further enshrined Mary. High on top of the Villa Maria Hall dome reposed an open-armed statue of the Virgin. In a back quadrangle, another Mary held baby Jesus as the Infant of Prague, credited with discovery of the campus well. Dozens of other images adorned alcoves and hallways. A typical issue of the campus newspaper reminded fellow students to "pay a tribute to Our Lady of the Annunciation canvas" in the library or "whisper a prayer . . . [in] the gallery of beautiful Madonna paintings" in Villa Maria.[16]

What did all these images and traditions of the Madonna at Immaculata mean? Well, they meant different things to different people, of course. Mary was no homogeneous model but a malleable symbol whose perfections could change to suit the occasion. Among other things, however, Mary signified appropriate feminine carriage and character. Specifically, when priests and prescriptive authors wanted to encourage girls' purity, gentility, modesty, and self-sacrifice, they cited Mary's example. For example, in best-selling youth manuals *The Young Man's Guide* and *The Catholic Girl's Guide*, Father F. X. Lasance recommended that Catholic girls ask Mary, sexually pure blossom herself, to help them carry themselves like flowers, in stillness and repose, to protect their purity. "Entreat Mary, your heavenly Mother, to watch over your flower, to protect it, to tend and cherish it," Father Lasance urged. His manuals enjoined sexual purity on both boys and girls but marshaled different metaphors. The boys' edition deployed battle imagery—"The Shield of Faith," "The Helmet of Hope"—to urge boys to charge forth as warriors for Christ. But the girls' manual metaphorized female virtues as various kinds of plants—"The Sunflower-Faith," "The Ivy-Hope"—whose placidity constituted morality. If Catholic girls just stayed still like flowers, he suggested, they could quiet desire, anchor waywardness. Sudden, quick, energetic movements were not only unseemly for young ladies; they bordered on sexual impurity. In short, good Catholic girls weren't fast.[17]

Leaders also imagined Mary as physically gentle, mild, and content. Monsignor Bonner, supporter of girls' basketball and nationally recognized progressive educator, was not immune to the romance of Mary. He gave numerous baccalaureate addresses in which he exhorted female graduates to follow the example of the Blessed Virgin, who worked at home without complaint or ambition, sacrificing herself for Jesus and domestic duties. "Show by your lives to a weary world the sweetness and gentleness of your Immaculate Mother . . . who . . . spent her life in none of the brilliant spheres for which many of our girls sigh today," Bonner said in one graduation speech, possibly given at Immaculata. "She simply lulled a little Babe to rest and pressed His baby face close to her mother heart."[18]

For educational purposes, Mary was also physically modest. On the cover of one typical prescriptive pamphlet, for example, was a picture of Mary, veiled and wearing a long dress with long sleeves, with the caption, "Mary-like Standards of Modesty in Dress." Inside, the pamphlet specified that "Marylike dresses require full coverage for the bodice, chest, shoulders, and back. . . . Marylike dresses do not admit as modest coverage transparent fabrics [or] flesh-colored fabrics." In conclusion, it recommended, girls should keep this pamphlet with them "at all times to use as a guide when buying clothes."[19]

Finally, Mary's stillness, mildness, and modesty complemented her special suffering, represented in the image of the Immaculate Heart, ubiquitous on a campus with sisters named for that devotion. Usually depicted as an X-ray view of Mary's heart—enflamed, pierced, or cinched with thorny roses—the Immaculate Heart showed the Blessed Mother's emotional suffering at her son's death as a physical wound. The motherhood that defined her womanhood also hurt the core of her body. Yet Mary bore the pain because she was willing to sacrifice her own desires while her son accomplished his mission. If in Philadelphia Mary enjoyed the lofty status of "Co-Redeemer," as Bonner sometimes called her, she redeemed, like Christ, through unmerited suffering.[20]

Bodies and Basketball at Immaculata

Of course, while Marian ideals were pervasive in Catholic communities, not all basketball players read the *Catholic Girls' Guide*, and not all heard Bonner's remarks on the Virgin. Furthermore, it is not clear that I.H.M. sisters agreed with clerics that following Mary's example called for stillness and mildness. College catalogs of the forties described the sisters' aim to produce the "clear-minded, right-principled, Christian Catholic woman" who was "spiritually and economically independent." In 1958–59, at the height of a national postwar backlash against women in the public sphere, the catalog nevertheless read, "Emphasis is placed upon . . . strength of will and purpose" to advance the nurture of "women who, as Catholic leaders, make a distinct contribution to every level of society."[21]

But while the sisters adjusted some clerical versions of ideal womanhood, they, too, believed in modesty. When players remembered the Immaculata environment as too "protective" or even "repressive," they usually referred to dress codes. The college abandoned school uniforms in 1940, but student handbooks continued to prescribe clothes until 1969: no pants, always stockings, no shorts, nothing faddish. Beyond written codes, Immaculata players remembered a vigilant atmosphere concerning attire. Wearing socks to their hemlines so their legs wouldn't show, students tried to avoid being stopped by sisters with rulers measuring skirt length. Dance mixers with men's schools were canceled when the twist came into vogue, and Jackie Kennedy's high boots "were considered awful." All dress regulations, students were to understand, protected what Christine Lammer DiCiocchio '70 called "absolute modesty."[22]

Vacillating between encouraging girls' leadership and regulating the length of their skirts, sisters' notions of ideal womanhood equivocated, as Immaculata team members recalled. On the one hand, said a class of '49 cheerleader, "those nuns wanted you to get out there and get those jobs. And, you know, be into a career." A player who graduated in 1953 agreed the sisters were "very worldly women" who "told us to go out there and make some mark and don't sit back and be just a little housewife." Women who emulated Mary, then, could be ambitious and strong. On the other hand, the sisters expected, with other Catholics, that most students would have children and thereafter keep house exclusively. Immaculatans following Mary's path should under no circumstances dress brazenly and sully purity.[23]

Of course, like prescriptive literature, rules and regulations revealed more about how the Catholic community *wanted* Immaculata girls to act than about how they actually did. Passionate admonitions to imitate Mary indicated in part that some Catholic girls did otherwise. But whether or not they liked the Marian model, the Virgin was a presence in their lives. In statues and stained-glass windows, sermons and lectures, Mary accompanied Immaculata girls everywhere. Buying a ball gown: "What would Mary do?" Deciding on a movie: "What would Mary do?" On a date with a boy: "What would Mary do?" They might have fantasized about iniquity but rarely followed through. "We had a nunlike quality about us," said Josephine Valentine of her 1938 class. Two decades later, Jean Doris '53 agreed that much normal mischief did not even occur to Immaculata girls. "We were like little angels," she said. Even in the sixties, said a former Immaculatan who left for the newly co-ed University of Dayton after her freshman year, the school enrolled "a lot of girls who were really goody two-shoes . . . like nuns, just not wearing the habit."[24]

Most Immaculata basketball players took for granted that you could play basketball and be like Mary at the same time. You played basketball in college and then seamlessly went on to marry, have children, and work at home. Unlike the DGWS physical educators, who strained to explain how basketball groomed girls to be good mothers, Immaculata players never had to rationalize this compatibility. As girls, they were free to play; as women, they would do the right thing. "So, I mean, it's sad stopping one [thing] and starting another, but that [new thing] is something else to do well," said Mary Frank McCormick '50. "That was what my goal was in life; I wanted to be a mother and wife, eventually, and so that was how I decided that I wasn't going to [play basketball] anymore."[25]

But while players rarely saw basketball and motherhood at odds, their community seemed intent on reminding them of what was around the corner. For example, in the pages of *The Immaculatan*, alongside accounts of brutal defenses and broken noses, reporters and columnists consistently dished on athletes' dates, boyfriends, domestic abilities, "pins," and engagements. Each successive coach's wedding was covered in detail, sometimes with accounts of the gown, flowers, and attendants. When Marie Schultes, coach from 1943 to 1946, got engaged and turned in her resignation, the article read, "Miss Schultes, we'll miss you, but ''tis a far, far better thing you do.'" Team alumnae got press when they brought husbands or babies to I.C. games. Dot Siehr Becker '51's new twin boys were photographed on the

Students work in Bethany, the home economics practice house, December 1961.
ROBERT HALVEY COLLECTION OF THE PHILADELPHIA ARCHIVES AND HISTORICAL RESEARCH CENTER.

spectator bus, sitting on either side of a basketball. "Mackie basketeers have just rounded up a successful season while the Becker twins . . . get an early start in court life," the caption read. And expectations of motherhood flowed back into the sports years. A 1946 *Immaculatan* photograph featured hockey player Margy McCormick playing with the home economics department baby-in-residence, while the accompanying article asked tongue-in-cheek, "Home and a career—Can a gal really have both?" It continued, "Look to Margy for the answer, which she firmly states in the affirmative. Not that it is easy—being star fullback of Immaculata's hockey team, and mother, to the practice-house baby that is."[26]

By the sixties and seventies, female athletes were becoming a national flashpoint, and the U.S. media began to address widespread perceptions of disharmony between girls' sports prowess and traditional roles. But for Immaculata players, it was a nonissue: a gal really could have both. In 1966 *The Immaculatan* reported proudly that team member Barbara Flanigan '68 had won runner-up in a contest judged by local sports reporters that spotlighted "the feminine sportswoman to show that you do not have to be mannish to be athletic." And as the 1973 Mighty Macs looked strong heading into their second national championship season, student Donna Anderson wrote that visiting crowds seemed to expect "six-foot, manly females to appear." But hometown fans knew, she continued, that among I.C. players, "the feminine approach was still sacred."[27]

Perhaps, as players' accounts would have it, these articles conjoining athletics and womanhood indicated merely that two threads made up one fabric of their lives. But is it also possible that student writers detected potential conflict between the two and addressed it in jokes and assurances about the "better thing" ahead for "ex-Mackie Mommies." Or perhaps the articles served the collective consciousness, dispensing gentle reminders to unconventional girls that they couldn't just hoop it up forever. Whatever the case, if basketball and motherhood did not explicitly clash, Catholic leaders still tended to the physical comportment of girls. And when leaders addressed Immaculata girls *as girls*—as future mothers—basketball players knew there was little use for stillness, gentleness, modesty, or martyrdom on the court.[28]

The Physical Pleasures of Basketball

On the basketball court, behaviors enjoined upon Catholic schoolgirls for sexual purity and gender identity weren't useful. After all, Immaculata players enjoyed a physical game that rebuffed static, modest, unselfish girls and rewarded mobile, grabbing, high-flying bodies. Players didn't mind. They just kept playing the game. And throughout the years, few players said they saw any contradiction between game pleasures and femininity. Or if they did, they adjusted the meaning of femininity to fit the game of basketball.

Motion

Immaculata basketball players loved to run. They loved to work the court, drip sweat, hone pivots, boost energy, relieve stress, and get tired.

Many players remembered the pure exhilaration of running. "I needed to liberate my body at 3:30 in the afternoon," said a player from the class of '57. "I wanted to *go*. I enjoyed running, anything . . . just [to] go out and play and have fun. . . . Sports was a physical outlet for me." Across the years, players repeated that basketball was an "outlet." "After you sat in classes all day, . . .

you go and you run around and clear your head a little bit," said guard Marie Olivieri Russell '66. "It was fun." Some said that outlet "balanced" their lives, which involved a lot of sitting still and absorbing instruction. Forward Fruff Fauerbach Timby '50 said an Immaculata sister once tried to persuade her that her academics would improve if she dropped basketball. "I told her without sports I would go nuts!"[29]

Practices, many Mackies remembered, "were a lot of fun" because you ran, sweated, competed. "It was a relief," said Mary Lou McCahon Noone '65, a rover who played both ends of the court during years of transition to the full-court game. "You went to practice and you just let it out." Over time, the frequency and intensity of Mackies practices varied. In the early years, team members attended a one-hour practice three times a week. In the fifties, the time stretched to two hours and, for some years in the sixties, five days a week. When Cathy Rush took over in the early seventies, she required a schedule of two hours three days a week, with optional Wednesday sessions. Within a few years, the championship teams ran miles in preseason, did five two-hour sessions all year, and spent Christmas break doing daily double practices. Whatever the time commitment, however, at basketball practice, Immaculata players moved. "You ran," said Helen Frank Dunigan '56, a forward who switched to guard after breaking her nose in a game. "Oh, you did everything you had to do to get in shape to do it."[30]

Games were even more fun than practices. Players relished putting their skills and bodies on the line when the stakes were high. Monica Burns Atkinson '51 said she liked working with fellow forwards to get "the ball in the basket and being clever enough to evade your [defender]," she said. "It was just fun working out with three people that know what they are doing and having some success." Margaret Monahan Hogan '63 also said she played forward, fielding passes and getting to the hoop, because "I liked to score and I liked to be in charge." Forward Meg Kenny Kean '58 said she remembered vividly "my first step onto the court for my first game and the thrill at making my first basket for I.C." Playing forward, Helen Frank Dunigan '56 said she loved trying out a new move, like her turnaround jump shot, so quick it made referees think she had done something illegal. "I can remember staying down in the gym playing just hours after school, just standing and turning and jumping," she said. Later, in a game, "you fake some girl out and [the refs] holler, 'Watch that Frank girl!' and by that time I had some girl out here and I was up there." Other players remembered the "happy-but-exhausted" feeling of playing well. "One game in particular, I played my very best," wrote a guard who graduated in 1952. "A great feeling." Playing second string, junior varsity, or even losing a game hardly diminished the pleasure. "Even on the backup team, making a basket was a big thrill," remembered a 1945 graduate. Likewise Sue Forsyth O'Grady '72, a senior substitute who played just a few seconds in a 1972 AIAW Mid-Atlantic Regionals game Immaculata was losing badly, wrote, "I knew it didn't matter . . . but it was just exciting to get in the game."[31]

In the early seventies, the Immaculata teams played schedules that included more than twenty games, but for most of these years, the basketball season was short, entailing fewer than ten games. Like Helen practicing after hours, many Immaculatans satisfied the "need to be active" by playing outside school. Forward Sister Marita David "Toddy" Kirsch said she practiced whenever she could because she "just liked the game" and commented that there were "never enough games to suit me." Many years later, forward Izanne Leonard Haak '70 remembered as her happiest moments in basketball simply "shooting baskets on my own on Saturday mornings."[32]

Always looking for more action, other players competed in noncollegiate leagues or other sports. Several Immaculata cagers played basketball as well as softball on Father Nall's Our Lady of Peace teams all through college. In the fifties and sixties, others played in recreational or summer leagues, in Philadelphia or at the Jersey shore. In the early seventies, at least three starters also played for the Teamsterettes, winning a world tournament of union teams in Indiana in 1973. Some pursued other athletics, usually softball or hockey, because they "needed a sport for that season." Forward Jean Doris '53, who described herself as a "jock," said she "would be lost without my sports." Others played different games "to keep in shape" for basketball season. "I used to play hockey just to get in shape for basketball," said Helen Frank Dunigan '56. "Never had a hockey stick in my hand until I went to Immaculata . . . [but] if you can run a hundred yards [on the hockey field], you could run that big basketball court."[33]

By most accounts, the Immaculata players ran more than most women's teams, because they tended to play their brothers' high-speed, fast-breaking, quick-scoring game. "Hustle," said Dee Cofer Cull '55. "We had to hustle or we sat." The men's Catholic colleges—Villanova, St. Joe's, and LaSalle— were known for fast-break offense and fierce defense. Catholic girls also "copied from the men" in using man-to-man instead of zone defenses, said Jenepher Shillingford, who coached the team from 1962 to 1970. "And maybe that [was] cultural because [most physical educators] felt women can't do man-to-man the whole game." Offensively, the Catholic game involved "more driving," Shillingford added. Players also remembered their teams as "faster" than others, with an up-tempo "give-and-go game." Throughout the years, Immaculata teams were often simply in better physical shape than opponents. With that history, they were poised to win big when the rules went full-court, as coach Cathy Rush could freely import physically intense strategies from the men's game that complemented her players' already athletic style.[34]

But earlier, during years when the rules did not allow women as much speed and space as men, Immaculata players developed compensatory ways of moving and scoring. Catholic girls played a long-shot offense even better than the boys—and, of course, before long shots counted for three points. "The high percentage shot in the men's game was always considered to be the lay-up," recalled Lucille Kyvallos, who coached at West Chester and Queens in the sixties and seventies. "This was not really based on the reality of the [women's] game. Young girls, especially those playing Catholic Youth Organization ball, were taking long outside shots and scoring consistently. . . . They were so skillful and accurate in their long-distance shooting that these really had to be considered high percentage shots."[35]

In all these ways, Immaculata players loved challenging their bodies, "sweating, going hard for two hours." If they weren't fast girls, at least they were not the type who kept still.[36]

Contact

Immaculata cagers also enjoyed contact with other players' bodies—both aggressive on-court contact and intimate off-court contact. The very first varsity players cherished, as their yearbook put it, the "dream of competitive activity" and "wholesome aggressiveness."[37]

The Mackies always "played hard," said rover Mary Jane Renshaw Lewandowski '64. They blanketed each other on defense, fought for rebounds, and dived for loose balls. Different kinds of girls played basketball at Immaculata, she wrote, but "ALL were *Tough*." The street game set the tone at Immaculata, and players not from Philadelphia felt the difference. "We never played like that in high school! What a powerhouse!" said Delaware native Fruff Fauerbach Timby '50. Those who couldn't take the heat retreated to the sidelines. A cheerleader raised in New Jersey said she tried out for the basketball team one year but soon found herself over her head in a "very physical game." She got a bloody lip and decided not to pursue it further.[38]

Officially, the Mackies were not allowed to throw illegal elbows or hips, recalled Helen Frank Dunigan '56, or coaches benched them. But pressing the limits, they were "aggressive." "Of course! If you can get away with it, do it," said Marian Collins Mullahy '54. "That's, you know, sports!" So players indulged in rough play when the situation warranted it. "You [didn't] want to take too much pushing and trash talk," said guard Janet Young Eline '74.

"I remember playing in a game where someone elbowed me and kept elbowing me, and I thought, I don't want to take this. So I kept watching the coach and when she didn't look, I"—Janet demonstrated a hard elbow—"and this girl's like, 'oooooh,' and I just laughed. . . . So you get away with what you can get away with."[39]

The bumping and banging felt good to some Immaculata players because it was an opportunity for physical aggression and release. Forward sharpshooter Mary Scharff '77 said playing hard "was a way for me to let out frustrations and things like that," while her teammate Sue Martin '78 told a reporter, "Exercise is a great way to work off aggressiveness and help you get along with people." High-contact play satisfied other players' sense of competition. "Winning is great, it's a great feeling," said Betty Ann Hoffman Quinn '73. "And to compete. Just beating somebody or having somebody beat you and then coming back and trying harder and maybe beating them the next time." Dozens of Immaculata players described themselves and teammates as "competitive, very competitive." "I am a competitive person," said a player from the class of '57. "If there is not a competition, I will invent it." And the Mackies didn't just want to compete—they wanted to win. "Everyone wanted to win," wrote Mary Jane Renshaw Lewandowski '64. Numerous players reported their happiest moments in basketball had to do with "winning all the time." Finally, a few players said aggression in basketball "probably" displaced sexual energy. "I don't think that I was really very . . . aware of feeling any kind of need like that or that I had really strong needs at that time, but that could have been a part of my whole upbringing," said Marie Olivieri Russell '66. "You need that activity." For whatever reason, Immaculata players liked hard contact. On the court, you left the gentle and mild self behind.[40]

Immaculata basketball players found opportunity in basketball not only for aggressive and competitive contact but also for more intimate bodily association as they changed, dressed, and traveled for games. Without a home court locker room during most of these years, boarders mostly changed in their dormitory rooms before practice or games. Commuters dressed in threes and fours "at different sites on campus," said forward Bunny Naughton DeArmond '66, such as a campus lavatory or the coach's office. In later years, after away games, players sometimes discreetly changed out of their uniforms or showered in the visitors' locker room. Players rarely saw each other fully naked, but they practiced and played in close quarters and knew the bodies of teammates often better than those of mothers, sisters, or other friends.[41]

Immaculatans would also spent time in close quarters on road trips. "The teams would tend to . . . enjoy each others' company because they would take trips together," remembered forward Mary Frank McCormick '50. "We spent a lot of time together." For road trips, money was always short, and the Mackies doubled and tripled up on hotel beds. "That was the way it had to go, or you didn't go," Mary continued. "You were trying to keep down [finances] and that was the way you did it." At a time when women who were friends hugged each other and held hands freely, players remembered sleeping in beds together as a normal and necessary part of doing things together as a team.[42]

It was normal and necessary, but it was still fun. Teammates were often very close friends, and they loved rooming on road trips because they loved their friends. From the release of aggression on each other's bodies to the physical proximity in hotel rooms, players experienced a deeper level of familiarity and intimacy among themselves than they often had with other girlfriends or family members.

Display

Basketball players at Immaculata also liked the sport because it gave them opportunities to be less modest. During practice, they got to wear otherwise banned shorts and T-shirts. During games, Immaculata players' bodies were on exhibition, clad in shorter-than-usual skirts, which regularly flew up in the heat of battle. They enjoyed being on display, being looked at—precisely the pleasures modesty was supposed to prevent. If Immaculata players came from the Catholic League, they were already hooked on the high of playing jam-packed doubleheaders at Convention Hall and high-stakes playoffs at the Palestra. But players also performed for other audiences: for each other, for men, for other women. In any case, at Immaculata, players who "loved the limelight" took further opportunity to show off and entertain.[43]

Players performed for each other and watched each other, delighting in the skill and beauty of each other's bodies in action. A forward who graduated in 1957 said she enrolled at Immaculata after she stumbled into an early fifties game between the Mackies and the Temple Owlettes, then still a hot women's rivalry. "I was absolutely floored" at the I.C. players' skills, she said. "These girls were way beyond me." Similarly, guard Anne Carroll Camp '51 remembered being happily "stunned" when a teammate won a big game with a half-court buzzer beater. "I . . . stood in disbelief at such a great feat," she recalled. Besides admiring other players' skills, Mackies appreciated the aesthetics of bodies in basketball. They described each other as "energetic," "healthy," "strong," and "fast as the wind." "At a time when women weren't, I guess, supposed to be conscious of strong, healthy bodies, we were," said Marian Collins Mullahy '54. "'Cause we couldn't play if we [weren't]." At least on the basketball court, they believed girls' bodies were supposed to be healthy and vigorous, not suffering and self-sacrificial. "The girls on our team were graceful and beautiful in my memory—long pony tails flying—guards' arms extended like very determined dancers," wrote guard Mary Murphy Schmelzer '62. "They moved like gazelles and thought like physicists."[44]

Some Immaculata players told me they remembered themselves or others showing off at practices or games because some crush—a boy or teacher—was in the audience. "Some had ulterior motives, e.g. . . . certain instructors attending games [whom they] wanted to impress," recalled Mary Jane Renshaw Lewandowski '64. Boyfriends and fiancés attended games, and at co-ed schools such as Temple or West Chester, male students might show up, too. A player from the class of '56 recalled vividly one shot she took to show off for the opposite sex. "A boy I had a mad crush on was watching," she recalled. "I took a long shot from center court and nailed it."[45]

Sometimes, players showed off for men, but most audiences over the years consisted of other women: classmates, friends, I.H.M. sisters, cheerleaders, and alumnae. Women athletes playing to a male audience reversed the usual dynamic of sports spectatorship in which women watched men but still fit general gender patterns in which men look and women are looked at. In contrast, Immaculata games featured girls doing a traditionally male activity under the gaze of other women. Not only a female audience but also Immaculata cheerleaders cheered for girls, celebrating their athletic prowess. It was considered prestigious to cheer for the basketball team—and certainly not unusual genderwise, "not if you've gone to all-girls schools," said Margaret Guinan Delaney '62, who served as team mascot her senior year.[46]

For Immaculata players, the pleasures of display and performance were self-evident and unremarkable. Throughout the years, players looked forward to games with big rivals such as Rosemont or West Chester, when they could count on fellow students and fans packing the home gym or loading one or two school buses for an away game. The Field House "would be crowded at a night time [game]," remembered Dee Cofer Cull '55. "It was mobbed. Yeah, lots of fun." Players tried to give the crowd what they wanted. "We made the competition exciting to watch," said rover Maureen Callahan Bigham '63. Some recalled satisfaction at making fans out of skeptics: "Those . . . who began to come to games and see us play . . . were surprised at the level of play and success," wrote guard Mary Jane Renshaw Lewandowski '64. Over the years, as the Immaculata teams made their mark in the Philadelphia area and then on the national sports scene, they found themselves attracting, and enjoying, the spotlight at a whole new level. Fans drove from nearby

Mary Frank '50 goes up for a loose ball in a field house game, February 1949. On her teammate (middle), you can see the garters that held up her stockings.

Photograph by Hagan-Halvey/Courtesy of Immaculata College.

states and packed into big borrowed gyms to see the Mighty Macs demolish another opponent. And players enjoyed being the center of attention. "I like it. . . . We like to have people screaming," forward Mary Scharff '77 told a reporter. "It really helps us get psyched."[47]

After the third championship in 1974, Immaculata played in the first-ever women's basketball game in New York City's Madison Square Garden. Coach Cathy Rush accepted an invitation from Garden promoters for Immaculata to play against perennial powerhouse and hometown favorite Queens College. On February 22, 1975, players, fans, alumnae, and Philadelphia sportswriters converged on the country's highest-profile sports venue, amazed to see Immaculata's name lit up on the marquee. The team came out of the locker room greeted by a sold-out crowd of twelve thousand and was startled to hear Helen Reddy's feminist anthem "I Am Woman" blaring on the loudspeakers. "It was an unbelievable experience," remembered Laureen Mann '78, who hailed from Queens and—with her uncle, Al McGuire, coach of Marquette University—fully appreciated the once-in-a-lifetime opportunity. Earlier that year, the Mighty Macs also played the first women's basketball game ever broadcast on live television. Matched against Maryland, Immaculata players performed for a national television audience.[48]

From early audiences of fellow students to seventies-era telecasts to millions, Immaculata team members liked people watching them play. On the court, it did not occur to them to that they should temper the fun of performance for the sake of modesty.

Catholic Femininity, Catholic Basketball

Pursuing physical pleasures, Immaculata players fractured the ideal of mild, modest, and suffering Catholic femininity. But they also reinforced the given model by working out a new, athletic womanhood that was morally if not physically consistent with norms. As good Catholic girls playing basketball, their bottom line was remaining acceptably feminine as well as pure and heterosexual. Within those limits, however, other niceties could go out the window. And players interpreted even those limits subjectively. In their minds, no matter how much they ran, no matter how rough they played, they remained ladies as long as they did not "act like guys." "We knew who we were and liked it," said Maureen Callahan Bigham '63. This circular, flexible understanding of femininity marked most players' discomfort with mannish play or people but left open the question of what it meant to act like ladies—or like guys. For them, femininity adapted to whatever they did on the court.[49]

At Immaculata, girls were trained to be ladies of the middle class, and at basketball practice, Immaculata coaches exhorted players to be ladies of the court. In doing so, they adopted a strategy common among women's coaches nationwide. "To offset the sociological stigma against women's athletics," remembered physical educator Mildred Barnes, "coaches often reminded their team about the importance of 'ladylike' behavior." In this usage, "being ladies" referred to gender more than class, involving physical appearance, gait, and demeanor. To be ladies, they wore long hair, walked lightly, smiled frequently, and behaved sweetly. Izanne Leonard Haak '70 said she still heard at Immaculata in the late sixties what her mother, a 1940s Mackies star, had told her: "You could play basketball and still be a lady." Throughout the years, most players got the same message.[50]

Players appreciated this principle, because it defended their on-court femininity even as other norms of Catholic womanhood challenged it. They could simultaneously be a "powerhouse," Fruff Fauerbach Timby '50 wrote, but "ladies . . . every one, on and off the court." They wanted basketball to set them apart from other girls but, in terms of gender identity, not too much. "An I.C. player could have been anyone of the student body," wrote forward Meg Kenny Kean '58. The rhetoric and practice of being ladies caulked fissures between basketball and community norms successfully enough that many players were genuinely perplexed at my suggestion that femininity and sports might clash. "It was odd for somebody to play, but that didn't make you less of a lady just to play a sport," said Mary Scharff '77. "We weren't looked at as outcasts . . . or doing something weird."[51]

Still, players acknowledged that basketball players' idea of femininity might differ from other girls.' When I asked survey respondents to classify teammates' gender type, less than half said they were "very feminine" or "somewhat feminine." Guard Mary Murphy Schmelzer '62 described her teammates as "very feminine" but then added, "as far as athletes go at least." Within femininity, players made room for themselves and teammates. They described themselves or others on the team as "jocks" and "tomboys" with no pejorative connotation. On the team, being boyish was viable option. Remembering a teammate whom she described as "very boyish," Christine Lammer DiCiocchio '70 said, "I can't imagine it would have been easy for her" outside sports. But she "was certainly accepted by the team and she was fun, too." For some self-described jocks, it was a point of pride to be the kind of girl who could play with the boys. "Basketball allowed me to find my niche! I not only played in school but outside I was able to compete with all the boys," wrote Terri Murphy McNally '63, who added she was "better than most in my neighborhood."[52]

Even when a certain player seemed threateningly "masculine or tomboy-ish," her teammates excused her anyway, typically attributing the trait to growing up with brothers. Mostly other teams, they said, had the masculine players. "We [were] all ladies . . . but some were more masculine than others, yes," said Dee Cofer Cull '55 of her teammates. "But never a threat. . . . Like when we would see other teams play, we might go 'Look a' dat bruiser' or something to that effect." Even on other teams, Dee concluded, that was okay. "Some girls are built differently, that's all."[53]

And, obversely, players could regard too much *femininity* as a threat to playing good basketball. "You're not a lady on the court," Gloria Rook Schmidt '64 said. "You're playing the game." Just as Immaculatans made ex-cuses for overly boyish players, they made excuses for ultrafemme team-mates. "There was a girl . . . who was very pretty and delicate, but an excel-lent player," said forward Marcella Rominger Lusby '52. Similarly, Sister Marita David "Toddy" Kirsch described another player as "a very ladylike guard, but she was good." She also said they teased mercilessly another team-mate, although she was "a great guard," because she insisted on starching her bloomers before every game.[54]

A majority of players resisted classifying themselves and their teammates in gender terms at all. Thirty-seven out of sixty-five survey respondents in-dicated that the team gender type was "different for different players." "Some were petite and delicate-looking," recalled guard Alvina DeLazzari Long '57. "Others looked as though they had played basketball with their brothers." Guard Marie Olivieri Russell '66 wrote that "all types of women played bas-ketball from very feminine to somewhat tomboyish." Others team members said they never noticed marked gender types. A cager who graduated in 1956 described fellow players as a "mixture—gender types were not prominent," while manager Sister M. Charles Edward, I.H.M., '60 (formerly Elisabeth Woodward) said, "I honestly didn't think of a 'type' of young woman for I.C. basketball." Still other respondents ignored the survey question and wrote out a nongendered answer. "Most were individuals who had high school sports experience and who had goals they hoped to achieve," wrote a forward from the class of '45. One former player criticized the question, writing "NO STEREOTYPE" and "strange question" beside it.[55]

Still, though most former Mackies insisted on a range of gender types, they nevertheless balked at the line beyond which players became "mascu-line." Forward Mary Frank McCormick '50 said, "I didn't like athletes or women that didn't act like women." On her teams, said rover Terri Murphy McNally '63, "All were ladies—no one was masculine." But basketball could be a rough game, and despite players' expertise at negotiating gender, basketball and femininity sometimes clashed, even in memory. Speaking to me, players would sometimes bifurcate their identities as girls and as athletes, even speaking of themselves as two different people on and off the court. "When you're out there on the court sweating and running around, you're not very feminine or weak," said a player from the class of '53. "But . . . you were out of context. It wasn't the you, the all-the-time you." Maureen Mooney '73 also wrote that she and her teammates were very feminine "*off the court*. On the court we played to the best of our athletic abilities to win the game." Marian Collins Mullahy '54 put it more bluntly. Playing basketball, "we weren't ladies," she said. "We were out there to win."[56]

Whether they tacitly reworked definitions of femininity on the court or simply held womanliness and sports together with their own bodies, Immaculata players' self-perceptions encompassed the pleasures of motion, contact, and display they enjoyed in the game.

Limits on Physical Pleasures of Basketball

While basketball called for more showy and aggressive physicality than Catholic leaders usually described in the ideal woman, the sport was still overwhelmingly supported by authorities, teachers, and parents. Most of what former players said they liked about the physicality of the game drew no objections. On the contrary, program participants remembered "widespread acceptance for girl athletes." Endorsing women's basketball and Marylike femininity at the same time, leaders sent a mixed message. But players rarely experienced this mixed message as a problem. Like all lives, theirs included different and competing institutional formations, casually coexisting and constantly remixing. But sometimes, when certain aspects of the game strayed outside already exceptional parameters, authorities set limits. And when those limits cut too close to pleasure, Immaculatans complained, resisted, and even took action for change.[57]

Limiting Motion

"Women's rules" basketball, formulated by the DGWS and played in most of the Northeast from 1892 to 1971, set limits on running. From 1938 to 1948, women's rules involved six players—three forwards on offense and three guards on defense—confined to their respective halves of the court. Players could bounce the ball only once before passing. In 1949 girls were allowed a "limited dribble" in which they could bounce the ball twice before passing. In the early sixties, the rules changed to allow a three-dribble limit and a "rover" on each team, one designated pointlike player who ran the full length of the

floor. In 1966 the unlimited dribble familiar to the men's game was introduced, and finally, in 1971, the DGWS approved a full-court five-player game.
Needless to say, until then, women's rules drastically limited how fast and how
far players could move. The strength of basketball traditions in Catholic
Philadelphia sheltered the community's young women from DGWS ideology
but not from its rules. In order to play against public schools, Catholic girls'
schools and colleges incorporated women's rules. This was not an effort, just
a fact. Full-court, unlimited-dribble school league play for women simply
"wasn't done," recalled Helen Frank Dunigan '56.[58]

But the girls' rules game was not, for many Catholic women, the only
game in town. They had often grown up playing full court in neighborhoods, playgrounds, and recreational leagues, with boys and girls, even occasionally on boys' teams. Even in the early forties, said a class of '45 player,
"if the coach had walked out we would've started up and down the floor."
Some women's summer leagues around the city and at the Jersey shore ran
full court as well. "In the fall [and] winter, so-called 'women's rules' were
slapped on us," remembered guard Rosemary McNichol Walsh '60. "Lucky
for me, I played in summer leagues at Narbeth and Ocean City, N.J." Many
Catholic girls who learned the game from brothers played the full-court
game first and had to learn the scaled-back version when they joined school
teams. Rover Gloria Rook Schmidt '64 first saw a girls' rules game in Catholic
grade school. "I started playing girls' basketball and the rules were different,
which I didn't like," she said. "Because I liked the full court at that time . . .
[the women's game] was slow." Guard Janet Young Eline '74 also learned full-
court first and remembered being whistled for dribbling the ball more than
twice in her first grade-school game. "I liked the boys' rules better," she said.
"I felt stifled, like, come on, let me get over on [the other] side, I want to go
get her and stop her with the ball."[59]

But, Gloria Rook Schmidt continued, Catholic girls "played by the rules.
You had no choice." A few Immaculata players said they took girls' rules for
granted. Guard Rosemary Duddy McFadden '46 said she just accepted that
"this is the girls' way of playing," while Marian Collins Mullahy '54 said it
"didn't bother me, really . . . boys did one thing, girls did another, and there
you go." Some also found reasonable the DGWS premise that women had
less stamina than men, at least at the time. Epiphany Pantaleo Collins '64
said she thought the physical training of girls lagged behind boys, warrant-
ing different games. "So we were very comfortable," she said.[60]

Far from comfortable for many teammates, girls' rules were an aberration
and an embarrassment. "Why can't girls play full [court]? I mean what is the
big deal here?" Betty Ann Hoffman Quinn '73 said she thought. "We can run,

you know." But instead of running, players spent half the game standing on one end of the court "like a telephone pole." The full-court game drew spectators, but the half-court game, among those who weren't used to it, drew derision. As Mighty Mac center Theresa Shank '74 told the *Christian Science Monitor*, people used to think women's basketball was just "girls in bloomers standing around pushing back their hair." So whatever new "freedom" came along, they cherished. In high school, "I started out [one] dribble," remembered Dee Cofer Cull '55. "So when I graduated it was just two dribbles, which we thought was the greatest. . . . More freedom."[61]

For practice scrimmages, Immaculata coaches sometimes indulged players' yen to run full-court but not always. The issue could make or break a coach in the team's eyes. Of ten coaches Immaculata hired from 1939 to 1975, some sympathized with men's rules advocates and occasionally ran full-court sessions for fun. Other coaches, wedded to the DGWS model, viewed the job at Immaculata as an opportunity to wean Catholic girls from the harmful, unladylike "run-and-gun" sport they loved and teach them a methodical, "by-the-numbers" game they loathed. Several players remembered a coach who was a "fitness freak," running whole practices of calisthenics instead of basketball. For one, Mary Jane Renshaw Lewandowski '64 made her dissatisfaction known, until she was rewarded with demotion to the junior varsity team her senior year. When Jenepher Shillingford took over the program in 1962, she tried to strike a winning balance between her girls' precocious athleticism and playbook strategy, an approach that arguably laid the groundwork for Immaculata teams' early seventies dominance. "We had set plays; Jen [Shillingford] demanded that," said Gloria Rook Schmidt '64. "You'd start running and gunning and if she didn't like it—if the balls were dropping, she was all right. As soon as they stopped, . . . then she called time."[62]

Whether complaining about the rules, finding full-court opportunities, or badgering rule-bound coaches, Immaculata players resisted restrictions on the motion of the game—and the implication that young Catholic women could not, or should not, run.

Limiting Contact

If Immaculata administrators and coaches merely acquiesced to rule limits on motion, they actively shaped and enforced controls on contact, both in the game and in the locker room.

While some Immaculata players liked the aggression and competition of the game, they heard from coaches and nuns that using too much physical force and vying with each other was inappropriate for Catholic young ladies.

A January 1953 game between alumnae and current Mackies. The Mackies are in pinnies and stockings, which sometimes fell around their knees.
ROBERT HALVEY COLLECTION OF THE PHILADELPHIA ARCHIVES AND HISTORICAL RESEARCH CENTER.

In Immaculata practices and games, "any contact would be a foul," said forward Sister Marita David "Toddy" Kirsch. "So you couldn't bump, push, or do any of that. You had to clear the person that you were going around, or it was a personal foul, or a technical." Helen Frank Dunigan '56 said they were strictly forbidden to shove or hip-check and had to apologize for physical force. "If you knock someone down, you say you're sorry and help him up," she said.[63]

Beyond teaching court manners, a few coaches "not into the competitiveness" tried to make basketball "prim and proper," said Mary Jane Renshaw Lewandowski '64. "You prettied yourself up and did all the Main Line stuff . . . wear the right clothes . . . and this is [supposed to be] all part of . . . playing basketball." Mary Jane said her coaches held a tight rein on aggression. "If I . . . made more than three attempts to steal a ball, I sat, because ladies didn't do that. Or [going] for a jump ball, if I hit a double hit, not a violation, but . . . I pulled it a little roughly, I sat. . . . I didn't see that as being quote, bad or wrong. But . . . the message we were given [was] that would not be tolerated." The Immaculata ethos guarded against too much aggression because, taken to an extreme, grappling for balls and fighting to win endangered players' femininity.[64]

Far more dangerous than too much aggressive contact on the court, however, was too much intimate contact off the court. Limiting nudity around other girls, the Immaculata basketball program observed an unwritten rule of Catholic culture, which players said they took for granted, that they arrive for games dressed and depart unshowered. Before games, players changed in their rooms or behind lavatory stall doors but rarely in full view in locker rooms. As early as the thirties, this unspoken rule stood out to team members when they traveled to away games. Josephine Valentine '38, who played forward on Immaculata protovarsity teams for two years, remembered entering the shared locker room at Temple University for the first time. "Most of the Temple players had no clothes on!" she said. "And it was the biggest eye-opener and shocker of our young lives." When I asked her if Catholic girls ever disrobed in front of each other, she said, "My goodness, no." It was the same in the fifties, said guard Alvina DeLazzari Long '57. "We traveled in our uniforms and did not change."[65]

The Field House bathroom and Alumnae Hall locker rooms remained unused except by opposing teams. The Field House didn't even have showers. "I just assumed that no one gave it a thought," said guard Mary Murphy Schmelzer '62. No one needed to give it a thought, because no Catholic girl would shower publicly, at home or away games. "I can't remember showering or changing before coming back" to school from away games, said guard Alvina DeLazzari Long '57. In the late sixties, little had changed. Immaculata players still used locker rooms at other schools "just to use the restrooms," changed awkwardly under their clothes, and never showered around each other. Even in the seventies, Janet Young Eline '74 said she and her teammates, who "were all very modest and never 'had' to shower or anything like that," were "aghast" at opposing teams' locker room comportment.

> So we would finish a game, towel off, change our clothes, and leave. You know, we went to these tournaments where you had to share a huge locker room with other schools, and these girls were walking around naked and sitting on chairs naked, drying their hair. We're like, "Oh, my God . . . let's get out of here." We were not comfortable at all with that. . . . [They] parade[d] around naked. Like, "I got my

shower, I guess I'll go find my towel." I'm like, why didn't she take her towel with her and keep it wrapped around her?

Janet concluded the story laughing. "It's funny looking back at that now," she said. "It must have been . . . a subconscious thing."[66]

The danger of too much intimate contact, at its outer limits, surpassed the hazard that girls would act like guys and approached the danger that girls would love like guys. Before the seventies, many kinds of same-sex interaction raised no red flags of homosexuality in U.S. or Catholic cultures. Holding hands, hugging, kissing, and sleeping together on road trips, Immaculata players did not necessarily signal any romantic or sexual feelings toward teammates. Some said it did not even occur to them at the time that girls could have romantic relationships. "We would not even think about doing [anything sexual]," said forward Mary Frank McCormick '50. "Or not doing it."[67]

It is highly possible that basketball players did not formally hear about homosexuality at all. If they did, Father Gorman might have mentioned it in their required sociology course on the family, which the course catalog said would deal with "the working mother, birth control, divorce, and feminism." But homosexuality might not have surfaced. "Certainly, the nuns never talked about that," said a player from the class of '53. Cardinal Dougherty had set this tone for his schools and, in a rare 1944 intervention in city politics, had blocked an initiative for sex education in public schools, too. If students did formally hear about same-sex love, it was within a Thomist framework that considered homosexual expression, along with premarital sex, birth control, and masturbation, a sinful distortion of the natural end of human sexuality: that is, reproduction within marriage. Manuals for Catholic parents and teachers sagely counseled against alarmism about what could be regarded as developmental phases, such as same-sex "crushes." But prescriptive literature for youth either didn't mention the topic or warned to "beware of" making friends with "men and women much older than yourself," because of the attendant "dangers of homosexuality." More often than not, silence was the approach. Pope Pius XII advised Catholics that telling adolescents about "aberrations in the sexual domain" symptomized a "harmful overestimation of [the value of] knowledge." In general, then, homosexuality "was something that nobody talked about," said the same class of '53 player.[68]

But players often comprehended homosexuality through nonofficial routes. Some got the concept because it was a frequent taunt from public school kids mocking Catholics kids for their strange, single-sex schools. "Outside, you hear that word, you hear 'lesbianism' as an accusation against you because you just happen to be in an all-girls' school," said Mimi McNamee, who played center for Sacred Heart Academy in the sixties. "That specter hung [over all of] us to some extent." Cheerleaders cheering for a girls' team occasionally got teased. At Immaculata, "it wasn't considered to be queer or, you know, offbeat," said cheerleader Geraldine Ferrari Burton '57. "I remember going to a University of Pennsylvania basketball game once, and they didn't have cheerleaders for the women's team, and they were making fun of us. And that was the first time that it occurred to me, 'What's wrong with this?' . . . Well, I was indignant. . . . You've got the problem, we don't." Even within the Catholic community, a tomboy could figure out what homosexuality was from innuendoes thrown her way. "I would hear . . . aunts and uncles saying, 'She acts kind of—,' and I would hear them say, 'Well, she'll grow out of it,'" said forward Mary Jane Renshaw Lewandowski '64. "They were referring to us as being . . . gay or homosexual, having those tendencies because you liked a baseball mitt instead of a doll." To diffuse the imputation, Immaculata teammates cracked "a lot of jokes," said the class of '53 player. "We would joke back and forth with each other, [saying about] somebody who was particularly aggressive and mannish in behavior on the court, 'She must not like men.'"[69]

Beyond jokes, some players got the concept of homosexuality because they felt it—or at least tried it. There was experimentation. Mary Jane Renshaw Lewandowski '64 said girls on her Catholic high school team "developed a type of homosexuality" she thought was "normal" and attributed to "close association." "Flirting or feeling somebody's boobs or something like that," she recalled. "And I'd say . . . 'Why are you guys doing this?' and they'd say, 'Oh, it's natural, we'll grow out of it.'" Some basketball players pursued experimentation to homosexual identity, teammates said. "There were certainly some women that did go down that path, and I think everyone knew it at the time," said the class of '53 player. By the seventies, when gay rights and other sexuality issues gained cultural visibility, everyone knew "there were gay girls on the team," said Dolly VanBuskirk Anderson '78. "That was no secret."[70]

Just as players dealt differently with teammates' gender styles, they also had different approaches to sexual identities. Some who felt the sting of social suspicion that girl athletes were mannish or homosexual defended their teams from it. A few survey respondents seemed to take my questions about gender type as accusations of homosexuality and answered accordingly: "All my class teammates are happily married and raised normal children," wrote an early fifties forward. But the majority of players seemed to regard their exposure to lesbian expression as normal or educational and defended teammates' "right to be their own individual." Janet Young Eline '74 even said she once told a homophobic teammate to "get a life." None of the players to whom I spoke, however, said they themselves were gay. None said they remembered anyone speaking to gay teammates about homosexuality. None said they remembered any gay teammate "ever coming out and saying, you know, 'I am.'"[71]

Catholic girls' locker room customs were supposed to protect against unsanctioned desires. Physical familiarity with teammates felt friendly and natural, but seeing each other naked might nudge you down a slippery slope. Gay, straight, or somewhere in between, Immaculata players kept their sexuality literally under wraps. Routinely changing and showering out of each others' view, they had absorbed the habit—from home, from school, from each other—of curtailing intimate contact, of signifying the sexual parts of their bodies as off-limits to other girls.

Limiting Display

Far surpassing Immaculata players' resistance to limits on motion or contact, however, limits on display in the form of uniform regulations maddened them. College administrators' concern for basketball players' modesty put Immaculata teams in impractical and outdated garb throughout these years. Regulating uniforms, they stepped in time with popes of the era, who singled out threats to girls' modesty in sports. "In gymnastic exercises and deportment, special care must be had of Christian modesty in young women and girls," wrote Pius XI in 1929, "which is so gravely impaired by any kind of exhibition in public." Similarly his successor, Pius XII, warned against immodesty in sports, defending hot, full-coverage gym uniforms for girls. According to the *Catholic Standard and Times*—the archdiocesan newspaper Philadelphia Catholics grabbed at the back of the church after Mass—Pius XII said that though some "contend that certain garments are more comfortable and more hygienic, . . . if they are dangerous to the soul they must be rejected."[72]

Accordingly, from 1939 to 1963, Immaculata teams wore "four layers of clothing" for games, wrote a player who graduated in 1956. Numerous others described the same ensemble. First, you put on underpants and a brassiere—not a comfortable sports bra, either, Dee Cofer Cull '55 reminded me. "They weren't around. Real bras. But, for the love of it." On top of undergarments each player wore white bloomers, a blouse, and full-length blue or black lisle stockings, all covered by a blue wool tunic with a sash and finished with socks and sneakers. Players like guard Rosemary McNichol Walsh '60 remembered with incredulity "just the amount of clothing we had to put on," while rover Marianne Specht Siecko '66 complained bitterly about "those horrible black tights we had to wear for games so our legs were covered." The seamed stockings, made of unstretchy lisle, a woven cotton, sagged badly, especially after the running and drenching of a normal game. They were also "hot" and hard to maintain, because every time a player hit the floor, they "would get a million runs and had to be sewn." The runs "drew even more attention to the stockings"—the last thing players wanted.[73]

To be sure, Immaculata was not alone in wearing heavy, skirted uniforms. Into the seventies, most East Coast, DGWS-administered regions clothed their teams similarly. It was really the stockings that set Immaculatans apart from opponents, even other Catholics. Until the invention of pantyhose in 1959, stockings required either round elasticized garters or a full apparatus of belts and snaps to hold them up. Players had nightmares about snaps popping during games. Temple-educated Mackies coach Marie Schultes McGuinness (1944–46) remembered being "flabbergasted" at the school requirement of legwear. "That meant garter belts on girdles. . . . And we practiced with the stockings on too!!" she wrote, drawing an unsmiley face next to her comment. McGuinness said she was glad "no one ever lost their stockings on the court," but guard Anne Carroll Camp '51, who played shortly after McGuinness's tenure, remembered a game in which she "lost garter in front of guys from Villanova who retrieved it from the court—embarrassment, etc.," she wrote. "Very difficult trying to play and keep stocking from falling to ankle." Another player was harassed during the 1946 Mythical Championship game by an "ardent male Temple fan" who "was distractingly insistent that she 'please' straighten her seams," according to a school newspaper column. In short, if Immaculatans enjoyed opportunities for being watched in basketball, the stockings drove them to despair. "Overall, we were feminine enough to want to look good," recalled guard Alvina DeLazzari Long '57, which was "impossible in black tights!"[74]

By comparison, in the thirties southeastern women's teams wore shorts, and in the forties AAU teams wore uniforms of brightly colored satin with short-shorts, sometimes including puffy sleeves or midriff-revealing tops. And even in the more staid DGWS-administered regions, only one or two Catholic colleges wore hose. Not even Catholic League *high school* teams in Philadelphia wore stockings. Moreover, Immaculata sisters allowed field hockey players of the same period to play bare-legged. Seemingly, administrators tailor-made the legwear rule for basketball, possibly to protect players' modesty in front of larger, mixed audiences.[75]

Players knew the costume was supposed to feminize highly visible young Catholic women, protect their bodies from the public eye, and keep them from showing too much skin. "Times had changed, but we were still in 1910—to be modest," wrote Margaret Klopfle Devinney '62. But they also

Mighty Macs in motion in a January 1974 contest.
ROBERT HALVEY COLLECTION OF THE PHILADELPHIA ARCHIVES AND
HISTORICAL RESEARCH CENTER.

knew their "Victorian" uniforms did just the opposite, exposing them to un-welcome looks, laughs, and remarks wherever they went. Forward Mary Frank McCormick '50 remembered "wisecracks" from opponents or specta-tors because of the black tights. Guard Alvina DeLazzari Long '57 recalled an away game at Penn when she was "embarrassed about our uniforms," and Epiphany Pantaleo Collins '64 said boys attending games "laughed" at their outfits. Finally, teams in the early sixties got fed up. After the 1962–63 sea-son, a delegation of Immaculata players visited college president Sister Mary of Lourdes and begged her to let them lose the stockings. "It was a fight—but we showed her how they were burning our legs," recalled rover Maureen Callahan Bigham '63. "She finally allowed us to shed them."[76]

Because of their initiative, in photographs for the 1963–64 season, the Mackies sported bare legs. And in 1965 the team purchased slacks to wear under their skirts for game warm-ups. But they continued to wear the wool tunics and blouses until 1972, partly because the school could not afford new uniforms but also because more current styles often featured shorts instead of skirts. Since the fifties, players had been practicing in shorts, but the college dress code forbade them in public. The hand-me-down, ill-fitting tunics in which the team won its first national championship were almost as old as the girls themselves. At that 1972 tournament, Denise Conway '74 told an *Im-maculatan* reporter, other teams "offered to burn our uniforms so we could get new ones." After Immaculata won the trophy that year, several chagrined team alumnae formed a fledgling booster club "for no other reason but to buy them new uniforms." Working with the administration, boosters purchased a set of just-above-the-knee skirts and short-sleeved tops, made of double-knit polyester. Still modest and ladylike, the modern style thrilled players.[77]

As East Coast teams increasingly switched to shorts, Immaculata players' skirts flew as they jumped for rebounds and laid up baskets. Still, college administration insisted on the traditionally feminine attire. Again in the early seventies, other teams and fans regularly "laughed" at the Immaculata teams' uniforms. "They just looked at us and were just in amazement that we were still wearing skirts," remembered forward Mary Scharff '77. "We got funny looks, and a few snide remarks from guys on the side . . . like, 'look, they're in skirts, look,' . . . because their team was in shorts." Finally, I.H.M. sisters allowed the Mighty Macs to wear shorts for the 1974–75 season.[78]

Apart from uniforms, however, players didn't mind their community's wish that they signify traditional femininity on the court. Like most young women, they wanted to look pretty, especially in public, especially in front of mixed crowds. So Immaculata players became known for appearing at games as "very dainty little ladies," said fan and administrator Sister Marian William Hoben '44, who later served as college president (1982–92). They wore jewelry, before rules disallowed it, and ornamented their long hair with ribbons and bows. Late sixties coach Jenepher Shillingford recalled the look. "Probably at the time that I was there, you know, we won't have short hair, we'll have long hair and we'll pull it back in a ponytail," she said. "And that will . . . create a certain image." In the seventies as well, remembered Janet Young Eline '74, "We wore bows and makeup and jewelry . . . we'd have our hair tied back and we'd always put nice pretty bows in our hair."[79]

Protecting team members from looking like guys, players as well as administrators trumpeted femininity over the noise of onlooking crowds. But when it came to ugly black stockings, old wool uniforms, and outdated skirts—when modesty interfered with looking good—players rebelled.

Pleasure and Pain

Immaculata athletes overwhelmingly remembered the physical pleasures of playing basketball. But sometimes they also recalled the painful limits of their bodies' ability and health. And a few said they ached to realize that the joys of basketball would soon give way to more traditional futures. The pain of these limits checked the pleasure of the game but also underlined all the more the physical and gender freedom players found in basketball.

Some players said lack of talent compromised their enjoyment. "I was very self-conscious—not very good," wrote Patricia Furey McDonnell '53. Several listed as their most difficult memory never being "a good player" or "not being as talented." "I wasn't as good a player as I wished but I tried," recalled forward Marcia Baylor Donnelly '58. When I contacted Mary Burke Flaherty '46, she said she didn't wish to talk because there were "quite a few players better than myself." While players of all heights and builds played basketball for most of these years, by the late sixties, the game got more competitive, and being tall helped. A couple players said they were too small for the game. "I was too short! My height was 5' 3" so I only played my freshman year," wrote Adrienne Friaglia Cyran '67.[80]

Across the years, players who got hurt in games or practices also experienced the limits of their bodies. Many listed injury as their most difficult experience: "Tearing cartilage in left knee." "Broke my left index finger." "Getting trampled in a game and someone stepping on my kneecap." "Spraining my ankle." More often than the pain of the injury itself, though, players remembered the difficulty of having to sit on the sidelines, "not being able to play," seeing "limited action," or missing a big game because of the flu. Immaculatans played through menstrual cramps as best they could, too. "You could tell when somebody wasn't running too hard. Cramps or something," said Dee Cofer Cull '55. But "you didn't want to [sit]," she said. "Unless you were really hurt, you didn't. Everybody on the team wanted [to play]. They'd play, except for a broken leg."[81]

For a few, even more painful than bodily limits on talent or participation were social assumptions that they would stop playing basketball after college. In a Catholic community that valued marriage and motherhood so highly, "not being taken seriously as an athlete was difficult," remembered rover Maureen Callahan Bigham '63. Many players could have continued basketball after college. From the forties, recreational, industrial, and even semipro leagues beckoned good players; in the seventies, a professional women's league briefly assembled. Before they had children, a few star players did play for local postcollege leagues such as the Camden Rockettes and the Suburban Girls' League. But most in the Catholic community—including many players—considered postgraduation hoops inappropriate. At public colleges or in noncollegiate leagues, players who were mothers would bring their children to games, and it "just didn't sit right with me," said forward Mary Frank McCormick '50, who also coached the Immaculata team from 1952 to 1956. "I always felt like the children were neglected or something."[82]

So some ex-Mackies who longed to join postcollege teams gave it up in the face of disapproval. Sister Marita David "Toddy" Kirsch was one of them. She played for a respectable team of alumnae from her parish high school, St. Katharine's, who called themselves the K-Club. She said she considered joining a women's industrial league, but it just wasn't the done thing for an

Theresa Shank '74 with Eddie Rush, Alumnae Hall, 1974.
PHOTOGRAPH BY H. ROSS WATSON, JR.

Immaculata girl. Or players got pregnant. One Mackie from the class of '57 hoped to play basketball after graduation but didn't have time as a single working woman. "I was thinking when I got married, I could go play [basketball] again," she said. "I didn't expect six children to get in the way." The one approved outlet available to ex-Mackies for postgraduation play was the season-opening exhibition game between the team and its alumnae scheduled yearly between 1955 and 1971. Team alums came out, babies in tow, and played to their hearts' content, regularly besting the younger Immaculata varsity. Otherwise deprived, ex-players said they found ways to get their basketball kicks. "I did play vicariously," said Dee Cofer Cull '55 said. "I coached, which was fine with me. I still had four boys that played basketball out back. You know, [I] got bumped and, oh yeah, I taught 'em how to play, I did. That was fun." Marian Collins Mullahy '54 said she and her husband watched their kids play basketball as often as possible. If she couldn't keep playing herself, she would not be like the mother of the family on the *Donna Reed Show*, who "ironed their pajamas, for heaven's sake," said Marian. "And I wanted to go out and do [things]—that's why we spent so much time in gyms. We loved it, we just loved it. I did not iron pajamas."[83]

The physical and sometimes emotional suffering players associated with basketball was not redemptive suffering, however. They simply considered lack of talent, health, or future opportunity to be sad and difficult. The culture of suffering regnant in Catholic discourses of the body throughout these years permeated their lives. But in the Catholic basketball subculture, players valued pleasure, and suffering was nothing more than suffering.

• • •

Immaculata players' physical enjoyment of the game pushed traditional Catholic notions of femininity. Playing basketball, they defended with their bodies the pleasures of motion, contact, and display. On the court, they liked feeling good and looking good; they complained and resisted when those ends were compromised. Of course, alternative physical experiences in basketball offered a mere loophole in an overarching Philadelphia Catholic ideology of gender, and Catholic authorities and culture worked hard to close it. But on the court, a site of overlapping versions of femininity, Immaculata players staged small protests, found temporary freedoms, and traveled just a bit outside prescribed gender roles, all hidden in plain view.

For players, however, testing Catholic gender norms never meant questioning whether they were Catholic. First and foremost, Immaculata players identified themselves not as women or basketball players but as Catholics. They took for granted that their lives—including their basketball games— were steeped in Catholic culture, conviction, and devotion. In fact, it was praying for the game that intensified some players' sense of a God who cared about their whole lives, even basketball.

CHAPTER 4

PRAYING FOR THE TEAM

Through basketball, I have argued, Immaculata players negotiated identity, class, and gender. Few of those I interviewed, however, would have put the significance of basketball in those terms. To them, if their sport had a deeper meaning, it lay in its connection to their Catholic faith. Like everything at Immaculata, basketball was religiously infused. Sometimes, players said, a game wasn't just a game but a divine lesson, even a cosmic event. The 1974 loss to Queens College was a case in point. It was the twenty-seventh of February, Ash Wednesday on the Catholic calendar, the start of the season of Lent, forty days of repentance and fasting until Easter Sunday. Observing the holy day, the two-time national champions all attended Mass, where the priest thumbed a cross of ashes on each of their foreheads. Then they boarded a bus for New York City. On the other end, national power Queens awaited them, hoping to avenge their loss to the Macs in the previous year's AIAW championship game. Immaculata was the team to beat. Riding to Queens with carloads of family and fans behind them, the Macs boasted a thirty-five-game winning streak—then the longest in college basketball—extending back through their undefeated season in 1973 and their first championship tournament in 1972. And the Macs were favored to win a third championship later that season. Buoyed on a crescendo of confidence, they took the hardwood against Queens. In a physical game with dozens of lead changes, they battled their Big Apple rivals. But two hours later, for the first time in two years, they walked off the court in defeat. Down by one point at the buzzer, Immaculata failed to drop a flurry of last-second shots.

In the locker room, players cried out their humiliation. Later, still weeping on the way home, someone remembered it was Ash Wednesday. The ashes had sweated off most foreheads, but the symbolism remained. It was a comfort somehow, to lose on the traditional Catholic day of repentance. No one suggested the team had something to repent, but they all remembered feeling crushed and embarrassed, as well as guilty to think they'd disappointed fans. But if they lost on the same day that Catholics worldwide marked their brows, somehow that was appropriate. Before Christ rose from the dead, said those ashen crosses, he had to die. And players came to feel God was telling them something about the loss by delivering it on Ash Wednesday. Was it a lesson in humility? A reminder to thank God in good times and bad? A sign that defeat shall yet end in triumph? Whatever each player concluded, star center Theresa Shank '74 later told *The Immaculatan*, "That game helped us to remember that some of God's greatest gifts are his refusals."[1]

Riding back on the bus, players planned to disembark and slink to their rooms, where they would nurse the loss and ponder the lessons. But Jesus did get up from the grave, and the Mighty Macs' Ash Wednesday was not over. Well past midnight, they pulled up to Villa Maria, gathered their things, and trudged into the great hall of the rotunda, only to be surprised by lights and music and shouting. The marble-and-tile stairwell was decked out like it was Christmas, the pep band was playing, and leaning out over every inch of two stories of balconies were Immaculata students who had stayed up and come out to cheer the Macs—after their *loss*. There had never been a late-night assembly for *wins*. "I think every student from campus was there, and every sister and alumnae were all around the rotunda, . . . screaming and cheering," recalled Sister Marian William Hoben, who had accompanied the team to Queens. Speechless with surprise, players were made to sit in a semicircle of folding chairs for an impromptu pep rally. "Once more in '74! Once more in 74!" the chanting and clapping resounded off marble pillars. Theresa Shank finally got up to speak. The students and sisters coming out to support them on this night meant more than any other night, she said. The team wouldn't let the loss put an end to their season, she continued, warming to the moment. They would practice hard and win big and, Theresa said in a rising voice, do Immaculata proud. "I promise you!" she shouted to the roaring assembly. "I will get you and this team will get you the national championship *once again*!" And they did. Twenty-five days later, Immaculata College celebrated Easter early, winning a third national trophy.[2]

Not only in dramatic championships but also in mundane practices and games, basketball and Catholicism melded in players' memories. Different players described the connection differently, but most agreed that God was somehow present in the game, as God played a part in everything in their lives. Team members prayed for basketball and believed God answered. It wasn't about mouthing pious words. In a diffusely Catholic context, prayers and devotions were "just part of our life at I.C.," as Lynn Hubbard Ouellette '66 put it. In conversations, players talked seamlessly about hooping with friends and praying for victory, driving past defenders and going to pregame masses, elbowing an opponent and feeling "a spiritual bond" with teammates. While I tried to discern any tension between playing basketball and living as Catholic women, most players said, like Josephine McFarland '42, "it never entered my mind" that basketball and Catholicism might clash, so thoroughly did they take for granted the relationship. Basketball was Catholic, and they liked it that way. It was more than a sport; it was part of their faith. Praying with the team was "fun" or made them "feel good," they said. Most Immaculata players enjoyed basketball in part because it offered a special forum for faith, where religion could be applied to a beloved activity. The Catholic context and devotional trappings of basketball enhanced the pleasure they already found in the game.[3]

Praying and going to Mass before games were not subversive; on the contrary, Immaculatans, like Catholic athletes across the country, were encouraged to see the spiritual in everything they did, including sports. So the spiritual often found itself far afield of sanctuary altars and parish festivals, showing up in playgrounds and gyms. While no player suggested any inherent connection between Catholicism and basketball, in the archdiocesan network of institutions, "it was *all* Catholic," and basketball became religious within the penumbra. I have already showed that basketball was culturally Catholic, a sport particularly cherished and cultivated in Catholic Philadelphia. But it became religiously Catholic. The favorite church game naturally called forth all the powers of prayer and all the codings of devotion.[4]

Praying for basketball flowed within norms of Catholic practice, but the sport stood at greater remove from direct institutional oversight than other sites of religious activity. Not only basketball but also other parareligious institutions, from confraternity lodge and butcher shop to bakery and kitchen table, gave Catholic Philadelphians many more occasions than weekly Mass to be Catholic. They received communion on Sunday but also bought Friday seafood at the corner grocery. They confessed their sins on Saturday but also debated interfaith marriage at the beauty parlor. In short, parareligious institutions were Catholic not only culturally but also religiously. Certainly, the vast majority of parareligious institutions supported and corroborated traditional Catholicism. The parallel Catholic universe was meant to, and did, insulate the faithful from secular and non-Catholic influence in their daily lives. But these Catholicized sites also gave ordinary people spaces and circumstances to improvise Catholicism at some distance from ecclesiastical supervision. For while faith infused basketball, so sometimes basketball talked back to faith. And not all theological questions and spiritual impulses generated on the court accorded with the priorities and practices of official Catholicism. For example, might God use a traditional church holy day to deliver a message to a basketball team? Ironically, then, the same institutions that were supposed to fortify Catholicism sometimes afforded believers subterfuge to apply theology and adapt practice without attracting church disapproval. Far from producing a uniform community and an unchallenged consensus, the Catholic subculture generated thousands who, like religious people everywhere, performed orthopraxy at church and experimented on the side. Precisely because the church endorsed basketball, players took the sport as an opportunity to customize their faith.

Philadelphia Catholic Religious Practice

Because a thick network of schools, parishes, and affiliated institutions connected Catholics to official church life, the mid-twentieth-century Archdiocese of Philadelphia boasted some of the highest rates of traditional religious participation in the country. Many U.S. bishops and priests struggled to conform diverse ethnic populations to Irish-dominated notions of "American" Catholic practice, emphasizing attendance at weekly Mass, reverence for clergy, and moderation in extraliturgical devotions. But in Philadelphia these dispositions were taken for granted, taught in a community little given to quarter ethnic particularism. In the name of catholicity—really a thin cloak for Irish norms—Cardinal Dougherty allowed no national parishes. Because parishes drew from surrounding neighborhoods, they still generally grouped Irish separately from Italian, German from Polish. But the policy discouraged interethnic political warfare and at least nominally homogenized practice one parish to the next. Meanwhile, the school system put immigrants' children in the same classrooms, learning the same orthodoxy. As a result, weekly Mass was, as historian Charles Morris put it, "carved deeply in neural pathways" of 90 percent of Philadelphia Catholics who attended each Sunday from the thirties through the early sixties. A full 99 percent of the Philadelphia faithful fulfilled the Easter duty of taking communion once a year. And most Philadelphia Catholics received communion at least once a month, a relatively high rate. Parishes saw high attendance for daily Mass, obligatory holy days, and many optional novenas, feast days, and seasonal liturgies. Tens of thousands also attended optional spiritual retreats each year. At the time of Dougherty's death in 1951, the men's center at Malvern and the women's center at Elkins Park might have constituted the largest retreat operation on the planet.[5]

Catholic Philadelphia was also, like most Catholic communities, a devotional culture in constant communication with Mary and the saints. If Philadelphia Catholics addressed the saints with more regulation from leaders, their devotion diminished in flamboyance not quantity. In particular, throughout Philadelphia, devotion to Mary of the Miraculous Medal, who appeared in an apparition to French Daughter of Charity Catherine Labouré in 1830, drew thousands for weekly Monday services, including Catholic teenagers on dates. Reputed to heal, the devotion was so popular that at the Miraculous Medal shrine at St. Vincent's Seminary chapel, located in working-class Germantown, priests held twelve services every Monday, which routinely drew between eight and ten thousand worshipers from 1930 to 1960.[6]

Apart from formal devotional rituals, Catholics in Philadelphia could consecrate anything, from a job interview to a new car, a child's illness to a blind date, by applying prayers, lighting candles, or festooning scapulars. A woman praying for her husband's upcoming operation could say a novena; a Catholic family leaving for vacation could hang a St. Christopher medal from the rearview mirror. Laity and clerics alike understood these private devotions as extensions of liturgical church life that, like the Mass, transformed daily mundanities into occasions of grace. Far from being discouraged, they made all of life "Catholic." And within devotional culture, in Philadelphia as elsewhere, women tended to feel more personally the need and responsibility for communicating with the saints. Raised to nurture family life and social relationships, women also sustained human communication with God and the saints.[7]

The tenor of Catholicism at Immaculata, whose sisters were usually products of the Philadelphia system, mirrored that of the archdiocese at large. Through the sixties, the I.H.M. sisters encouraged formal religious observance at a weekly flurry of services and automatically enrolled everyone in the Sodality, a club for devotion to Mary. They started each class with prayers and required students to write at the top of assignments "J.M.J." (for Jesus, Mary, and Joseph) or AMDG (for *ad majoram deam gloriam*, "all for the greater glory of God"). They advocated petitioning the saints, especially Mary, Teresa of Avila, and Alphonsus Liguori, all patrons of the Immaculate Heart community.

In addition, the sisters kept Immaculata current with trends in Catholic higher education, such as the twenties' and thirties' Catholic intellectual revival that restructured curricula around neo-Thomistic theology. The renaissance of Thomism was soon put to what Philip Gleason called the "ideological function" of creating a "Catholic culture." This Catholic culture, "self-consciously countercultural" in its opposition to the modern secular world, propounded Catholicism as a holistic "way of life" orienting both the highest holy days and the smallest chores toward a religious whole. In this new outlook, educator Gerald B. Phelan wrote in 1932, "Religion is not a course in the ordinary sense of the term. It is a life. As such it should control and guide all activity, academic and otherwise, of the Catholic student." In the Catholic-college–rich Philadelphia area, thousands of Catholics who might otherwise not have attended college at all were exposed to this elite, supradevotional Catholicism. All Immaculatans, including basketball players, studied theology and philosophy in a neo-Thomist framework. Immaculata in 1930 already required a religion curriculum similar to that of local men's colleges: six semesters of theology and philosophy and then, for Catholic students, an additional semester of both religion and church history every year.[8]

If the Immaculata sisters were seen as more progressive than many orders before the Second Vatican Council, they appeared more conservative afterward. With the rest of the Philadelphia archdiocese, they approached Vatican II reforms with caution. As many sisters shed traditional garb, the I.H.M.s reaffirmed the order's full habit, including the veil. The sisters promoted Vatican II with special seminars, but little of the new church spirit markedly altered campus life. Neither did social activism, which on many Catholic campuses coalesced with Vatican II to redefine lay American consciousness, disturb the school's hilltop tranquility. Pete Seeger and George McGovern visited the campus in 1968; there were occasional lectures on ecumenism or environmentalism or editorials supporting Catholic radicalism. But there were few challenges to the authority of sisters or the church. "That just wasn't in the can of my experience," said cheerleader Geraldine Ferrari Burton '57. "And people would say, 'Well, that's because Catholic kids are sheep, they just did what they were told.' I was never a sheep, never. But there were certain givens. You were a student. You weren't in charge. That was the way it was." Several sisters and players remembered the highlight of campus activism came when students marched to the sisters' Gillet Hall home singing demands for dress code changes to the tune of "We Shall Overcome." Sisters misunderstood and thought the students had arrived to serenade them. Immaculata was not Berkeley.[9]

And Immaculata basketball players were not religious rebels. In this pervasively Catholicized milieu, they took for granted that daily life was punctuated with formal observance and intertwined with spontaneous prayers. "We spent so much time in church, it seemed," said Frances Gercke Campbell '45. "And Catholic grade school and then the academy and then Immaculata. And you know there was such a thing as sin then, and the Ten Commandments. It was before love came." Thirty years later, though, players still said they toed given lines. "We never rebelled against anything," remembered Mary Scharff '77. "We believe[d] in God, we're Catholic. . . . I believed in prayer, I believed in Mass, in church, and . . . all that. It wasn't in my eyes anything to go against." At Immaculata, some players attended daily Mass or contemplated religious vocations. After graduation, many said, Catholicism became even more important, as they married and raised children in the faith.[10]

To casual observation, then, the Catholic Philadelphia landscape featured few undisciplined crevices where heterodoxy might sprout. But high rates of formal religious practice did not necessarily translate into religious hegemony. If everything was Catholic, there was room to improvise. Could you have a funeral for a dead pet? Should you give your Protestant neighbor a rosary? Might you say a novena for the softball team? Why not?

Could you go to a weekday mass for your team's big game or pin Miraculous Medals to your basketball uniform? Immaculata players did. And, in doing so, they experimented with their tradition, tested its assumptions, and pushed its logic. Thoroughly within the Catholic world but away from theology classes, basketball provided an arena of spiritual exploration. Some players found in basketball a fresh and compelling reason to pray. Others took basketball as a case in point that anything in life could be a religious experience. For some, connections between Catholicism and basketball led to questions: Could God use basketball to work his will in their lives? Was there something special, even holy, about the spirit they felt among teammates? Was it worthy of faith to pray for basketball games? On the other hand, was it worthy of basketball to tie it up with the church? Wondering and exploring, players worked out parts of their personal theologies and religious practices on the basketball court.

Immaculata Basketball and Religious Practice

Numerous prayers and rituals marked Immaculata players' experience of basketball. From a special basketball prayer to foul-line signs of the cross, from religious medals to pregame masses, these devotions, many players said, made both sports and Catholicism more meaningful.

The basketball team in the chapel, with warm-up jackets and veils, 1960. COURTESY OF IMMACULATA COLLEGE.

Praying to the "God of Players"

Almost all former players told me prayer featured prominently in rituals surrounding basketball. When they prayed for basketball, they often said prayers drawn from Catholic tradition, such as the Hail Mary or the Our Father, both heavyweight appeals for any occasion. But through the seventies, at the start of every game, Immaculata players also said another prayer, tailor-made for athletes' concerns. It started, "O God of Players, hear our prayer." "We all leaned into a circle with one hand upon another player's hand and recited [it] together," said Fruff Fauerbach Timby '50. When I spoke with Immaculata hoopsters decades later, many could still recite the prayer in full:

> *O God of Players, hear our prayer*
> *To play this game and play it fair,*
> *To conquer, win, but if to lose*
> *Not to revile nor to abuse*
> *But with understanding start again,*
> *Give us the strength, O Lord. Amen.*

No one recalled the origin of this prayer. Players who went to I.H.M. high schools, such as Villa Maria and St. Katharine's in Wayne, said they learned it before coming to Immaculata, so it might have been a prayer written by an Immaculate Heart nun and disseminated among her sisters. A few said they heard other Catholic schools saying it, too. Whoever its author, however, she did not mention girls, basketball, or Catholicism specifically. Instead, its words petitioned God regarding a generic team sport. And when Immaculata players said this prayer season after season, it was significant as much for the context as for the words themselves.[11]

For one thing, when players and coach gathered on the court in front of fans and prayed together, it was a rare instance of Catholic laywomen praying together in public, without a priest or sister. Of course, laywomen prayed together all the time, in homes and at meetings. But very rarely did they say prayers in public without the leadership of priests or nuns. Even more unusual for Catholic laywomen, sometimes the Mackies prayed "O God of Players" in front of Protestant crowds, making this unusual mode of Catholic prayer visible to non-Catholics. And, finally, this prayer featured young women supplicating heaven for something other than family members and relationships. Unlike most prayer duties accorded their gender, "O God of Players" petitioned for a basketball game. Standing on the court, hands in a pile, requesting God's help for the upcoming contest, Immaculata players broke form as to how and for what Catholic women should pray.

The words of the prayer also mattered, embedding assumptions about God not found in traditional Catholic prayers. Immaculatans who prayed "O God of Players" addressed a God who cared about athletes—*girl* athletes, since they were the ones praying it. The prayer specified no gender, but when Immaculatans appealed to this God, they assumed he heard their prayers for basketball just as well as their brothers' prayers for football. Moreover, the Mackies supplicated this God directly, with no mediating saint. Catholic prayers of private petition often appealed to a saint known to patronize a cause—such as St. Anne, patron of pregnant women, or St. Joseph, the patron of laborers—and Catholic women carried the community burden of these prayers via saints. But in "O God of Players," young Catholic women went straight to the top, circumventing even Mary and Jesus. There was a patron saint of sports, St. Christopher. But Christopher was vastly better known for another of his jobs, safeguarding travel. In this team prayer, God himself served as patron of athletics. Named for his sponsorship, the Almighty himself was the "God of Players."

The words of the prayer also voiced many requests. The first one listed, "to play . . . fair," assumed that a sportsmanlike game, honor-bound by rules, should be the team's primary concern. Fair play included losing contests gracefully, even apprehending losses as God's will: "if to lose / . . . with understanding start again." While being good sports invoked a set of widely held American athletic values, Immaculata players often identified general traits of sportsmanship as "Catholic," including losing honorably. A few players agreed that they should pray "to do one's best, not necessarily be victorious," as Anne Carroll Camp '51 wrote. Mary Scharff '77 said that because the team prayed, "We knew whether we won or lost, that's what was meant to be."[12]

But when most Immaculata players remembered "O God of Players," they did not, despite its words, remember its primary petition as a request to play fair and lose honorably. Instead, they intended the prayer to solicit other forms of help, not explicitly stated. Health and safety were among foremost requests in their minds—"that no one got injured" or "that everybody would come home safely." Margaret Monahan Hogan '63 said she and her teammates prayed to "use well the talents given by God." But even safety and health couldn't compete with players' dominant concern, which, according to many, was "to conquer" and "win." Though this request came second in the prayer's wording, it was first in players' hearts. More than any other aim, they prayed to beat opponents. "I prayed to win," said Dee Cofer Cull '55. "I don't know what the others prayed for. But I'm not pussyfooting around, I prayed to win." The God of Players cared not only about basketball but also about the score.[13]

Players sometimes allowed that God could be spotty granting requests for particular victories. Dee Cofer Cull '55 wrote bluntly, "sometimes [prayers] worked—Other times—NOT." But, in their minds, this possibility did not compromise the appropriateness of asking. "My conviction [was that] a prayer during a tough time period on the court often helped," recalled Meg Kenny Kean '58, "and if it didn't work that time perhaps it would later—and often did." Alvina DeLazzari Long '57 remembered "praying for something you didn't always receive but not giving up on it." Despite tough losses, to most players, it was clear that God always welcomed sports requests and often answered them. "Of course, we prayed to win," said Marian Collins Mullahy '54. "And that was part of it all—boy did we win."[14]

Other Basketball Rituals

In the seventies, the Immaculata team still collectively recited "O God of Players" but added other traditions, too. Cagers and coach Cathy Rush appended an elaborate "pre-game ritual of song and prayer" intended "to get everyone pumped up." Part of this pregame ritual was an informal litany of the saints in which each player would petition her favorite saint, for example, "St. Christopher, pray for us." With less oversight praying in gyms than in churches, players introduced the occasional winking irreverence. When St. Christopher was demoted from sainthood, Marianne Crawford Stanley '76 changed her line in the litany. "Mr. Christopher, play for us," she would pray, much to the mirth of the whole circle. But in the midst of laughter, as Sue Forsyth O'Grady '72 wrote, the ritual "reminded us . . . that God could help us do our best, even if a game was *just* a game." In fact, it was especially in the championship years that the Immaculata teams credited God with what one reporter called their "faintly miraculous" success. "We all believed God answered prayers," said team manager Jean Brashears Vause '74. "When things looked down a few prayers could not hurt," said Maureen Mooney '73, "and as history shows, someone was listening." Mary Scharff '77 gave voice to her team's widely shared suspicions that God had a lot to do with their uncanny national-title streak. "Why are we winning?" she said they used to wonder. "Is it just because you're good, or is there a little bit of help from upstairs, that he's really behind you? And we all believed that . . . you have so much power behind you from the Almighty that you're doing as well as you are. . . . We always thought that we had a lot of help from the outside and it wasn't visible help."[15]

Assumptions about God's attention to courtside petitions carried over into players' other basketball-related solicitations. Sometimes they simply prayed on their own, for example "to make the varsity team" or to "plead" for teammates and friends at tryouts. Commuters who missed team rites would duck into their parish churches for a quick prayer or a weekday mass. Together, the team often visited the campus chapel together before games. Maureen Mooney '73 said she remembered sitting with teammates in the chapel, "very quiet but praying for the same thing . . . the ability and strength to win the next game for the team, our famil[ies], friends and fans." Other collective religious activities included praying "the rosary aloud as a group" on the team bus and walking in silence between classes on game day "to offer it up for the game." Not ceasing to pray during games, players called on God with a quick sign of the cross before foul shots or a murmured invocation at in-bounds. "Before a foul shot, I'd pray, because I stunk taking foul shots and prayers didn't help," remembered Dee Cofer Cull '55. I asked her if she got mad when she missed shots for which she'd prayed. "No, we won too many games to shake my faith," she said. "Fortunately I never had to win a game with a foul shot."[16]

At crucial points in the action, benchwarmers and cheerleaders "pray[ed] like crazy for the girls on the court," they said. Mothers and fathers added daughters' games to their Sunday Mass intentions and lofted prayers as well as cheers from the sidelines. In the seventies, songs with religious themes regularly accompanied fans' cheers. Volunteers would mimeograph sheets of hymn lyrics adapted for basketball use by Sister Marian William Hoben '44, then college director of development. Including lines such as "Rise and shine and give God your glory," these sheets would be passed out to fans at games and sung heartily. A favorite was the Mighty Macs' apocalyptic theme song, "When the Macs Go Marching In." The St. Joe's fans came to be known for their adaptation of this song later, but the Mackies said St. Joe's got it from them.[17]

Throughout these years, even the loftiest of Catholic rituals, the Mass itself, could be applied to the consecration of basketball. "If we had an important game, we went to Mass," recalled Rosemary Duddy McFadden '46. A few remembered "Mass the next day" after games, or going to Mass together on road trips, sometimes having brought with them a college chaplain, who would deliver a "fitting homily" for game day. After the third national championship, in March 1975, in keeping with the seventies trend of themed masses, the entire Immaculata community was invited to a "eucharistic celebration to honor the 'Macs'—National Champions," as the mass program announced. The call to worship read, "We come together to shout praise, to share friendship, and to offer thanksgiving for exhilarating moments of accomplishment. We celebrate the daring and the endurance of the athlete, the excellence of fair play, self-discipline and teamwork, and the sweet joy of victory. For our basketball team, we have cause to praise the Lord, and we ask to *be in that number when the 'Macs' come marching in.*" This basketball-themed mass also featured a reading of 1 Corinthians in which Paul exhorts his listeners to run the race "so as to win . . . a crown that is imperishable"; a gospel selection from Matthew in which Jesus guaranteed the power of prayer "if two of you join your voices on earth to pray for anything whatever"; and offertory gifts of a basketball and noisemakers along with the customary bread and wine. In this mass, all the weight of church and biblical tradition supported praying for the team.[18]

Mary's Intercession for Basketball

God cared about basketball, and so did Catholic players' feminine role model, the Blessed Virgin Mary. Players nicknamed her "B.V.M." and during games invoked her aid regularly. In response, she intervened at crucial moments. When a 1956 graduate hit a half-court shot in front of the boy she liked, she said, "I owed that one to B.V.M." Many canards about the graceful and serene Virgin chafed against the rough-and-tumble realities of basketball, but that did not stop players from assuming her interest in games.[19]

Praying for Mary's help, players used the more common mediated form of petitionary prayer rather than the forthright "O God of Players." For basketball, as for every other need in Immaculatans' lives, Mary the Mother of God was the primary mediator; one of her titles was Mediatrix of Heaven.

Reciting the rosary on the bus or crediting Mary with big baskets, Immaculata players took the model of Catholic womanhood onto the court with them. During time-outs, on-court forwards and guards might huddle to pray several rounds of Hail Mary, remembered Mary Frank McCormick '50, since during most of these years, coaches weren't allowed to consult during these breaks. "So lots of times the coach wasn't even in the huddle," Mary said. "We probably figured we'd make that extra foul shot if we said the Hail Mary at the time-out instead of . . . talking about the shot." For basketball as well as all other needs, the "Blessed Mother [was] always the person that we prayed to," remembered Sister Marita David "Toddy" Kirsch.[20]

If players weren't actively seeking Mary's help, they often wore her images on their team uniforms. The popular Philadelphia devotion to the Miraculous Medal found its way onto the basketball court when enthusiastic I.H.M. sisters began giving players the small silver medallions Mary originally described in her apparition to Catherine Labouré. The Mackies were only too happy to place confidence in the powerful symbol, worn around their necks on chains or pinned with a ribbon to their tunics. In the early seventies, some sisters also gave team members little blue enamel pins in the shape of the Madonna's veiled head, bowed in prayer, which players wore pinned to their uniforms. Soon, game rules disallowed jewelry, but the Mighty Macs refused to play without the Mary pins. "I was like, we have to wear this pin; the nuns gave it to us," remembered Janet Young Eline '74. "And so we did . . . we tucked them down in the bottom of our tunics . . . so you couldn't see them." Players took their devotion—and their formula for success—seriously enough to find ways to defy the regulation.[21]

I.H.M. Sisters' Prayers for Basketball

The sisters who gave team members Miraculous Medals and Mary pins were themselves earthly mediators in the communion of saints, especially commissioned in their vocations to pray on others' behalf. Sister Marian William Hoben '44 said she and other sisters frequently prayed for the basketball team because "prayer was very, very essential to whatever we were doing," she said. In attendance for every Mighty Macs game, former Immaculata president Sister Mary of Lourdes said she "would never think of starting a game without praying." "Why pray for basketball?" I asked her. Not so much to win, Sister Mary of Lourdes said, but to put "them under protection." As for winning, she said, "it can't help you to pray beforehand for anything." Her unprepared students who madly prayed before chemistry exams, she said, were deluding themselves. But, she added with a half-suppressed smile, praying to win "can't do any harm, . . . either." Ultimately, different sisters might have held different views on praying for games. But as older women mediating for younger women's basketball activities—especially as nuns, whose prayers were popularly regarded as particularly efficacious—the I.H.M.s affirmed the appropriateness of feminine prayers on the subject of sports.[22]

Basketball players remembered many nuns throughout the years praying for the team. Chronically overcommitted and underpaid, sisters could not always find enough time or enough cars to attend. "But [they] always wished us well and prayed," recalled a student fan from the class of '47. "Especially if we were leaving the campus," recalled Helen Frank Dunigan '56, the sisters said, "'Hey, good luck, don't forget we'll pray for you.' . . . They prayed for your safety to get there . . . and get back . . . and then to play a good game. They didn't really care if you won."[23]

But when sisters did attend, their presence was dramatic, especially if the opposing team was not Catholic and not used to cadres of nuns in full habit. The I.H.M.s arrived en masse, filed in all at once, and turned entire sections of bleachers dark blue and white. They were at least impressive and at most intimidating. Identically dressed and veiled, the sisters signified religiosity; cheering at games, they blessed the proceedings. "You could see the sisters in the stands praying constantly for us," said Mary Scharff '77. "You had this really good feeling about everything because it wasn't like we were out on our own." The sisters were flanked by families and friends, all together called by one campus reporter the "rosary-rooters."[24]

Visiting Camilla Hall

When the Immaculata teams started winning at the national level in the early seventies, special relationships developed between team members and sisters at Camilla Hall, the on-campus home for aging and sickly I.H.M. nuns. At Camilla, it became a favorite pastime for sisters to follow and pray for the Mighty Macs. In turn, it became a tradition for the basketball luminaries to stop by and visit the elderly nuns. Some Mighty Macs particularly credited Camilla Hall and its "prayer power" as the force behind their victories. If nuns' prayers were especially efficacious, perhaps old and dying sisters' petitions were even more potent. Whatever the case, championship-era players rarely pronounced the words "Camilla Hall" without an added tone of reverence.[25]

But for the Camilla sisters themselves, along with their I.H.M. nurses and caretakers, there was no mystique about their prayers. For them, praying for the team was just part of the fun and diversion of following the team. With time to pay attention to big games and minute stats alike, sisters followed the team even more intensely after local radio station WCOJ started broadcasting the Mighty Macs live. The sisters would put the broadcast on the inter-com system at Camilla, so nurses doing rounds could follow the action. They would also set up a radio on the windowsill of the common lounge, where many wheelchair-bound nuns gathered around to listen. Together, the sisters prayed before each game and interjected prayers throughout, especially if the Macs took a turn for the worse. "If somebody would say, 'They're losing, they're losing!' everybody'd go to the chapel . . . wheeling their wheelchairs in to pray . . . for them in chapel," said Sister Marian William Hoben.[26]

Players said they began to hear stories of the Camilla sisters' patronage and gradually realized "the power of so many silent yet boisterous sisters at Camilla," remembered Lorrie Gable Finelli '78. "They helped us so much in all of their prayers," agreed Mary Scharff '77. "They were behind us and sup-porting us and . . . we decided . . . hey, let's support them, too." At coach Cathy Rush's initiative, the Mighty Macs began making regular team visits to Camilla Hall, bonding with the little sub-community of infirm nuns and their nurses. The sisters thought "it was just fabulous that we would stop just to visit them," said Mary Scharff '77. The team even began to hold pep ral-lies at Camilla. Many players told me that visits with the Camilla Hall sisters, which started in a team effort to give something back for prayers rendered, quickly transcended duty. They enjoyed going to see the sisters and treasured new relationships. Several Mighty Macs continued to visit Camilla Hall friends long after graduation. In this case, praying for the team brought to-gether the basketball team and retired sisters, enriching two groups of the Immaculata community that otherwise would rarely have interacted.[27]

Basketball and Religious Pleasure

Not only at Camilla but also on the court, on the bus, between classes, and in the chapel, players remembered religious activities associated with bas-ketball. The mere pairing of basketball and Catholicism already constituted unconventional religious practice for young female cagers, who were praying for unusual things in unusual ways. Beyond that, many basketball players said devotions and athletics mutually enhanced each other, as they felt prayers more intensely when they were about basketball and experienced basketball more intensely when they prayed.

Many said various basketball rituals helped produce a sense of together-ness and purpose. "Praying together helped a team spirit and camaraderie," remembered Patricia Furey McDonnell '53, or "just a great spiritual bond," said a class of 1956 player, "which is inevitable when individuals are direct-ing their efforts to a common cause." Collective chapel visits could also gal-vanize team determination. Cheerleader Joan Davis Tynen '54 said chapel visits involved a "great feeling [of] bonding . . . and supporting a good strong committed group of girl athletes," while a 1952 graduate said she treasured a "memory of prayer in unison" with her teammates. Chapel visits, often attended in uniform, also showcased the school's prestigious ball club in a venue off the court. "It was a great feeling," said Dee Cofer Cull '55, "to be with your uniformed teammates, praying." Margaret Monahan Hogan '63 agreed that in the chapel she "felt it was good to be part of this group of young women; it was fun."[28]

For other players, the pleasure of religious devotions surrounding basketball was not how they felt but how they "worked": praying or wearing Miraculous Medals had salutary effects on their play. Some believed there was a direct cause-and-effect link between prayers fully said and games well played. "All [the prayers and rituals] needed to be kept and honored," said Meg Kenny Kean '58, who "felt something was missing if skipped." A few others said prayer might even make up the difference when effort and talent failed, functioning as "insurance," suggested Lorrie Gable Finelli '78. More loosely, many team members believed religious rituals helped them play better. Alvina DeLazzari Long '57 said she understood "group prayer as a source of strength," while Ann McSorley Lukens '53 said devotions "centered the team to compete well."[29]

Others did not link prayer to team bonding or success but said for different reasons they simply enjoyed doing something "spiritual" in association with their favorite sport. A class of 1952 player said the prayers, cheers, and sisters in the stands made her feel a "closeness with my faith." Sister Marita David "Toddy" Kirsch said she went to Mass in her parish church before games just "to get that feeling of support from the Lord." Prayers recited for games, like prayers recited for everything at Immaculata, "added much to the enjoyment of college life," remembered Evie Adams Atkinson '46. Lorrie Gable Finelli '78 said the familiarity of Catholic rituals calmed her down before games: the "repetition," she said, was a "comfort." For another player, class of '51, the rituals served "not really any purpose," she suggested, except they "made you feel good."[30]

Different Immaculata players said the rituals felt good for different reasons, but they all knew that praying for basketball set them apart from other teams, distinguishing them as Catholics. Most took for granted identification not just as basketball players but as Catholic basketball players. Especially before games with public schools, they were self-conscious of praying before games and did it partly as a point of religious pride. Players also became more aware of identification as Catholics in the presence of their own Protestant coaches. After 1962, when Jenepher Shillingford became Immaculata's first Protestant basketball coach, college administrators increasingly hired non-Catholics from area physical education programs to fill positions as instructors, coaches, and directors in the athletic department. Immaculatans continued embellishing basketball with Catholic devotions but noticed them more around Shillingford, as when they had to explain things to their Methodist coach. For her part, Shillingford set precedent by joining team prayers and attending daily Mass. "I learned to say Mass. I went every day," she told me. Before ecumenism was a common Catholic vocabulary word, Shillingford's participation in Catholic rituals impressed her players. She "attended chapel with us prior to each game," remembered Maureen Callahan Bigham '63, and the team "thought that was great of her."[31]

In 1970 Jen Shillingford was promoted to director of athletics and promptly hired twenty-one-year-old Cathy Rush, still working on her physical education degree at West Chester, as new basketball coach. Rush was a Baptist, but, like Shillingford, she prayed and attended Mass with her players. She also started the team visits to Camilla Hall and in general "never said anything against [Catholicism] in any way, shape, or form." Perhaps emboldened because of Rush's youthful approachability, the new coach's players made religious difference a topic of humor, teasing her that she should convert to Catholicism. "I think we thought maybe if she becomes a Catholic we would never stop winning," said Sister Marian William Hoben '44. "So . . . the girls were . . . giving her rosaries . . . and she was wearing medals and they were sprinkling holy water" on her. Players were delighted when their jocular proselytizing paid off, as Rush began to volunteer that Catholic prayers and devotions, especially the Camilla Hall sisters' intercessions, might have helped bring about the school's three-year championship run. "When the sisters started going crazy and following us, [Rush] just thought, there's something [to] this," recalled Mary Scharff '77. The unexpected success "enlightened her into [thinking], there's something with this Catholic[ism] that's right." Rush was already hugely popular at Immaculata because her teams won, but she got extra acclaim for being a Baptist who affirmed the school's Catholic identity, even to the secular press. When a reporter asked her after the first championship what it took to win a national title, she said, "Well, when you're from a small Catholic girls' school like Immaculata, it takes a lot of prayer." Always media-savvy, Rush even made Catholic jokes like an insider. "We don't have scholarships at Immaculata," she told a reporter in 1974, "but we have a couple 'Hail Marys' and a few used rosary beads."[32]

In the presence of Protestant coaches, Immaculata players' difference as Catholic athletes was highlighted but also positively reinforced. Shillingford and Rush seemed to put aside religious difference to join Catholic activities, for the sake of the team. Certainly on the coaches' part, interfaith bonding in part served the end of team cohesion, but it also went deeper than diplomacy. At least players thought so. And it is possible that admiration of coaches' openness to Catholicism indicated beginnings of their own regard for other faiths, in a religious community otherwise wary of Protestants. For many Immaculatans, these coaches were the first Protestants with whom they had significant personal interaction. They seemed nice, never disparaged Catholicism. On the contrary, they went to both Mass and Protestant services with little sense of contradiction. For cradle Catholics in Philadelphia, this seemingly effortless crossing of the Catholic-Protestant divide presented a rare and intimate glimpse of interfaith practice. Notwithstanding players' favorable impressions of Protestant coaches, I can only speculate how much the experience changed their religious outlooks. But for all Immaculata players from the early sixties, basketball included immediate experience of deep respect and fruitful contact between Catholic and Protestant women. If the sport affirmed their religious identity, it might also have smoothed faith's sharpest edges.

Basketball and the Holistic Life

Most cagers remembered prayer and other devotional rituals as the cement between sports and faith. At the same time, several players linked the two not so much because of rites and artifacts as because basketball was part of a holistic Catholic life. Rather than pray for basketball as if to consecrate a secular activity, these players assumed basketball was already sacred, if played by Catholics who understood their whole lives as an ongoing offering to God. No activity, no matter how mundane or trivial, fell outside the sphere of grace. A 1953 graduate said she came to understand through basketball "that religion is in every facet of life," while Dolores Giordano Prokapus '56 said she viewed basketball as Catholic because it was "just part of my life—acknowledging God's presence in all activities." Several players said they learned to depend on God in their daily lives through sports. "Anything we do with God's help, even playing basketball," remembered Patricia Furey McDonnell '53, while a cheerleader who graduated in 1957 affirmed that "you need God for everything in your life—even sports!" Basketball was religious because somehow it, too, was included in God's continuing restoration of humanity. Suddenly meaningful beyond its secular status as leisure or entertainment, basketball could become satisfying as part of a whole life consecrated to God.[33]

This understanding of mystical meaning in mundane activities had a long history in Catholicism, but in the Immaculata context it arose with the ascendancy of neo-Thomism, which overlay and intermingled with Catholic devotional culture at Immaculata from the twenties through the sixties. Physical activity was one dimension of a Thomistic "whole life." In the 1948–49 Immaculata catalog, the curriculum description newly reflected a Catholic Renaissance emphasis on holistic education. "Knowledge and learning must be integrated with life . . . the *whole* student must be educated," it read. Immaculata students would learn not just in the classroom, but "through their experiences in chapel, . . . library, laboratories, residence halls, and on the athletic field."[34]

Many former Immaculata players spoke to me of basketball as one of diverse activities of a Catholic's life that could and should be ordered toward God to make a person complete and whole. Many sat through theology classes taught by eminent local priests who used the language of Thomism to describe incorporating everyday activities into the veritable sacrament of life itself. In addition, in other classes and around campus, nuns related subjects and activities back to God, communicating that "*all* extracurricular activities" were, as former I.C. manager Sister M. Charles Edward Woodward '62 wrote, "an integral part of the wholeistic approach to education." Sister Loretta Maria Tenbusch remembered teaching her freshman composition students that the physical world, including sports, ranked among God's great gifts to humanity. "He has given us all these gifts," she said she always taught, "including the physical, so important, so precious."[35]

More than classroom teaching, however, the I.H.M. sisters' lives and examples made the philosophical vocabulary of Thomism live and breathe. The sisters prayed for the girls' basketball games and junior balls no less than they prayed for their final exams and Sodality meetings. Throughout the years, not just after Vatican II, most players said that despite the Mass requirement and moral legalisms, Immaculata sisters tried to create a diffuse spiritual environment rather than "push" Catholicism. Jean Doris '53, for example, remembered "no pressures to be 'Catholic.'" If there was proselytizing, it came in the form of sisters seeming to regard all college activities, no matter how big or small, as potential ways to glorify God. It was the sisters, Marian Collins Mullahy '54 said, who taught that you should use what God gave you as a way to praise and honor him. Marian was tall and athletic; therefore, she should play basketball. "There was an inspiration there," she said. "If you didn't do what you could do, you were losing it."[36]

Usually, devotional Catholicism was associated with popular church culture, while the philosophy of holism seemed to originate with Catholic theologians. But on the basketball court of a Catholic women's college, the two outlooks worked together. Prayer for basketball suggested everyday life was holy, and the holiness of everyday life called forth prayers for basketball. As manager Sister M. Charles Edward Woodward '62 said, "The praying helped me see a connection between God and daily life." While players learned Catholic cultural theory in the classroom, they translated it into the unstudied pleasure of lived faith on the basketball court. Basketball was Catholic, explained Mary Scharff '77, but "it's nothing different than anything else. It's who you are and what you believe in."[37]

God's Providence and the Spirit of the Team

A few players suggested that basketball was more than one consecrated activity among many. For them, basketball channeled a dramatic sense of divine presence because the sport played pivotal roles in God's plan for their lives and sometimes even the wider world.

Rosemary Duddy McFadden '46 grew up as the baby in a family of five older brothers and played basketball from 1938 to 1942 at Reading Catholic High School in Reading, Pennsylvania. I reached her at her home in nearby Allentown, where she and her husband raised twelve children and never went on vacation, she said, until they drove their twelfth child to Notre Dame. Rosemary said that, after high school, she told her parents that "if I was going [to college], I'd like to take phys-ed." But no Catholic colleges offered physical education majors, and her parents wanted her to go "somewhere safe," that is, to a Catholic school. So Rosemary's older brother, a Philadelphia priest, suggested Immaculata's program in dietetics as the next best thing. She enrolled at Immaculata and made the basketball team. Part of the late-forties wave of great I.C. squads, Rosemary said she was now "glad" her brother steered her to Immaculata, because the school brought her "closer to God." "I don't think the other colleges would have done that for me," she said. And her choice of Immaculata was God's way of leading her to a career in physical education after all. After playing four seasons at Immaculata, Rosemary heard about a Catholic high school in Allentown that needed a physical educator. She applied and got the job, the answer to years of prayers. Soon she founded the high school's girls' basketball team. "God works in strange ways," she said. "God takes care of you."[38]

For Mary Jane Renshaw Lewandowski '64, who grew up the oldest of seven in a poor extended family in the Manayunk section of Philadelphia, involvement with basketball cleared a way out of the "slums" and "turn[ed] around my life as an adolescent." As she neared the end of grade school, Mary Jane said, she started hanging out with a "gang" of girls who were "drinking and running around with guys and doing all sorts of things you shouldn't do at that age." But she and her crew changed when they discovered basketball. Playing both for the local city recreation center and the parish CYO team, they "got steered away from" trouble, Mary Jane said. Moreover, after she became a model ballplayer and student, her parish priest offered her a scholarship to Immaculata. "And I always wanted to go to Immaculata even as a kid," she said. "It was like a dream, like 'Oh my God, I will never go there.'" In her assessment, basketball secured her moral health. "Some people might say, '[Basketball is] a silly thing,' but it has been my saving grace," she said. As a young adult, Mary Jane continued her association with basketball by officiating women's contests and again experienced the game's powers of rescue. Struggling to recover from personal and family crises, she found refereeing games "kept me busy" and served as "a barometer for all sorts of things in my life, not just where I [was] physically," she said. "It also told me where I was spiritually or morally . . . by the way I responded to the game." She continued to officiate Philadelphia area games for years.[39]

For Mary Scharff '77, who coached Immaculata's basketball team in the 1990s, the game was a gift from God that literally saved her life. When I talked to Mary in her Alumnae Hall office in January 1997, her hair had just recently grown back after her latest round of chemotherapy for brain cancer. Raised in a New Jersey family of brothers, Mary helped take Immaculata to one national championship and several more semifinals, shooting long-range swooshers and diving for loose balls. Traveling with the Mighty Macs to Australia after her sophomore year, she began to suffer blackouts and underwent a successful operation in 1979. But several years later, the tumor recurred, and Mary endured two more operations. Today, she believes that playing basketball kept her healthy during school and that glowing memories of team glory days sustained her through medical ordeals. "I don't believe I ever could have survived my surgeries if it wasn't for playing basketball," she said. "I was able to . . . play and enjoy life even though there were bad times afterwards." Moreover, basketball gave her illness a vocational meaning, expressed in her coaching years. "God was keeping me alive through basketball to be able to continue to [coach] and encourage kids," she said. At Immaculata, the sisters and players saw her as a mentor who taught about life as much as basketball. She showed Immaculata players how to set picks but also what to do if she blacked out during practice.[40]

Rosemary, Mary Jane, and Mary experienced basketball as part of God's plan for their lives personally. They were only a few of many, however, who believed their basketball experiences had purpose even beyond their individual lives. Most did not presume to specify what that larger purpose might be. It was "all a matter of faith . . . that, you know, things are for a reason," said Pauline Callahan Earl '57. "You don't always know what the reasons are, but you just have to have faith."[41]

Former Immaculata players sometimes expressed their sense of collective participation in something larger than themselves with the word "spirit." In the American sports lexicon, references to spirit generally mean "team spirit" or "school spirit," phrases that only a few Immaculatans used. Much more often, they referred a "good spirit" or just "spirit" that suggested, if not the Holy Spirit itself, a spiritual feeling or presence among the basketball players larger than the sum of their parts. This spirit graced the basketball players and sometimes, through them, a larger community. Recalling pregame locker room camaraderie, cheerleader Joan Davis Tynen '54 said she cherished "the beautiful spirit! . . . It was fun to participate in the spirit of the I.C. [basketball] environment." Players linked team prayers to this experience of spirit. Maureen Callahan Bigham '63 said devotions surrounding the basketball games "were unifying, they fed our spirit, [and] kept us close in heart and mind to one another."[42]

Perceptions of God's providence and spirit pervaded players' memories of the program. Especially among those who played on and followed the team during the championship years, many came to feel the Immaculata community had been collectively blessed by God for some purpose only dimly understood. Sister Marian William Hoben '44 indicated that nuns and players alike believed they were partaking in some unknown way in "the work of the Lord in trying to bring about a victory." By any measure, the championship years were remarkable. National media as well as Immaculata stalwarts were astonished when the Catholic girls' college of eight hundred students won successive women's titles. Even members of the secular press found themselves half-joking about the supernatural to explain the phenomenon. Years later, championship team point guard Denise Conway Crawford '74 said even now her only explanation for the victories was that they were "providential."[43]

The Immaculata community largely encouraged providential explanations. Arriving on campus the fall after the second national championship, Mary Scharff '77 said she immediately felt "caught up" in the college "atmosphere, the aura." After a short time, the aura "just totally turned your mind around," she said, to believe that something special was happening at Immaculata. When the team flew back from their first championship tournament in Normal, Illinois, a throng of fans welcomed them at the airport with a sign that read, "IC Alumnae Welcomes 'Miraculous' Mighty Macs." Even rare losses came to have mystical significance, like the 1974 Ash Wednesday loss to Queens.[44]

When I pressed players to describe what God might have been doing through the championships, there were several speculations. The main one seemed almost too obvious to spell out: God was spreading the joy they felt as a basketball team to other people, to fans near and far who caught the spirit when they watched an Immaculata game. Players gave other suggestions more reluctantly. Perhaps God was showing team members how much could be accomplished with God's help. Perhaps God was using this little Catholic school to open doors for other women who wanted to play basketball. Perhaps God was showing the country what great things could come from an unlikely group of girls and nuns who happened to pray. But even listing possibilities encroached, they implied, on the real point of the victories: God's pure gift, God's inscrutable grace, God's boundless love. In the championship years, Mary Scharff '77 explained, they just felt the hand of God in their lives. "There was a sense where you just believed that something took place in you coming here. It wasn't just the fact that, oh, you were lucky," she said. "To this day people say that [the championships were] amazing. . . . It was just something powerful unbeknownst to us." Certainly, some people, including some players, doubted divine assistance in the Immaculata victories. But as the winning seasons went on, Mary said, "even if you were very, very leery" about crediting the Lord, "you just believed it more and more as time went by."[45]

While traditional Catholicism certainly included a general conception of providence, it figured more prominently in Protestant vocabularies. Similarly, Philadelphia Catholicism manifested a decidedly low pneumatology compared to many Protestant churches. Ideas of providence and spirit were perfectly orthodox in themselves but reeked to many Catholic authorities of general Protestant flavor, if not incipient antinomianism, that could ultimately compromise church mediation. Immaculata sisters, big-time consecrators of basketball, still drew lines in the sand beyond which basketball threatened priorities and "perspective." Sports could not and should not become a substitute church, a sort of cult. Even Sister Marian William Hoben '44, a huge Mighty Mac fan, linked winning to "athletics in their proper perspective." In a speech to a 1980s Middle States Association conference on college sports, Sister Marian William said Immaculata won precisely because basketball was *not* the most important thing on campus. Religion and education were. If there were any lesson to be learned from Immaculata's success, she said, it was that good and well-rounded girls do finish first.[46]

But it is likely that some players did experience basketball as powerfully as a religion and that, for a time, it was at least as compelling and important, if not more. Perhaps that is the suggestion of ideas like "providence" and "spirit." Just a game in the world's eyes, basketball was so much more to many players. Still, it is not clear what framework players used to understand God's providence in their athletic careers. Nor is it clear what exactly some meant by "spirit." Were ideas of providence and spirit outgrowths of devotionalism and holism, in which everyday events took on supernatural significance? Did the Catholic environment sacralize secular athletic concepts of "team spirit" and "school spirit"? Did players absorb these ideas from the wider culture and enfold them in their narratives years later? I'm not sure. But it is certain that religious interpretations of experience often arise from too many interweaving sources to disentangle—from institutional theology and Sunday sermons to overheard conversation and casual reading. The Immaculata community's witness to God's presence in basketball was no different. In fact, basketball's parainstitutional status, at once overdetermined by the church and free of its regulation, provided a hothouse climate for young Catholic women to graft different religious elements together.

Limits of Praying for the Team

On the one hand, Philadelphia leaders encouraged Catholics to pray for anything, but, on the other hand, devotions flourishing away from clerical supervision could compromise institutional authority. In Philadelphia, so-called popular excesses were less of an issue than in many dioceses, but some basketball players still heard disparaging remarks about sports-related prayers. Most such remarks voiced an age-old Christian caution that one should not link petitions with outcomes too mechanistically, in a way that reduced faith to formulas or, worse, trapped God in human whims. Instead, this line of thinking went, the aim of prayer was faith that perdured in spite of our limited perceptions of how and when God addressed our needs. Sister Marie Roseanne Bonfini '57, academic dean at the time of the championships, linked basketball success to players' "deep faith" but called some prayers "fetishes" and some devotions "superstitious." Even Sister Mary of Lourdes, who as president told a reporter after the first championship that she thought "prayer really did it," nevertheless encouraged team members not to think of prayer as some kind of win-o-matic machine. "Just because I said that Hail Mary isn't going to make the basket go in," she said, "but it's the faith that you have, that you have an inner help." The sisters could hardly discourage talking to the Lord about basketball, especially when players learned through their sport to "pray regularly and to understand you could pray for anything," as Margaret Monahan Hogan '63 wrote. But the sisters also could not control some players' quid pro quo theology of prayer.[47]

"O God of Players, hear our prayer . . .": before a game, with coach Jenepher
Shillingford and daughter Anne, 1962.

Still, along with some sisters, a few team members found religious practices and attitudes associated with basketball distasteful. Basketball was an
inappropriate topic for prayer, said a player who graduated in 1957, since
Catholicism rightly understood was more serious than mere athletics. "I
mean, sports were sports," she explained. Making foul shots or winning a
game, agreed a cheerleader from the class of '49, is "not what you ask the
Lord for." She continued, "One thing that really annoyed me was when [play-
ers] would bless themselves before a foul shot––that drove me crazy." The
1957 graduate, in particular, thought "praying for a win" was "kind of ridiculous." Growing up with Protestants on her dad's side of the family, she said a
non-Catholic "asked me the question along the line what we were praying

for" before games. The inquiry "must have turned my brain on," she said. After that, she said she stopped asking God to orchestrate victories. "You just never expected God to come down and help play and win a basketball game," she said. A related problem, said other players, was that praying for basketball compromised personal responsibility. Marie Olivieri Russell '66 said she thought the team should pray "for assistance in our human endeavors" but "then apply all the personal skill we could." Lorrie Gable Finelli '78 also said "there was a separation" between basketball and Catholicism because "talent won games, not prayer!"[48]

Several players further questioned praying to win basketball games because such petitions begged the question of whose side God took. When the opposing school was another Catholic team likewise praying to win, the petitions were especially "mindless," said the 1957 graduate. Jean Doris '53 painted the picture. "So here you are playing St. Herbert's, and they are blessing themselves, [too]," Jean said. "Is God going to listen? . . . Give me a break." Finally, some indicated they believed sports and faith were or should be distinct by interpreting basketball as a neutral activity only superficially coated by religious veneer. There was "nothing" Catholic about basketball, "if you mean generic basketball," wrote Mary Mawhinney Puglielli '46. Basketball in itself was "neither 'Catholic' nor 'not Catholic,'" explained Fruff Fauerbach Timby '50. Similarly, Terri Murphy McNally '63 said, "I was Catholic—basketball wasn't."[49]

In all these cautions, it is possible that sisters and basketball players were reflecting charges absorbed from a Protestant mainstream often suspicious of Catholic models of prayer. Certainly, Catholic tradition itself warned against praying to manipulate God, but Protestant critics also repeatedly assessed Catholic modes of petition and repetition as immature and simple. It was beneath rational Christians to pray by rote, specify outcomes, or fantasize an Almighty concerned with trivialities like sports, critics implied. But if some quarters of Catholic spirituality absorbed Protestant-like disdain of prayer traditions, at least a few athletic Protestants seemed to absorb Catholic-like practice. Fruff Fauerbach Timby '50 told the story of a game against the University of Pennsylvania, before which opposing, mostly non-Catholic players decided they could outpray Immaculata. "One of the [Penn] players told me that in a discussion on their team bus to the game, they came to the decision that I.C. would say 100 Hail Marys, so the Penn team, to a player, said 101 Hail Marys!" Penn proceeded to win the game—by one point. Fruff was shocked that opposing players believed Catholic prayer operated so causally, even though, she admitted, the strategy "worked." "Can you imagine that?!" she wrote.[50]

Some players, then, questioned the theological underpinnings of connecting basketball and faith. But even those who challenged the link implicitly acknowledged that prayers surrounding basketball affected and honed their personal religious ideas and practices. While players who liked the prayers said their faith was strengthened, those who didn't like the prayers still found basketball clarified their Catholicism, filtering real prayer from deplorable fluff. For them, prayers for basketball became a touchstone for what Catholicism was *not*—or should not be, in their opinions. Negotiating the tension between praying constantly and praying appropriately, these Immaculatans modified game-time prayers after concluding certain kinds of petitions insulted God.

Finally, a sizable handful of former Immaculata players flatly rejected a connection between basketball and Catholicism, devotionally, holistically, or otherwise. For them, basketball was not and should not be part of Catholicism. But, whether they liked it or not, they were compelled to pray along with the rest of the team. Like every institutionally affiliated activity in Catholic Philadelphia, basketball was overcoded with devotions without anyone even thinking about it. Praying for basketball was "like saying the creed at Mass," explained Pauline Callahan Earl '57. "You say it, but how often do you really reflect upon what you're saying? It just comes right out. . . . Automatic." Catholicism, everyone agreed, was "intertwined" with basketball and everything else.[51]

Even so, it seems from certain survey responses and interviews that some players went to lengths to dissociate basketball from faith. While the large majority of survey respondents indicated several or many kinds of devotions that surrounded basketball, a handful also said there was "nothing" Catholic about basketball or that basketball petitions meant "nothing." There was "nothing specifically religious" about basketball in her mind, wrote Dolores Giordano Prokapus '56. But this is hard to fathom. How could players go to pre-game masses, pray for wins, and wear Miraculous Medals for contests attended by cheering nuns and yet say there was "nothing" Catholic about basketball?[52]

There are several plausible explanations. It is possible that religious practices surrounding basketball at Immaculata were so interwoven with the fabric of Catholic life that to some they were rendered undetectable or forgettable. "I can't say that [basketball] was Catholic or religious in particular," explained Margaret Klopfle Devinney '62. "Because my life was limited to experience among family, school friends, [and] parish friends, it was *all* Catholic—and I suppose all of the religious practices and values surrounding most activities worked together, but rather unobtrusively." It is also possible that former players were genuinely puzzled at my questions about the relationship between religion and basketball. "I never thought of basketball as a particularly Catholic experience," remembered a graduate of 1957. Similarly, Pauline Callahan Earl '57 said, "I've never even tried to put the two together."[53]

Other players who said there was nothing Catholic about basketball seemed to mean that the prayers and devotions held no meaning for them because they were not temperamentally very religious. They did not object to others' Catholic world making but said the faith didn't impress itself on them very deeply. Jean Doris '53 said she counted on her own athletic efforts and just didn't believe in the prayers and devotions. She even flouted the occasional team vow to keep silence on game day as an offering to God. "I [was] the one that's playing and I [was] the one that's talking." Christine Lammer DiCiocchio '70 said basketball might have been connected to Catholicism for more devout teammates, "but that wasn't part of my makeup." Sue Forsyth O'Grady '72 suggested that basketball was part of a church strategy to keep potentially disaffected young people close. The connection was structural, nothing more. "I don't think basketball in itself was a part of Catholicism," she said, "but rather a way to keep us involved longer in the Catholic community."[54]

Still other players who said there was "nothing" Catholic about basketball did not overlook, forget, or ignore the religious codings of the Immaculata game. They just disliked them. The very question of Catholic devotions associated with basketball seemed to irritate. One player from the sixties marked "0" devotions on the survey, that the purpose of such devotions was "none," that Catholicism and basketball were "separate," and that "0" was religious or Catholic about basketball. She also indicated that Immaculata was "too isolated" for her and that while she "had fun" playing basketball, fellow students were "mostly unsupportive." A few years later, another player also indicated she remembered no external markings of Catholicism in basketball.[55]

Without follow-up interviews, it is hard to tell what such responses mean. There is no evidence that in some years the Immaculata teams did not go to Mass or that they ever stopped invoking Mary in the huddle. But it is clear that a few players liked basketball and religion better when they did not overlap. Perhaps these women, too, felt that Catholicism's traditions were abused by application to basketball. Or perhaps their responses indicate a resistance to Catholicism, or Immaculata's version of Catholicism, or to the faith's reach into every corner of life. In other words, a few players might have enjoyed basketball because it felt *less* Catholic than church or school and offered respite from the rest of Catholic-saturated life.

Players who resisted Catholic markings in basketball had one thing in common with teammates, however: they liked basketball. If they ignored or disparaged the prayers, the game nevertheless offered certain pleasures. In a sense, then, players were still saying something about Catholicism when they said there was "nothing" Catholic about basketball. For them, Catholicism was not the comprehensive universe it claimed to be. For them, that was a pleasure.

• • •

Most former players enjoyed the spiritual aspects of basketball at Immaculata. These included practices of prayer and ritual, as well as ideas of holism, providence, and spirit. For a few, on the other hand, basketball yielded the pleasure of freedom from religion. Players' religious lives were forged largely in the practices of devotional Catholicism and the spirituality of neo-Thomism. But the game generated new practices, raised theological questions, and strengthened religious conviction. What should you pray for? Is everything Catholic? Does God enjoy basketball? Does God, maybe, enjoy our pleasure? On the court, young women found comfort in familiarities of Catholicism but also took advantage of the game's religious marginality to forge their own ideas about the "God of Players."

Immaculatans almost never said God was on their side because they were Catholic. But there were definite sides in players' sense of competition with other teams. As Immaculata teams increasingly traveled and played against non-Catholic teams, ways of distinguishing "us" from "them" multiplied as well.

CHAPTER 5

LADIES OF THE COURT

In 1934 Josephine Valentine '38 arrived at Immaculata's campus from a coal town in northern Pennsylvania. Her new college lay far west of the big city, bordered by single-lane, often unpaved country roads. Beyond the reach of most public transportation, Josephine and her resident classmates had few options to leave campus. There was the occasional trip in a friend's car or a date to a big dance. Otherwise, residents stayed put. Unless they happened to play basketball, that is. The basketball team went places. I reached Josephine by telephone at her apartment in northeast Philadelphia in July 1998. Eighty-one years old, she talked at length about her memories of playing basketball at Immaculata, which involved travel even before the team got varsity status for good in 1939. The team trekked all over the city "in a bus and everything—it was a really big deal for us." She liked two things about traveling: the ride itself and the chance to see new people and places. At each school, she said, the team got to see an "entirely different kind of place, kind of people."[1]

Years later, the Immaculata squads would travel far beyond Philadelphia. On a cold Tuesday morning in the spring of 1974, members of the back-to-back national championship Mighty Macs boarded a bus to Kansas to capture a national trophy for the third time. Immaculata's success meant the team no longer traveled unnoticed. Families, nuns, fans, a nurse, and a priest would fill three more buses, following the team in a twenty-eight-hour caravan to the prairie. But just like Josephine Valentine in 1934, players in 1974 recalled the same twofold delight of travel: both the "fun unrivaled" of bus trips with teammates and the wonder of people and places they visited. They breathed deeply at the sight of the flat Kansas horizon and gazed after tumbleweeds billowing behind the bus. Arriving at Kansas State, they tried not to stare at other tournament players, girls with different looks, clothes, accents, and beliefs. Traveling brought the team together, players said. It also made them reach out to others.[2]

Between 1939 and 1975, the varsity squad always played locally but gradually expanded its schedule to include other mid-Atlantic venues and then national and even international sites. Immaculata players almost uniformly remembered road trips as part of the pleasure of basketball. The travel itself was fun. And it was also enjoyable to see and meet different people: other Catholic girls but also non-Catholics, both white and black. The fun of meeting different people had two sides. Sometimes, Immaculata players found themselves identifying with women of other backgrounds because of common experience in basketball, despite a church culture that often looked warily on such contact. Other times, there was pleasure in highlighting their difference from other teams, perhaps to bond more closely with teammates, perhaps to chisel by contrast their own identity as Catholic ladies. Traveling, Immaculata players expanded their horizons but also secured them.

Scholars of sport have often observed that athletes crossed social boundaries because sports allows forms of contact, expression, and mobility not usually tolerated in middle-class and wealthy ranks. From Babe Didrikson and Notre Dame's Four Horsemen to Jackie Robinson and Muhammad Ali, athletes led the edge in public consciousness of civil rights for women, Catholics, African Americans, Muslims. But sports, like other social rituals in which people take time out from normal life, also reinforces boundaries, because any contact with new people and places is provisional and limited. Games, then, can highlight difference as well as cultivate understanding. Traveling for a matchup on the other side of town, Immaculata athletes experienced the common humanity of others, playing the same game by the same rules, but they also had opportunities to encounter and construct difference up close. As they discovered both the similarity and strangeness of others, these young Catholic women, like many travelers, came away with a fresh view of others and, corollarily, a new sense of themselves. Likewise, while the basketball court sometimes provided a temporary level playing field for groups of different classes, races, or religions, teams also always carried social disparaties and ready-made interpretations of difference into the game. Like all communities, the Philadelphia Catholic community traded heavily in opinions of outsiders—and in the meaning of contact, or lack of contact, with them.[3]

When Immaculata basketball players met public schoolers, rich Catholics, or black women in their travels, they both challenged and reproduced their community's received notions of "others." In the process, players fluidly reimagined their own identity as Catholic women to serve different interests of commonality and contrast with other teams. Specifically, contrasting themselves with other teams, Immaculata players often used the gender identifier "ladies" with or instead of the religious identifier "Catholic." The importance of "being ladies" has come up in previous chapters. When players described gender types on the team, "ladies" was a word that policed athletic women to stay on the near side of femininity. Then again, when players described class expectations at Immaculata, they said all students were to comport themselves like "ladies," carrying Catholic status aspirations onto the court. But in discussions of travel, players used the word "ladies" in yet a third way, to express what was, to them, "Catholic" about playing basketball. I would ask players what, if anything, set them apart as Catholic athletes. And when the word "ladies" arose in these discussions, players embraced it to contrast themselves favorably with other teams. In other words, "ladies" stood in for "Catholic," functioning as a religious identifier in disguise. And while players sometimes resisted being ladies as part of Catholic discourses of gender and class, they liked being ladies when comparing themselves to other teams. Still, the word "ladies" did not signify one coherent contrast to all other teams. Instead, talking of road trips and travel, Immaculata players called themselves "ladies" to indicate shifting qualities, each marking specific differences from opposing teams: while the Mackies were ladies, the other team came from a public school, or, while the Mackies were ladies, the other team all majored in physical education.

Since social identities both reflect and interpret reality, exploring the Immaculata basketball players' perceptions of themselves and other teams does not disclose the actual character of any team. Players' shifting definitions of ladies—and of unladylike others—reveal their own interests, not some objective state. Working with Immaculata players' accounts, I cannot say whether this team actually served the best postgame snack or that team really played dirty. But I do narrate how the Mackies distinguished themselves from other teams. While these stories tell little about opposing players, they do reveal more of Immaculata players' desires and satisfactions. When they traveled, they met others—and figured out more about themselves.

Philadelphia Catholics, Travel, and Others

Many Philadelphia Catholic women traveled frequently, especially women from poor, working-class, or middle-class families who commuted to school or work. But not all travel was fun travel. For commuting Immaculata basketball players, for example, travel from home to school and work was a burden. Riding public transportation, commuters bonded with other dayhops, saw the city, and came into contact with different people. They got to preview aspects of travel that resident players would experience for the first time on the team bus. But most commuters said they didn't enjoy that kind of travel. Naturally, a universe of meaning separated lower-class travel from leisure travel. Public transportation's associations with poverty, need, and labor signified differently—and to its users, felt different—from leisure travel's connotations of wealth, freedom, and fun. Immaculata basketball players, both commuters and boarders, relished the classier form of travel: on a school bus rather than public transportation, with friends rather than strangers, for fun rather than necessity.

Opportunities for leisure travel and all its attendant pleasures came few and far between for Immaculata students. College regulations restricted travel. As at many women's schools, Immaculata girls signed in and out of the dormitories, observed a curfew, and obtained written parental permission to visit another girl's house. "If you were used to running around and going on dates with boys," said former student Sister Therese Marita Dignam '53, "it was too restrictive." Before many students had cars, and before Routes 76 and 202 became multilane highways, geography also isolated Immaculata from the world. The campus lay beyond the Paoli stop of the Main Line trolley and was linked by only one or two daily buses to West Chester, the closest town to the south. Many Immaculata boarders of the sixties, like Josephine Valentine thirty years earlier, arrived on campus in September and rarely left until Thanksgiving, even if they lived in Philadelphia. If they did leave, they risked missing buses, classes, and dinner, not to mention paying for expensive taxi rides back.[4]

In the forties and fifties, players recalled occasionally hitchhiking to town to eat pizza or see a movie, though thumbing rides was strictly prohibited and warranted suspension. Sometimes, players broke the rule because hitchhiking was the only way to see important Big Five or Catholic League games in town. Trying to catch a high school game, Sister Agnes Frederick Blee, S.N.D., formerly Beverly Blee '47, remembered going with other players "by thumb—our only possibility of getting there on time." When a car stopped to pick them up, who should be in the driver's seat but Immaculata's president, Monsignor Francis Furey, also on his way to the game. "He was delightful, understanding," Sister Agnes said, though he gave them a "faint warning," too. "We all had a good laugh and a good ride," she said.[5]

There were some avenues for venture off campus. By the fifties, some students had cars, and players could ride with friends and teammates for visits home or city entertainment. Several college extracurricular activities offered the chance to travel locally and meet new people, including the Temperance Society, the Interracial Club, and the Sodality. If Immaculata women traveled, however, they usually visited other Catholic places and people, reflecting more of the same Catholic environment. Only the basketball team and, to a lesser extent, the field hockey team brought Immaculatans regularly into contact with non-Catholics.[6]

At Immaculata, there were sometimes a few random Protestants on campus; non-Catholic students had been admitted since the school's 1921 founding. And as the sixties progressed, the sisters more often invited Protestant speakers to campus and encouraged students to take advantage of ecumenical opportunities. But even in the sixties and seventies, most sisters and students had grown up in Philadelphia's traditional parish-centered Catholic neighborhoods, in which parents and teachers discouraged contact with Protestants, mandated parochial school, patronized Catholic-owned stores, and policed parish boundaries. "In my neighborhood, we maybe had two non-Catholic families on the whole street," recalled a player who graduated in 1957. Of course, players remembered some Catholic-Protestant heat simmering in the city's melting pot. Their parents fought prejudice on the job; they felt the sting of media anti-Catholicism; they heard snickers about their ethnic names and poor neighborhoods. Still, if interreligious tension simmered, it rarely boiled over, because, in Philadelphia, Protestants and Catholics were largely isolated from each other. "[There] was no antagonism, none whatever," said this 1957 graduate. "It was as if we lived in two different worlds."[7]

And within the isolated Catholic community, different ethnic groups mixed with relatively less drama than in New York, Chicago, and Pittsburgh, where bishops had allowed the creation of so-called national churches: a St. Boniface for the Germans, an Our Lady of Mount Carmel for the Italians, and so on. In Philadelphia, to be sure, national groups famously clustered in specific regions of city, such as the Italians in South Philly. But Cardinal Dougherty, bent on ecclesiastical uniformity, never sanctioned the national parish system. Later-arriving immigrants mostly had to fit into established, Irish-dominated parishes—and mostly they did, though sometimes despite deep resistance. When ethnic groups clashed, Dougherty backed up his integration policies, even occasionally using force to break down "last-stand Irish parishioners barricaded inside the church," as historian Charles Morris described these scenes. Even as Catholic Philadelphians increasingly moved to the suburbs, many mixed-ethnicity, majority-Catholic neighborhoods thrived around historic local parishes throughout the seventies. In Philadelphia's enclaves of Irish, German, Italian, Polish, and Czech Catholics, the gospel of unity preached from the top defused much intrareligious conflict. In most basketball players' memories, being Irish or Italian was less important than being Catholic and from Philly.[8]

As different immigrant families stabilized socially and economically, they began to send their daughters to Immaculata and other Catholic women's colleges in the area. Ethnically, Immaculata reflected the Philadelphia Catholic community, plus an I.H.M. presence in the Caribbean and South America. Throughout the years, Irish and German names appeared in the college yearbook most consistently, as well as occasional Italian, Scottish, English, Polish, and Czech names. Because the I.H.M. order maintained mission schools in Peru and Chile, they funneled to Immaculata a steady stream of young aristocratic women from South America, who joined the Club Español and helped prepare its gala Spanish Night each year. From the thirties onward, the college also welcomed students native to Puerto Rico, the Philippines, and even China. Several former players mentioned campus prejudice against the privileged South Americans; others heard "snide remarks and jokes about South Philly." But, on the whole, former players said ethnic issues at Immaculata rarely surfaced.[9]

Racial issues, even less visible on campus, were mostly present by their absence, and players usually left them unremarked. But when players remembered what they called "mixed" neighborhoods, they still meant "absolutely all white" neighborhoods. An American minority in the face of an Anglo Protestant mainstream, Philadelphia Catholics proudly and defiantly claimed their national and religious heritage. But also, finding themselves enmeshed in U.S. racial coding, they preferred to identify with white people—the same Anglo Protestants—rather than black people. Claiming whiteness, for Catholics and others, was a set of practices. In ideological terms, it could involve stereotyping, disparaging, and fearing black people; in material terms, it meant taking collective care not to work, live, socialize, date, or intermarry with African Americans. In Catholic neighborhoods, Catholics were white, and, as former Catholic League center Mimi McNamee said, "you didn't cross those lines."[10]

From Dougherty's appointment in 1918 to the beginning of World War II, Philadelphia's black Catholics, only a fraction of the city's total 10 percent black population, grew from a half-dozen families to between ten and fifteen thousand people. In the face of a sizable black Catholic community and numerous potential converts, European Catholic resistance and indifference plagued diocesan leaders, as well as a band of Catholic interracialists, including Monsignor Edward Cunnie and Mother Katharine Drexel. Warning that African Americans would be lost to proselytizing Protestants or godless

Communists, progressives exhorted and excoriated to little popular effect. Many Philadelphia Catholic schools and institutions remained segregated in defiance of archdiocese policy for years, and few white Catholics ever came into significant contact with black coreligionists—or any black people.[11]

After World War II, as millions of African Americans migrated to northeastern urban centers, Philadelphia's European Catholics increasingly encountered black people on the street, at work, at church, and at school. With increased contact, the years also brought seismic changes in racial dynamics, from civil rights to black activism. The changes brought to the surface many European American Catholics' racialized fear and hostility. They protected strong parish-centered neighborhoods from *all* outsiders by selling houses only to parishioners and running off non-Catholic buyers. But few resisted occasional white Protestant or Jewish neighbors in the ways they opposed black residents—Catholic or not—with harassment and rocks. In these cases, Philadelphia's white Catholics policed bodies and territories on the principle of race, not religion.[12]

At Immaculata, some sisters and students swam against the tide of fellow Catholics, who actively and passively coded religious identity with white identity. As early as 1936, the college sponsored an Interracial Club, inspired by Father John LaFarge's 1934-founded Catholic Interracial Council. Student editors at *The Immaculatan* elaborately covered club members' work to catechize black children in Philadelphia and Camden, New Jersey. In the 1950s Immaculata members of the National Federation of Catholic College Students brought its civil-rights–inspired message to campus. Speakers such as James Farmer, Ralph Ellison, Alex Haley, and Romare Bearden, as well as a black theater troupe and a black history conference, highlighted issues of race on campus.[13]

In a trickle, African American women enrolled at Immaculata. In the 1950s the president-treasurer team of Sister Mary of Lourdes McDevitt and Sister Cor Immaculata Connors began recruiting black Catholic young women to the college, though they could offer only a few academic scholarships. In the sixties Sister Virginia Assumpta McNabb visited West Philadelphia Catholic high schools to find African Americans who qualified for federal Equal Opportunity Grants. From photographs, it is not clear whether the first black Immaculatan enrolled in the late forties or early fifties, because her class year was not specified. But a photograph of her, unidentified like all on the page, appears in the 1952 yearbook. From then on, students assumed an unwritten policy of "one black a class on a scholarship," remembered Marian Collins Mullahy '54. "That's how it was going to be . . . one per class." The numbers corroborate popular assumption: from the late forties to the

The 1962 team with the school's first Protestant coach, Jenepher Shillingford.
COURTESY OF IMMACULATA COLLEGE.

early seventies, only one, two, or zero African Americans per year entered Immaculata.[14]

These low numbers were typical of most Catholic colleges, of course. And in the presixties context of entrenched European Catholic whiteness, only a handful of black Catholics considered Catholic campuses their own. Pictured in campus activities from chorus to field hockey, the few black Immaculatans made their way against the backdrop of white Catholic racism and national black-white turmoil. Up close, they dealt with lack of awareness among teachers and students, who throughout these years reported no racial tension on campus. "Race . . . wasn't an issue at the time," said a player from the class of 1953. "It was kind of treated matter-of-fact." But she and other respondents admitted Immaculata might not have been appealing to black women. Sisters and students "didn't do much to open things up in any way," she said. "I'm not so sure . . . many [black students] would have wanted to go there." In terms of leading the charge for integration, recalled Marian Collins Mullahy '54, Catholics "were standing still."[15]

For most Immaculatans, then, contact with those outside the white Catholic environment was extremely limited. Occasionally, a former player reported contact with non-Catholic or black people before college, if she grew up in a religiously mixed neighborhood, attended a nominally integrated school, or worked around Protestants and Jews. But the vast majority of Immaculata basketball players lived in a world logistically circumscribed by home, school, church, and work, and socially confined to other European American Catholics they met along the way.[16]

Seeing New Places

Immaculata women might have visited Penn for a student conference or attended a ball at Villanova, but few activities offered as much opportunity for travel as basketball. Throughout the years, as I have described, Immaculata teams rarely played games at home. And sometimes a freshman's first away basketball game took her for the first time in her life somewhere besides neighborhood, parish, and school. As early as 1939, Immaculata traveled to Lakewood in eastern New Jersey to play Georgian Court, a Sisters of Mercy school. Between 1942 and 1946, the team also took road trips to the nonsectarian College of St. Joseph's in Brooklyn, New York; Panzer College of Physical Education and Hygiene in East Orange, New Jersey; Mount St. Joseph's in Emmitsburg, Maryland; and Marywood College, another I.H.M. school hours upstate in Scranton. Trips got lengthier and more frequent as the years progressed. In 1966 the team traveled to Virginia to play William and Mary College the next day and then stayed for the weekend to tour historic Williamsburg. In 1972 the team took standby flights to Normal, Illinois, to compete in the first AIAW national tournament. It was the first time some players had traveled by airplane. In 1973 Theresa Shank Grentz '74 traveled to the Soviet Union as a member of the United States World Games team. And in the summer of '74, after a triumphant third national championship, the AIAW and Australia's Victorian Basketball Association sponsored the Mighty Macs on a playing tour of Australia, everyone's first international experience. Philadelphia Catholic girls might not have traveled for fun much, but Immaculata basketball players did.

As the teams traveled to new places, they also met new people. Naturally, Immaculata always played games with other Catholic colleges in the Philadelphia area. Their Catholic archrival was Rosemont College, further east on the Main Line, but Immaculata played Chestnut Hill, Drexel, Gwynedd-Mercy, Holy Family, and Cabrini as well. They also regularly scrimmaged Catholic League high school teams and clubs of alumnae, both from Immaculata and from St. Vincent's College in Latrobe, Pennsylvania.

But Immaculata never played an all-Catholic schedule. From the beginning of varsity competition, the school's teams also contested non-Catholic public and private institutions. In the varsity's first year, Immaculata played Swarthmore, a Quaker school, and West Chester State Teachers' College. Shortly, the Mackies' schedule filled out with regular contests against Temple, Penn, Glassboro State, and Ursinus, whose rosters included a diversity of young women, wealthy and poor, Protestant and Catholic, white and black. Not all area Catholic schools played non-Catholic institutions as often as Immaculata did, if at all. Stronger in basketball than most of its Catholic sisters, Immaculata scheduled those schools because they sponsored physical education programs and could field worthy competition for the Catholic powerhouse. Then, in 1970, when Cathy Rush took charge of the team, the Mackies played for the first time a historically black school, Cheyney College, located just ten miles south. And after that, the team began taking on national-caliber opponents from all regions of the country, including South Dakota, Mississippi, California, and Texas. Outside basketball, few Immaculata players had regular contact with anyone non-Catholic, much less southerners and Californians. But basketball brought players of different backgrounds into more contact than usual, in spaces where common goals of fun and competition at least temporarily eclipsed tensions of religion, race, and region.

If Immaculata players met Protestants before coming to college, it often happened in civic sports leagues. City-sponsored recreation centers cut across religious and racial lines to teach games and field teams. In the forties, Pauline Callahan Earl '57 learned to play basketball at a rec center across the street from her home. "Not too many black [people] . . . were in that area where I lived," she said. "But we would go to other recreation centers and play other teams. We had like a little traveling team." In Catholic neighborhoods, the recreation center sometimes just fielded the local parish CYO squad as its own but scheduled the Catholic kids against white and black Protestant youth across town. "Our high school CYO team represented, and played for, a rec center in the area," reported Mary Murphy Schmelzer '62. "I met my first group of non-Catholic friends playing playground ball for the city. . . . Basketball was the most nonsectarian thing I did." In addition to recreation centers, Mackies played with and against non-Catholics in other formal and informal venues. A graduate of 1957 remembered her parents sending her to the local Young Men's Christian Association (YMCA) as an additional sports outlet. In an era when the YMCA was known as an evangelical Protestant institution, "Catholics did not go to the YMCA," she said. "I was very surprised when I got older and found out I wasn't supposed to be there." When Helen Frank Dunigan '56 played for Father Walter Nall's renowned Our Lady of Peace teams, she said, the enthusiastic priest "used to troop us all over the place," playing not only other parishes but also any industrial or civic team he could schedule.[17]

Starting in the midforties, Father Nall also regularly scheduled Our Lady of Peace to play a team in a predominantly black housing project in Chester, Helen and others remembered. Like many projects, the complex was arranged as a square of buildings around a common courtyard. But as a twelve-year-old seeing public housing culture for the first time, Helen said she was wide-eyed. "Everyone contributed their backyard," Helen said, "and they all sat out on their roofs and everything. . . . They'd bring their couches right out." She and her teammates, paler than usual, trailed behind Father Nall as he walked assuredly toward the courtyard. "We had never been exposed to anything like that," Helen said. "All these black people [were] hanging out all [over] the place. . . . It was like something closing in on you, because I was never exposed to it." But the experience changed her, Helen said. "Maybe over the long run it gave you the idea that, yeah, these are these people," she said. "And they have a right to play ball just like I did."[18]

At Immaculata, the expansive basketball schedule gave young Catholic women rare contact with black and white, Catholic and non-Catholic, inaugurating "a lot of opportunities that I hadn't had up to that point, with travel and meeting people from different places," said Janet Young Eline '74. "It was great." Traveling for basketball, players remembered a handful of particular pleasures, from riding the bus to eating special food, from seeing new places to bonding with teammates.[19]

Traveling with the Team

Players I interviewed said over and over that apart from seeing new places and meeting new people, they enjoyed the traveling itself: "the fun we had getting there and back." Team members would meet the bus at a designated time of departure, usually outside the main campus building, Villa Maria. In some years, the bus was owned by the school and steered by familiar drivers the players befriended. When the few overused school buses broke down or couldn't transport all the fans, Immaculata rented buses from the local Shoreline company. After the usual hassle of getting all the gear loaded and all the players boarded, the bus pulled out of the campus driveway onto King Road, and the girls settled into a "wonderful time on the bus."[20]

Some remembered just looking out the window and taking in the view. "I learned the city, suburbs and outlying counties playing," remembered Mary Murphy Schmelzer '62. Others said they remembered most the "general sense of fun" on road trips. "We had a ball on the bus," remembered Izanne Leonard Haak '70. "We laughed and told stories. I loved the bus trips." Many players throughout the years remembered the whole interior rocking with "singing on the bus all the way home," recalled team manager Joan Biegler Snyder '53, "especially if we won," added a player from the class of 1957. Others said they prayed together or played "cards or charades" along the way. Players with cars sometimes drove separate loads of teammates, designating different vehicles "smoking" and "nonsmoking," experimenting with back routes, and getting lost. It was even exciting to get caught in the occasional blizzard or ice storm.[21]

In 1972 team travel went to another level when the squad boarded an airplane for the first time together, to go to Illinois. Janet Young Eline '74 remembered being "amazed at O'Hare" airport in Chicago. More excited about staying in a hotel than playing in the national tournament, team members stayed up most of the night watching television and cavorting and played their first few games on almost no sleep.[22]

Eating Special Food

Often, what Immaculata players remembered about travel for basketball was eating at restaurants, getting snacks, or being treated to a meal. Food was naturally pleasurable, of course. But for players who most often ate meals at school or at home, who couldn't often afford restaurants, part of the fun of travel was special food. Eating out could mean even more of a treat for basketball players whose household chores included helping their mothers cook.

First, there were snacks to anticipate. Until the 1960s, the Philadelphia girls' basketball version of Gatorade was orange slices, provided by the host school for game-time sustenance. Each season, Immaculata recruited a student to serve as "orange girl," whose job was to cut and serve oranges to both teams. After games came more refreshments, also provided by the home team, as it was the custom through the sixties for players to stay after court battles to mingle with opponents. "Each school had a unique treat, for example, ice cream sodas at I.C., sticky buns at Ursinus, soft pretzels at Penn," said Margaret Monahan Hogan '63. "It was a nice opportunity to socialize." Immaculata's special snack was root beer floats. When teams visited Immaculata, they rendezvoused after the game at the campus snack shop, Valley View, and got a round of floats. And when Immaculata hit the road, they looked forward to other gustatory delights. "That was the fun of playing," said Evie Adams Atkinson '46. "You had . . . hot chocolate and cookies. . . . And there were certain places you liked to go for the games because you knew the cookies were really better than others."[23]

By the late sixties, as competition heated up, this genteel tradition died out. But players were still hungry after games. Lorrie Gable Finelli '78 remembered she and her teammates "would be starving, and we would torture our drivers to stop at food stores and get treats that we wanted," she said. "Mint cookies, chips, all junk food!" Sometimes, players and fans associated particular foods with particular places. Sister Virginia Assumpta McNabb remembered riding with carfuls of fans and nuns up to the New York game at Madison Square Garden and "stopping at the bagel shops on the way." Watching the historic game, she said, "we [were] all sitting there eating bagels." At the 1975 national tournament in Mississippi, local teams served the Immaculata crowd catfish and hush puppies.[24]

In addition to snacks, basketball players could look forward to out-of-the-ordinary meals. Frequently, the team and fans would stop at a restaurant for a postgame late lunch or dinner. "We always went out to eat afterwards," recalled manager Sister M. Charles Edward Woodward '60. Sometimes, the team stopped partly for practical reasons, having played at a time or distance that kept them away from campus after the dining room closed. But mostly they stopped to eat out because it was part of the fun of being on the team. Sometimes, a campus priest would treat the girls. In 1950, when the team took one of its first longer trips, playing Mount St. Joseph's in Emmitsburg, Maryland, religion professor and campus chaplain Father Francis Walsh "drove us down the night before and bought us all a big steak dinner," said Fruff Fauerbach Timby '50. If no one was footing the bill, some girls could not afford to eat out. One cheerleader from the class of 1949 recalled a story told by her friend, a Mackie starter from a poor family. "They would stop someplace and have hamburgers and Cokes and whatnot," the cheerleader said. "And I guess it was the coach [who] knew somehow that [my friend] didn't have the money to buy anything. And somehow it was always handled so that [she] was able to buy what everybody else was able to buy."[25]

Seeing the World

Former players said they loved not only traveling and eating out but also seeing new places they otherwise might not have seen. For most of them, like Josephine Valentine '38, just going across town to see another campus was fun. "You got to travel and see some of the other colleges," remembered Rosemary Duddy McFadden '46. Another player, class of 1953, also said, "I like[d] to see the other schools and what their campuses were like."[26]

In the seventies, when Immaculata teams started to play at the national level, players treasured the experience of visiting locales beyond Delaware County. Playing basketball "allowed a[n] expanded view of the U.S.," said Lorrie Gable Finelli '78, "that I never would have had, had I not played." She said the experience was "a great confidence builder." Similarly, Mary Scharff

'77 remembered basketball as a "tremendous experience" because she was "able to travel all over the country."[27]

Bonding with the Team

Wherever they went on road trips, the team went as a group, and former players throughout the years remembered bonding with each other as part of the fun of basketball travel. Evie Adams Atkinson '46 said she remembered most about road trips simply "the fun of being together . . . and enjoying one another's company." Likewise, Dee Cofer Cull '55 said she recalled "just fond memories of being with your teammates." Others mentioned "camaraderie" and "conviviality" on the bus trips.[28]

Teammates might have remembered feeling close to each other for away games or road trips because at those times they not only played together; they lived together. "Those special times were a function of the twelve of us being together," explained Lorrie Gable Finelli '78. In addition, players might also have felt close during trips because the newness and "otherness" they perceived in unfamiliar surroundings relativized tensions among them and bonded them more tightly. In non-Catholic venues, they were a foreign curiosity, coming from an all-girls' Catholic college and wearing quaint costumes. Outside Philadelphia, they constituted some audiences' first contact with Catholics. Moreover, they usually won their games, building a reputation that created heat and animus ahead of their arrival in any gym. After three championships, players' sense of the outside world's otherness, even antagonism, made them "very intradependent upon one another," Lorrie said. "Everybody wanted to beat us. So, you had to depend on each other, and that's who you depended on."[29]

Whether enjoying rides or food, new places or good friends, players experienced travel for basketball as "VERY EXCITING," as a 1952 graduate wrote in capital letters. As exciting as eating in a restaurant or journeying beyond county lines, however, was meeting the new people in those new places.[30]

Meeting New People

Through basketball, young Catholic women whose worlds usually included mostly fellow white coreligionists came into contact with different kinds of people. For Evie Adams Atkinson '46, this was a new experience. "You had to go meet other girls while you're playing, you had to speak to them," she said. "And usually afterwards there was cookies, and you'd be talking to people that you didn't even know. So, it sort of kind of brought you out of your shell." Dee Cofer Cull '55 remembered meeting "some great people from other teams," while Mary Murphy Schmelzer '62 said she "cherished the after-game camaraderie . . . we made many friends that way." For Josephine McFarland '42, the experience of interacting with opposing players "taught me how to get along with all kinds of people." Dolores Giordano Prokapus '56 echoed her, remembering that through basketball she learned "to respect others."[31]

But former Immaculata team members did not regard all other players they met as the same. Over the years, Immaculata played many different kinds of schools, from Moravian College, associated with the Moravian church, to Panzer, a physical education and hygiene school. From a wide variety of opposing institutions, players remembered a range of differences with other teams, from what they considered the mysterious southern ways of Mississippi State to the hypercompetitive ballast of Wayland Baptist. But there were patterns of remarks that emerged amid the variety. In particular, I noticed players tended to talk about otherness of four main kinds: other Catholic schools; non-Catholic schools; institutions that offered physical education degrees; and black colleges.

Often, players identified particular things they enjoyed about each kind of institution, such as familiarity at other Catholic schools or quality competition at physical education colleges. But when they tried to describe what was "Catholic" about basketball at Immaculata, they identified with each group particular things they did not like. For Immaculata players from every period, girls from Rosemont were snobbish; from Penn, foul-mouthed; and from West Chester, unfeminine. Immaculatans also told stories that posited black opponents as dangerous. Very rarely did Immaculatans say the difference between themselves and other teams was a religious difference. But they implied a moral difference. Immaculatans were ladies of the court, and others, for various reasons, were not.

In one sense, Immaculata basketeers experienced displeasure encountering what they regarded as unsavory characteristics in others. But, in another sense, it was evident that when players discoursed on opponents, they liked describing the contrast between themselves and others. I did not talk to other teams; I cannot say how opponents really acted on the basketball court, much less how opponents in turn regarded Immaculata. What was clear, however, was that Immaculata players believed they acted better in a range of ways, and comparison with others teams made the point well. Travel bonded Immaculata team members in part, then, because contact with other teams powerfully contributed to their self-understanding as young Catholic ladies. Or, as in the case with Rosemont, young Catholic ladies who could still play kick-butt basketball.

Playing Other Catholic Schools

Immaculata and Rosemont were only two of more than a half-dozen nearby women's schools that graduates of local Catholic high schools could attend. By the late sixties and early seventies, Villanova, LaSalle, and St. Joseph's also accepted women for enrollment. For most of these years, however, Immaculata's two most significant sister schools—or competitors, depending on how you looked at it—were Rosemont, founded by the Society of the Holy Child, and the College of Chestnut Hill, a Sisters of St. Joseph school. Of the three, Immaculata served the least privileged population. "There was three," said Marian Collins Mullahy '54, and "Immaculata was third." In compensation, Immaculatans prided themselves on drawing the more "athletic" girls. "There were some very girly girls at the other two," Marian said.[32]

Chestnut Hill lay within northwest city limits just east of Fairmont Park and was surrounded by working-class and middle-class neighborhoods. Like Immaculate Heart sisters, St. Joseph's nuns at Chestnut Hill drew Catholic women from across the class spectrum with tuition reasonable enough to match that mission. Rosemont, on the other hand, drew from the high end of the economic spectrum. Its lush campus sat right in the city, on prime Main Line real estate near Villanova, Swarthmore, Haverford, and Bryn Mawr. More cosmopolitan and more expensive than Immaculata or Chestnut Hill, Rosemont enrolled girls largely from middle- and upper-class Catholic families, whose daughters had already attended Catholic private academies rather than diocesan high schools. Many former players said their only three choices for college had been Immaculata, Chestnut Hill, and Rosemont, but that Rosemont was "too expensive." Marie Olivieri Russell '66, whose first-generation immigrant parents opened a general store not far from Rosemont, said with her Italian last name and working-class family, she never applied to Rosemont. "Maybe I didn't think I was appropriate for it," she reflected. "It was clearly a school at that time that was much more wealthy, considered to be all the rich kids."[33]

While all three schools drew Catholic League basketball players, Immaculata consistently attracted more of them, and the best of them. "We always beat all the Catholic schools," remembered Marie, which was true for her midsixties years at Immaculata and for most other years as well. It is clear that many basketball players could not attend Rosemont because of expense, but it is less clear why Immaculata fielded better teams than Chestnut Hill, which was located so much closer to the city. Some players explained it in terms of tradition. "Your reputation does those things," said Helen Frank Dunigan '56. "I think it was just the idea that if you went out [to Immaculata], you could at least play with some people that are interest-ed in playing." Margaret Guinan Delaney '62 said she always got the im-pression that "the better basketball players came to Immaculata" because of the school's "support of basketball." Most likely both reputation and sup-port, as well as an uncanny series of good coaches and standout players, worked together to elevate Immaculata above Chestnut Hill in the sport.[34]

Playing other Catholic schools, Immaculata players felt familiarity and comfort with opponents who shared backgrounds and values as well as reli-gion. They and Catholic adversaries had often already competed with or against each other in the Catholic League or on CYO teams. Many of their parents were relatives or neighbors. They all attended schools that didn't schedule games on holy days of obligation and where no one looked twice at bleachers full of nuns. For a period, at least one other Catholic college team even suffered playing basketball in full-length lisle stockings. Playing anoth-er Catholic school was like playing family.[35]

The family feel hardly made games inconsequential, however. Immacula-ta squads seemed to like playing other Catholic teams partly because I.C. often handily won. Moreover, for many years, the only game players said they absolutely had to win was a family game, the intra-Catholic contest with Rosemont. With Rosemont, however, the competitive spur wasn't just sibling rivalry. It was class rivalry. There were some sparks with Chestnut Hill, play-ers said, but populated as it was with girls similar to those at Immaculata, the competition was "more nebulous." It was Rosemont's "snootier" profile that fired in the Mackies a burning desire to win. Rosemont girls, the most lady-like ladies of the Catholic world, had more wealth, a better campus, better opportunities, and, many Immaculatans believed, better men. If Immacula-ta had any claim to being ladies themselves, they had to beat Rosemont. "The biggest event of the season was the game versus Rosemont College," said Terri Murphy McNally '63, "and we always beat them during my four years." Meg Kenny Kean '58 even said her happiest basketball memory was "beating Rosemont." Almost every year, Immaculata got the victory, but the thrill did-n't fade until the seventies.[36]

Former players especially prided themselves on vanquishing Rosemont because it proved, at least in one small way, that Immaculata was superior. Through the team, Immaculatans could brag they were every inch ladies, just like Rosemonters—but they were ladies who happened to take care of busi-ness on the basketball court. For the purposes of this matchup, in fact, Im-maculatans were all the more ladies because they came up through the tough, gritty neighborhoods of the working class, as opposed to being born ladies like Rosemont's belles. As a member of the Immaculata team, "you conducted yourself as a lady at all times," said Gloria Rook Schmidt '64. But in the heat of the game, she said, "we weren't afraid to . . . get [our] . . . knees [dirty] or our elbows or something," unlike their prim rivals. Immaculata girls were ladies, but, against Rosemont, they made sure to define the term short of any refinement that would compromise winning the ball game.[37]

Not only players but the whole Immaculata student body felt the charge. Throughout the forties and fifties, classmates competed in anti-Rosemont poster contests and turned out in force for the games. They pounced on their rival school's tradition of observing a formal campuswide tea time every afternoon. Cheering at games, Immaculata students would support their team by chanting "Tear Down Tea Town!" and "The Rose Is Dead!" or by pinning tea bags to their lapels like corsages.[38]

Of course, the ritzier school's players still laid more social claim to the status of ladies. And behind Immaculatans' antics burned the collective sting of relative economic deprivation, social marginalization, and geographic isolation, all too obvious when they visited Rosemont's campus. For the feel of family, players liked to play other Catholic teams. But also they really enjoyed disliking Rosemont.

Playing Non-Catholic Schools

Over the years, Immaculata played many non-Catholic schools, private and public, religious and secular. Outside the women's basketball hothouse of Philadelphia, the Mackies usually beat non-Catholic as well as Catholic teams. In the Philadelphia area, however, non-Catholic schools had an advantage of numbers, drawing potential players from a larger population. Schools that offered physical education degrees attracted an even higher concentration of skilled non-Catholic *and* Catholic athletes. But even with those advantages, public schools barely matched the Catholic League talent pool, and Immaculata squads consistently competed with the best area teams. Throughout these years, Immaculata posted winning records in every year except one and usually lost only one or two games a season. But often those one or two losses came at the hands of strong non-Catholic teams.

Immaculata players enjoyed playing non-Catholic schools partly because they got to meet other people besides Catholics. Evie Adams Atkinson '46, for example, said her basketball experience "dealing with people outside the Catholic faith . . . helped me to be more understanding and more tolerant of other religions." Even many years later, in the seventies, Janet Young Eline '74 also said basketball first put her in touch with the non-Catholic world. "I mean, we were the best religion; they told us that," she said. "But you had to respect other people and their religion."[39]

Through athletics, Immaculatans made contact with non-Catholics even on campus. After 1962, when college president Sister Mary of Lourdes McDevitt first hired a Protestant, Methodist Jenepher Shillingford, to coach the basketball team, Immaculatans began to interact with an unusually high proportion of non-Catholics in an athletic department staff that soon also included Quakers and Baptists. In Protestant coaches' company, the basketball players received an education in ecumenism as well as athletics. For example, when the team stopped for postgame sandwiches, daily Mass-goer Shillingford would draw the line at observing Catholic meatless Fridays, ordering a ham-filled hoagie while her players ate tuna subs. But no former players remembered tension in relationships between Catholic players and Protestant coaches. Religion "wasn't an issue, I would say," said Marie Olivieri Russell '66, adding that the sisters endorsed her coaches as "a very good example of true Christians." Shillingford said she and her boss, Sister Mary of Lourdes, talked about religion frequently and "understood each other."[40]

Beyond Immaculata's religiously integrated athletic department, Catholic-Protestant conflict occasionally surfaced. A few players remembered games that sparked credal invective, as when non-Catholic athletes made jokes Immaculata players found offensive. For example, a player from the class of 1952 remembered she "did not like it when [opponents] made fun of the Immaculate Conception," the controversial Marian doctrine for which their college was named. And in the context of general Catholic-Protestant tension, "it always somehow seemed more of a victory when we beat a specifically non-Catholic institution," admitted Mary Murphy Schmelzer '62. "Except they tended to be not very good," she added. Players often proudly said that, bar none, Immaculata was "always the best basketball team in the area"—a claim staking territory beyond the Catholic world. In most seasons, except a few years in the sixties, the claim was true.[41]

In most players' accounts, however, explicit mention of Catholic-Protestant tension was noticeably absent. When I asked Margaret Guinan Delaney '62 directly whether she thought Immaculata's competition with non-Catholic schools involved religious tension, she said, "No, . . . not in my eyes anyway." Likewise, most other players didn't remember anti-Catholicism from other teams or anti-Protestant animus on their own. How should I interpret this? Wasn't tension with Protestantism always the primary conflict underlying American Catholic reality? Wasn't Catholic-Protestant antagonism a fact of life in Philadelphia? What, then, could Immaculatans' seeming oblivion to the issue mean? I don't know for sure. Perhaps the tension was so pervasive it was normal or unnoticeable. Perhaps the socially suspended space of sports did dramatically relieve its constant pressure. Perhaps Catholics and

Protestants in Philly were usually so isolated that interfaith basketball games amounted to first contact, where rules of politesse and good faith held sway. Or perhaps tip-off had a way of putting in Mackies' minds more immediate and, to them, more important things than religious identity.[42]

Players rarely said they experienced religious conflict in ball games, but they did say there was something Catholic about their team, epitomized in always acting like ladies. "Ladies" was their way of saying "Catholic" without saying it. Likewise, speaking of non-Catholic schools, players didn't say their opponents were Protestants. They said something else, something very specific and consistent: non-Catholic teams tended to use lots of curse words on the court. In their minds, non-Catholic schools were different from Immaculata not because they were Protestant or public but because players from those teams used foul and aggressive language. For the Mackies, an important part of being "ladies" was not swearing, questioning calls, or verbally riling opponents. So while Immaculata players did not make a big deal of religious difference, still they suggested that they upheld higher moral standards than non-Catholic opponents.

While I had to press former players for thoughts on Catholic-Protestant dynamics in basketball, many volunteered stories of non-Catholic teams' cursing. "I can remember playing against some teams that I thought, whew, really hard people. Anything but ladies," said Helen Frank Dunigan '56. "You would have thought they were, you know, the proverbial truck driver," she continued. "Which is maybe not fair to the truck drivers." The "language," as players put it, always surfaced at non-Catholic schools: Penn, Temple, West Chester. "When we played [Penn], . . . the language from those players was much different on the court . . . than that of I.C. players," recalled Anne Carroll Camp '51, "particularly under the basket." Dee Cofer Cull '55 remembered non-Catholic schools the same way. Against Penn and Temple, "you might have heard a few curse words," she said. "It was a different type of game. . . . I don't know how different, but yeah, [we were] ladylike. That's the word, ladylike."[43]

Like Dee, other Immaculata players contrasted swearing and cursing opponents with themselves as ladies. "When you think of a lady," said Gloria Rook Schmidt '64, "they don't use the language. . . . If a ref called something, that was it. . . . There was never any type of questioning. . . . You might have thought it, but you didn't dare say it." Janet Young Eline '74 said being "ladies" meant that for Immaculatans there was "no such thing as trash talking," under penalty of coaches pulling the offender from the game. Keeping language clean signified the moral, even Catholic, dimension of being ladies. It was Catholic to make sure "the cheers [were] all clean-cut and hopeful," said Ann McSorley Lukens

'53. For religious reasons, "we never used [bad language] when we played," said Mary Scharff '77. "We believe in God, we're Catholic, and we just don't want to go against anything that he would want us to do."[44]

Immaculata players' self-identification as Catholic ladies through issues of language reflected in part Catholic leaders' concern for female external piety and middle-class respectability. Usage considered coarse or rough, much less vulgarity and swearing, simply was not tolerated in girls' Catholic schools at any level. And for young women raised in that environment, abstention from cursing naturally followed from good morals, refined femininity, and deference to authority, all lacking in players who swore. But Immaculata players, who brought up issues of language only when they spoke of contact with non-Catholic schools, possibly signaled another contrast as well. For them, pure speech perhaps stood for the difference between Catholic and non-Catholic schools. Imagining their own pristine language compared with others' purported dirty words could have functioned partly to signify, fairly or unfairly, difference from "publics."

So perhaps this distinction of language was religious after all, displacing Catholic friction with the Protestant world too submerged or confrontational to express. Confrontational, especially, for *girls* to express. The Mackies' notable lack of feeling against non-Catholics *as non-Catholics* presents the possibility that Catholic-Protestant dynamics did not pervade communities so inescapably as we thought. Or at least not the female half of communities. Or, if they did, those dynamics sometimes went by other names than religious antagonism.

Playing Physical Education Majors

The Immaculata teams did not lose many games, but their one or two losses per season came at the hands of a few local powerhouses: Temple, Ursinus, and West Chester, all of which sponsored top-flight physical education programs. There, young women who wanted to make careers of sports or just liked athletics could learn to coach, officiate, teach, and administer. Through the forties, Temple's teams dominated city women's basketball, but Immaculata gradually decreased the margins of their victories, gathering strength and incentive with each passing year. In those years, "Temple was usually an emotional game," remembered a graduate of 1945, "one we *had* to win." When Immaculata finally beat Temple by one point in March 1946, snapping the Owlettes' thirty-one game winning streak as well, players and fans were beside themselves with joy. "We did it and we bragged plenty," recalled a cheerleader, class of 1947. "We were so proud."[45]

After Immaculata beat Temple a second time in 1947, the Owlettes' glory began to fade, while Ursinus and West Chester rose to give Immaculata its best competition. Teachers and students packed games with their new "big rivals." In the fifties and sixties, Immaculata players remembered, "beating Ursinus and West Chester" felt especially satisfying, and "always losing to Ursinus & West Chester" blemished otherwise outstanding seasons. But even if players "knew [we] were going to get crushed," as Christine Lammer Di-Ciocchio '70 put it, they looked forward to the tightly fought games. "We knew that Ursinus was going to be good, that was one of our big schools," said Gloria Rook Schmidt '64. "And West Chester, they were [good]."[46]

The Catholic team's sense of rivalry with Temple, Ursinus, and West Chester thrived partly because the games were tight. But the deeper charge owed to the difference between schools that had physical education majors and schools that didn't. Immaculata didn't. As enthusiastic about women's athletics as Immaculata was, Catholic colleges did not envision physical education as an appropriate major in liberal arts curricula; much less did they consider sports a respectable career for women. For some athletically gifted Catholic girls, this lack ruled out Catholic higher education. They enrolled at Temple or West Chester or even transferred out of Immaculata or Chestnut Hill, playing for the publics against former Catholic League teammates. Of course, Catholic schools, including Immaculata, depended on local physical education schools to supply coaches. Not only the school's later Protestant coaches but also earlier Catholic coaches—such as Marie Schultes McGuinness, who graduated from Temple in 1945—were physical educators trained at non-Catholic schools. Still, it was out of the question for Immaculata itself to offer a physical education degree. The huge program in home economics notwithstanding, Catholic education was about liberal arts, not trades and skills, and somehow physical education fell beneath standards.[47]

Practically, this difference between Immaculata and physical education schools meant other schools could field teams twelve deep of the cream of talent in any sport. But to Immaculata hoopsters, the difference was more than practical. To them, a team full of physical education majors suggested opponents' schooling consisted entirely of playing sports and further that opponents were not smart enough or feminine enough to do anything else. "We were students, they were jocks," said Betty Ann Hoffman Quinn '73. "We were students that happened to play good basketball, and we were going to get a good education, and get good jobs afterwards." In contrast, "it wasn't as tough to go to college and be a phys ed major. . . . Their courses are golf . . . you know, they do sports all day and it's really not that hard," she said.

Her teammates' "overall impression," she added, was that phys-ed opponents "were more masculine than we were."[48]

In other contexts, Mackies asserted their own right to enjoy basketball more than school or to decide for themselves what was feminine. They said basketball helped them focus on academics and required a lot of smarts in its own right. And did not some of them long for the chance to major in physical education themselves? But comparing themselves to physical education majors, none of this came into play. In this context, they implied, basketball was unworthy of serious commitment and beneath intellectual consideration. In other words, if they were to remain proper Catholic ladies, there must be limits to basketball's importance, and physical education majors exceeded them.

Over and over, Immaculata players proudly pointed out that, while opponents "major[ed] in basketball," their own teammates concentrated in various arts and sciences—and still played outstanding ball. "I remember hearing the team names and majors announced before a big game at West Chester," wrote a cheerleader who graduated in 1963. "All the I.C. players majored in chemistry, el[ementary] ed[ucation], history, French, etc. All the West Chester team majored in phys ed!" Margaret Guinan Delaney '62 added, "We thought that was pretty neat, that we could be competitive with them."[49]

To a certain extent, these comments reflected widespread Catholic assumptions about what counted as good education for girls. But the real edge slicing through commonplaces of Catholic education was a set of implications about physical education majors in particular, whose choice at least marked distorted values and probably signified low intellect. In this context, Immaculata players considered basketball merely an extracurricular activity, while for physical education majors, they said, basketball *was* their curriculum. "We were playing for fun," explained Helen Frank Dunigan '56, whereas "those girls were playing for marks."[50]

Closely related to the imputation about phys-ed opponents' underdeveloped values or minds was a slur that the major distorted physique and even gender. Immaculata players studied phys-ed opponents' height and girth. West Chester and Ursinus fielded "very big masculine-looking girls," said Terri Murphy McNally '63. Gloria Rook Schmidt '64 agreed. "Some of those girls were so damn big it was pathetic," she said. "I remember walking in and going, 'I have to play her?'"[51]

Talking about Immaculata team gender types, players defended styles from boyish to girly. But comparing themselves to opponents from physical education programs, they were suddenly all ultrafeminine and small, almost frail. A graduate of 1953 said she was always "surprised" at "how feminine [Immaculata] players were compared to our opponents." In contrast, Immaculata players thought of themselves as "small," even as the "flea squad," said Gloria Rook Schmidt '64. Whatever their actual corporeal dimensions, Immaculata players prided themselves that they "were not physical education majors who had to prove they were tough, nor did we have to act like guys," explained Maureen Callahan Bigham '63. Throughout the years, the Mackies included players tall and short, round and slender, stocky and lithe. But always, as Mary Scharff '77 said, "we [were] supposed to act . . . like ladies. . . . Let's walk like a lady, let's not walk with any kind of a manly walk."[52]

From the forties through the sixties, Immaculata also played physical education schools out of the area, such as Glassboro State and East Stroudsburg, whose teams *The Immaculatan* repeatedly called the "fizz-eds." Then Immaculata began to play at a national level, and the squad increasingly matched up against other state schools that offered physical education degrees, among them Washington State, whose center, remembered Janet Young Eline '74, was "a gigantic girl." In tournament programs, other teams' players were listed "all the way down [the roster], phys-ed, phys-ed," Janet said. "Get to Immaculata, and there was no phys-ed major." In 1975 the AIAW national tournament for the first time included teams that actually offered athletic scholarships, such as the Wayland Baptist Flying Queens. The Mighty Macs played the Flying Queens in the quarterfinals and beat them, snapping their twenty-one-game winning streak. "The idea of beating a scholarship school meant a lot to us," coach Cathy Rush told a reporter.[53]

Although all the physical education schools were also non-Catholic institutions, players never mentioned it and dismissed it as irrelevant when I pointed it out. According to them, the antipathy between these schools and Immaculata was about phys-ed, not about religious tension. Still, the physical education major usefully marked not only the two communities' different education philosophies but also Immaculatans' wish somehow to be better than public school counterparts. Perhaps their avowal of smarter, prettier Immaculata teams displaced, again, less expressible feelings about Catholics and Protestants. And perhaps it suggests, again, that Catholic-Protestant dynamics might appear in submerged forms—forms that look more like sniping about how a girl walks and what classes she takes.[54]

Conjecture aside, however, it is clear that many players contrasted themselves with phys-ed counterparts to assert self-regard as balanced, intelligent, and feminine basketball players. Immaculatans liked games with physical education schools for the "heightened sense of competition" but also for the fresh opportunity to hone their identities as Catholic ladies.[55]

Immaculata vs. Cheyney, 1975.
Courtesy of Immaculata College.

Playing Historically Black Schools

Through the 1973–74 season, Immaculata players remembered few black fellow students and played basketball on totally white teams. But long before the first two black players joined Immaculata's squad in the fall of 1974, Philadelphia was a basketball hotspot for black women as well as white. In the thirties and early forties—just as the Immaculata varsity played its first few seasons— a team of women sponsored by the city's black newspaper, the *Philadelphia Tribune*, tore up the pro and semipro circuits. From the twenties and thirties, local black college Cheyney, as well as Temple University, drew players from West Philadelphia schools to build impressive programs. Tapping a neglected talent pool, Philadelphia's other non-Catholic colleges gradually integrated their classrooms and teams from the 1880s through the 1930s, while historically black Lincoln University went co-ed in the fifties and shortly fielded a team. Playing black women on squads from Temple, Penn, West Chester, and

Ursinus throughout these years, Immaculata players through basketball came into regular contact with a few African Americans.[56]

As the sixties progressed, the sport of basketball reflected increasing U.S. social integration as well as concomitant tensions. In the professional leagues, for example, the white-identified, stodgier National Basketball Association (NBA) found itself upstaged by the black-identified, freestyling American Basketball Association (ABA). The huge popularity of ABA star Julius "Dr. J" Erving might have been the single largest factor pushing the NBA to merge with the ABA. When it did, for the 1975–76 season, Dr. J played for the local Philadelphia 76ers, while basketball fans and players continued to debate the merits of the orthodox "white" game versus the improvisational "black" game. Six years earlier, in 1970, Immaculata coach Cathy Rush had taken her team to its first contest at a historically black school, Cheyney College, a national-caliber team in Immaculata's backyard. In subsequent years, Immaculata played another powerhouse, predominantly black Federal City— now the University of the District of Columbia—in Landover, Maryland, as well as Lincoln University and Morgan State, near Baltimore. Rarely hosting games in the seventies, Immaculata mostly traveled to these schools' home courts, coming into contact with audiences of African Americans in places white Catholic women didn't usually go.[57]

Throughout the years, Immaculata team members remembered encounters with black players in new parts of town as wondrous and "eye-awakening experiences." Mary Scharff '77 told the story of playing in a black college gymnasium for the first time. "They looked at us funny when we walked in, and I guess you could say we looked at them," she said. "Because we weren't used to just total black and white, and we would walk into a gym and see nothing but the black people there." In black venues, Immaculata players could experience themselves as a minority for the first time. Moreover, seeing themselves through their black audience's eyes, some Immaculatans grasped their own strangeness. To black players, Immaculatans suddenly realized, they were "a bunch of white Catholic girls who won't get undressed in the locker room," said Betty Ann Hoffman Quinn '73. "They [must] have been like, these girls are weird."[58]

In addition to memories of mind-opening encounters, Immaculata players also got pointed messages that racial prejudice would not be tolerated on the team. "We played people of other races, and we were told to can it because there were some [who were] bigoted," recalled Dee Cofer Cull '55. "We had a girl [who] was terrible with Temple, who had colored players. She would not play on the same side of the court. And [coach Mary Frank] said, 'If you don't play [with them], you will sit.' And [she] sat. . . . Simple as that."

On the whole, players felt good that "there [weren't] any . . . problems between us and them, or even the fans. . . . Overall, they respected us, we respected them," said Mary Scharff '77. "You know, I just realized that, OK,
they're a different color and, you know, so what?" When three African American women joined the Mighty Macs in 1975, white teammates said "it didn't
faze us in any way," as Mary put it. "You know it was just, they were girls!"
she said. "You know, they were women in college, we were all playing one
thing, and we were all doing it for the same reason."[59]

Immaculata players had reason to be proud of healthy interracial activity.
During years when Catholic postimmigrant families had "become white," in
Noel Ignatiev's memorable phrase, when most Catholics lagged behind the
civil rights movement, when Catholics, especially Catholic girls, didn't cross
racial lines, and when Philadelphia Catholic neighborhoods hosted incidents
of antiblack violence, the mere fact that Immaculata players interacted with
black women on the basketball court took on revolutionary proportions.[60]

Throughout these years, however, most Immaculata players came from
homes and communities where religious identity was tightly intertwined
with—and sometimes overshadowed by—racial identity. Talking about
Catholics of European origin, players said they were Irish or Italian or Polish. But talking about black players, they were white. And white Catholic liberalism, like other white liberalisms, had limits. As scholars of race have argued, twentieth-century white interracialism took for granted that race was
a biological fact and thereby, in the midst of worthy efforts, helped natural-
ize and harden arbitrary categories of white and black. At least three characteristics of white liberals resulted from the assumption that race was something genetic. First, white progressives, like white conservatives, tended to
regard black people as "other" to whites in a foundational way. That is, race
was more of a difference than other differences, such as religion, language, or
nationality. Second, while white progressives worked to undermine stereotypes, they tended to retain several centuries' worth of European American
perception that black people were essentially threatening. At its root, of
course, this sense encoded an opposite myth that white people were essentially safe and protected whites from responsibility for harm done to blacks.
Black people, not white people, were the dangerous ones. Third, if there were
attempts to elude the white-black pas de deux, it came in the form of so-
called color blindness. Laudable for its intentions to transcend race, the
white liberal appeal to racial color blindness was inclined to whitewash reality, absorbing black people and culture that whites found acceptable without
addressing wider social imbalances. In all these ways, white progressives anchored interracial sensibilities and actions squarely within white privilege.[61]

Only with reference to black players did Immaculata athletes talk about themselves as white women. Consistently, too, they interpreted interaction between white and black players to confirm racially loaded differences between them. Formally taught that Christ saw no color and personally outraged at inequality, Immaculata players never said being white made them better than black women. And, on the post-1974 teams, there is no evidence white players treated black teammates differently. When three African Americans—Deneice Gray, Sue Martin, and Lydia Sims—joined the team for the 1974–75 season, white players countered racial difference with steadfast color blindness. "They came on board and played and geez, . . . you don't even look at the fact that they're black," said a forward. "It doesn't make any difference what color their skin is." On a national championship team, within which any disunity could threaten success, the color-blind approach seems generally to have flattened race as a factor. Still, players from all years tended to understand the difference between themselves and black players as somehow richer—biologically, culturally, or both—than that between themselves and, say, white non-Catholics. As deep as Catholic-Protestant differences ran in Philadelphia, white-black differences ran deeper.[62]

Talking about black players on other teams, Immaculatans were not colorblind. In fact, throughout the years, Immaculata players tended to recall African American opponents as aggressive and dangerous, while, in contrast, they themselves were meek and peaceable. In the second season of varsity play, in 1940, Immaculata started scheduling games with Temple University, for which the team would travel by bus through the neighborhoods surrounding campus. In white Philadelphia, Temple was well known for being in a "different" part of the city; poor and black people lived there, and better-off citizens feared for their safety. Immaculatans arriving at Temple expressed surprise when they got from the bus to the gym without getting mugged. Once inside the gym, they still felt the danger outside emanating from the Temple team, though most of its members were white. On the court, "these Temple girls [were] much more aggressive," remembered a 1930s player. In contrast, the Immaculata girls "would not think of hitting," she said. "We were more timid, more polite." The Immaculatans' qualities of reserve and courtesy marked them as Catholic ladies, signifying for them a racial contrast to black opponents.[63]

When the Immaculata teams began playing historically black colleges, players' perceptions of difference—and danger—mounted. Against the "unnecessarily rough" and "notoriously aggressive" Federal City team, the college newspaper reported, the Mighty Macs had to withstand an onslaught of unspecified "scare tactics and psych techniques." Perhaps players just found it scary to be around black people. A 1970s Immaculata player described audiences of "large masses of black people" who seemed about to bring down the bleachers, acting "crazy and hollering and screaming." She said the "rocking and rolling" black venues made her feel "intimidated and afraid." "In my mind," she said she thought, "man, we better stick together, don't go straggling off any place." Another teammate said she figured she and her teammates were "safe" as long as "we didn't start any fights and we got in and out." But coaches, players, and fans clearly imagined not only danger but violence as real possibilities and were prepped for what to do should they be physically assaulted. Even "if their bones were all mashed," said an Immaculata fan, "they were supposed to rise up with dignity and creep away."[64]

With Immaculatans fearful of violence and unused to verbal sparring, black teams' game-time rhetorical jabs did not go over well. A 1970s player recalled Federal City team members trying to rile Immaculatans on the court, "Like, 'I'm going to knock your pearly whites out,' you know," she said. Trash talking coupled with the usual physicality of the game heightened fear of black assault. The same 1970s player said the Cheyney team "beat us physically so bad" that "when the game was over, the coach said, 'Go straight to the bus.' We did and we got out of there, because we were concerned that they were just going to tear us apart physically again." Although Immaculata women usually proudly represented themselves as aggressive players of "street" ball, in comparison with black players they suddenly pictured themselves as weak and fragile. "Our street ball . . . and their street ball . . . were totally different," the same player explained. "Like, if you don't see blood, keep playing. I think that was their mentality. We're, oh, my fingernail." Black women's allegedly more aggressive game followed, she suggested, from their biologically different bodies. "I think they're built physically stronger. . . . I mean, they just looked it. And at the time, they had the Afros and trying to guard them, it was like, could you move your hair?" This player in no way saw herself as superior to black women. Still, her ruminations about blood, hair, and physique outline Catholic girls' self-constitution as white, without ever mentioning skin color.[65]

According to my sources, in physical terms, black players acted out, while Immaculata players suffered innocently. Corollarily, in social terms, black players nurtured hostility, while Immaculata players took the high road. For example, many Mighty Macs believed that black teams were racially prejudiced against them, while they themselves held no preconceptions. "They were more racially against us, . . . discriminatory against us, than we were against them. I mean, they would say slanderous, slurring things while we were out on the court," remembered a 1970s player. The Immaculata team, she said, "came to play a basketball game, and you guys are . . . acting like you're ready to kill us." According to other players and fans, African American opponents also racially harassed black members of the Immaculata team, "Uncle-Tom type stuff," asking them why they were playing with the "whiteys."[66]

In the context of early seventies racial tension in the Northeast, it is quite possible Immaculatans faced antagonism from black teams. Many black players learned as tough a game as their white counterparts. They also could have deliberately used well-known white phobias to intimidate Immaculatans and taken advantage of an unusually level playing field to get in some verbal and physical digs. But Immaculata players, beyond describing aggressive black play, suggested it flowed unilaterally from black to white. On the contrary, there is no evidence that Immaculatans suspended their usually assertive style of play for the sake of black opponents, whom they usually defeated. Serving as athletic director in the seventies, Jen Shillingford said of I.C.'s meetings with historically black colleges, "I don't know that anybody was rougher than anybody else. Immaculata could dish it out, too. They sharpened their elbows and came out to play." And far from being innocent of racializing games, one team captain told a reporter in 1975 how she and another starter created a fictional letter, supposedly from Federal City, to read to her team as "a little something to get us up." In the fake letter, Federal City insulted various Immaculata players, including black players for playing for a white team. (In a huge upset of the three-time national champions, Federal City and coach Bessie Stockard won this game, 61–52). This incident shows how difficult it is to tell whether Immaculatans' perceptions originated on the court or in their Catholic culture's investment in whiteness.[67]

From within that culture, Immaculata team members' identity as Catholic ladies depended partly on particular contrasts with black opponents: they did not act crazy, play roughly, stoop to dirty tactics, or harbor racial animosity. "You stick to what you know wins games," said a 1970s player. "We did not unravel as a result of their style of play. Or their behavior, or whatever they did." In the heat of battle, said another 1970s graduate, "we did not embrace . . . getting crazy—I mean, certainly enthusiasm, but not kicking things or throwing things." The Immaculata players said they acted like ladies, "very proud of who we were," and certainly above taking or giving racial insult. Instead, "we walked in as ladies and held our heads up high," one said. "And when the game was over, even after we beat them, you know there wasn't any loud screaming or yelling. . . . And that's how we . . . acted, win or lose, and that's how we walked out of the gymnasium, with our heads held high."[68]

Were Immaculata's contests with black teams another kind of submerged Catholic-Protestant hostility? Perhaps: most opposing black players were

Protestants. But in Immaculata players' minds, that fact was entirely eclipsed by the exceptional meeting of black and white; no one suggested religious sources of conflict. In this small Philadelphia instance, as in many instances, Catholic-Protestant tension smoldered, but white-black conflict burned.

Immaculata players contested African American opponents on the frontiers of Catholic racial interaction and prided themselves on unusual and formative contact with black women through basketball. But they also prided themselves, if less explicitly, on being different from black women. They remembered games against black players and remembered they behaved like ladies. Catholic ladies. *White* Catholic ladies.

· · ·

When Immaculata basketball players traveled with the team, they enjoyed both "going different places" and "playing different teams." Venturing outside the usual geographic and social boundaries of the Catholic community, part of players' pleasure in new places and new people came from constructing their own sense of self. It was fun "to meet the others from N, S, E & W" and "see . . . the different school campuses," as one cheerleader put it. It was also fun to come back home and "appreciat[e] our own." They were at all times Catholic ladies. But what it meant to be Catholic ladies changed according to the constructed class, moral, intellectual, or racial difference of the opposing team. Identifying their team alternately as more skilled, refined, feminine, or peaceable, Immaculata players tailored ideas about opponents to shape identity as Catholic ladies.[69]

Basketball was one way of figuring out what it meant to be young Catholic women in a very big world. In the seventies, Immaculata players slowly realized, basketball changed not only their own lives but also the lives of thousands in the communities that watched them play.

CHAPTER 8

CHAMPIONSHIPS AND COMMUNITY

As she stood at the Alumnae Hall podium that Sunday afternoon in March 1972, presidential duties were the last thing on Sister Mary of Lourdes's mind. Before her sat a reunion of hundreds of alumnae, both newly minted and white-haired, ready to socialize and donate. A charismatic public speaker, Sister Mary of Lourdes took a deep breath and launched into a humorous monologue, taking alumnae back to their school years of yore. But as she talked, her thoughts went again and again halfway across the country, to a place she had never seen, Southern Illinois State University, in Normal, Illinois. There, at that very hour, her beloved basketball team was playing in the final game of the first-ever women's national basketball tournament. The alumnae sitting before her were fans of basketball, too, of course, but in 1972 few off campus knew there was such a thing as a women's national tournament, much less that the Mackies had qualified for it. Only Sister Mary of Lourdes's fellow nuns, lining the back row of the auditorium, fathomed how big the game was—and how fast the seemingly composed president's heart was fluttering. They had orders to interrupt her with any news from Normal.

About ten minutes into the talk, one of the back-row sisters approached the stage and touched Sister Mary of Lourdes's elbow. There had been a phone call from coach Cathy Rush, she said and then whispered a few words more. The president beamed and quickly begged the pardon of her audience. "You may not have heard, but we are very proud our basketball team is playing for the national championship," she said. "We just got a call that the Mackies are up at the half." The alumnae murmured to each other and looked bewildered, so Sister Mary of Lourdes collected herself to proceed. But all she could think was, defense, girls, defense in the second half.[1]

The Mackies were not supposed to be playing for a national championship. In the early seventies, as state universities gathered the bodies and resources to stock increasingly good teams, Immaculata was still a tiny Catholic women's college out in the Chester County sticks. The Mackies had no recruitment budget, no scholarship players, and no physical education major. Its five starters all commuted to campus early every morning, carpooling through the city's darkness to make practice at six. Coach Rush was a twenty-four-year-old recent mother paid $450 a year to do something part-time with the team. She scuffled with officials even to get invited to the mid-Atlantic regional qualifying tournament, held in Towson, Maryland. Sure, to everyone's surprise, the Mackies had gone 24–1 their second year with Rush. But that one loss had come only eight days before, when Rush's alma mater, neighboring powerhouse West Chester, thrashed the Mackies 70–38 in the regional finals. Since the top two teams went on to Normal, Immaculata made the cut. But barely. Their second-place finish seeded them fifteenth in the sixteen-team national tournament. As far as other teams were concerned, Immaculata didn't belong there at all.[2]

The Mackies qualified for the national tourney but almost couldn't go, because the college had no money to send them by plane, and there wasn't time to drive. For four days, Immaculata nuns furiously phoned in all favors, raising funds for the team to travel. Sister Mary of Lourdes tapped each college trustee to send one kid, and development head Sister Marian William Hoben strong-armed local businesses to contribute. The players themselves sold toothbrushes by the armful to defray expenses. When it was time to drive to the airport on Wednesday, there was only enough money to fly eight players and one coach. On standby.[3]

It was not an auspicious start. "Oh, say a prayer they win one game, the poor kids," the sisters said among themselves. Thursday night, they got a call. The Mackies had won their first game. "Great," said Sister Marian William. "Now that's done, now we're off the hook." Friday morning, the sisters got another call. The team had won a second game. Later that night, the phone rang a third time with good news. And after that, there was only one more game to play. Sunday afternoon in Normal, Immaculata would face none other than crosstown rival West Chester for the national championship.[4]

An hour into the Alumnae Hall proceedings, fifty minutes after the halftime report, the back row of sisters began to rustle, giggle, and fidget, while alumnae looked around to see what was going on. Sister Mary of Lourdes stopped speaking. Again, a nun approached the stage from the back, touched the president's elbow, whispered in her ear. This time Sister Mary of Lourdes did not check her glee, laughing and crying the news into the microphone. Only minutes before, Immaculata had defeated West Chester by four points to become national champions. The sisters were already beside themselves, laughing and clapping and jumping. Astonished alumnae joined the impromptu celebration. Sister Mary of Lourdes snuck out to call the team. She reached Cathy Rush at the hotel in Normal. "I want you to fly home first-class," she said. "We'll figure out how to pay for it later."[5]

A few local reporters caught wind of the news from Normal. "It was a little like Santa Barbara Junior College dumping the UCLA cagers," wrote George Heaslip of the *Daily Local News*. "There's just no way to describe the immensity of Immaculata's upset 52–48 over mighty West Chester State." As it turned out, that Sunday in 1972 was only the beginning of the biggest surprise in the history of the college—and perhaps in the history of women's basketball. For the next two years, Immaculata would repeat as national champions. For the next four years, Immaculata would play in the title game. For the next five years, Immaculata would win the Mid-Atlantic Regionals. Soon, the team had a national following. They sold out gymnasiums wherever they went. Reporters and photographers attended practice sessions. National magazines splashed their faces across feature pages. Players would be named to Kodak All-American, Street and Smith, Olympic Games, Goodwill Games, and Pan-American Games teams. The team inspired the first women's college basketball poll. And by the time Cathy Rush left the school in 1977, her record was 149–15. She and her "Mighty Macs"—as Heaslip christened them after their first title—had won 91 percent of their games for seven years. For players, fans, and families, the experience of winning at that level was not just fun but outrageous, surreal, rapturous. And it was all the more gratifying for being so highly improbable.[6]

From the start of those surprising years, players understood their victories as a blessing, if not a miracle. This was not a pious veneer painted on top of pleasure by a preening Catholicism. Rather, it was the only logical sense players could make of their good fortune. Sensing the hand of God, persuading teammates of it, and receiving confirmation with each passing year, Mighty Macs said the wins always seemed bigger than the team, than just players and coach. Instead, the championships were about the whole community that materialized around Immaculata basketball. National titles pushed players to reach beyond the circle of the team to find mooring amid fame and success. In turn, fame and success pushed players into ever-widening circles of community, as they began to touch—and be touched by—people who followed them and admired them all over the country. The ways the Mighty Macs moved and reshaped communities—communities of Immaculata College, Philadelphia Catholics, local fans, and American women—multiplied the miracle of their championship years.

Still, natural factors helped explain the Immaculata phenomenon. By the early seventies, former Mackies were coaching Philadelphia Catholic high school teams and sending graduates to the college. At Immaculata, new players met the youthful Rush, a coach fully at home with the 1971-instituted full-court game and brash enough to try anything. Rush had played at West Chester under women's basketball radical Lucille Kyvallos and gained a sixth sense for where the game was going. Within days of taking the job at Immaculata, Rush had players running miles to get in shape and began teaching men's game strategies: physical picks, man-to-man coverage, trapping defenses. The new coach soon realized she had stumbled on a national-caliber lineup that marvelously complemented star center Theresa Shank.[7]

But even the fortuitous meeting of players and coach did not add up to three national titles. "It was just too flukey, . . . to have had basically a bunch of girls who could play ball and happened to be there at the same time," said Lorrie Gable Finelli '78. After exhausting explanations, most Immaculata team members and fans attributed the championships to sisters' prayers and the Lord's responses. Why did they win? "God must have wanted it that way," forward Rene Muth Portland '75 told a reporter in 1992.[8]

While no earthly logic fully accounted for the Mighty Macs' success, changes in church and nation partly accounted for the communities that tightened around them. The championship years coincided with Vatican II and sixties backlashes, as well as Vietnam, Watergate, and the feminist movement. Fans loved the Immaculata teams because they won—but also, perhaps, because they represented the best of the old and the new together. The Mighty Macs looked and acted like throwbacks to the fifties. But they played basketball like they had arrived from the future. For Philadelphia Catholics and the American public, both witnessing the end of idealistic eras, the winning women's team both preserved vanishing values and augured worthwhile change. As victories piled up, spectators thronged, and three dozen basketball players found themselves in a position rare for young women—almost unique for Catholic young women—as thousands paid attention to what they said and did.

Interacting with different kinds of people on and off campus, Immaculata teams of the seventies did the same as Mackies of the past, but on a larger scale. Championship players loved their sport for all the reasons other Immaculatans did, including the plain old high of winning all the time. But they loved winning partly because it gave them new powers and freedoms. Moving in constant limelight, Immaculata players gradually realized that various groups or communities, from little girls to local journalists, imagined the team somehow represented *them*. People identified with them. And that identification gave them chances to affirm and shape constituencies of fans. The Mighty Macs not only played games; they also talked to reporters, signed autographs, expounded their faith, and lingered with youngsters. In the process, they touched communities in ways that sometimes preserved old values and sometimes challenged them.[9]

Immaculata College, 1965–75

By the early seventies, Catholics had arrived on the American scene. Already on the threshold of middle-class respectability in the early sixties, Catholics rode President John F. Kennedy's patrician coattails to mainstream religious acceptance as well. But after Kennedy's 1963 assassination, the country seemed plunged into unrest, tragedy, and war for the rest of the decade, as utopian folk music and haunting spirituals played in the background. Catholics had arrived—but on the scene of a nation more self-consciously fragmented than any time since the Civil War.

In a church newly interfaced with American society, changing women's roles chafed. While the Vatican affirmed prohibitions on artificial birth control in the 1968 encyclical *Humanae vitae*, "women's lib" activism was poised to reset the terms of U.S. gender dynamics. For years, Catholic clerics had disputed secular and liberal Protestant versions of women's rights. But the new encyclical cemented official Catholic opposition to early seventies feminism. Catholic women sympathetic to the "libbers"—or just sympathetic to the Pill—increasingly found themselves squeezed between church and conscience.[10]

Also, in the midst of burning cities, hippie demonstrations, and feminist activism, the U.S. Catholic church struggled with its own internal revolution, implemented in stages as documents from the Second Vatican Council reverberated across American pews. Many faithful who missed Latin Mass and communion fasts were further baffled to hear about ecumenism and the priesthood of the laity. For others, the church changed too little, too late. Disillusioned on both ends of the spectrum, priests left dioceses, sisters left orders, and collegians left Catholic universities. In the late sixties and early seventies, when Georgetown, Holy Cross, and Notre Dame began to admit women, many Immaculatans and their Catholic sisters left women's colleges to go co-ed.

In Philadelphia, however, one of the most conservative dioceses in the nation, there were fewer visible changes than elsewhere. Traditional bishops and priests implemented mandates slowly and even grudgingly. And while many religious communities quickly modified public garb, the Immaculate Heart sisters wished to avoid what superior Mother Maria Claudia Honsberger called "secularist renewal" and reaffirmed the full habit of veil and dress. In 1974 Mother Claudia listed other aspects of secularist renewal, which she believed opposed the true spirit of Vatican II, in the *Catholic Standard and Times*: "lack of prayer, overemphasis on permissiveness and personal satisfaction, a forgetting of penance and sacrifice." Some sisters continued to teach as if Vatican II had never happened, students recalled. "[The church] had the ecumenical council and all that business, and at religion class they were saying, 'Everyone is going to hell except Catholics and your mission is to go out and save the world,'" said a player from the sixties. "It was repressive."[11]

Still, students and sisters at Immaculata trudged along with national and church trends. In the seventies, the school enrolled greater numbers of adult and continuing-education students, more of whom were not Catholic. Students entered classrooms headed increasingly by lay faculty, as membership in the orders began to decline. And, like most college communities, Immaculata felt the effects of social change that irresistibly broke over the baby-boom generation. Through the late sixties and early seventies, student groups and forward-thinking I.H.M.s scheduled speakers on hip topics, from Native Americans and mysticism to witchcraft and feminism. A few students caught the deepest implications of nationwide student unrest and challenged school structure itself. They wanted different classes, more freedom, more input. They wrote passionate editorials stating their demands. Two underground newspapers, *The Soapbox* and *The Option*, briefly emerged to challenge the faculty-moderated *Immaculatan*. And, in the spring of 1969, *The Immaculatan* itself published an open letter from drumbeating freshman Sheila Konczweski, who lamented the "oppressive piousness" at Immaculata. "Religion seems to permeate the courses which fill the freshman roster, whereas, the religion course itself seems to be lacking a true Christian spirit and atmosphere." From the sisters' perspective, "there was a lot of unrest among students," said Sister Virginia Assumpta McNabb, college admissions officer who also served as dormitory monitor in those years. "Maybe it was the Vietnam War, maybe it was women getting their voice, whatever. But . . . we had many, many problems in the dorms where students didn't want restrictions, which we still had. . . . They did have to sign in and out when they left the dorms. They didn't want to do that." From some students' perspectives, however, friction energized the college environment. "It was probably the best time to be a Catholic college student," said Marie Olivieri Russell '66. "A cool time to be young, actually. . . . I got my Christian conscience, and I never gave it back. No matter what they told me."[12]

At the same time, Immaculata was a college full of traditional Philadelphia Catholic daughters whose approach to changes in church and country ranged from oblivious to resistant. The "very small handful" of students who agitated for curriculum reform and social change were widely considered "weirdos," said Christine Lammer DiCiocchio '70. Most students instead worked deferentially with the administration, headed until 1972 by the vastly popular Sister Mary of Lourdes, to talk through minor campus conflicts. There were no political protests or faculty-student standoffs and little experimentation with drugs or sex of the kind that characterized many campuses of the era. Many late sixties and seventies players remembered feeling sheltered from the outside world. Some said they finished college largely unaware of Vatican II and turn-of-the-decade turmoil. Lorrie Gable Finelli '78 said when she left Immaculata, she began to wonder "where I'[d] been for four years; I fe[lt] like [I was] on Planet X." But, she said, "in that bubble, that's what we knew."[13]

Everyone at Immaculata in 1972, however, was aware that the basketball team was enjoying a phenomenal season. Always a nice distraction from work and classes, basketball in the seventies offered, at the least, a far more pleasant preoccupation than unsettling developments in church and nation. At the most, it is possible that basketball represented more immediate and relevant change than other distant events. Women's hoops was Philadelphia Catholic heritage, but now, with the Immaculata team's success, the old tradition suddenly looked fresh and modern. Women—Catholic women—as top-flight athletes? If nothing else bridged the gap of the generation, basketball could. Winning had drawn around the team fans of many different types: old and young, women and men, religious and laity. All winter, fans had marked their calendars, stepped out to games, and cheered boisterously as they watched the Mackies alternately demolish and scrape by opponents on their way to an undefeated regular season. When they defeated West Chester in the finals at Normal, news spread fast. There was no question but to get folks out to the airport. When the team came through the gate, six hundred proud fans shouted cheers, waved posters, and threw confetti. They were going to celebrate their miracle even if no one else in the country even knew it happened.[14]

At the airport after the first championship, March 1972. Left to right are Theresa Shank, Sister Mary of Lourdes McDevitt, Maureen Stuhlman, Janet Young, Coach Cathy Rush, Denise Conway, Janet Ruch, and Maureen Mooney.
ROBERT HALVEY COLLECTION OF THE PHILADELPHIA ARCHIVES AND HISTORICAL RESEARCH CENTER.

The Championship Years

The first championship surprised few people more than the players themselves. Visiting Immaculata as a high school senior in 1970, Janet Young Eline '74 "watched a game and thought, this is not a great basketball team by any shot," she said. "It was just to have fun and take our minds off academics." Theresa Shank Grentz '74 came to Immaculata as a fluke. Her senior year, the Shank family's row house tragically burned to the ground. Suddenly impoverished, Theresa saw her hopes to attend college out of state—and play big-time basketball—dashed. The local default, Immaculata was the end of her dreams, not the beginning.[15]

Even after Janet, Theresa, and their teammates went undefeated in the 1971–72 regular season, most of them knew little of the new women's collegiate tournament, much less that they could qualify. "We got invited to the national tournament as the [fifteenth] seed, but who knew? We didn't know what a seed was," point guard Denise Conway Crawford '74 recounted to a reporter. When they got to Normal, where the AIAW had scheduled opening ceremonies and other formalities, Immaculata players felt like they were living a fantasy. "Opening ceremonies, you mean like the Olympics?" they asked Cathy Rush. Even then, players said they largely treated the first national tournament as a lark, staying up late, watching hotel television, and eating junk food. "It was still like, 'We've got this game, let's play the game, now we're done, let's go have some fun,'" recalled Janet. In the first game, unknown Immaculata easily knocked off previously undefeated South Dakota State. In the semifinals, they upset the tournament's top seed, Mississippi University for Women. "My mother . . . remembers that I would call and say, 'Well, we just won that game,'" said Janet. "Then I'd call again, 'We won again. We won again.'" For the final game, against West Chester, Rush adjusted some matchups and told her team to play good defense, while Theresa Shank made some big shots in the last minutes. Naive and relaxed, the team made an impressive average of 50 percent of their field goal attempts in the tournament.[16]

After the first championship, the Immaculata phenomenon took on a life of its own. First, the school came "alive in a tidal wave of enthusiasm," remembered Maureen Mooney '73's father, Leo Mooney. "During basketball season, it was all anyone talked about," said Lorrie Gable Finelli '78. "It was very hard to explain but everyone was excited." Then, media attention started. At first, only a few keen-eyed local sportswriters realized what had happened in their backyard; most barely noticed women's sports. "I didn't even know they'd gone to full court," said one sportswriter after hearing the news. But over the summer, it sank in that little Immaculata had just implausibly won the first-ever women's college basketball championship. It was a Cinderella story for the ages. And it drew more people, Catholics and non-Catholics, into the community of Immaculata fans.[17]

In the following 1972–73 season, every game warranted local sports section coverage. As word traveled, big matchups drew hundreds and sometimes thousands of fans. Basketball team alumnae brought husbands and children to games. Chester County locals glommed on to the thrilling team tucked among their cornfields. Philadelphia Catholics beamed to claim the collegiate flowering of Catholic League girls. And true-blue lovers of basketball came to see the Mighty Macs play an old-school game of teamwork and hustle, passing and passion, so often missing in the pros and even men's college ball. Immaculata sold bumper stickers and T-shirts to spread the good news further. They even cranked up a tiny public relations office to churn out regular press releases. By the time the Macs appeared in their second national tournament, there was a "very large community associated with basketball," said Sister Marian William Hoben '44. "There was something about the whole team that everyone loved so much."[18]

What was the appeal? Some loved the Immaculata girls because they played basketball "the way we remembered it," recalled sportswriter Mel Greenberg, that is, the way men played in the fifties and sixties. Chester County fan Rolf Brachwitz agreed. "The ladies' game ran rings around the guys," he said. Making basketball look fun to play, the Mighty Macs made basketball pleasurable to watch. "The theme for the Mighty Macs [is] 'I F-E-E-L GOOD.' And they did," wrote student reporter Donna Anderson, describing the Macs' warming up to James Brown's hit song. "They smiled as they worked the ball with ease, enjoying every move, every play. . . . I 'oohed' at the way Marianne Crawford could handle the ball and 'awed' at the agility of Theresa Shank as she scored 22 points in the second game. . . . It seemed as if every game had this pleasure."[19]

Fans were also drawn close by the team's closeness. Sister Marian William said team members seemed to take "such good care of one another." Reporters remarked on the team's "warm, sisterly feeling." When new players came on board, older girls mentored them in the family feel of the team, teaching them "this love, . . . this brotherhood bit," Rene Muth '76 told reporter Skip Myslenski. And Rush never partook of the coaching style of berating or screaming at players. "Watching Immaculata," wrote Myslenski for the *Philadelphia Inquirer* magazine, "one remembers Vince Lombardi saying his Packers won the Super Bowl because they love one another."[20]

Operating with no sports budget and no scholarship money, however, everyone knew the Mighty Macs' winning ways couldn't last. Perhaps the fan base of Immaculata basketball grew thicker and tighter because signs of the times urged people to enjoy success while it lasted. As the Macs launched their second championship season, the U.S. Congress passed the Education Amendments of 1972, modeled on 1964 civil rights legislation, making federal educational discrimination against women illegal. A controversial segment called Title IX required public institutions to offer comparable opportunities—including athletic programs and scholarships—for men and women. Met with legal opposition from big football universities, Title IX languished in court battles until the summer of 1975. Still, the provision affected women's sports immediately, as athletic departments swelled with unprecedented allocations. With new money to recruit and finance players, state schools quickly bypassed small basketball anomalies. Everyone watching Immaculata, from sportswriters and fans to sisters and players, saw the handwriting on the wall. "It was a very narrow window," said Betty Ann Hoffman Quinn '72. "I mean, you could see it. You knew it was going to change and it did." Fan and college admissions officer Sister Virginia Assumpta McNabb agreed. "We knew it would pass, you know, when you're up against Mississippi and Tennessee and all those other big huge universities," she said. "It was unbelievable it lasted three years."[21]

In the 1972–73 season, the Mighty Macs never lost, from opener to championship game. The team beat second-ranked West Chester again, as well as several other top-ten teams. The closest contest all season came in the national tournament semifinals at Queens College, in New York. Playing Southern Connecticut State, Immaculata trailed the whole game and was down by twelve with three minutes to go. At that point, center Theresa Shank—whom *Sports Illustrated* would soon call "the Bill Walton of women's basketball"—looked at the scoreboard and took over the game. She scored six points on field goals and fouls, another two on an inbounds steal, and the winning deuce on a last-second tap-in. Immaculata settled any lingering questions about their dominance the next day, beating Queens by seven for a second national championship.[22]

The Queens squad, coached by Cathy Rush's former West Chester coach Kyvallos, avenged the loss late in the following season, dealing the Mighty Macs the hard-fought one-point loss on Ash Wednesday 1974 that broke their thirty-five–game winning streak. But the Mighty Macs regrouped and refused to lose for the rest of the 1974 season. They arrived at tournament host Kansas State University to defend their title after driving twenty-eight hours in a three-bus entourage of students, sisters, and families. Again, the semifinals nearly finished them, as William Penn College missed the upset by just three points. When Immaculata easily defeated Mississippi College the next day, they garnered the national laurels for the third time in three years. The trinity of trophies made them a bona fide national phenomenon. Not just the *Philadelphia Inquirer* but the *New York Times*, the *Wall Street Journal*, the *Christian Science Monitor*, *Sports Illustrated*, and *Ms. Magazine* covered the story.

In those three years, Immaculata changed forever the way players, fans, and the media thought of women's basketball, so recently a half-court, six-player, limited-dribble affair. The Mighty Macs' game was not your grandmother's basketball. Some commentators called the team's fundamentally sound style the hardiest game played by women or men. And since women's rules had added the thirty-second clock in 1974, years before the men, it was arguably the most exciting game, too. Still, many could hardly believe their eyes. "Men, you are not going to believe this," wrote Philadelphia's *Evening Bulletin* sportswriter Jim Barniak, "but Immaculata's Marianne Crawford, a girl, scooped up this loose ball, dribbled between her legs to get past one East Stroudsburg defender, then took off on a three-on-two fast break. She dribbled a while left-handed, then right-handed, a few stutter steps here and there, then looked left and threw right to the lovely Rene Muth for two points." The writer breathlessly paused and then issued a challenge. "If there is a better guard in Philadelphia than Marianne Crawford, it's a boy, and if so, I want to see them go one-on-one." Converted by Marianne's razzle-dazzle at the point, Barniak went on to bemoan the injustice that male players of her caliber routinely attracted scholarships and perks, while their female peer commuted and worked two jobs to pay tuition. Marianne and her teammates didn't just change the game. They changed minds.[23]

The fellowship the Mighty Macs gathered around them and the changes they brought about should not be overestimated. Fans gathered at games bonded only temporarily, and the national public of sports-page readers merely grazed on Mighty Mac news. Moreover, the coming-out of the women's game through Immaculata's three championships did not change the country like the American sixties and did not change the Catholic Church like Vatican II. But for some Immaculata players and fans, for a few years, the championships might have seemed more important—or at least more compelling—than other supposedly bigger events. On campus, basketball was "more important, definitely," than other current events, said Mary Scharff '77. Perhaps for some the team even seemed to address and solve big issues. Fan Rolf Brachwitz explained his love for the Mighty Macs to a reporter in 1975. "It's the kids and the coach," he said. "What turns me on is their attitude. It's not business to them, it's fun. . . . I think their attitude is the key to solving some of the world's problems." Brachwitz might have been alone in voicing it, but if local and national attention indicated anything, he was not alone in feeling it.[24]

Building an Immaculata Basketball Community

The Immaculata basketball team won games, but to players, victory meant much more than impressive box scores. It meant touching people of all sorts: students and sisters, family and fans, local and national. It meant little girls who saw the team of young women as role models. Playing basketball, the Mighty Macs affirmed communities: as Immaculatans, as Philadelphians, as Catholics, and as women. The team enjoyed playing basketball partly because others, in ever-widening circles, enjoyed them.

Building the Immaculata Community

At a time of change, basketball brought the Immaculata community together. Sisters and students, players and cheerleaders, alumnae and parents said they gloried in the "electrifying" championship years because "basketball pull[ed] us together." Sister Virginia Assumpta contrasted student unrest with basketball enthusiasm. "To the school I think it brought a great deal of cohesiveness," she said. "Everybody got behind the team. Everybody went to all the games. . . . So, it was just exciting to be here at that time."[25]

When the Macs started winning big, a whole bandwagon of new nuns joined stalwart I.H.M. lovers of basketball. Dozens of sisters packed home games, carpooled for away games, and followed the team on road trips. Sister Marian William Hoben '44 penned hundreds of lines of Mighty Macs songs and cheers, which she distributed at games for fans to bellow. Barniak reported with some amazement a scene perfectly normal for the Immaculata crowd. "Yesterday, during the heat of battle, a nun from the balcony stood up and in her shrillest falsetto yelled, 'Watch the pick and roll!'" Back on campus, other nuns prayed for the team, excused missed classes, and listened on the radio. After one of Theresa Shank's heroic games, Sister Loretta Maria Tenbusch and her English class decorated their class member's chair. "That was typical of the involvement of the school," said Sister Loretta Maria. "It wasn't just one girl, one game. We were all in it together."[26]

Some sisters just loved hoops. Others appreciated new attention for the school. And still others connected to the younger generation through basketball—at a time when much else disconnected them—idealizing players as "women of deep faith." Team members "could have been models for the whole university," said Sister Loretta Maria. "They were not a bunch of rebellious people angry with the world." Whatever the reasons, sisters of the Immaculate Heart of Mary adored the team. Several nuns I interviewed recalled the championship years with tears in their eyes. "People say it was a Cinderella team," said Sister Marie Albert Kunberger '51, a professor of home economics. "It was a Cinderella *time*."[27]

Another key group of supporters was Immaculata alumnae, especially those who had played basketball at the school in years past. Raising families or working in the area, former I.C. players came out to games to cheer for the team and socialize with each other. "When my son was little, when they were playing all those big games, I dressed him up in blue and white, and we went," said Gloria Rook Schmidt '64. "And your friends were there. You'd walk in and see people." Former players were "proud" to have "lit the flame" that blazed into later championships and bragged to friends about their own playing days. "I would just . . . say, 'I played basketball, too, at Immaculata.'

And they would go, 'What?!'" reported Margaret Guinan Delaney '62. "So, I got a lot of mileage out of it." Alumnae marveled at how far the game had come. "I was jealous; I wanted to be out there playing with them," remembered Jean Doris '53. They also marveled that, though rules had changed, Immaculata uniforms had not. Two alumnae from the fifties, who "virtually went to every game" with husbands and children in tow, started a booster club to raise funds to costume the team properly.[28]

The whole college got in on the act. Administrators declared school holidays so Immaculatans could travel to regional tournaments. Students packed into friends' cars to follow their team around the city, as well as to Illinois, Kansas, and Mississippi. "Basketball pulls us together here," one student told reporter Bill Verigan. "The school is really out in the sticks. . . . I never get to Philadelphia except when the team plays there. . . . Basketball provides our spirit, our social meetings." Campus custodian Jimmy Brazes gave the team good-luck shamrock pins to wear for a St. Patrick's Day game. And when the team's streak ended on Ash Wednesday 1974, the entire campus population threw a spontaneous midnight pep rally in the Rotunda, Villa Maria's splendid, three-story central hall.[29]

Along with sisters, alumnae, and students, parents made up an enthusiastic—and loud—component of the cheering section. It was Rene Muth's mother and father who decided, after an unceremonious loss in their daughter's first season, that Immaculata's fans were too quiet. To the next game, they brought from the family hardware store a supply of galvanized metal buckets and dowels to bang like drums and drumsticks. After that, the raucous so-called bucket brigade appeared at every game, sometimes a hundred parents strong. They easily drowned out other teams' bands and made Immaculata fans notorious. At the 1975 national tournament, AIAW officials, acting on complaints from an unidentified rival team, banned the buckets, much to the Immaculata fans' outrage.[30]

For most of those years, loaned buckets were the only band instruments Immaculata could afford. Winning brought the school community together, but so did adversity. When seniors on the 1972 team started playing, the college had no gym. "They had to endure a lot of hardships just to play basketball," said Sister Virginia Assumpta. "They got so much enjoyment out of it, and then when they started winning, . . . then everybody got the fever." When they started winning, everything got expensive, too. Eventually, the school tried to put a few resources behind the team. Before the 1974 tournament, point guard Denise Conway '74 proudly told *The Immaculatan*, the team's new and expanded support crew included "four managers, cheerleaders, a band, and a mascot." They soon expected "different uniforms [and] new warm-ups" to arrive. But neither the school nor parents could underwrite the staff and travel needs of a number-one team. Cathy Rush hired assistant coaches out of her own pocket. Theresa Shank thumbed her way to campus three times a week. The team stayed four to a room for tournaments and had no meal budget. They hand-washed and hang-dried their one uniform apiece in hotel bathrooms and usually had to put them on again still damp. When the job of managing the team surpassed student qualifications, athletic director Jenepher Shillingford agreed to do it because the college couldn't hire additional staff. "They were crazy days," Shillingford said. "I would drive [an hour] to Pottstown to have the program printed because it was about ten dollars cheaper." Cheerleaders bought their own outfits. The financial adversity was real and unpleasant. But it bonded an Immaculata basketball community that met challenge after challenge to go the next step. And college poverty also became part of the Immaculata mystique, adding to fan pride, media fascination, and team "incentive," as Sister Mary of Lourdes put it.[31]

Immaculata players sensed the cohesion they helped forge in the college community, and it awed them. "The sisters all wanted to come to games, parents wanted to come, and just the community, the Immaculata community," said Mary Scharff '77. Players knew they enjoyed basketball, but others' fulfillment added to their own. They tried to pay back in wins "all the hours [fans] spent following us" and all the money they raised for travel. They counted on fans, especially the sisters, just to be there. Usually, it was the fans who cheered the players. But once, when a carload of nuns got lost and filed into an away game late, Immaculata players on the floor stopped and cheered *them*.[32]

Building the Catholic Community

Most Immaculata championship players cherished their public association with the sisters—and with the Catholic school and faith they represented. They were Catholics and proud of it. If many only dimly recognized controversies inside the church, all knew Catholicism was a strange and even ignominious faith to many outsiders. Partly, the thrill of success was the vindication of their religion. Not always expressed in religious terms, players took for granted that the benefit of Catholic culture, education, and morality proved itself on the basketball court. After Immaculata's first title, wrote father Leo Mooney only half tongue-in-cheek, the quest for more national championships was "elevated" to the level of a "crusade."[33]

Not only the fact that Mighty Macs won but also the way they won—surmounting obstacles of size, poverty, and obscurity—justified Catholicism. At the first three AIAW national tournaments, Immaculata was the only Catholic college and one of very few private schools without a physical education major. "When we got there, they're like, 'Immaculata what? What's that?'" recalled Janet Young Eline '74. When the Macs won all three tournaments, "we were breaking a big barrier . . . in that we were coming from a Catholic college," said Mary Scharff '77. "As opposed to a big university, we were a Catholic women's college. That was breaking a barrier in itself."[34]

Not only at Immaculata but across the Philadelphia archdiocese, Catholics saw in the Mighty Macs a highly visible validation of their faith and culture at a time of church change and struggle. The diocesan paper, the *Catholic Standard and Times*, was among the first papers to get the scoop on the national championship in Normal and the following year ran a much-quoted article entitled "Is UCLA the Immaculata of the West?" Readers of the *Standard and Times* caught on and started coming to games. Usually, different Philadelphia families rooted for rival Big Five teams, depending on where fathers and brothers went to school. But they commonly identified with the women's college where Catholic basketball had bloomed for the whole country to see. Even girls' high school rivalries chilled in support of the Mighty Macs. Sacred Heart Academy player Mimi McNamee grew up in the sixties hating rival Villa Maria Academy and by extension Immaculata, taught by the same order of nuns. But when she read about the Mighty Macs, she regarded them as her team, because they were Catholic. "It was *us*," she said.[35]

The Mighty Macs drew Philadelphia Catholics together and could also, they believed, improve non-Catholic impressions of the faith. Watching a little Catholic school hit it big in sports made Catholicism more appealing than the usual public fare about bishops and birth control. Their own coach, Cathy Rush, was a case in point. A Baptist graduate of well-funded West Chester, she recognized the wonder of a tiny Catholic college doing what Immaculata had done. "This team is not only a champion in basketball, but also in life," Rush told the *Catholic Standard and Times*. "They are a credit to their religion, their families, and now to their school." "She was always for [Catholicism]," said Mary Scharff '77. "And then when all the sisters started going crazy and following us, she just thought . . . there's something with this Catholic education that's right." Players liked to see basketball moxie persuade non-Catholics that there was a certain "something" about their faith. After defeating Southern Connecticut in the 1973 national semifinals, Immaculata players were tickled when all the Southern Conn girls wore their shorts on their heads like nuns' veils to cheer the Macs in the finals.[36]

In the Philadelphia area, many non-Catholics had seen Catholic women's basketball and were used to the uniforms, the prayers, and the nuns. But as the team traveled the rest of the country, they soon realized that some non-Catholics had no clue about their religion. In one program the school was listed as "Immaculate State College." Sisters fielded questions as to whether players were postulants in the order. And the national media alternately exoticized and infantilized the sisters, captioning their photos "Little Sisters of the Floor" or "Heavenly Help." But the I.H.M.s tolerated it, because it put their team and Catholicism in the news in a positive way. Perhaps it could change non-Catholics' impressions to see pictures of nuns screaming at referees.[37]

To be truthful, the sisters didn't just tolerate attention; they liked it and helped it along. In 1974 they impishly volunteered one of their own, shy Sister Regina Socorro Kovalik, for an ingenious picture shot by Bryn Mawr photographer Ross Watson Jr. Taking a low upward angle on Sister Regina standing beneath the backboard and holding a basketball on her hip, Watson contributed his photo for a story in the short-lived *Sports Philadelphia* magazine. Published, the young nun stood framed by a pun: "How Many Men Are On Philadelphia's Best Basketball Team? None." The title was clever. But Watson's composition was inspired. Backboard angles appeared as a cross hovering behind Sister Regina's shoulders, and the basketball hoop seemed to halo her head. She cradled the ball on her hip like a mother carrying an infant, while the nuns' traditional wedding band shone prominently on her left hand. The caption asked the gender of the city's best team, but the photograph itself mischievously posed other questions. Was this woman a devotee of Catholicism or basketball? Was the fruit of her womb a baby or a ball? And was she married to God or the game?[38]

Volunteering Sister Regina for the photo, certainly the nuns did not intend to raise such questions. Nevertheless, the questions get at more of the early seventies relationship between basketball and Catholicism—and between women and their church—than some Immaculata participants might have admitted. And, more patently, the photograph accurately portrayed a community enthralled with a game that made their heavy-laden faith seem lighter and brighter. Sister Regina under the basket suggested it was simple and easy to love basketball at a time when loving Catholicism wasn't. Dull and vague answering questions about Vatican II and social changes, sisters and players beamed and wept remembering Immaculata basketball. More than anything else happening in those years, the championships made them proud to be Catholic. It is even possible that, for some players, sisters, and fans, basketball moved them more than anything in traditional religious practice. Games, and the community feel they engendered, certainly juiced everyone more than the awkward, newfangled Masses. Those years served, as

Title page of a winter 1974 *Sports Philadelphia* article by Herm Rogul, which showed Sister Regina Socorro cradling a basketball on her hip.
Photograph by H. Ross Watson Jr.

it were, as God's last blessing on a passing separatist culture. "It was a glorious time . . . such a gift," said Sister Marian William. "Everything was great."[39]

Building the Philadelphia Community

Citizens of Philadelphia found special meaning in the Mighty Macs, too. As the team kept winning, more and more Chester and Delaware County residents attended games to have fun, support the local team, and feel the sense of community. *Daily Local News* reporter Randy Shantz described the Macs' "fanatical following" as "the envy of all women's teams and many college men's programs throughout the Delaware Valley." In "a tremendous sports city," said Mary Scharff '77, "all of a sudden there was . . . a little tiny all-girls' Catholic college . . . becoming the national champion. And then everybody woke up and said, 'What is this? What's going on here?' . . . All these people from all over wanted to come see the games." As the press stepped up its coverage, players were recognized on the street and lionized in the neighborhoods. "If you were talented in sports and you played for Immaculata, it was the only team getting press at the time," said Lorrie Gable Finelli '78. "People from my neighborhood [thought] I was the next best thing to [sliced] bread."[40]

Fans followed the team because they won but also because, they said, the team exuded a warm, communal feeling. Jeanine Driscoll, who played basketball at a Downingtown public high school in the early seventies, was attracted to "a sense of community at the games, a community of players, coaches, and fans." Rolf "Bugs" Brachwitz was another local fan who said he came out for the sense of community. An auto mechanic who attended his first game after Sue Martin '78 brought him her Volkswagen Bug, Brachwitz became a Mighty Macs fixture. "There were five people on the court, but there was a sixth being, the sum," he said. "The sixth being was more than the sum of the parts. . . . I choke up when I think about it." Improvising in his shop, Bugs fashioned himself a long, thin, eight-foot horn that he played boisterously at every game, earning a second nickname, "The Horn Man." The instrument, sounded as a call to battle and a witness to triumph, became an artifact of the Immaculata basketball community. When the Mighty Macs traveled to Madison Square Garden, Bugs made the trip with his horn, but stadium security stopped him "because they thought it was a weapon," said Immaculata athletic director Jen Shillingford, who talked to officials on his behalf. "I thought the man was going to cry, and I couldn't get it past . . . anybody." Bugs got his horn back after the game.[41]

After games, Immaculata players were besieged for autographs, and at home they received abundant fan mail. Hundreds joined the new booster club—"people not involved with Immaculata at all and some of them perhaps not Catholic," said an alumnae player from the class of 1957. Team members liked seeing the fun spread. "I thought it was just great they wanted my autograph," said Janet Young Eline '74. "It just told me that they enjoyed what they were watching, and I just kind of entertained them. You know, give [them] some enjoyment for a little bit of time at least." Lorrie Gable Finelli '78 also saw playing for the Mighty Macs as a service to the wider community that in turn supported them. "There was such an outpouring of support and gratitude and enjoyment from the community. Not Immaculata, . . . but the people of the area," Lorrie said. "I think we did allow people to enjoy their life a little better, and I think that we . . . collectively provided a service for an area that was fairly quiet and now had something to be really energized about."[42]

Among the most energized of all fans, key local sportscasters said the Macs were not just another story but a crew of girls that changed their lives. There were highs and lows to Immaculata relations with the press. Most sportswriters barely noticed the first championship and, when they did, mostly noticed "pretty" and "blonde" Cathy Rush. Others succumbed to chauvinist sports humor. In 1973 a *Philadelphia Evening News* picture of the Macs' tournament play was captioned "They Bounce Better Than the Guys Do," and when the cross-river Camden, N.J., *Courier-Post* covered Cathy Rush's 1974 appearance at the Philadelphia Sports Writers Association banquet—the first time a woman had been invited—the reporter included an honoree's remark that if he played for Rush, he'd "certainly feel motivated."[43]

But on the Immaculata beat, hard-nosed sports analysts softened. Maybe it was because the Philadelphia Sixers set a record for NBA losses in 1972–73, and journalists liked seeing someone win. But some, especially local reporters assigned to cover the Macs, said the sense of community they found with the team far outdistanced game thrills. "I find it so pleasant to think back on that time," said Dennis Daylor, who covered the Macs for the *Suburban Advertiser* in Wayne, Pennsylvania. The Immaculata players were "an extension of family" and gave him professionally "the happiest time of my life," Daylor said. "Not only were they a great team, but they were really nice kids," remembered Art Douglas, play-by-play announcer for local radio station WCOJ—the station to which the Camilla Hall sisters tuned their dials, known as the "Mighty Mac Voice of Chester County." Douglas said the Macs once played a game on his birthday and at halftime came out to present him with a cake and candles. Frank Farley, who did WCOJ's color commentary with Douglas, relished association with the team, which he said gave him the best gift of his career. "In life, everyone has a pinnacle you want to achieve," he said, "[and] being with the Macs in Madison Square Garden, the Mecca of sports, was that mission accomplished for Art Douglas and me."[44]

Even further, *Philadelphia Inquirer* sportswriter Mel Greenberg, known alternately as "the godfather of women's basketball" and "Mr. Women's Basketball," credited the Immaculata teams as "the catalyst of my existence." A particular fan of Marianne Crawford Stanley '76, Greenberg attended the Immaculata postseason banquet her senior year. "I remember the nuns singing and the whole atmosphere. I thought to myself, 'If I don't do something, all this is going to die.'" Shortly after that, Greenberg started calling coaches to compile the first women's basketball poll, which served as a national clearinghouse for information coaches needed. "You have to understand, the game was really in the dark ages," he told a reporter in March 2000. "Some of the coaches didn't even know the records of their next opponent." Greenberg continued to coordinate the poll, later published by the Associated Press. "Immaculata was responsible for the polls, no question about it," he said. "It's kind of funny how a Jewish guy found inspiration at a Catholic girls' school."[45]

Building the Community of Women

In Immaculata's second championship year, the same newspapers that covered Mighty Macs games also debated women's place in society. "Women's lib," the Equals Rights Amendment, and *Roe v. Wade* made headlines in 1972 through 1975. But almost no event of early seventies feminism fired popular imagination as much as the now-famous, nationally televised September 1973 tennis match between Billie Jean King and avowed male chauvinist Bobby Riggs. King won. It was possibly, as journalist Robert Lipsyte dubbed it, "the most spectacular public event of the modern women's movement." When the revolution arrived, sports ushered it in.[46]

Hardly a team of Billie Jean Kings, Immaculata players in the seventies inadvertently landed themselves on the front lines of the feminist movement. As they changed minds about women's basketball, they also changed minds about women. They did not consider themselves feminist and, true to their Catholic background, often repudiated aims of the libbers. But playing basketball as fine and fierce as any guys, they walked the walk, if they didn't talk the talk. Moreover, nurtured in a hothouse of Catholic support, team members took for granted that they could make the women's game exciting and approached their new opportunities with confidence. From that angle, "they were a few steps ahead in equality," said Immaculata student and fan Barbara Glunz Miller '71.[47]

In hindsight, it could seem ironic that Immaculata, a conservative Catholic college that never raised a finger for feminism, ended up three-time national champions rather than, say, its neighbor, West Chester State, a bastion of progressivism whose physical educators fought for years to organize the first women's tournaments. Indeed, some rival coaches seethed that Immaculata won the first championships, getting the glory for others' hard work. On the other hand, it is possible that Immaculatans played with great freedom precisely because they never took part in women's activism. They had grown up playing with boys, not demanding to play with boys. They assumed support of girls' hoops rather than asked for it. To them, the full-court game was not playing like men; it was just playing like athletes. Sidestepping the fight for equality, perhaps they had more energy for basketball. In any case, feminism "passed me by big time," said Lorrie Gable Finelli '78. "And I really think that it passed all of us by." She continued to explain. "We were doing what we knew. And, whether it was ignorance, whether it was blindness, apathy, you know, we were playing basketball, and we didn't care if people liked it or they didn't," she said. "We didn't care if Billie Jean King was playing center court. I don't remember having discussions whether we're female athletes or women's libbers. . . . And because we were at Immaculata, I don't think we had to deal with those issues because we were accepted from day one as we were."[48]

Coach Cathy Rush proved a woman of like mind with her players, if by a different route. Having played basketball at West Chester in the late sixties, Rush knew the political wranglings of physical educators. But as a young coach released from the half-court game, she saw the women's future in men's techniques. And she had ample time to study those techniques, attending numerous NBA games with her husband, Ed Rush, a league referee. "She was close to the highest level of the game," Theresa Shank Grentz '74 told a reporter in April 2000. "She taught things that were never taught at that time. We learned the techniques of man-to-man defense and boxing out back when everyone else played zones." In 1976, after *Daily Local News* reporter Randy Shantz watched Rush's team win a game with her experimental "platoon system," in which she used substitutions to alternate entire squads, he called her "the greatest innovator in the women's game today."[49]

Rush also adopted male coaches' habits of carefully organizing practices and fully researching opponents. In her second season, she figured out how to beat West Chester for the 1972 title, just a week after the team had slaughtered Immaculata in the regional tournament. Rush "was one of the first to think, wait a minute. Let's look at this team, figure out how to exploit it," said Jenepher Shillingford. "Let's look at our weapons and see how we can employ them. She did it naturally. You know, it was like, this is how you win a game."[50]

Rush got Immaculata to win games—big games—and then lunged at all the "women's first" opportunities success brought. In January 1975 Immaculata played the first nationally televised women's basketball game, against the University of Maryland. Both teams played sloppily, but the Mighty Macs won 80–48 anyway. When the Washington-area station WMAL–Channel 7 cut to a regularly scheduled program with 1:38 left in regulation, hundreds called to complain, and area journalists cried foul.[51]

A month later, when Immaculata played Queens at Madison Square Garden, Rush exhorted her team to play at a level more worthy of the national venue. It was another first for women, and Immaculata had the chance to prove girls' hoops could fill the Garden. On game day, the Garden had sold out its twelve thousand seats, and the arena brimmed with what *Wall Street Journal* reporter Gail Bronson described as a "tense, noisy atmosphere, more typical of a World Series game." But, technically, the women's matchup only served as the opening act for a men's game between Fairfield and Massachusetts. Had all these people just come to watch the NCAA men? After Immaculata defeated Queens in a tightly played game, that question was answered, as six thousand fans got up and left the stadium, while only half stayed to watch the men. Shortly afterward, Garden promoters' doubt that a women's game could draw fans seemed absurd. "What in the name of Bella Azbug, are Fairfield and Massachusetts doing in the feature game of a doubleheader that includes the defending national champ and a team that has gone to the nationals the past four years?" asked reporter Dave Hirshey in the New York *Daily News*. Other members of the press further asked why promoters paid the two women's teams only half as much as the men though they had obviously drawn at least half the crowd.[52]

Together, the televised game and the Madison Square Garden contest drew more fans to Immaculata basketball, publicized female athletes' genius, and proved that people would watch women's sports. Honored in *Sports Illustrated*'s International Women's Year roundup of 1975 athletic milestones, Immaculata players enjoyed their status as national representatives of women's basketball. "I'm not a women's lib-type person, but I'm glad that the public, male and female, is finally recognizing women's basketball for what it is," Marie Liguori '77 told a reporter in 1975. "The best thing about all the attention is that it's a big step forward for the game itself."[53]

Many players, however, said they saw the advance for the game less in the lights and cameras and more in the faces of worshipful young girls who saw the Mighty Macs play. Throngs of aspiring hoopsters kept team members signing autographs for hours after games. "They just wanted to come up and talk to us. . . . It was so fabulous," said Mary Scharff '77. "The little girls were, like, finally there was somebody to look up to other than a guy, and we were their . . . heroes." The girl-fans themselves said the Macs were their "role models." "I'd sit and watch the guards and point guards, and try to hold in memory their moves," said high school player Jeanine Driscoll. "I knew I was purposely watching to learn more about the game." More than that, she said, "the impact was that girls and women can be good people, good students, good athletes. . . . I wanted to be like them." Boys cheered the Mighty Macs, too. Brian McGlinchey, son of Immaculata alumna Wanda McGlinchey Ryan '57, was five years old when his mother started taking him to games. "My current love of basketball is firmly rooted in my childhood experience rooting for the Mighty Macs," he said. "I didn't think myself less of a 'man' for following a women's team. Perhaps my attendance . . . was actually one of life's lessons that taught me to respect women."[54]

Basketball and Community Change

Immaculata champions pulled into the spotlight with them constituencies of Immaculatans, Catholics, Philadelphians, and women. Unlikely fame for a bunch of Catholic girls was fun. It was also subversive. On or off campus, dealing with Catholics or non-Catholics, Immaculata collegians rarely found themselves at the top of social hierarchies. But in this sports windfall, players were uniquely authorized to influence those around them. And the team's actions did not just build folks up but also challenged them to change.

Challenging the Immaculata Community

As much as basketball unified and endorsed the Immaculata community, it also made its future contours clear. College administrators could not sustain big-time basketball without Immaculata becoming a very different place. If Immaculata continued to sponsor its team at the highest levels, they knew, it would have to offer more diverse programs, attract wealthier students, hire more lay teachers, build a bigger gym, offer athletic scholarships, and pay a full coaching staff, among other things. And while they relished the excitement of basketball, most sisters and students were "trying to maintain what was Immaculata for all the years that had been," said Lorrie Gable Finelli '78. "Change was not going to happen, and it certainly was not going to happen fast. . . . The majority of females at the school, that's why they were there. So, you were looking at a minority of women . . . who wanted change." Some were outright suspicious of basketball success. A few students even com-plained to new college president Sister Marie Antoine Buggy (1972–82) that they did not appreciate Immaculata becoming a "jock college."[55]

Even from the first tournament trip to Normal, events made clear that Immaculata administrators had little stomach for the priorities of big-time basketball. After sisters and players spent four frenzied days raising money, only eight players accompanied Rush to Illinois, which meant three team members—including one senior—had to stay behind. The decision left nuns heartsick. Parents of excluded players were outraged. The grounded team-mates themselves tried to understand, but they hurt, too. "I felt somewhat apart because of that," said one of the players. "You know, I had been set apart. And there's always this undercurrent of 'maybe I don't belong.'" When the team came home victorious, Immaculata celebrated, but quiet "anguish" over players who stayed home deepened, too. As necessary as it seemed at the time, the determination not to send the whole team left scars. Back on cam-pus, when the championship squad posed for its commemorative photo, some of the same excluded players inexplicably did not make the shoot. Al-ways competitive about basketball, Immaculatans had not foreseen a day when championships would come—as they often do—at the expense of bench players. Arguably as early as the spring of 1972, sisters began "drawing back" from big-time basketball rather than "aggressively going forward." The case of the left-behind players was only one of many new and uncomfortable situations the successful program posed. Non-Catholic students from dis-tant states enrolled purely to try out for basketball. Conflict erupted in the athletic department over fund allocation. Team members floated through college life in an increasingly exceptional atmosphere, missing days of class for photo shoots and road trips. "Many of the sisters were cautious and un-familiar with the changing of Immaculata thr[ough] basketball," Lorrie Gable Finelli '78 wrote.[6]

For the most part, Immaculata players, like their fellow students and teachers, said they liked Immaculata the way it was, without basketball run-ning the show. It became a point of pride—even a team myth—that "none of us went to I.C. to play basketball." The myth was partly true. "Our wins were always exciting, but it was, like, 'Get back on the airplane with your books,'" said Janet Young Eline '74. "I mean . . . basketball, that's on the side, but you're really here for your academics." But the myth was also partly false. The whole Catholic League always knew players could find good ball at Im-maculata, and soon the whole country knew, too. After the first champi-onship, some incoming players were frank that they only came to I.C. to play for Rush. Nevertheless, the official line, from Philadelphia players as well as the sisters, was that Immaculata kept athletics in "proper perspective": "no recruiting," "no scholarships," and "plenty of moral support," said Sister Marian William Hoben '44, addressing a mideighties Middle States Association gathering. "Basketball was a game to be played and enjoyed." The school ideal was frequently affirmed by journalists who, jaded by the ills of big-money sports, celebrated Immaculata's impoverished purity. Everyone said schoolwork came first at Immaculata partly because it did—but also because basketball success immediately threatened to change that.[57]

Cathy Rush also largely endorsed Immaculata's old way of doing things. Perhaps nothing spoke louder of her affinity for Immaculata priorities than her retirement in 1977. When Title IX took the women's game toward a new era of recruiting and scholarships, Rush left coaching, started a summer basketball camp program, and never looked back. Still, there were moments in her seven years at Immaculata when she might have welcomed some changes. The school vastly underpaid her, topping out at $1,800 per year, and she occasionally wondered aloud if the school appreciated the exposure basketball brought. Rush argued to reallocate physical education funds for basketball, which led to confrontations with other members of the athletic department. She begged for need-based scholarships for her players, who sometimes had trouble making tuition payments. And in asking for changes, she sometimes crossed invisible lines with the nuns—a situation her players attributed to her "not being Catholic." Their coach was "trying to be politically correct and not step on toes, but trying to move her team and what she needed into a bigger spotlight, [with] more finances and revenue," said Lorrie Gable Finelli '78. "So, I think she was caught between a rock and a hard place. She didn't completely understand the mentality. If you don't grow up in that, it's very, very strict, conservative."[58]

Some players might have welcomed a few changes, too, like not having to work at a convenience store until one in the morning for the privilege of representing the school. Playing basketball, some athletes' perspectives on Immaculata changed. Traveling the country, seeing other teams' resources, interacting with non-Catholics, and talking to journalists, the sport gave the Mighty Macs a "more liberal" liberal arts degree, said Lorrie. They realized that, emotional and spiritual support notwithstanding, the I.H.M.s were "probably trying to keep a fairly conservative grip on the community." When Cathy Rush left Immaculata, several basketball players transferred out. For the team as well as sisters, basketball not only cohered the Immaculata community but also changed it. Perhaps athletic success stitched the community together along the very tear it created, a sudden rip of the old Immaculata from the new.[59]

Challenging the Catholic Community

Seeing the world outside the Philadelphia Catholic community also gave players new perspective on their faith. If classes only intellectually conveyed, for example, the ecumenical spirit of Vatican II, players got it practically by hanging around Cathy Rush, who adored the sisters but was not above jokes. "She'd say, 'Oh, here come the penguins,'" said Dolly VanBuskirk Anderson '78. The nuns got her back, though, saying "'Oh, let's get you converted,'" said Janet Young Eline '74. "The jesting was all in fun." But as Catholic girls witnessed the good-natured back-and-forth between religious authority figures and a respected coach, a growing appreciation of the non-Catholic world wedged between them and the conservative elements of their faith community. For them, Cathy Rush was proof positive that good people came from different faiths. "She's a good moral person," Janet said. "I guess she had some good religious training in her childhood, too. I guess Baptists can do that."[60]

After the first championship, a few players of other religious backgrounds joined the team, from Protestants to nonreligious. Catholic teammates knew some sisters interacted more circumspectly with non-Catholic players. "Bless the sisters," said a Presbyterian player, "they really used to give me the hairy eyeball." Three African American women joined the team for the 1974–75 season as well. With these new teammates, players became friends with women whom many in the Catholic community distrusted on two fronts, religious and racial. But it was the real-life ordeal of one of their own that brought Catholic players face-to-face with Catholicism as their community lived it. Shortly before the 1975 national tournament, star point guard Marianne Crawford found out she was pregnant. She played almost every minute of the tournament and made the Kodak All-American team for her efforts. But by the summer, the news was out. Marrying her boyfriend of five years, Rich Stanley, Marianne delivered a baby girl, Michelle, in October.[61]

Marianne and Rich had been planning to marry anyway, and Marianne always assumed she would keep playing ball. Despite the marriage, however, many Immaculata sisters, players, and alumnae were "shocked" and "stunned." Marianne was the captain of what was, in the eyes of many, not only a great basketball team but a morally immaculate one. And for midseventies Catholics, pregnancy before marriage was still "a real conversation piece," said Jenepher Shillingford. Some community members questioned whether Marianne should be allowed to remain on the team. Sister Mary of Lourdes, who left Immaculata in 1972 to serve as a local high school principal, heard about the ruckus over at Immaculata. "They certainly weren't happy about it, and I don't think anybody thought she should have been playing," she said.[62]

Meanwhile, Marianne's Mighty Mac teammates watched events unfold. They knew how scandalized sisters and fans felt; they felt some of it themselves. They also knew the unwritten rule of a Catholic women's college: that without marrying, Marianne would have been expelled. Still, faced with a situation involving a beloved teammate, her well-liked boyfriend, and a new baby girl, players balked at the stigma. They embraced her. So did a handful of I.H.M.s. So did fellow students, who would take baby Michelle to the dorms during practice. And so did Cathy Rush, who insisted Marianne be allowed to play. Initially, Rush's stance could have derived as much from naïveté as principle. Oblivious to the weight of Catholic teaching, Rush had even jokingly harassed Marianne for not using birth control. Whatever the source of her position, however, Rush's commitment to Marianne deepened when she realized the ostracism she might face, not to mention the poverty, as a mother, wife, student, and basketball player. Several times after Michelle's birth, the new little family lived at Rush's house while they got on their feet.[63]

Players followed their Baptist coach's example, rallying around Marianne, against some of their own and fellow Catholics' instincts. But the lesson for all of them went beyond ecumenism. In this case, their actions said, it wasn't about being Catholic or Protestant or even right or wrong. It was about loving a friend. And, gradually, the force of coach and team support won others over. Eleven days after delivering, Marianne showed up at practice feeling "a little weak" and started doing scaled-back workouts to get ready for the season. "That's what she wanted to do," said Sister Mary of Lourdes. Shortly, players elected Marianne team captain for the second straight year.[64]

And as the season got under way, the scandal blew over. Naysayers quieted and then frankly admired the young woman who braved ignominy and went on to lead her team to a national semifinals finish in 1976. When Marianne graduated, Rush promptly hired her as assistant coach. And when Rush retired from coaching in 1977, several Immaculata players transferred to Virginia's Old Dominion University, which had just signed a new head coach: Marianne Crawford Stanley.

Challenging the Non-Catholic Community

While the team still interfaced with Catholic culture, they increasingly moved and played in the outside world. They played non-Catholic teams, dealt with secular media, and performed for the culturally Protestant public that followed their exploits. Ever since Kennedy was elected president in 1960, Catholics inhabited an America where overt anti-Catholic bigotry had diminished. But everyday alienation between Catholics and "Americans" remained. And in the early seventies, most Immaculata players still came from Philadelphia neighborhoods with immigrant relatives, large families, private schools, and isolated ways. When the church-raised basketball players entered secular arenas—dressed in skirted uniforms, accompanied by nuns, and serenaded by the blue-collar bucket brigade—they inevitably dealt with their exotic identity as Catholics and their contested identity as Americans.

But "sports have a tendency to be more accepting of everyone's differences," as Cathy Rush put it. And championships have a way of paving paths for acceptance all the more. Earning trophies, the Catholic girls also earned social capital. Not just on the basketball court but in public spaces from gyms and hotels to restaurants and award banquets, Immaculatans moved with confidence among people and events designed to honor their presence. For Catholics in the secular United States, it was an unusual sense of belonging. For whole championship seasons, basketball could make them feel at home in America.

Still, in otherwise non-Catholic tournament crowds, they stood out. Players couldn't hide their uniforms and fans, their long hair and St. Patrick's Day green ribbons. But talking to the press, they carried their Catholicism lightly. "We didn't make the fact that we were Catholic stand out," said Janet Young Eline '74. "We were just regular people." Downplaying Catholicism was not part of some scripted plan to build bridges to the American public. Probably players really just felt like average all-American girls. Or it is possible they liked breathing rare air and didn't think faith should be a basketball issue. Or they could have tempered Catholic identity as a defense against public curiosity. Whatever the motivation, they helped make the Catholic angle in sports-page reports mellow and positive. Writers tended to convey Immaculata players' religious affiliation as a charming quirk rather than a separatist identity. In the atmosphere of celebrity, Catholicism served as color commentary on the Mighty Macs' American dream come true.[65]

Did Immaculata players change minds about Catholicism? There are no facts and figures. But like Catholic sports celebrities from Knute Rockne and Rocky Marciano to Joe DiMaggio and Floyd Patterson, the Mighty Macs, on a smaller scale, contributed to a stock of public images of Catholics excelling in popular, unthreateningly "American" pursuits.

Championing the Community of Women

While the majority of reporters carried on a sports-page love affair with the Mighty Macs, not all media attention was so benign. Looking for an edgier angle, some reporters focused on the team's unconventional femininity. At a time when female athletes represented the vanguard of women's lib, they also

Theresa Shank signing autographs, February 1974.

threatened the male bastion of sports. Sometimes, Immaculatans inspired portrayals as creatures just past the era of "bloomers and blushes," too delicate and beautiful to sweat, along with other abundant physical descriptors. At other times, reporters regarded the team as "Amazons" so bereft of femininity "they seemed surprised we even combed our hair," said Theresa Shank Grentz '74.[66]

Underattuned to feminism and overschooled in grace, Rush and the Mighty Macs, one of the earliest and biggest women's sports stories, unwittingly broke in numerous male writers. With patience and humor, they answered ridiculous questions—such as what dress sizes they wore or whether male journalists could "equally" enter the Immaculata locker room for postgame interviews. It also probably eased rapport with the male media that, off the court, the Macs preferred conventional female attire of dresses and jewelry.[67]

Immaculata players did not speak as feminists. Instead, true to their backgrounds, they advocated both women's sports *and* women's traditional roles.

They could be "pioneers" but not the "women's lib-type" at the same time, they said, and brushed aside the popular equation of the two. As 1974 Player of the Year Theresa Shank Grentz insisted, traditional femininity and progressive sports unproblematically meshed. "After a game, we set our hair and get dressed up and boys take us out to dinner," she said. "We don't look anything like the awful stereotypes of female athletes."[68]

But some reporters capitalized on Immaculatans' endorsement of traditional femininity and heard little else. Articles assured sports-page readers that the best women's basketball team in the nation decried women's lib and had no problem with makeup. In particular, some reporters transformed Cathy Rush, whom players knew as a brilliant strategist and fierce taskmaster, into a hapless and harmless Barbie doll. Rush was a lifelong athlete who at five years old tried to turn into a boy by kissing her elbow, because she "thought boys had it easier." After playing basketball and majoring in phys-ed at West Chester, Rush coached at a local public middle school and high school. Then, as a young wife and mother, she got restless staying home and took the part-time Immaculata job to while away some pleasant hours while husband Ed traveled as an official for the NBA. She always firmly said family came before basketball. Nevertheless, Rush anticipated the later "super-woman" phenomenon by two decades, steadily building an ace program while her baby son played in a portable crib nearby. "Cathy . . . was like a sponge," said athletic director Jenepher Shillingford. "She was a young, wonderful gal who was just doing this as a little pastime and then suddenly got into it."[69]

But in the media's hands, Rush's life turned into endless commentary fetishizing her beauty, fashion sense, pregnancies, children, and husband, in articles such as "Immaculata's Formula: Defense and Diapers" and "Pregnant Coach Leads Team to Championship." If the articles mentioned her coaching, they often also insinuated that the young woman whose winning percentage approached UCLA men's coach John Wooden only succeeded because her NBA-ref husband coached from behind the scenes. And when Rush carefully explained to the press that she was not a feminist because she worried "equality" could send boys flooding to girls' teams, the headline opportunistically screamed, "'Knock It Off, Libbers!' Pleads Cathy Rush."[70]

While many sportswriters cultivated a reassuringly conventional image of Rush, they struggled to reconcile her players' ferocity with their femininity. Asked time and again about hairstyles and boyfriends, players made some headway convincing reporters they were girls like any other girls. Writing for the *Main Line Times*, Mary Boardman happily reported that "the image of 'female jocks' most clearly does not apply to them. On the contrary, they think a pleasing appearance is important, . . . and sports represent only one of their varied, meaningful activities."[71]

Other journalists were not so persuaded. At the 1975 national tournament, rival Wayland Baptist players passed Immaculatans in the hotel and talked some trash, calling them "ugly." It was only the latest insult from Wayland, whose coach, Dean Weese, had told the press, "We won eight AAU titles before Immaculata even thought of basketball, but I understand you media people in New York don't know anything about Texas, don't know anything about the Flying Queens." The Macs proceeded to school Wayland in a blood match that left Weese screaming and his players in tears. But the press heard about the "ugly" remark. Shortly after, Cathy Rush found herself defending her players' looks, while a Macs fan and salon owner invited the whole team over for a makeover, "to shed the 'ugly' label for all time." Then, following them to the salon, the *Philadelphia Inquirer* ran a story called "The Uglies Become the Swans," with a large photo spread. The next day, picked up by the Associated Press, the story was reprinted in hundreds of papers as far away as Wisconsin, California, and Kentucky. No other Mighty Macs story—not even coverage of the championships—got nearly such wide circulation.[72]

Constantly trapped between being ladies or libbers, the Mighty Macs grew tired of insisting they were as feminine as the next girl. "If I'm a female jock, where is my jock strap?" Dolly VanBuskirk Anderson '78 asked. "It was crazy." Players gradually became more guarded with the press. And sometimes they tried to talk about femininity differently. Instead of straining to pair athleticism with the fairer sex, Immaculatans began to say womanhood was whatever women did. A few reporters published their words. In 1973 Theresa Shank Grentz '74 told a reporter that a "feminine" sport was any sport in which females participated, while Marianne Crawford Stanley '76 described herself, in the reporter's words, as "just a great basketball player who just happens to be a woman." Another reporter quoted Marie Liguori '77 saying her teammates were just people "who love to play basketball, that's all." Immaculata basketeers who dealt daily with stereotypes began to broaden their own ideas of what counted as feminine. Short of endorsing feminism, they pushed beyond traditional Catholic limits, hinting to the press of a world in which no particular activity constituted—or compromised—womanhood.[73]

• • •

Enjoying status as authority figures and role models in the circles that supported them, the Mighty Macs affirmed and questioned communities of Immaculatans and Philadelphians, Catholics and non-Catholics, women and men. In turn, the team gave fans an alternative community, with which, in fragmented times, many identified for different reasons.

The Mighty Macs never became feminists. The resistance to "lib" in barrier-breaking Immaculata players stemmed mostly, of course, from upbringing in a faith culture with long-standing suspicion of feminism. But there might have been other factors as well. Perhaps for Immaculatans, who grew up in the women's basketball hothouse of Catholic Philadelphia, there was simply little contradiction between womanhood and athletics. Perhaps Catholic women who played basketball anticipated some freedoms of body, gender, and identity sought by secular feminism. Or maybe church support of the game they loved cultivated loyalty to an institution that, by the seventies, other Catholic women were criticizing.

In any case, the Immaculata champions did their small part to help liberate national attitudes. As *Main Line Times* editors wrote, "a lot more doubting men would be won over to feminism by playing a game of taps with Theresa Shank than all the words Gloria Steinem could ever write." But Immaculata players weren't concerned about winning over men—or women—to feminism. Nor were they out to change their school, town, church, or nation. They just wanted little girls across the country to have as much fun as they did, breaking free of a defender on the open court, dribbling and spinning through traffic, and pulling up for the sweet jumper. For them, that was emancipation.[74]

IMMACULATA BASKETBALL AND
U.S. RELIGIOUS HISTORY

As the seventies progressed, Title IX began to shape women's basketball. The AIAW began to include scholarship-granting schools in its national tournament in 1973, and in 1975 Delta State, with scholarship players, won the victory trophy away from three-time champion Immaculata. Cathy Rush coached the school to the AIAW tournament finals again in 1976, where they lost a second time to Delta State, and to the semifinals in 1977, where they lost to Louisiana State University. The balance of power was shifting. As public university programs suddenly found themselves with money to recruit and fund the best athletes, they eclipsed the brief heyday of small anomalies like Immaculata, Queens, and Federal City. The shift benefited thousands of women, who could now, like their male counterparts, go to school on athletic scholarships. And it improved the game of women's basketball, which could now offer young girls goals and models as they fell in love with basketball in increasing numbers across the country.

Title IX also brought some unanticipated setbacks, however. The era of women's control of women's athletics was suddenly over. Coeducational institutions that combined programs to save money usually put men over women's sports programs; gradually, men replaced women as coaches of women's teams, as well. Also in the years after Title IX, the men's collegiate sports governing body, the National Collegiate Athletics Association (NCAA), noticed the new market and new money in women's basketball and in 1981 persuaded the AIAW to merge. The NCAA offered the experience and power needed to regulate the big-money enterprise women's basketball

Jimmy Kennedy, nephew of Rene Muth '76, picking up confetti at the airport after the 1974 championship.
PHOTOGRAPH BY WELCHMAN/COURTESY OF IMMACULATA COLLEGE.

was quickly becoming. But the organization's monopoly on collegiate sports created as well as solved problems in the women's game.[1]

By the time fans, journalists, and participants started to notice the few downsides to Title IX, the spotlight on Immaculata had faded. College administrators consciously chose not to try to keep up with scholarship-granting schools, instead taking steps to reorient campus sports life away from big-time basketball and toward physical education for all. Cathy Rush retired after the 1977 season and started in Philadelphia a successful series of summer basketball camps. Her players went on to careers as teachers, mothers, doctors, businesswomen, and coaches at all levels, from NCAA Division I to parish CYO teams. National-caliber players no longer considered going to Immaculata. The formerly Immaculata-bound Catholic League girls with huge basketball talent now enrolled at schools that paid them to play. And the sisters, students, and teams of Immaculata got used to a quieter campus, where only the national championship trophies displayed in glass cases in Alumnae Hall stood as silent witnesses to past basketball glory.

• • •

The story of basketball at Immaculata College has just begun to receive the attention it deserves in the history of American sports. But, as I have tried to suggest, this same story—both the seventies glory days and the three previous decades of unheralded fun for young Catholic women—also witnesses to underattended dimensions of American Catholic history. Immaculata basketball players loved their sport because it both nestled them in the Catholic community and distinguished them from it. In turn, the church community mostly embraced and sometimes defended against its girl ballplayers. But it didn't defend very hard. Mostly, it just stood there, another spectator watching with awe as the shots went up and the points rained down.[2]

I leave this story wondering about other ordinary Catholics hidden in plain view, affirming and subverting Catholicism in spaces and practices we haven't yet noticed. If an overwhelmingly conservative and rigorously gendered Catholic subculture nurtured girls' basketball, I wonder what else we miss because we're not looking in the right places. Might we discover something new if we explored piety in neighborhood playgroups, teachers' lounges, or urban botanicas? And if Catholic women hoopsters changed their religious milieu just by having fun in an activity the church encouraged, I wonder what practices we have overlooked because we're not asking the right people. Might we discover something fresh if we asked musicians about playing polka, caterers about cooking church dinners, bishops about golf outings?

If we looked in those places and asked those people, I imagine the history of U.S. Catholicism—largely framed by themes of immigration and nativism, devotionalism and Thomism, ethnicity and acculturation, Americanism and Vatican II—would change. We would start to ask for whom, when, and why these themes were important. For example, were the Immaculata basketball players more preoccupied with becoming Americans or with honing their jump shots? Did they think more about the Virgin Mary, model mother, or the Virgin Mary, supernatural cheerleader? Did they care more about the changes of Vatican II or roster changes for next season? Obviously, these are not really either/or questions. But their answers are more ambivalent than we previously imagined. And overall it is clear that playing basketball affected how these Catholic women thought about identity, gender, and religion—and that basketball tells us something new about Catholicism. With these new locations and practitioners, we stumble upon different themes—such as pleasure and pain, subjection and identity, whiteness and blackness, compromise and resistance. And as fresh themes increasingly reveal Catholicisms under daily revision by those who call themselves Catholics, we might find ourselves narrating a new Catholic history from "way, way below."[3]

The story of Immaculata basketball also affirms new approaches to U.S. religious history. If basketball at Immaculata reveals heterogeneity in what had appeared the unrelenting conformism of mid-twentieth-century Philadelphia Catholicism, surely other less homogenizing faiths might also turn out to be composites of everyday accommodation and resistance. But to see religion in America this way, we need to look away from specifically religious practices. On the margins of institutional piety, we can start to see what lived religion looks like: Methodist camp kids dialing psychic hotlines, Muslim clerics planting community gardens, and Jewish women organizing cooking clubs.

Looking off to the side of explicitly religious practice does not deny or devalue institutional religion. Rather, it takes it more seriously, not as a coherent, disembodied entity but as a group of people constantly engaging with others, in harmony and dissonance, from different positions of power. Studies of bishops as well as basketball players, convents as well as gymnasiums, could disclose the full extent to which lived religion makes up institutions. Lived religion also takes ordinary religious people more seriously, suggesting that we might learn to see institutional piety differently when a Presbyterian likes professional wrestling, a Buddhist loves to shop at Wal-Mart, or an A.M.E. deacon enjoys chatting online.

Ultimately, I can only imagine how it would look to plot U.S. religious history by multiple stories of lived religion. But this story of Immaculata basketball—and others like it—does suggest we may find new spaces, new players, and new themes if we look for them *within* the churches and synagogues, denominations and conferences, mosques and temples we think we already know.

. . .

In this project, I discovered anew that narrating always distorts as much as it clarifies, however particular and local the narrative. Or, to put it another way, I realized that narrating is always as much art as fact. I sometimes wished I could just compile all the women's memories or edit them into a documentary film. I wished that words could just point instead of interpret. But then this project would not be a book but something else. So I told a story, this story, their story, and mine, too. And in the process I constantly found myself humbled at the density of meaning and the ineffability of memory. Now, after living with players' recollections for four years, I remember Immaculata basketball, too.

I remember meeting with Sister Mary of Lourdes McDevitt and her buddy, Sister Cor Immaculata Connors, both in their eighties, in the cool living room of a tree-shaded convent in Wayne, Pennsylvania. Sister Mary of Lourdes kept making us both laugh, and Sister Cor served a quavering tray of juice and cookies. Sister Mary of Lourdes said several times that she had no idea how she ended up in the convent, much less the most celebrated president of Immaculata. Growing up playing basketball, baseball, tennis, football, and swimming, she always longed just to teach physical education and coach basketball. "And then here I landed," she said. "I don't know why I didn't get to be a phys ed teacher." She looked at me appraisingly and said, "I think I could take you on anytime."[4]

I remember visiting Dee Cofer Cull, a graduate of 1955 and team captain, whom one of her teammates described as "a tiny thing with springs in her feet." She was now divorced and worked in a bakery in Media, Pennsylvania. I found her at the shop just as a huge thunderstorm gathered outside to darken the late summer afternoon. Looking with her at a black-and-white team picture that showed her plump dark lips and outrageous dimpled smile, I said, "How did your lips get that color without lipstick?" She said, "I don't know. Maybe I was sucking on one of those Italian ices or something." She paused and said, "My husband said that's why he married me, my smile." When I left, she packed two huge bags of pastries for me to take home to my family.[5]

I remember reading a story on a survey from Sue Forsyth O'Grady '72, a senior on the first championship team, who said she sat on the bench most of the time but loved playing anyway. She got engaged to her boyfriend as a sophomore at Immaculata and was married for her last two college years. Recalling what first came to mind about the locker room, she wrote she remembered one day after practice "realizing that I had bent one of the prongs on my engagement ring," loosening the diamond. As I read her words, I wondered—and I still do—why she remembered that particular moment and what it meant.[6]

I cannot say what their memories mean. Or mine. In this book, I have been making meaning, too, embracing and contesting their words. And returning to them again and again. Sue's account of her diamond, jarred during that rough-and-tumble practice, stayed with me. A treasured diamond, set in a ring, emblem of future marriage and touchstone of womanhood, almost lost on the court. For me, it signaled the small, ordinary ways these young women athletes changed their religious environment. They might never have consciously or broadly questioned the path of traditional Catholic womanhood laid out before them. But they found in basketball a strategy, a lever, a loosening of limits, tangible in their very bodies, as they practiced, played, prayed, and delighted in basketball, day after day.

APPENDIX A:
IMMACULATA COLLEGE BASKETBALL SURVEY

Answers anonymous—please use other side or additional sheets if necessary*

1. What is your age? _____
   graduation year? _____
   hometown? _____
   high school? _____
   ethnic or racial background? _____
   religious affiliation? (Circle one)
        Roman Catholic   other (please specify)_____
   association with basketball program? (Circle one)
        player   cheerleader   manager
   Were you a commuter or resident student? _____

2. What was your father's education level and profession? _____
   Your mother's?_____

3. Would you describe your family as poor, working-class, middle-class or upper-class
   when you attended Immaculata? _____

4. Did you play/manage/cheer for sports other than basketball in college? ____
   If so, what ones? _____

*This survey was mailed in the spring of 1998. In the spring of 2002 I mailed requests for
permission to use respondents' real names.*

5. How would you rate your general experience in college? Circle one:
    1 — very negative
    2 — mostly negative
    3 — equally good and bad
    4 — mostly positive
    5 — very positive
    Please explain:

6. How would you rate teacher and administration (sisters and lay) support of the basketball program? Circle one:
    1 — very unsupportive
    2 — mostly unsupportive
    3 — both supportive and unsupportive
    4 — mostly supportive
    5 — very supportive
    Please explain:

7. How would you rate Church (priests, archdiocese) support of women's basketball? Circle one:
    1 — very unsupportive
    2 — mostly unsupportive
    3 — both supportive and unsupportive
    4 — mostly supportive
    5 — very supportive
    Please explain:

8. How would you rate your fellow students' support of the basketball team? Circle one:
    1 — very unsupportive
    2 — mostly unsupportive
    3 — equally supportive and unsupportive
    4 — mostly supportive
    5 — very supportive
    Please explain:

9. What other campus groups did you belong to?

10. What did you do for fun in college (e.g. hanging out, dances, dates, hobbies)?

11. What kinds of benefits and values did your association with basketball give you?

12. What do you remember was Catholic about your basketball experience? Check all that apply, and please specify:
    1. practice rituals _____
    2. game rituals _____

3. locker room rituals _____
4. pre-game rituals _____
5. post-game rituals _____
6. private prayer _____
7. collective prayer _____
8. uniforms or other apparel (medals, jewelry) _____
9. sisters/chaplain _____
10. team mascot _____
11. cheers _____
12. fans _____
13. other _____
What purpose did these Catholic features of basketball serve, in your experience?

13. Did your teachers and/or the Church seem to view basketball as part of Catholicism or separate from it? How so?

14. What, if anything, was Catholic/religious about basketball **to you**?

15. Has Catholicism/religion been a part of your life since college? _____ If yes, how so?

16. Were there any disadvantages to your association with basketball in your opinion?

17. Compared to other sports and activities available at Immaculata, was basketball more or less popular than other activities? How so?

18. What was the Immaculata basketball "type" of young woman? Circle one:
   1 — very tomboyish
   2 — somewhat tomboyish
   3 — different for different players
   4 — somewhat feminine
   5 — very feminine
   Please explain:

19. What is the first story or memory that comes to mind about you or someone else **trying out for the team**?

20. What is the first story or memory that comes to mind about the **locker room** or **restroom** where the team met and changed before and after games and practice?

21. What is the first story or memory that comes to mind about the **games** you played, cheered, or managed (memories of the events, or of physical or emotional feelings)?

22. What is the first story or memory that comes to mind about **going to chapel** together or **visiting Camilla Hall** as a team?

23. What is the first story or memory that comes to mind about the team **road trips** and **away games**?

24. What is the first story or memory that comes to mind about **championship** games, **tournament** games or **postseason** play?

25. What is your happiest memory from your Immaculata basketball experience?

26. What is your most difficult memory from your Immaculata basketball experience?

27. Would you currently describe yourself as poor, working-class, middle-class or upper-class? _____
    What is/was your work? _____
    Are/were you single, religious, married, widowed or divorced? _____
    If married or religious, at what age did you marry/enter? _____
    How many children, if any, do you have? _____

28. What would you *estimate* was the percentage of your Immaculata classmates who left Immaculata for financial or other reasons? _____% These women, not listed in the Alumnae Directory, are hard to find. Would you be willing to share names, addresses and phone numbers of basketball players, cheerleaders or managers whom you know and who did not graduate? If so, please list below.

THANK YOU for your time and help!   Please send to:

Julie Byrne
[address]
[fax]

APPENDIX B:
SURVEYS, INTERVIEWS, CORRESPONDENCE,
AND UNPUBLISHED MEMOIRS

All sources are former basketball players unless otherwise noted.

Surveys

Kathryn Bansbach Lyons '37	KBL37, age 82, ques. 5.9.98
Helen McElroy '44	HM44, age 74, ques. 6.13.98
Player '44	Player '44, age 74, ques. 7.22.98
Irene Schultes Jordan '45	ISJ45, age 73, ques. 6.1.98
Player A '45	Player A '45, age 73, ques. 5.18.98
Player B '45	Player B '45, age 74, ques. 6.27.98
Eva "Evie" Adams Atkinson '46	EAA46, age 72, ques. 6.15.98
Mary Mawhinney Puglielli '46	MMP46, age 74, ques. 5.6.98
Sister Agnes Frederick Blee, S.N.D., '47	AFB+47, age 71, ques. 6.18.98
Student '47	Student '47, age 72, ques. 5.20.98
Player A '48	Player A '48, age 71, ques. 7.10.98
Fruff Fauerbach Timby '50	FFT50, age 70, ques. 7.1.98
Anne Carroll Camp '51	ACC51, age 68, ques. 5.10.98
Player '51	Player '51, age 69, ques. 5.20.98
Helen Stoerlein Connors '52 (*cheerleader*)	HSC52, age 67, ques. 5.18.98
Marcella Rominger Lusby '52	MRL52, age 68, ques. 5.20.98
Player A '52	Player A '52, age 66, ques. 5.4.98
Player B '52	Player B '52, age 67, ques. 6.18.98
Player C '52	Player C '52, age 68, ques. 6.20.98
Jean Doris '53	JD53, age 66, ques. 5.10.98
Joan Clements Fromm '53	JCF53, age 66, ques. 7.27.98

Ann McSorley Lukens '53	AML53, age 67, ques. 5.22.98
Patricia Furey McDonnell '53	PFM53, age 66, ques. 5.15.98
Joan Biegler Snyder '53 (*manager*)	JBS53, age 67, ques. 6.13.98
Player A '53	Player A '53, age 66, ques. 5.8.98
Joan Davis Tynen '54 (*cheerleader*)	JDT54, age 65, ques. 5.28.98
Dolores "Dee" Cofer Cull '55	DCC55, age 65, ques. 6.27.98
Manager '55	Manager '55, age 64, ques. 6.30.98
Bernadette Ellis McBeth '56 (*cheerleader*)	BEM56, age 63, ques. 10.6.98
Dolores Giordano Prokapus '56	DGP56, age 62, ques. 6.5.98
Player '56	Player '56, age 63, ques. 5.4.98
Geraldine Ferrari Burton '57 (*cheerleader*)	GFB57, age 63, ques. 6.23.98
Alvina DeLazzari Long '57	ADL57, age 62, ques. 7.20.98
Cheerleader '57	Cheerleader '57, age 62, ques. 5.15.98
Player '57	Player '57, age 62, ques. 6.17.98
Marcia Baylor Donnelly '58	MBD58, age 61, ques. 9.22.98
Margaret Mary "Meg" Kenny Kean '58	MMKK58, age 62, ques. 7.9.98
Player '59	Player '59, age 61, ques. 6.20.98
Rosemary McNichol Walsh '60	RMW60, age 60, ques. 5.23.98
Margaret Klopfle Devinney '62	MKD62, age 57, ques. 7.28.98
Mary Murphy Schmelzer '62	MMS62, age 57, ques. 5.24.98
Sister M. Charles Edward Woodward, I.H.M., '62 (*manager*)	MCEW+62, age 57, ques. 6.2.98
Maureen Callahan Bigham '63	MCB63, age 56, ques. 5.23.98
Margaret Monahan Hogan '63	MMH63, age 57, ques. 6.10.98
Therese "Terri" Murphy McNally '63	TMM63, age 56, ques. 5.25.98
Cheerleader '63	Cheerleader '63, age 57, ques. 5.18.98
Mary Jane Renshaw Lewandowski '64	MJRL64, age 58, ques. 8.4.98
Mary Louise McCahon Noone '65	MLMN65, age 54, ques. 6.22.98
Bernadette "Bunny" Naughton DeArmond '66	BND66, age 54, ques. 6.1.98
Lynn Hubbard Ouellette '66 ("*orange girl*")	LHO66, age 52, ques. 6.23.98
Marie Olivieri Russell '66	MOR66, age 53, ques. 6.27.98
Marianne Specht Siecko '66	MSS66, age 53, ques. 6.17.98
Adrienne Friaglia Cyran '67	AFC67, age 52, ques. 5.10.98
Barbara Flanigan '68	BF68, age 51, ques. 8.17.98
Izanne Leonard Haak '70	ILH70, age 49, ques. 5.8.98
Patricia LaRocco '71	PL71, age 48, ques. 5.10.98
Susan Forsyth O'Grady '72	SFO72, age 48, ques. 6.24.98
Maureen Mooney '73	MM73, age 46, ques. 9.3.98
Janet Young Eline '74	JYE74, age 45, ques. 8.8.98
Jean Brashears Vause '74 (*manager*)	JBV74, age 45, ques. 6.5.98
Player '75	Player '75, age 45, ques. 5.10.98

Dolly VanBuskirk Anderson '78   DVA78, age 43, ques. 7.26.99

Lorrie Gable Finelli '78   LGF78, age 41, ques. 5.15.98

Laureen Mann '78   LM78, age 42, ques. 5.26.98

Interviews

Immaculata Graduates

Sister Mary of Lourdes McDevitt,   MLM+36, age 83, int. 6.30.98; age 87,
   I.H.M. '36 (*president* emerita)   int. 8.16.02

Josephine Valentine '38   JV38, age 81, int. 7.20.98

Josephine McFarland '42   JM42, age 77, int. 7.20.98

Anna Maria Reilly '43   AMR43, age 76, int. 7.21.98

Sister Marian William Hoben,   MWH+44, age 74, int. 10.16.97
   I.H.M. '44 (*president* emerita)

Player '44   Player '44, age 74, int. 6.23.98

Frances Gercke Campbell '45   FGC45, age 74, int. 5.12.9

Player B '45   Player B '45, age 74, int. 7.24.98

Player C '45   Player C '45, age 74, int. 6.24.98

Eva "Evie" Adams Atkinson '46   EAA46, age 72, int. 6.17.98

Mary A. Burke Flaherty '46   MABF46, age 73, int. 7.24.98

Rosemary Duddy McFadden '46   RDM46, age 73, int. 7.9.98

Student '47   Student '47, age 72, int. 7.29.98

Cheerleader '49   Cheerleader '49, age 70, int. 7.23.98

Mary Frank McCormick '50   MFM50, age 69, int. 3.17.98

Sister Cecile Marie Phelan, I.H.M. '50   CMP+50, age 69, int. 6.25.98, int. 8.6.98
   (*student, professor*)

Monica Burns Atkinson '51   MBA51, age 68, int. 7.22.98

Sister Marie Albert Kunberger,   MAK+51, age 68, int. 1.1.98, int. 8.6.98
   I.H.M. '51 (*student, professor*)

Player C '52   Player C '52, age 68, int. 6.3.98

Sister Therese Marita Dignam,   TMD+53, age 66, int. 7.2.98, int. 8.6.98
   I.H.M. '53 (*student*)

Jean Doris '53   JD53, age 66, int. 6.8.98

Player B '53   Player B '53, age 66, int. 5.11.98

Mary Frances Heaney Backe '54   MFHB54, age 65, int. 8.26.98
   (*cheerleader*)

Marian Collins Mullahy '54   MCM54, age 65, int. 6.17.98, int. 6.23.98

Manager '54   Manager '54, age 65, int. 7.21.98

Dolores "Dee" Cofer Cull '55   DCC55, age 65, int. 6.26.98

Helen Frank Dunigan '56   HFD56, age 63, int. 7.23.98

Sister Marie Roseanne Bonfini,   MRB+57, age 61, int. 10.16.97
   I.H.M. '57 (*president* emerita)

Geraldine Ferrari Burton '57   GFB57, age 63, int. 6.14.98
   (*cheerleader*)

Pauline Callahan Earl '57   PCE57, age 62, int. 7.23.98

Player '57	Player '57, age 62, int. 6.11.98
Joanne Seemans Kolen '58	JSK58, age 61, int. 6.23.98
Margaret Guinan Delaney '62	MGD62, age 57, int. 7.21.98
Epiphany Pantaleo Collins '64	EPC64, age 55, int. 6.11.98
Mary Jane Renshaw Lewandowski '64	MJRL64, age 58, int. 8.4.98
Gloria Rook Schmidt '64	GRS64, age 55, int. 8.5.98
Cheerleader '64	Cheerleader '64, age 55, int. 7.20.98
Mary Louise McCahon Noone '65	MLMN65, age 54, int. 6.22.98
Marie Olivieri Russell '66	MOR66, age 53, int. 6.26.98
Kathleen Clark '70 (*student, professor*)	KC70, age 49, int. 6.10.98
Christine Lammer DiCiocchio '70	CLD70, age 49, int. 6.8.98
Barbara Glunz Miller '71 (*student*)	BGM71, age 48, int. 7.30.98
Elizabeth "Betty Ann" Hoffman Quinn '73	EAHQ73, age 46, int. 7.2.98
Janet Young Eline '74	JYE74, age 45, int. 8.8.98
Mary Scharff '77	MS77, age 42, int. 10.16.97
Dolly VanBuskirk Anderson '78	DVA78, age 43, int. 7.9.99
Lorrie Gable Finelli '78	LGF78, age 41, int. 7.23.98

Other Interviews

Sister Mary Hayes, S.N.D. (*professor, Trinity College, Washington, D.C.*)	MH+, int. 5.15.97
Sister Marita David "Toddy" Kirsch, I.H.M.	MDK+, age 71, int. 1.9.98; age 75, int. 8.21.02
Sister Virginia Assumpta McNabb, I.H.M. (*professor*)	VAM+, age 65, int. 6.25.98
Margaret "Mimi" McNamee (*Sacred Heart Academy player*)	MM, age 44, int. 5.8.98
Player	Player, age 60, int. 6.6.98
Cathy Rush (*coach, 1970–77*)	CR, age 53, int. 8.20.02
Jenepher Shillingford (*coach, 1962–70*)	JS, age 66, int. 8.25.99; age 69, int. 8.20.02
Student	Student, age 51, int. 7.12.98
Sister Loretta Maria Tenbusch, I.H.M. (*professor*)	LMT+, age 78, int. 10.17.97

Correspondence

Kathryn Bansbach Lyons '37	KBL37, age 83, corr. 5.2.98
Helen McElroy '44	HM44, age 74, corr. 6.15.98
Frances Gercke Campbell '45	FGC45, age 75, corr. 5.16.98
Player B '45	Player B '45, age 74, corr. 5.30.98
Player B '48	Player B '48, age 72, corr. 5.16.98
Joan Davis Tynen '54	JDT54, age 65, corr. 5.28.98
Manager '55	Manager '55, age 64, corr. 6.30.98
Player '57	Player '57, age 62, corr. 6.1.98

Mary Murphy Schmelzer '62	MMS62, age 57, corr. 7.26.00 (email)
Margaret Monahan Hogan '63	MMH63, age 57, corr. 6.1.98; age 58, corr. 11.22.99 (email)
Barbara Flanigan '68	BF68, age 51, corr. 8.17.98

Unpublished Memoirs

Marie Schultes McGuinness (*coach, 1944–46*), "I was 20 years old in 1943 . . ."	MSM, age 75, mem. 7.13.98.
Leo Mooney, "The Mighty Macs—Brigadoon Revisited" (sent with completed survey by daughter Maureen Mooney '73)	LM, mem. 9.3.98.

NOTES

Introduction: Philadelphia Hoop and Catholic Fun

1. "Owlettes Lose 1st in 4 Years to Immaculata," *Philadelphia Record*, March 6, 1946, Archbishop Furey Scrapbook, Gabriele Library Archives, Immaculata College, Pennsylvania (ICGLA). This article states that the crowd of more than a thousand was "a record for Conwell Hall."

2. "Managers Settle '46 Basketball Schedule," *The Immaculatan* (TI) 13, no. 3 (December 14, 1945): 6. Issues of *The Immaculatan* can be found at ICGLA.

3. "Mythical City Championship," "city crown," and "city title" were phrases used by former Immaculata players I interviewed as well as journalists for the college and local papers. Fruff Fauerbach Timby '50 wrote, "When we beat [Temple], among ourselves, we won the 'city' title; there was no such rank at that time" (FFT50, age 70, ques. 21, 7.1.98). In an article in *The Immaculatan*, the author wrote that Immaculata maintained its "hold on the mythical City Championship for the second consecutive year" ("Immaculata Beats Temple to Take City Crown," TI 14, no. 6 [April 23, 1947]: 3).

4. Dora Lurie predicted Temple's defeat in "Small Gymnasium Fails to Daunt Immaculata: Looms as Threat to Temple's Streak," *Philadelphia Inquirer*, March 3, 1946, Archbishop Furey Scrapbook, ICGLA. Newspaper reports after the game included Harvey Pollack, "Immaculata Girls Snap Temple String," *Philadelphia Evening Bulletin*, March 6, 1946; and Dora Lurie, "Temple Loses to Immaculata: 31-Game Streak Ends as Main Line Girls Win Thriller, 33–32," *Philadelphia Inquirer*, March 6, 1946, both in Archbishop Furey Scrapbook, ICGLA.

5. For game details, I drew on Pollack, "Immaculata Girls"; Lurie, "Temple Loses"; "Mainliners Crush Wise Old Owlettes, 33–32," TI 13, no. 5 (March 25, 1946): 5; and Helen O. Mankin, "Unbeaten Immaculata Girls Win City Court Title," *Philadelphia Evening Bulletin*, March 16, 1946, Archbishop Furey Scrapbook, ICGLA.

6. MDK+, age 71, int. 1.9.98. The screaming timekeeper is mentioned in Jeanmarie Dunn, "I.C. by Jeanmarie," TI 13, no. 5 (March 25, 1946): 5. Eva Adams Atkinson '46 remembered Furey's declaration of a holiday: EAA46, age 72, ques. 25, 6.15.98.

7. MDK+, age 71, int. 1.9.98; MMP46, age 74, ques. 25, 5.6.98. Another player who said this win over Temple was her happiest basketball memory was EAA46, age 72, ques. 25, 6.15.98.

8. A body of U.S. Catholic social history shows how particular Catholic communities or groups lived their faith in creative tension with their church and the wider culture. Robert A. Orsi launched this scholarship with *The Madonna of 115th Street: Faith and Community in Italian Harlem, 1880–1950* (New Haven: Yale University Press, 1985). Other studies include Orsi's *Thank You, St. Jude: Women's Devotion to the Patron Saint of Hopeless Causes* (New Haven: Yale University Press, 1996); Thomas A. Tweed, *Our Lady of the Exile: Diasporic Religion at a Cuban Catholic Shrine in Miami* (New York: Oxford, 1997); Paula M. Kane, *Separatism and Subculture: Boston Catholicism, 1900–1920* (Chapel Hill: University of North Carolina Press, 1994); Karen McCarthy Brown, *Mama Lola: A Voudou Priestess in Brooklyn* (Berkeley: University of California Press, 1991); John T. McGreevy, *Parish Boundaries: The Catholic Encounter with Race in the Twentieth-Century Urban North* (Chicago: University of Chicago Press, 1996); and Colleen McDannell, *Material Christianity: Religion and Popular Culture in America* (New Haven: Yale University Press, 1995). I owe my personal introduction to the social study of Catholicism to my father, Donald E. Byrne Jr., who took me on field trips to Catholic street festivals in Pennsylvania's coal regions in the late seventies. See Donald E. Byrne Jr., "Folklore and the Study of American Religion," in *Encyclopedia of the American Religious Experience: Studies of Traditions and Movements*, ed. Charles H. Lippy and Peter W. Williams (New York: Scribner's, 1988), 1:85–100. In the present study, I hope to join these scholars, who have helped break down the historiography of Catholic exceptionalism and incorporate Catholic history into the broader project of U.S. social history. Furthermore, in exploring how second- and third-generation American Catholics created local faith practices at odds with national characterizations, scholars slowly correct the periodization of Catholicism as a church unified through the fifties and suddenly fragmented in the sixties. On challenging consensus themes in narratives of American religious history, see Thomas A. Tweed, "Introduction: Narrating U.S. Religious History," in *Retelling U.S. Religious History*, ed. Thomas A. Tweed (Berkeley: University of California Press, 1997), pp. 1–23. For background on nineteenth- and twentieth-century Philadelphia Catholicism, see Dennis Clark, *The Irish in Philadelphia: Ten Generations of Urban Experience* (Philadelphia: Temple University Press, 1973); and Dale B. Light, *Rome and the New Republic: Conflict and Community in Philadelphia Catholicism Between the Revolution and the Civil War* (Notre Dame, Ind.: University of Notre Dame Press, 1996).

9. Thomas J. Donaghy, F.S.C., *Philadelphia's Finest: A History of Education in the Catholic Archdiocese, 1692–1970* (Philadelphia: American Catholic Historical Society, 1972), p. 234. For figures on school attendance, see Charles Morris, *American Catholic: The Saints and Sinners Who Built America's Most Powerful Church* (New York: New York Times Books/Random House, 1997), p. 174. McGreevy also wrote that northern urban cities with strong school systems, including Philadelphia, educated as much as 40 percent of the total student population by the midsixties. Breaking down the same numbers

racially, he noted that Philadelphia's Catholic secondary schools educated *60* percent of all non–African American city high schoolers (*Parish Boundaries*, pp. 236–37).

10. For enrollment figures, I consulted a timeline of Immaculata College history compiled by Sandra Rollison and Sister Trinita Marie Amorosi, I.H.M., part of the 1996 seventy-fifth anniversary of the college's founding and located in the ICGLA. The team's name changed over time. For most of these years, Immaculata players were known as the Mackies, named for the school and its Im*mac*ulate Heart sisters, whom students familiarly called "the Macks." In 1965 the student body voted as mascot the Scottish terrier, for the prefix "Mac" on many Scottish names. See "Scottish Terrier 'Mac' Elected New IC Mascot," TI 33, no. 3 (November 23, 1965): 4. In 1972, when the team won the first national championship, local reporter George Heaslip dubbed them "the Mighty Macs," and the nickname stuck. See Heaslip, "Immaculata Girls Win National Cage Title," *Daily Local News* (West Chester, Pa.), March 20, 1972, p. 11. Before the AIAW 1972 tournament, there had been three years of national invitational contests to determine U.S. college champions. But 1972 was the first year in which the AIAW sponsored regional play-offs to determine the sixteen teams to attend the national tournament. For that reason, the 1972 trophy was the first "official" one. See Joan S. Hult and Marianna Trekell, eds., *A Century of Women's Basketball: From Frailty to Final Four* (Reston, Va.: National Association for Girls and Women in Sport, 1991), p. 429.

11. EPC64, age 55, int. 6.11.98; Player B '45, age 74, int. 7.24.98; DCC55, age 65, int. 6.26.98.

12. MCM54, age 65, int. 6.23.98; Player A '48, age 71, ques. 21, 7.10.98; Player A '53, age 66, ques. 21, 5.8.98; MOR66, age 53, int. 6.26.98; DCC55, age 65, int. 6.26.98. Other players who used the word "fun" to describe their general basketball experience included HM44, age 74, ques. 20, 6.13.98; ISJ45, age 73, ques. 21, 6.1.98; EAA46, age 72, int. 6.17.98; AFB+47, age 71, ques. 11, 6.18.98; MBA51, age 68, int. 7.22.98; ACC51, age 68, ques. 11, 5.10.98; JD53, age 66, ques. 25, 5.10.98; JCF53, age 66, ques. 23, 7.27.98; HFD56, age 63, int. 7.23.98; Player '59, age 61, ques. 18, 6.20.98; EPC64, age 55, int. 6.11.98; MLMN65, age 54, int. 6.22.98; JYE74, age 45, int. 8.8.98; Player '75, age 45, ques. 11, 5.10.98; and LGF78, age 41, ques. 21, 5.15.98, and int. 7.23.98. Players who volunteered that basketball was "important" to them included: MDK+, age 71, int. 1.9.98; MOR66, age 53, int. 6.26.98; CLD70, age 49, int. 6.8.98; SFO72, age 48, ques. 6, 6.24.98; and Player '75, age 45, ques. 11, 5.10.98. Others used the word "enjoyment" or forms of it, including Player B '45, age 74, int. 7.24.98; JCF53, age 66, ques. 21, 7.27.98; MCM54, age 65, int. 6.23.98; Player '59, age 61, ques. 11 and 26, 6.20.98; EPC64, age 55, int. 6.11.98; and BND66, age 54, ques. 11, 6.1.98. Two players said they felt "joy" in the game: MKD62, age 57, ques. 25, 7.28.98; and LGF78, age 41, ques. 21, 5.15.98. Players who used the word "pleasure" included MDK+, age 71, int. 1.9.98, and LGF78, age 41, int. 7.23.98. Others recalled "good times" in basketball: AFB+47, age 71, 6.18.98; Player '51, age 69, ques. 25, 5.20.98; MMKK58, age 62, ques. 11, 7.9.98; and ILH70, age 49, ques. 21, 5.8.98. Several players said basketball gave them "happiness," among them, MMKK58, age 62, ques. 11, 7.9.98; and JYE74, age 45, int. 8.8.98. A number of players said they "loved" basketball: JM42, age 77, int. 7.20.98; Player C '45, age 74, int. 6.24.98; FFT50, age 70, ques. 18, 7.1.98; CLD70, age 49, int. 6.8.98; and LM78, age 42, ques. 17, 5.26.98. Others said basketball was "thrilling," "exciting," or "wonderful": Player A '53, age 66, ques. 26, 5.8.98; ISJ45, age 73, ques. 24, 6.1.98;

and EAA46, age 72, int. 6.17.98, respectively. Players' memories of fun did not vary according to whether they were good players or were on winning teams. Team members who described themselves as benchwarmers or who played in losing seasons seemed to count these experiences insignificant in comparison to the fundamental pleasure of the sport. Adrienne Friaglia Cyran '67 said she was too short to play effectively, but she had "fun though while I played" (AFC67, age 52, ques. 26, 5.10.98). A 1953 graduate said she was "klutzy," but basketball "was a sport I enjoyed": "It was fun" (Player B '53, age 66, int. 5.11.98). Barbara Flanigan '68 remembered that in her playing years, 1964–68, "Immaculata was an underdog" but said she "loved basketball" (BF68, age 51, ques. 21, 8.17.98).

13. PCE57, age 62, int. 7.23.98; LGF78, age 41, int. 7.23.98.

14. On the "culture of suffering," see Robert A. Orsi, "'Mildred, Is It Fun to Be a Cripple?' The Culture of Suffering in Mid-Twentieth-Century American Catholicism," *South Atlantic Quarterly* 93, no. 3 (summer 1994): 547–90.

15. Poststructuralist definitions of pleasure tend to uncouple desire from universal good or beauty and instead locate pleasure in the body, as both a social and physical entity. But since pleasure and desire are both experiences, they are, like all experiences, always constructed and mediated by the social order, or several competing orders. Philosophers Gilles Deleuze and Félix Guattari, for example, admit the unlikely possibility that desire ever fully escapes institutionalization. But they do suggest ways of noticing partially uncolonized desire, located both inside and outside institutions and regenerated in the clash of competing orders. As they see it, uncolonized desire reveals social fault lines and therefore "lines of flight" to temporarily discarded or disordered space. See Deleuze and Guattari, *Anti-Oedipus: Capitalism and Schizophrenia*, trans. Robert Hurley, Mark Seem, and Helen R. Lane (Minneapolis: University of Minnesota Press, 1983), pp. 51–137; and idem, *A Thousand Plateaus: Capitalism and Schizophrenia*, trans. Brian Massumi (Minneapolis: University of Minnesota Press, 1987), pp. 3, 213. It is the possibility that uncolonized desire works with and against institutions from the inside that fuels the insight that pleasure might signal small-scale political activity. For examples mentioned from scholars of the subaltern, see Albert J. Raboteau, *Slave Religion: The "Invisible Institution" in the Antebellum South* (Oxford: Oxford University Press, 1978); Tera Hunter, *To 'Joy My Freedom: Southern Black Women's Lives and Labors After the Civil War* (Cambridge: Harvard University Press, 1997); Robin D. G. Kelley, *Race Rebels: Culture, Politics, and the Black Working Class* (New York: Free/Macmillan, 1994); Dick Hebdige, *Subculture: The Meaning of Style* (London: Methuen, 1979); C. L. R. James, *Beyond a Boundary* (Durham: Duke University Press), 1993; and Jennie Livingston, dir., *Paris Is Burning* (Academy Entertainment, 1992). Raboteau as well as other scholars of religion have considered the link between faith and subaltern politics. See, for example, Evelyn Brooks Higgenbotham, *Righteous Discontent: The Women's Movement in the Black Baptist Church, 1880–1920* (Cambridge: Harvard University Press, 1993); Nell Irvin Painter, *Sojourner Truth: A Life, a Symbol* (New York: Norton, 1996); Karen E. Fields, *Revival and Rebellion in Colonial Central Africa* (Princeton: Princeton University Press, 1985); Jean Comaroff and John Comaroff, *Of Revelation and Revolution: Christianity, Colonialism, and Consciousness in South Africa*, vol. 1 (Chicago: University of Chicago Press, 1991); Richard Price, *Alabi's World* (Baltimore: Johns Hopkins University Press, 1990); James C. Scott, *Domination and the Arts of Resistance: Hidden Transcripts* (New Haven: Yale University

Press, 1990); Ranajit Guha, *Elementary Aspects of Peasant Insurgence in Colonial India* (Delhi: Oxford University Press, 1983); and David Hardiman, *Feeding the Baniya: Peasants and Usurers in Western India* (Delhi: Oxford University Press, 1996). For some commentary on U.S. scholars' resistance to understanding religion, particularly Catholicism, as a factor in popular politics, see John T. McGreevy, "Thinking on One's Own: Catholicism in the American Intellectual Imagination," *Journal of American History* 84, no. 1 (June 1997): 97–131; Roger N. Lancaster, "Marxism and Religion: A Critique," in *Thanks to God and the Revolution: Popular Religion and Class Consciousness in the New Nicaragua* (New York: Columbia University Press, 1988), pp. 164–94; Leslie Woodcock Tentler, "On the Margins: The State of American Catholic History," *American Quarterly* 45, no. 1 (March 1993): 104–27; and Jenny Franchot, "Invisible Domain: Religion and American Literary Studies," *American Literature* 67, no. 4 (December 1995): 833–42.

16. Many survey respondents indicated they did enjoy other extracurricular activities such as singing in the chorus and working on the yearbook. For Tuesday night sodalities, see Morris, *American Catholic*, p. 177. For details of the Elkins Park diocese retreat center for women, see Hugh J. Nolan, "The Native Son," in *The History of the Archdiocese of Philadelphia*, ed. James F. Connelly (Wynnewood, Pa.: Unigraphics Incorporated, 1976), p. 410.

17. David D. Hall, ed., *Lived Religion in America: Toward a History of Practice* (Princeton: Princeton University Press, 1997). For the purposes of this project, I understand lived religion as anything self-described religious people say and do. This material and historical approach brackets the supernatural dimensions of religion that many faithful consider its essence. I agree that religion is not lived within purely historical boundaries. I do not bracket the supernatural because it is not real but because it is largely unnameable. So, telling this story, I have declined to put words to the supernatural. I trust this is a form of witnessing its reality.

18. Morris, *American Catholic*, p. 170.

19. Nolan, "Native Son," p. 346; Donaghy, *Philadelphia's Finest*, p. 234. Morris wrote that Dougherty was the Philadelphia prelate priests called simply "the Cardinal" for years after his death (*American Catholic*, p. 172). McGreevy noted the non-African American Catholic population of Philadelphia in 1952 was 41 percent in *Parish Boundaries*, p. 132.

20. Donaghy, *Philadelphia's Finest*, p. 234. On school attendance, see Morris, *American Catholic*, p. 174.

21. The phrase "unique in the entire country" comes from Nolan, "Native Son," p. 378. Sister Mary of Lourdes McDevitt '36, president *emerita* of Immaculata College (1954–72), said in an interview that she often heard the joke that nuns worked for "a dollar a day" but that the jest "wasn't too far off—that's the way we survived" (MLM+36, age 83, int. 6.30.98). For attendance figures, see Morris, *American Catholic*, p. 174; and James F. Connelly, "John Cardinal Krol," in *The History of the Archdiocese of Philadelphia*, p. 546.

22. MLM+36, age 83, int. 6.30.98.

23. GRS64, age 55, int. 8.5.98; MKD62, age 57, ques. 14, 7.28.98.

24. Morris described Philadelphia Catholicism under Dougherty as a "state-within-a-state" (*American Catholic*, p. 173). For an account of the modern disciplining institution, see Michel Foucault, *Discipline and Punish: The Birth of the Prison*, trans. Alan Sheridan (New York: Vintage/Random House, 1979).

25. Judith Butler suggested that the historical subject is best understood as a site or moment between the institution and the individual: the subject embodies her subjection but changes it simply by inhabiting it in her singular, material particularity. See Judith Butler, *The Psychic Life of Power: Theories in Subjection* (Stanford: Stanford University Press, 1997).

26. EAA46, age 72, int. 6.17.98.

27. As with all voluntary surveys, it is likely that those who returned the Immaculata basketball survey remembered their Immaculata basketball experience on the whole more strongly—positively or negatively—than those who did not. The mailing included nearly three hundred players who were listed on rosters or mentioned in game write-ups in *The Immaculatan* and newspapers, excluding thirty-three deceased former players. But rosters and articles did not give comprehensive lists of players, and I was not able to identify team members who might never have appeared in these sources. For that reason, I might have missed talking to players who never made any lists because they played less or quit the team. Therefore I also might have missed players who had more negative experiences. Furthermore, my only source of addresses was the Immaculata Alumnae Office. Because the Alumnae Office did not keep records for nongraduates, I did not send surveys to players who never graduated. This last uncontacted group (seventy-seven women) is significant because over the years (1939–69), on average a third of all entering freshmen did not graduate. Many students, including some basketball players, left for financial or academic reasons or because they got pregnant or married. While these attrition rates reflected the norm for women's colleges at the time, presumably some also left Immaculata because they had an unsatisfactory experience, and I missed talking to them. All surveys and interview tapes are in my possession. I have benefited from other scholars' work on the history of women's basketball. The following books integrate interviews with female athletes and coaches into the text: Susan K. Cahn, *Coming on Strong: Gender and Sexuality in Twentieth-Century Women's Sport* (New York: Free/Macmillan, 1994); and Janice Kaplan, *Women and Sports* (New York: Viking, 1979). Invaluable essays and memoirs on the women's game can be found in Hult and Trekell, *A Century of Women's Basketball.* Other academic studies of women's basketball include: Elva Bishop and Katherine Fulton, "Shooting Stars: The Heyday of Industrial Women's Basketball," *Southern Exposure* 7, no. 3 (1979): 50–56; Barbara Schrodt, "Vancouver's Dynastic Domination of Canadian Senior Women's Basketball, 1942–1967," *Canadian Journal of History of Sport* 26, no. 2 (1995): 19–32; Janice A. Beran, *From Six-on-Six to Full-Court Press: A Century of Iowa Girls' Basketball* (Ames: Iowa State University Press, 1993); Sylvia Faye Nadler, "A Developmental History of the Wayland Hutcherson Flying Queens from 1910–1979" (Ph.D. diss., East Texas State University, 1980); Joanne Lannin, *A History of Basketball for Girls and Women* (Minneapolis: Lerner, 2000); Pamela Grundy, "Bloomers and Beyond: North Carolina Women's Basketball Uniforms, 1901–1997," *Southern Cultures* 3, no. 3 (1997): 52–67; and idem, "From Amazons to Glamazons: The Rise and Fall of North Carolina Women's Basketball, 1920–1960," *Journal of American History* 87, no. 1 (June 2000): 112–46.

28. Clippings in the Archbishop Furey Scrapbook and other Gabriele Library Archives files did not always include page numbers of the original articles; neither were they themselves fully paginated. Where original page numbers were not available, I cite articles' lo-

cations in the archives files, for example: "Owlettes Lose 1st in 4 Years to Immaculata," *Philadelphia Record*, March 6, 1946, Archbishop Furey Scrapbook, ICGLA.

29. Questions could arise as to the reliability of memories as a source, especially memories of childhood or youth recounted by adults. But I assume that memories of youth are no more or less reliable than other kinds of narrative evidence, such as adult accounts gathered in ethnographies. Whether youth or adult, past memory or contemporaneous narrative, sources in oral history and ethnography interpret and construct meaning in and across time, and none have an unmediated relationship to reality. In this study, I granted interpretive authority to players' memories and cross-checked accounts with other sources where I could.

30. PCE57, age 62, int. 7.23.98.

31. The John W. Hallahan Girls' High School Alumnae Association, *Hallahan: The Story of Fifty Years of Free, Higher Education for Catholic Girls in Philadelphia* (Philadelphia: Campus Publishing/Zamsky Studios, 1951), Philadelphia Archdiocese Historical Research Center, St. Charles Borromeo Seminary, Overbrook, Pennsylvania (PAHRC), p. 31.

32. Monsignor Bonner expounded the unique role of student athletics in "The Value of Athletics to Boys," undated, Monsignor John Bonner Collection at the PAHRC (MJBC), box 1, folder 14, item 3, p. 2. For Catholic League founding dates, see John Bonner, address to the Catholic High School Athletic League of Philadelphia, untitled, undated (probably 1925), MJBC, box 1, folder 15, item 2, p. 1; and *Vita*, February 16, 1945, MJBC, box 5, folder 10, item 11. For Bonner as coach, see John Bonner, speech in thanks for tribute, untitled, undated, MJBC, box 1, folder 12, item 2, p. 4. For Bonner's description of Catholic League events, see Bonner, address to the Catholic High School Athletic League, p. 3. On Bonner's progressive proclivities, see Francis J. Ryan, "Monsignor John Bonner and Progressive Education in the Archdiocese of Philadelphia, 1925–1945," *Records of the American Catholic Historical Society of Philadelphia* 102, nos. 1–2 (spring 1991): 17–43. Under Bonner, Catholic schools developed advanced sports programs, including unusual girls' varsity teams, but not necessarily commensurate physical education programs, the lack of which in Catholic schools state accreditors constantly decried (Morris, *American Catholic*, p. 184). Philadelphia Catholic educators long recognized the benefits of physical education, especially for girls, evident in years of superintendents' *Report of the Parish Schools* from the turn of the century (PAHRC). But, despite good intentions, until the late sixties Catholic educators slighted physical education in favor of more exciting—and less costly—team sports.

33. JS, age 66, int. 8.25.98; MLM+36, age 83, 6.30.98. On Hallahan's basketball program, see Ryan, "Monsignor John Bonner," p. 24. Those who mentioned playing against Liz Ann Kelly included Dee Cofer Cull '55 (DCC55, age 65, int. 6.26.98); cheerleader Bernadette Ellis McBeth '56 (BEM56, age 63, ques. 21, 10.6.98); and Pauline Earl Callahan '57 (PCE57, age 62, int. 7.23.98).

34. On the relationship between Dougherty and Greenfield, see Morris, *American Catholic*, p. 188.

35. Morris described Dougherty as "shy and private" (*American Catholic*, p. 170). See also Nolan, who characterized him as socially formal and professionally secretive ("Native Son," p. 346). Reverend Joseph G. Cox memorialized Bonner's charisma in an obituary, "Right Reverend Monsignor John J. Bonner, D.D., Superintendent of Schools,

1926–1945," published on the first page of the March 1946 issue of *School Lore*, an arch-diocesan teachers' newsletter that Bonner founded (PAHRC). Judging from his papers, Bonner was constantly asked to speak and deliver sermons at alumnae gatherings, sisters' retreats, girls' high school graduations, and women's college commencements. In 1951 Hallahan alumnae published a fiftieth-anniversary history in which they credited Bonner alone with the progress of the schools and celebrated him as a "visionary." "Everyone wanted to see him, hear him, talk to him," they wrote. The "epitome of every sanguine hope of Catholic education," Bonner was "gracious, zealous for lay leadership, his brilliant mind avid for the success of the schools" (Hallahan Alumnae, *Hallahan: The Story*, pp. 31–32, 39–41, in PAHRC). On the tension between Bonner and Dougherty, see Ryan, "Monsignor John Bonner," p. 37; Donaghy, *Philadelphia's Finest*, p. 213; and Morris, *American Catholic*, pp. 185–86. For the correspondence between the two in which Dougherty refused to grant Bonner assistants, see the following items in the Cardinal Dougherty Papers at PAHRC: 80.1187 (May 24, 1930); 80.1188 (May 28, 1930); and 80.1231 (May 31, 1939). The only extracurricular activity ever cited in Bonner's reports to Dougherty was music. See John Bonner, *Report of the Parish Schools, Archdiocese of Philadelphia, 1932–33* (Philadelphia: Diocesan School Board, 1933), p. 13; and *Report of the Parish Schools, Archdiocese of Philadelphia, 1944–45* (Philadelphia: Diocesan School Board, 1945), p. 10, both in PAHRC.

36. On the rivalry between Hallahan and West Catholic, see Hallahan Alumnae, *Hallahan: The Story*, p. 41. Paula D. Welch and Harold A. Lerch, in *History of American Physical Education and Sport* (Springfield, Ill.: C. C. Thomas, 1981), noted that most U.S. physical educators in the thirties considered basketball for women an "acute problem of national significance" (p. 249). Regional exceptions to public high school and college bans on competitive play included parts of Oklahoma, Georgia, Iowa, Tennessee, Texas, and North Dakota. See Welch and Lerch, *History of American Physical Education*, p. 253, as well as Mildred Barnes, "Coaching and Game Reflections, 1940s to 1980s," in *A Century of Women's Basketball*, ed. Hult and Trekell, pp. 339–40. In some places, African American women as a group played competitive ball by men's rules sooner than their white counterparts did. See Cahn, *Coming on Strong*, p. 89, as well as Cindy Himes Gissendanner, "African-American Women and Competitive Sport, 1920–1960," in *Women, Sport, and Culture*, ed. Susan Birrell and Cheryl L. Cole (Champaign, Ill.: Human Kinetics, 1994), p. 83. Basketball for college women in the East at this time was largely governed by the Division of Girls' and Women's Sports (DGWS), a committee of female physical educators auxiliary to the American Association for Health, Physical Education, and Recreation. In 1971 the DGWS became the Association for Intercollegiate Athletics for Women, or AIAW, and in 1981 the AIAW merged with the National Collegiate Athletics Association, the NCAA. Other early DGWS name changes are detailed in Joan S. Hult, "The Saga of Competition: Basketball Battles and Governance War," in *A Century of Women's Basketball*, ed. Hult and Trekell, p. 223. For simplicity's sake, I refer to the organization as the DGWS until 1971 and the AIAW afterward. Immaculata College and its local competitor schools played under DGWS rules. Since the organization discouraged women from the competitive dimensions of basketball, northeastern high school and college teams did not play regional tournaments and championships until the late sixties; an exception was the

Catholic League, whose girls' teams played among themselves for a championship each year. The DGWS did not govern nationally, however, and neither did it have jurisdiction over noncollege teams. Many high school, collegiate, industrial, club, semiprofessional, and professional women's basketball teams throughout the country, especially in parts of the South, Midwest, and West, followed various non-DGWS rulebooks. The major non-DGWS voice for governance of women's sports was the Midwest-based Amateur Athletic Union (AAU). Supporting amateur athletics at all ages, AAU women's basketball teams, including some college teams, played by rules much closer to Naismith's original game from the 1920s. And, as the AAU favored competition in women's sports, its teams competed in local and regional tournaments. Hosting its first national invitational tournament in 1926, the AAU matched up college and club teams that played by men's rules. Only in 1965, when the DGWS and AAU formed a joint rules committee, was the stage set for nationwide uniform governance of women's basketball. The first college-only national invitational tournament was held at West Chester State in 1969. See Welch and Lerch, *History of American Physical Education*, p. 249; Hult and Trekell, *A Century of Women's Basketball*, pp. 429–30; and Nadler, "A Developmental History," pp. 26, 32–33. Like other women's basketball hotspots, Philadelphia nurtured not only collegiate but also noncollegiate, non-DGWS teams, a few of which Immaculata played, such as the Valley Forge Nurses. The history of these industrial and independent teams, composed of working women, including Catholics, remains largely unknown. On independent and industrial teams in the city, see Frank Fitzpatrick, "Where It All Began," *Philadelphia Inquirer Magazine*, March 26, 2000, p. 9.

37. John Bonner, "While the Catholic high school system," fragment of speech or radio address, untitled and undated, after 1940, MJBC, box 1, folder 12, item 3, p. 2; John Bonner, dedication of Knute Rockne Memorial Hall at Sacred Heart in Allentown, Pa., untitled speech (September 20, 1942), MJBC, box 2, folder 7, item 6, p. 1. MLM+36, age 87, int. 8.16.02.

38. DCC55, age 65, int. 6.26.98. A number of other players and sisters said similar things.

39. Bonner, dedication of Knute Rockne Memorial Hall, pp. 1–2. This address, delivered during World War II, also contained a patriotic rationale for athletics, common in American sports ideology but unusual in Bonner's promotions. On physical education themes during wartime, see Welch and Lerch, *History of American Physical Education*, pp. 127–28, 176–83.

40. Bonner, dedication of Knute Rockne Memorial Hall, p. 1. Sister Mary of Lourdes said the sisters popularly called the Philadelphia schools "the System": MLM+36, age 83, int. 6.30.98. While I am exploring the unusual relationship in Philadelphia between Catholicism and women's basketball, the relationship between Catholicism and men's sports was well established, as many U.S. Catholic communities generated athletes, fans, team loyalties, and deep-rooted sports cultures. Many observers have written on the love affair between sports and Catholics, who, while they were marginalized religiously, economically, and socially, found on the football field or baseball diamond a literal, if temporary, level playing field. Similarly, C. L. R. James on cricket and John Edgar Wideman on basketball have described the centrality of sports in marginalized communities. See James, *Beyond a Boundary*; and John Edgar Wideman, *Hoop Roots: Love, Race, and Basketball*

(Boston: Houghton Mifflin, 2001). But women's basketball does not quite fit the standard interpretation of sports as assimilation for the sons of slaves, colonials, and immigrants. Some studies of "cultural Catholicism" go further than historical connections to link Catholicism and sports aesthetically or even theologically, for example, in James T. Fisher's provocative essay, "Clearing the Streets of the Catholic Lost Generation," in *Catholic Lives, Contemporary America*, ed. Thomas J. Ferraro (Durham: Duke University Press, 1997), pp. 76–103. But, however strong the U.S. Catholic community's affinity for sports, I didn't find that its athletes or leaders considered the connection anything but circumstantial. No player I interviewed, for example, said basketball was inherently Catholic; in fact, many explicitly rejected that idea. "It was only that I played for a Catholic institution," explained Maureen Callahan Bigham '63 (MCB63, age 56, ques. 13, 5.23.98).

41. MGD62, age 57, int. 7.21.98.

42. Tricia Brown estimated the percentage of East Coast intramural and varsity women's teams in an article commemorating the ninetieth anniversary of the first women's collegiate game at Smith. See Tricia Brown, "A Step Back into the History of Basketball," *NCAA News* 20, no. 12 (March 23, 1983): 9.

43. On Foster, see Nancy Cole Dosch, "'The Sacrifice of the Maidens' or Healthy Sportswomen? The Medical Debate Over Women's Basketball," in *A Century of Women's Basketball*, ed. Hult and Trekell, p. 127.

44. JS, age 66, int. 8.25.99. See Hult and Trekell, *A Century of Women's Basketball*, pp. 427–30.

45. JS, age 66, int. 8.25.99.

46. Ibid.

47. Iowa high school girls' leagues already approached mythic status in the twenties, as Janice A. Beran describes in "Iowa, Longtime 'Hot Bed' of Girls' Basketball," in *A Century of Women's Basketball*, ed. Hult and Trekell, pp. 181–205, as well as in *From Six-on-Six to Full-Court Press*.

48. MCM54, age 65, int. 6.23.98.

49. Bishop Bernard Sheil of Chicago founded the Catholic Youth Organization (CYO) in 1930 to provide wholesome activities for urban Catholic youth. The CYO was based in parishes, not schools, and in Chicago it showcased boys' boxing. Bonner's earlier Catholic League linked athletics structurally to schools and philosophically to education from its inception. On the CYO and Bishop Sheil, see Steven A. Reiss, *City Games: The Evolution of American Urban Society and the Rise of Sports* (Urbana: University of Illinois Press, 1989), pp. 101–2; and Gerald R. Gems, "Sport, Religion and Americanization: Bishop Sheil and the Catholic Youth Organization," *International Journal of the History of Sport* 10, no. 2 (1993): 233–41. While other northeastern cities had CYO chapters in the middle and late thirties, the earliest account I received of an Immaculata player participating in the CYO comes from the midforties, from Patricia Furey McDonnell '53 (PFM53, age 66, ques. 7, 5.15.98). For the CYO in other cities, see Florence D. Cohalan, *A Popular History of the Archdiocese of New York* (Yonkers, N.Y.: United States Catholic Historical Society, 1983), p. 255; Robert H. Lord, John E. Sexton, and Edward T. Harrington, *History of the Archdiocese of Boston in the Various Stages of Its Development, 1604–1943* (Boston: Pilot Publishing, 1945), 3:668–69.

50. MFM50, age 69, int. 3.17.98; MM, age 44, int. 5.8.98; JS, age 66, int. 8.25.99.

51. MKD62, age 57, ques. 13, 7.28.98. A cheerleader from the class of '49, who attended Notre Dame Moylan for high school, said girls' league ball was "the big, big thing" (Cheerleader '49, age 70, int. 7.23.98). Maureen Callahan Bigham '63 said basketball was "deeply associated" with her religion (MCB63, age 56, ques. 14, 5.23.98).

52. On the Philadelphia Tribune Girls, see Cahn, *Coming on Strong*, pp. 92–94; Gissendanner, "African-American Women," p. 84; and Lannin, *A History of Basketball*, p. 41.

53. MCB63, age 56, ques. 19, 5.23.98. The player who said she started in Catholic high school but was "out of my league" at Immaculata was Pauline Callahan Earl '57: PCE57, age 62, int. 7.23.98. Therese Murphy McNally '63, among others, mentioned starting team shake-ups after 1959 (TMM63, age 56, ques. 19, 5.25.98).

54. JM42, age 77, int. 7.20.98. For student agitation, see the "Sportettes" column by Georgeanna Franey, basketball player and member of the Athletic Association, a club run and subsidized by students: "Sportettes," TI 3, no. 1 (October 18, 1935): 3; TI 3, no. 3 (December 16, 1935): 3; and TI 3, no. 4 (February 14, 1936): 3.

55. "I.H.M. Sisters Observe 125th Year," *Catholic Standard and Times* (November 19, 1970), microfilm, "I.C. in print," roll 2, ICGLA. In 1970 the I.H.M.s were educating 50 percent of the children enrolled in archdiocese schools.

56. On Dougherty's drives to Immaculata, see Nolan, "Native Son," p. 364. Dougherty intimidated his priests but by all accounts had excellent relationships with and deep personal affection for archdiocesan sisters. Sister Mary of Lourdes McDevitt '36 described him as "a good man," "a man you'd sit down and have a conversation with" (MLM+36, age 83, int. 6.30.98). See also Morris, *American Catholic*, p. 192, on Dougherty's relationship with women. Bonner, who taught theology at Immaculata for several years, called the college "home" in his Immaculata College commencement address, untitled, undated (probably during World War II), MJBC, box 1, folder 5, item 1, p. 1.

57. KC70, age 49, int. 6.10.98. Sister Mary of Lourdes described the Immaculate Heart Sisters' policy of "diversified" degrees (MLM+36, age 83, int. 6.30.98). See also Connelly, "John Cardinal Krol," p. 307. Former Immaculata president Sister Marie Roseanne Bonfini '57 (1992–2002) said the sisters "insert something of the spiritual" into every activity, no matter how seemingly secular (MRB+57, age 61, int. 10.16.97).

58. EAA46, age 72, ques. 13, 6.15.98. Between 1918 and 1951, I.H.M. numbers grew from 774 to 1,816, according to Nolan, "The Native Son," p. 411. Several interviewees mentioned Immaculata priests' financial support, including JBS53, age 67, ques. 7, 6.13.98; Player '56, age 63, ques. 7, 5.4.98; and FFT50, age 70, ques. 7, 7.1.98.

59. Among others, Mary Murphy Schmelzer '62 remembered Sister Mary of Lourdes running interference between players' obligations and sisters' demands (MMS62, age 57, ques. 6, 5.24.98). A player from the class of '56 said Sister Mary of Lourdes looked after the team's financial needs (Player '56, age 63, ques. 17, 5.4.98).

60. MLM+36, age 83, int. 6.30.98.

61. JV38, age 81, int. 7.20.98; GFB57, age 62, int. 6.14.98; Cheerleader '63, age 57, ques. 25, 5.18.98.

62. For Philadelphia Catholic resistance to social change, see McGreevy, *Parish Boundaries*, pp. 91–92, 175–76, 256–60. McGreevy also mentions Krol's longtime resistance to lay activism (p. 216). Daniel Carroll said O'Hara was the "last of the old order" in "The O'Hara Years," in *The History of the Archdiocese of Philadelphia*, ed. Connelly, p. 468. For

an overview of O'Hara's policies, see Carroll, "The O'Hara Years." For an overview of Krol's policies, see Connelly, "John Cardinal Krol."

1. Making the Team, Making Identity

1. Fifty-four girls tried out for the 1939–40 Immaculata basketball team; see "Basketball Occupies Minds of Sports Enthusiasts," *The Immaculatan* (TI) 7, no. 3 (December 20, 1939): 4. Players who said they tried out with no basketball experience included Josephine Valentine '38, from upstate Pennsylvania (JV38, age 81, int. 7.20.98); a team member from Washington, D.C., class of '56 (Player '56, age 63, ques. 26, 5.4.98); and a player native to New York state, class of '52 (Player A '52, age 66, ques. 19, 5.4.98).

2. MDK+, age 71, int. 1.9.98.

3. MCM54, age 65, int. 6.23.98.

4. PL71, age 48, ques. 19, 5.10.98. Thirty girls attended the 1969 tryouts; see "Basketball Season Underway; Pro Rules to Be Followed," TI 37, no. 4 (December 12, 1969): 4. Dolly VanBuskirk Anderson '78 estimated the number of attendees for the 1974 tryouts (DVA78, age 43, int. 7.9.99).

5. AML53, age 67, ques. 19, 5.22.98; Player C '52, age 68, ques. 19, 6.20.98; MKD62, age 57, ques. 19, 7.28.98; AML53, age 67, ques. 22, 5.22.98. The phrase "joy at being part of a wonderful group" comes from a survey returned by Margaret Klopfle Devinney '62 (MKD62, age 57, ques. 25, 7.28.98). The phrase "being part of the team" is from Alvina DeLazzari Long '57 (ADL57, age 62, ques. 25, 7.20.98).

6. Player B '45, age 74, int. 7.24.98; Player B '53, age 66, int. 5.11.98; MMKK58, age 62, ques. 17, 7.9.98; MFM50, age 69, int. 3.17.98.

7. EAA46, age 72, int. 6.17.98; JYE74, age 45, ques. 19, 8.8.98.

8. HFD56, age 63, int. 7.23.98; EAA46, age 72, int. 6.17.98. The phrases "special friends," "best friends," "in the whole world," and "unmatched" come from, respectively, FFT50, age 70, ques. 11, 7.1.98; MOR66, age 53, ques. 25, 6.27.98; LGF78, age 41, ques. 25, 5.15.98; and LGF78, age 41, int. 7.23.98.

9. "Miss Donohue Selects 1957 Basketball Team," TI 24, no. 3 (December 19, 1956): 6; MCM54, age 65, int. 6.23.98; Player B '45, age 74, int. 7.24.98. The phrase "a select few" comes from Alvina DeLazzari Long '57 (ADL57, age 62, ques. 25, 7.20.98). The phrases "pride," "wearing the I.C. jacket," "sense of belonging," and "wonderful group of girl athletes" come from, respectively, AML53, age 67, ques. 21, 5.22.98; MMKK58, age 62, ques. 25, 7.9.98; Player C '52, age 68, ques. 24, 6.20.98; and DGP56, age 62, ques. 25, 6.5.98. Marian Collins Mullahy '54 said team members thought of themselves as "different" (MCM54, age 65, int. 6.17.98).

10. MGD62, age 57, int. 7.21.98; EAHQ73, age 46, int. 7.2.98. I gleaned information on Izanne Leonard Haak '70 and her mother from Izanne's survey (ILH70, age 49, ques. 2, 5.8.98) and from "Two Immaculatans Win Forward Positions on All-Philadelphia Girls' Basketball Team," TI 12, no. 6 (April 24, 1945): 4.

11. HFD56, age 63, int. 7.23.98; MFM50, age 69, int. 3.17.98.

12. MSM, age 75, mem. 7.13.98; MMS62, age 57, ques. 18, 5.24.98.

13. Player '56, age 63, ques. 25, 5.4.98; CLD70, age 49, int. 6.8.98. By any standards, Immaculata's coaches were a forward-looking lot, and players kept going there to reap the

benefits. For example, between 1941 and 1946, Marie Schultes McGuinness, later called the "Knute Rockne" of Immaculata, fashioned a seven-year-old program into a local powerhouse. And Cathy Rush, the women's game "pioneer" of the early seventies, imported tactics from the men's game to capitalize on her street-smart players. Reporter Mike Scully called Schultes Immaculata's "Knute Rockne" in "Marie McGuiness Is Macs' Answer to Knute Rockne," unknown newspaper, 1975, microfilm, "I.C. in print," roll 11, Gabriele Library Archives, Immaculata College, Pennsylvania (ICGLA). Frank Fitzpatrick said Rush was a "pioneer" of the women's game in "Where It All Began," *Philadelphia Inquirer Magazine*, March 26, 2000, p. 30.

14. MOR66, age 53, ques. 20, 6.27.98; this is also the source of "good role model . . . ." Several Immaculata coaches who were Catholics left their jobs when they got married, including Marie Schultes and Mary Frank.

15. Immaculata's tradition of training basketball referees owed much to Shillingford, who, said Gloria Rook Schmidt '64, was "pretty active in all the associations" and saw the opportunity for her players to make money, gain experience, and seed the area with good officials. "That's why you had so many referees . . . because of her," said Gloria, who officiated games for years afterward (GRS64, age 55, int. 8.5.98). Kathryn Peterson was pictured in a photograph in the yearbook: "Basketball Team," photograph of team and captain K. Peterson, *The Gleaner 1929*, p. 102, ICGLA. Her life story was featured in "Play Is Her Work," *Philadelphia Inquirer Magazine*, August 8, 1965, microfilm, "I.C. in print," roll 2, ICGLA. Margaret Guinan Delaney '62 said a teammate started the summer league (MGD62, age 57, int. 7.21.98). For basketball at the Native American mission, see "Joan Gagliardi Reports on Life in Winnebago: Activities Range from Parish Work to Basketball," TI 31, no. 3 (December 18, 1963): 5. For the Malvern project, see "AA Head Sparks Athletic Program," TI 32, no. 6 (March 10, 1965): 6.

16. JS, age 66, int. 8.25.99.

17. EAA46, age 72, int. 6.17.98.

18. MLMN65, age 54, int. 6.22.98.

19. Sister Marie Albert Kunberger '51, who entered the novitiate after graduation, remembered conniving with college president Monsignor Vincent Burns (1946–54) to attend a big game she and some fellow novices wanted to see at their high school alma mater. They had assigned chapel seats at the required afternoon hours' devotion and would surely miss the game, so Monsignor Burns agreed to meet them secretly in back of Villa Maria, after he took off his vestments and sneaked out a back way, to drive them to the game (MAK+51, age 68, int. 8.6.98). Joanne Seemans Kolen '58 said it was the nuns' "favorite sport" (JSK58, age 61, int. 6.23.98). Helen Frank Dunigan '56 said basketball was the nuns' "outlet" (HFD56, age 63, int. 7.23.98).

20. MMH63, age 58, corr. 11.22.99; MLM+36, age 83, int. 6.30.98; FFT50, age 70, ques. 6, 7.1.98. Marcella Rominger Lusby '52 said Sister Mary of Lourdes was the team's "top supporter by far" (MRL52, age 68, ques. 6, 5.20.98). Jenepher Shillingford called Sister Mary of Lourdes a "fantastic athlete" (JS, age 66, int. 8.25.99).

21. MMS62, age 57, ques. 6, 5.24.98; JBV74, age 45, ques. 6, 6.5.98. Bernadette "Bunny" Naughton DeArmond '66 mentioned sisters' "flexibility" for players (BND66, age 54, ques. 6, 6.1.98), while Margaret Klopfle Devinney '62 said they "rearranged" schedules (MKD62, age 57, ques. 6, 7.28.98).

22. Charles R. Morris described the mid–twentieth-century Philadelphia priestly image in *American Catholic: The Saints and Sinners Who Built America's Most Powerful Church* (New York: New York Times Books/Random House, 1997), p. 178.

23. In several interviews, I heard about priests coaching CYO teams, including TMM63, age 56, ques. 7, 5.25.98; MMS62, age 57, ques. 7, 5.24.98; MKD62, age 57, ques. 7, 7.28.98; and MCB63, age 56, ques. 7, 5.23.98. Only one player ever mentioned a male lay coach, her own father, who coached her CYO team (MMS62, age 57, ques. 7, 5.24.98). Mary Frank McCormick '50 remembered Father Nall calling the Our Lady of Peace team "his girls" (MFM50, age 69, int. 3.17.98).

24. MFM50, age 69, int. 3.17.98; HFD56, age 63, int. 7.23.98. Dee Cofer Cull '55 said Father Nall's team traveled as far as Jackson, New York (DCC55, age 65, int. 6.26.98).

25. HFD56, age 63, int. 7.23.98; MFM50, age 69, int. 3.17.98. *The Immaculatan* reported in 1955 that Father Nall's Our Lady of Peace team had at that point not lost a game in nine years ("Wedding Bells Ring Out for All-Star Mary Frank," TI 22, no. 7 [May 29, 1955]: 4).

26. MCB63, age 56, ques. 7, 5.23.98; MJRL64, age 58, ques. 7, 8.4.98; ADL57, age 62, ques. 14, 7.20.98. Rosemary McNichol Walsh '60 mentioned parish-based adult women's sports programs (RMW60, age 60, ques. 7, 5.23.98). Anne Carroll Camp '51 and Margaret Klopfle Devinney '62 mentioned priests' allocation of gym time and funds (ACC51, age 68, ques. 7, 5.10.98; MKD62, age 57, ques. 7, 7.28.98).

27. EAA46, age 72, int. 6.17.98. Cheerleader Joan Davis Tynen '54 said priests came to games (JDT54, age 65, ques. 7, 5.28.98). On the dinner and home movies, see "Fr. Gorman Honors Team After Unbeaten Season," TI 13, no. 7 (May 31, 1946): 8; and "A.A. Treks to Lake for Picnic; Dinners Honor Basketball Team," TI 17, no. 7 (May 31, 1950): 8. The Mansion House event is mentioned in Jeanmarie Dunn, "I.C. by Jeanmarie," TI 13, no. 6 (April 15, 1946): 4.

28. DCC55, age 65, int. 6.26.98. Sister Marie Albert Kunberger '51 explained Father Gorman's support of Immaculata sports: MAK+51, age 68, int. 8.6.98. The electronic scoreboard he purchased is mentioned in "Tid Bits," TI 17, no. 5 (March 25, 1950): 6.

29. MBA51, age 68, int. 7.22.98; PCE57, age 62, int. 7.23.98; BF68, age 51, ques. 12, 8.17.98; EPC64, age 55, int. 6.11.98.

30. PCE57, age 62, int. 7.23.98; EAHQ73, age 46, int. 7.2.98. The story of the club-switching father is from Player '57, age 62, int. 6.11.98.

31. HFD56, age 63, int. 7.23.98; PCE57, age 62, int. 7.23.98; EPC64, age 55, int. 6.11.98. Epiphany Pantaleo Collins '64 also said she was both "daughter and son" to her dad.

32. MCB63, age 56, ques. 25, 5.23.98. The quotation from Marianne Crawford Stanley '76 and information on fathers' roles come from Herm Rogul, "Marianne a Winner," *Evening Bulletin*, December 7, 1974, microfilm, "I.C. in print," roll 11, ICGLA. Rene Muth Portland '75's words about the fathers going "hysterical" and her brother's wedding can be found in Herm Rogul, "Immaculata Closes Up Store," *Evening Bulletin*, January 25, 1974, microfilm, "I.C. in print," roll 11, ICGLA.

33. MFM50, age 69, int. 3.17.98; MLMN65, age 54, int. 6.22.98; JYE74, age 45, int. 8.8.98; MGD62, age 57, int. 7.21.98. Others who said they or others on the team had grown up playing basketball with their brothers included Player A '48, age 71, ques. 21, 7.10.98; MBA51, age 68, int. 7.22.98; MRL52, age 68, ques. 18, 5.20.98; and RDM46, age 73, int. 7.9.98.

34. DCC55, age 65, int. 6.26.98; GRS64, age 55, int. 8.5.98; JYE74, age 45, int. 8.8.98.

35. EAA46, age 72, int. 6.17.98; ACC51, age 68, ques. 7, 5.10.98.

36. FFT50, age 70, ques. 24, 7.1.98.

37. MFM50, age 69, int. 3.17.98.

38. EAA46, age 72, int. 6.17.98; Player B '53, age 66, int. 5.11.98.

39. DCC55, age 65, int. 6.26.98; MLMN65, age 54, int. 6.22.98. Helen and Tim Dunigan's remarks came from HFD56, age 63, int. 7.23.98. Other players who remarked on suitors in attendance included EPC64, age 55, int. 6.11.98; MFM50, age 69, int. 3.17.98; and MGD62, age 57, int. 7.21.98. *Immaculatan* columnist Jeanmarie Dunn reported on audience regulars in "I.C. by Jeanmarie," TI 13, no. 5 (March 25, 1946): 5; Janet Young Eline '74 and Betty Ann Hoffman Quinn '73 noted the same (JYE74, age 45, int. 8.8.98; EAHQ73, age 46, int. 7.2.98).

40. MFM50, age 69, int. 3.17.98; JYE74, age 45, int. 8.8.98; MWH+44, age 74, int. 10.16.97.

41. CLD70, age 49, int. 6.8.98; MFM50, age 69, int. 3.17.98; MCM54, age 65, int. 6.23.98; MOR66, age 53, int. 6.26.98. Mary Frank McCormick '50 said there was "most definitely" a type of young man attracted to basketball players (MFM50, age 69, int. 3.17.98). Ann Killion told the story of Marianne and Rich Stanley's courtship in "Her Days in Court," *San Jose Mercury News West*, November 24, 1996, p. 18.

42. On priests' dominance in theological instruction, see Philip Gleason, *Contending with Modernity: Catholic Higher Education in the Twentieth Century* (New York: Oxford University Press, 1995), p. 141. At Immaculata, theology and philosophy were the only departments where priests were always in the majority. Sisters served as members of the religion and philosophy departments from the late forties but did not teach theological courses until the late fifties. Even then, Sister Mary Cosmas taught softer, introductory Christology and ecclesiology, while priest colleagues taught the abstract, upper-level moral theology, dogma, and sacramental theology courses. See *Immaculata College Catalog, 1948–49*, pp. 61–63, and *Immaculata College Catalog, 1958–59*, p. 80, both ICGLA.

43. HFD56, age 63, int. 7.23.98. For most of this time, field hockey, a less prominent program, was also a women-only space on campus. In the early seventies, Immaculata began to hire male physical educators, who never coached the basketball team. See *The Gleaner 1970*, p. 51, ICGLA. Mary Jane Renshaw Lewandowski put "Fathers" in quotation marks in her survey (MJRL64, age 58, ques. 7, 8.4.98).

44. MLM+36, age 87, int. 8.16.02.

45. FFT50, age 70, ques. 18, 7.1.98; Player, 1940s; JYE74, age 45, int. 8.8.98; Player A '53, age 66, ques. 16, 5.8.98. Theresa Shank Grentz '74 told reporter Lindquist she chose to play rather than help her mother clean (Jean Lindquist, "Theresa Shank Plays Basketball Just 'Like One of the Boys,'" *Today's Post* [Philadelphia], October 3, 1973, p. 15). In my interview with Mary Frank McCormick '50, she referred to traditional young women's work as what girls "were supposed to do" (MFM50, age 69, int. 3.17.98). Seven survey respondents said fellow students were "very unsupportive" or "mostly unsupportive," while thirteen said they were "equally supportive and unsupportive."

46. MLMN65, age 54, int. 6.22.98; EAHQ73, age 46, int. 7.2.98; HM44, age 74, ques. 23, 6.13.98; FFT50, age 70, ques. 6, 7.1.98. Maureen Callahan Bigham '63 said some sisters would not be "caught dead in the gym" (MCB63, age 56, ques. 6, 5.23.98). Of sixty-five respondents to the survey, only two said they felt the sisters were "very unsupportive" or "mostly unsupportive"; nine said they were "equally supportive and unsupportive."

47. MFM50, age 69, int. 3.17.98; MBA51, age 68, int. 7.22.98; FFT50, age 70, ques. 18, 7.1.98; Player A '53, age 66, ques. 7, 5.8.98; Player '57, age 62, int. 6.11.98; JYE74, age 45, int. 8.8.98.

48. Player A '53, age 66, ques. 7, 5.8.98; MJRL64, age 58, ques. 7, 8.4.98. Lorrie Gable Finelli '78 said she thought some priests were "unaware" of changes in women's roles (LGF78, age 41, ques. 7, 5.15.98). On the survey, only five of the sixty-five respondents rated the priests and archdiocese as "very unsupportive" or "mostly unsupportive"; fourteen rated them "equally supportive and unsupportive." Seventeen abstained from responding to this question, an unusual rate. It is not clear what these nonresponses mean, but it is possible players found the question confusing or even irrelevant. Perhaps, as I have suggested, girls' basketball was one of the rare Catholic activities in which clerical presence, or the lack of it, mattered little.

2. Practicing Basketball, Practicing Class

1. Sources on the field house fire included "Immaculata College Field House Is Destroyed in $750,000 Blaze," *Daily Local News* (West Chester, Pa.), November 18, 1967; and "They Dance at Immaculata College Despite Fire that Destroyed Gym," *Catholic Standard and Times*, November 24, 1967, both on microfilm, "I.C. in print," roll 2, Gabriele Library Archives, Immaculata College, Pennsylvania (ICGLA).

2. JS, age 66, int. 8.25.99; MLM+36, age 83, int. 6.30.98.

3. FFT50, age 70, ques. 8, 7.1.98. Jenepher Shillingford said losing the field house was "a real blow" and that she and Sister Mary of Lourdes were "petrified" surveying the damage (JS, age 66, int. 8.25.99). Sister Mary of Lourdes described school use of the building in "They Dance at Immaculata College Despite Fire." She also characterized school finances as always barely breaking even (MLM+36, age 83, int. 6.30.98).

4. Immaculata players came from poor to upper-middle-class households, according to their self-descriptions on the surveys. The school did not keep records on student demographics until the seventies, so I was not able to compare basketball players' family incomes to those of the general student body and national averages. Instead, on surveys and in interviews, I asked players about their families' economic status relative to schoolmates and other Catholics and about their parents' education levels. Out of sixty-five survey respondents, three regarded their families as poor, eighteen as working class, thirty-seven as middle class, and six as upper class. One respondent did not answer the question. Again out of sixty-five, the largest group of respondents said their fathers had completed only a grade school education (eighteen), while almost as many said their fathers had completed college or professional school (seventeen). A great number of players were the first generation of women in their families to finish college; only thirteen said their mothers had completed college or professional school. Almost half the mothers (thirty out of sixty-five) had completed high school. Self-perception has drawbacks as evidence of class. For example, a slight majority of survey respondents (thirty-seven out of sixty-five) characterized their families as middle class, but Philadelphia Catholics' perception likely gauged class relative to the Catholic community, on the whole less wealthy than mainline Protestants during these years. For example, Mary Mawhinney Puglielli '46, who listed her high school–educated father as a "railroader" while her mother worked at home, des-

ignated her family "middle class" (MMP46, age 74, ques. 3, 5.6.98). Nevertheless, players' self-described status along with their stories revealed significant class disparities at school and on the team. Most often these differences broke down as a distinction between commuters and boarders. Commuting players often said they could afford to attend Immaculata at all only because of its relatively low cost or with help from academic scholarships. A few said they could not afford team travel and uniform expenses. Many took jobs to supplement funds for school as well as contribute to family finances. In contrast, basketball players who boarded tended to describe a more comfortable existence, mentioning family vacations to the Jersey shore, for example. Sometimes the commuter/boarder distinction indicated nothing about class, because in some instances poor students on scholarships lived on campus (Player '56, age 63, ques. 3 and 5, 5.4.98; JYE74, age 45, int. 8.8.98), while some well-off students commuted (PCE57, age 62, int. 7.23.98). Even so, the correspondence of status as commuter or boarder usually corresponded to anecdotal financial indicators. And even when it did not, campus stereotypes of commuters as poorer and boarders as wealthier were still in play.

5. MS77, age 42, int. 10.16.97. On the space of games and rituals, see Catherine Bell, *Ritual Theory, Ritual Practice* (New York: Oxford University Press, 1992); Pierre Bourdieu, *The Logic of Practice*, trans. Richard Nice (Stanford: Stanford University Press, 1990); Henri Lefebvre, *The Production of Space*, trans. Donald Nicholson-Smith (Oxford: Blackwell, 1991); Yi-fu Tuan, *Space and Place: The Perspective of Experience* (Minneapolis: University of Minnesota Press, 1977); and Jonathan Z. Smith, *To Take Place: Toward Theory in Ritual* (Chicago: University of Chicago Press, 1987).

6. EAA46, age 72, int. 6.17.98. In "Drive Opens for New Gym Building," *The Immaculatan* (TI) 6, no. 7 (May 31, 1939): 1, the author called Gorman Hall a "great handicap."

7. MDK+, age 71, int. 1.9.98. A fan from the class of '47 said play in Gorman Hall was a "feat" (Student '47, age 72, ques. 8, 5.20.98). Fruff Fauerbach Timby '50 described van rides to off-campus gyms (FFT50, age 70, ques. 20, 7.1.98).

8. EAA46, age 72, int. 6.17.98; FFT50, age 70, ques. 19, 7.1.98. For details on borrowed gyms, I also drew on my interview with Sister Marita David Kirsch (MDK+, age 71, int. 1.9.98).

9. The rental of Turners Hall was mentioned in "Managers Settle '46 Basketball Schedule; I.C. Chooses Turners Hall for Home Court Games," TI 13, no. 3 (December 14, 1945): 6. The venue was probabaly the former Turngemein, a German athletic club located at Broad and Columbia and renamed to suit American sensibilities. Mary Frank McCormick '50 said the school occasionally borrowed the West Catholic gym (MFM50, age 69, int. 3.17.98); Fruff Fauerbach Timby '50 also mentioned West Catholic (FFT50, age 70, ques. 8, 7.1.98). For more information on scheduling, I consulted "Immaculata's Varsity Officially Opens Basketball Season," TI 16, no. 4 (February 23, 1949): 6. On inadequate transportation, see "Varsity Teams Arrange Intercollegiate Meets," TI 10, no. 1 (October 23, 1942): 6. Manager Joan Biegler Snyder '53, who arranged team bus service, said she was "always fearful it would not show up" (JBS53, age 67, ques. 23, 6.13.98). Some years, the lack of available transportation decreased student body attendance at basketball games. They "participated when they could," said a player from the class of '45 (Player B '45, age 74, ques. 8, 6.27.98). Fruff Fauerbach Timby '50 also wrote, "Whoever could go would go" (FFT50, age 70, ques. 8, 7.1.98).

10. For information on college finances, I relied on interviews with Sister Virginia Assumpta McNabb (VAM+, age 65, int. 6.25.98) and Sister Mary of Lourdes McDevitt (MLM+36, age 83, int. 6.30.98). It was Sister Mary of Lourdes who said the school managed to "look great on the books" but that solvency measures had included her sacrificing her salary, which otherwise would have gone to the I.H.M. community's general funds.

11. The Gymnasium and Auditorium Fund is dated in Sandra Rollison and Sister Trinita Marie Amorosi, I.H.M., timeline of Immaculata College history, prepared by decades for the 1996 seventy-fifth anniversary of the college's founding, ICGLA. President Furey's quote is in "Drive Opens For New Gym Building," TI 6, no. 7 (May 31, 1939): 1. Rollison and Amorosi, timeline, also dated Cardinal Dougherty's permission. For the laying of the cornerstone, see a photograph captioned "The Long-Awaited Field House," as well as "Bishop Lays Field House Cornerstone," both in TI 17, no. 1 (October 24, 1949): 1. On the building's inaugural game, see the photograph captioned "Action Galore," TI 17, no. 4 (February 23, 1950): 5.

12. BND66, age 54, ques. 25, 6.1.98; FFT50, age 70, ques. 20, 7.1.98. Mary Frank McCormick '50 reported one bathroom in the new field house (MFM50, age 69, int. 3.17.98). Mary Murphy Schmelzer '62 described the two rows of chairs surrounding the court (MMS62, age 57, ques. 8, 5.24.98).

13. JS, age 66, int. 8.25.99; MLM+36, age 83, int. 6.30.98. The federal grant was reported in "Work on Alumnae Hall Begins at Immaculata," *Philadelphia Evening Bulletin*, January 16, 1969, microfilm, "I.C. in print," roll 2, ICGLA. Pat Fanning detailed the building's progress and use during the 1971 season in "Basketball Opens Season with Win," TI 38, no. 6 (February 18, 1971): 4; and "IC Basketball Team Boasts New Coach," TI 38, no. 4 (December 10, 1970): 4. See also "Federal Funds Will Help Replace Field House," *Daily Local News* (West Chester, Pa.), July 2, 1968; "Immaculata Starts Hall," *Philadelphia Inquirer*, January 16, 1969; and "Immaculata Dedicates Alumnae Hall," *The Archive* (Downingtown, Pa.), November 18, 1970; all on microfilm, "I.C. in print," roll 2, ICGLA. Mary Scharff '77, Sister Marian William Hoben '44, and Leo Mooney, Maureen Mooney '73's father, recalled setting up folding chairs and renting gyms during the championship years (MS77, age 42, int. 10.16.97; MWH+44, age 74, int. 10.16.97; and LM, mem. 9.3.98).

14. MFM50, age 69, 3.17.98. The anonymous columnist wrote "You and I.C.," TI 16, no. 3 (December 13, 1948): 6.

15. EAHQ73, age 46, int. 7.2.98. The *Immaculatan* article mentioned is "Managers Settle."

16. Player '57, age 62, int. 6.11.98; AMR43, age 76, int. 7.21.98; Player B '52, age 67, extra notes, ques. 6.18.98. Sister Marie Roseanne Bonfini '57, former Immaculata president (1992–2002), said team "solidarity" strengthened in adversity (MRB+57, age 61, int. 10.16.97). An *Immaculatan* writer called playing in Gorman "hide-and-seek" in "Juniors Lead in Intramural Games," TI 16, no. 5 (March 24, 1949): 6. Among several who suggested that the lack of a physical education major and athletic scholarships at Immaculata meant that its teams played with more freedom and pleasure was Helen Frank Dunigan '56 (HFD56, age 63, int. 7.23.98).

17. Stan Hochman, "Move Over, UCLA, Immaculata Also Flying No. 1 Flag," *Philadelphia Daily News*, March 21, 1972, microfilm, "I.C. in print," roll 11, ICGLA.

18. GFB57, age 63, int. 6.14.98; GRS64, age 55, int. 8.5.98. Jay Dolan cites a national survey conducted in the 1940s that placed two-thirds of Catholics in the poor and working classes, 25 percent in the middle class, and 9 percent in the upper class. By the early 1960s, he goes on to say, "Catholics had made a decisive move into the middle class." See Jay P. Dolan, *The American Catholic Experience: A History from Colonial Times to the Present* (Notre Dame, Ind.: University of Notre Dame Press, 1992), p. 357.

19. CLD70, age 49, int. 6.8.98. On families' financial contributions to Catholic schools in Philadelphia, see Charles R. Morris, *American Catholic: The Saints and Sinners Who Built America's Most Powerful Church* (New York: New York Times Books/Random House, 1997), p. 187.

20. MH+, int. 5.15.97; CMP+50, age 69, int. 6.25.98, int. 8.6.98. For the character of the Immaculate Heart community, I drew on interviews with Sister Virginia Assumpta McNabb (VAM+, age 65, int. 6.25.98) and Sister Mary of Lourdes McDevitt '36 (MLM+36, age 83, int. 6.30.98). Figures on Immaculata tuition and board come from *Immaculata College Catalog, 1948–49*, p. 19, and *Immaculata College Catalog, 1958–59*, p. 23, both in ICGLA. For Immaculata requirements, see *Immaculata College Catalog, 1958–59*, which describes a core curriculum heavy with religion, philosophy, English, and foreign languages (p. 34, ICGLA). For more on Immaculata professional programs, I drew on interviews with academic affairs staff member Sister Therese Marita Dignam '53 (TMD+53, age 66, int. 7.2.98, int. 8.6.98) and former home economics professor Sister Marie Albert Kunberger '51 (MAK+51, age 68, int. 1.1.98, int. 8.6.98). Surpassed only by basketball, the Immaculata home economics program got more local newspaper coverage than any other aspect of college life. For a few examples, see Barbara Barnes, "Prize College Rooms: Immaculata Students' Color Schemes Match Their Eyes," *Philadelphia Evening Bulletin*, October 26, 1940, Archbishop Furey Scrapbook, ICGLA; "Bethany House: Unique Experiment in Education," *Daily Local News* (West Chester, Pa.), November 1, 1958; and "Little Mothers," *Sunday Bulletin Magazine*, May 20, 1962, both on microfilm, "I.C. in print," roll 2, ICGLA. All the above were printed with huge photo spreads. For trends in national Catholic higher education, see Philip Gleason, *Contending with Modernity: Catholic Higher Education in the Twentieth Century* (New York: Oxford University Press, 1995).

21. Player B '53, age 66, int. 5.11.98; MS77, age 42, int. 10.16.97.

22. EPC64, age 55, int. 6.11.98.

23. On basketball and class, see Joan S. Hult, "Introduction to Part I: The Early Years of Basketball," in *A Century of Women's Basketball: From Frailty to Final Four*, ed. Joan S. Hult and Marianna Trekell (Reston, Va.: National Association for Girls and Women in Sport, 1991), pp. 10–13.

24. Player '57, age 62, int. 6.11.98; VAM+, age 65, int. 6.25.98. Player, age 60, int. 6.6.98. Players who mentioned working jobs while attending school included MJRL64, age 58, ques. 10, 8.4.98; JYE74, age 45, int. 8.8.98; MMH63, age 57, ques. 10, 6.10.98; and Player B '53, age 66, int. 5.11.98. Sister Virginia Assumpta confirmed students often dropped out because it was a "brother's turn to go to college" (VAM+, age 65, int. 6.25.98). Sister Therese Marita Dignam '53 of the Office of Academic Affairs explained other reasons for attrition, common across the Catholic women's higher-education spectrum. Some students, she said, never intended to enroll except for a one- or two-year experience. Some

left to specialize in programs not available at Immaculata or just didn't like the school. Some dropped out to address life crises or got poor grades after "too much socializing" (TMD+53, age 66, int. 7.2.98, int. 8.6.98). It was difficult to tell whether basketball players' rate of attrition was the same as the general student body. Since my main method of finding players was to look up their listing in the alumnae directory, it was hard to track those who did not graduate. Nevertheless, the numbers looked similar. I found about two hundred and fifty former players in the alumnae directory and failed to find there about eighty women who had been listed on basketball rosters at some point. This suggests that roughly 32 percent of basketball players, like the rest of their fellow students, did not complete their degrees. See Immaculata College Alumnae Office, *Immaculata College 1997 Alumnae Directory* (Immaculata, Pa.: Publishing Concepts, 1997).

25. EPC64, age 55, int. 6.11.98; Student Association of Immaculata College, *Living the Immaculata Way: Student Handbook 1950*, unpaginated reproduction, ICGLA. The visit of the proponent of "the natural look" is reported in Anita Morales, "Prospective 'Pin-ups' Meet the One and Only John R. Powers: Natural Girl Creed Preached by Head of Famous Modeling School," TI 12, no. 5 (March 23, 1945): 3.

26. EPC64, age 55, int. 6.11.98; GRS64, age 55, int. 8.5.98; MKD62, age 57, ques. 5, 7.28.98.

27. Mary Frank McCormick '50, like many others, said she remembered "no class tension" at the school (MFM50, age 69, int. 3.17.98). I estimated commuter and boarder proportions at Immaculata and on the basketball teams from interviews, surveys, newspaper articles, and other sources. Marguerite Horan Gowan termed resident life "ideal" in "Immaculata College Stands High . . . ," *Catholic Standard and Times*, May 29, 1936, Archbishop Furey Scrapbook, ICGLA. Sister Marie Roseanne Bonfini '57, former Immaculata president (1992–2002), said boarding was "part of the experience" (MRB+57, age 61, int. 10.16.97).

28. JV38, age 81, int. 7.20.98; MGD62, age 57, int. 7.21.98; EAA46, age 72, int. 6.17.98. Christine Lammer DiCiocchio '70 said it was "more fun" to be a boarder (CLD70, age 49, int. 6.8.98); Dee Cofer Cull '55 and Mary Lou McCahon Noone '65, who also spent time both as commuters and boarders, agreed (DCC55, age 65, int. 6.26.98; MLMN65, age 54, int. 6.22.98).

29. EPC64, age 55, int. 6.11.98; PCE57, age 62, int. 7.23.98; Player B '53, age 66, int. 5.11.98. Patricia Furey McDonnell '53 said commuters "missed out on a lot" (PFM53, age 66, ques. 10, 5.15.98).

30. EPC64, age 55, int. 6.11.98, who also said commuters were perceived as those who "could not afford to board"; HFD56, age 63, int. 7.23.98.

31. HFD56, age 63, int. 7.23.98; Player B '45, age 74, int. 7.24.98; MOR66, age 53, ques. 10, 6.27.98. For college regulations on curfews and callers, see 1950s college handbooks, ICGLA. For religious requirements, see *Immaculata College Handbook, 1954*, p. 17, ICGLA. Margaret Guinan Delaney '62 said the college was "isolated" and "way out" of town (MGD62, age 57, int. 7.21.98). A number of players mentioned fun in friends' cars or on buses: JD53, age 66, int. 6.8.98; MOR66, age 53, int. 6.26.98; PCE57, age 62, int. 7.23.98; Player B '53, age 66, int. 5.11.98; and CLD70, age 49, int. 6.8.98. Helen Frank Dunigan '56 mentioned the commuter lockers (HFD56, age 63, int. 7.23.98). Gloria Rook Schmidt '64 said commuters met to play across the city (GRS64, age 55, int. 8.5.98).

32. Maureen Callahan Bigham '63 and Christine Lammer DiCiocchio '70 said commuters changed in various restrooms across campus (MCB63, age 56, ques. 20, 5.23.98; CLD70, age 49, int. 6.8.98). Fruff Fauerbach Timby '50 and Mary Frank McCormick '50 remembered riding public buses home in sweat-soaked uniforms (FFT50, age 70, ques. 20, 7.1.98; MFM50, age 69, int. 3.17.98).

33. BF68, age 51, ques. 17, 8.17.98; PCE57, age 62, int. 7.23.98; Player A '53, age 66, ques. 20, 5.8.98; MCM54, age 65, int. 6.23.98. Rosemary McNichol Walsh '60 recalled her long commutes after games (RMW60, age 60, ques. 26, 5.23.98). Sister Marita David Kirsch's trip involved taking the Paoli local (MDK+, age 71, 1.9.98). Pauline Callahan Earl '57 said her trip lasted a half-hour each way (PCE57, age 62, int. 7.23.98); Anne Carroll Camp '51 said she traveled a full hour each way (ACC51, age 68, ques. 5, 5.10.98); Frances Gercke Campbell '45 said she traveled up to two and a half hours each way (FGC45, age 74, int. 5.12.98).

34. MDK+, age 71, 1.9.98.

35. JSK58, age 60, int. 6.23.98; MSS66, age 53, ques. 9 and 21, 6.17.98; BGM71, age 48, int. 7.30.98. Pauline Callahan Earl '57 said the "names" were commuters (PCE57, age 62, int. 7.23.98). On commuters as team captains, I relied on survey data, which showed that more than half the team captains who responded to the survey were commuters.

36. MSS66, age 53, ques. 11, 6.17.98; MLMN65, age 54, int. 6.22.98; EAA46, age 72, int. 6.17.98; ACC51, age 68, ques. 23, 5.10.98; PFM53, age 66, ques. 25, 5.15.98. Other interviewees who said commuters and boarders rarely met apart from practice included TMD+53, age 66, int. 7.2.98, int. 8.6.98; VAM+, age 65, int. 6.25.98; and MGD62, age 57, int. 7.21.98. Jean Doris '53 said she relished the rare chance to sleep overnight at Immaculata (JD53, age 66, ques. 23, 5.10.98).

37. JYE74, age 45, int. 8.8.98.

38. MDK+, age 71, 1.9.98; MGD62, age 57, int. 7.21.98; MS77, age 42, int. 10.16.97.

39. ILH70, age 49, ques. 21, 5.8.98.

3. Bodies in Basketball

1. EAA46, age 72, int. 6.15.98.

2. MDK+, age 71, int. 1.9.98. The phrases "absolute joy, energy" and "fun" come from Lorrie Gable Finelli '78 (LGF78, age 41, ques. 21, 5.15.98). The phrase "loved to play basketball" comes from Player C '45, age 74, int. 6.24.98. Those who used the words "fun," "love," "joy," or "enjoyment" specifically to describe playing the game of basketball or listed "playing the game" as their "happiest" memory included BF68, age 51, ques. 21, 8.17.98; Player B '45, age 74, ques. 25, 6.27.98; MBA51, age 68, int. 7.22.98; JD53, age 66, ques. 24 and 25, 5.10.98; JCF53, age 53, ques. 21, 7.27.98; AFC67, age 52, ques. 26, 5.10.98; Player '57, age 62, int. 6.11.98; Player A '48, age 71, ques. 20, 7.10.98; EPC64, age 55, int. 6.11.98; and Player B '53, age 66, int. 5.11.98.

3. John Edgar Wideman, "Playing Dennis Rodman," *New Yorker*, April 29 and May 6, 1996, p. 94; EAHQ73, age 46, int. 7.2.98.

4. Bodies are always also racialized and class-ified bodies. For organizational purposes, I have discussed class in chapter 2 and race in chapter 5, dealing in this chapter with gender and sexuality. To represent players' memories and interpretations faithfully, I assumed

Catholic women's bodily pleasure was a broadly physical rather than discreetly sexual phenomenon. The players to whom I spoke described a wide variety of bodily experience, usually not directly sexual, including feelings of vigor, fatigue, elation, aggression, and performance. In this approach, I took cues from Deleuze and Guattari, who criticized the Freudian reduction of physical pleasure to sexuality, thereby also reducing it to private realms and political irrelevance. See Gilles Deleuze and Félix Guattari, *Anti-Oedipus: Capitalism and Schizophrenia*, trans. Robert Hurley, Mark Seem, Helen R. Lane (Minneapolis: University of Minnesota Press, 1983); and idem, *A Thousand Plateaus: Capitalism and Schizophrenia*, trans. Brian Massumi (Minneapolis: University of Minnesota Press, 1987).

5. Charles R. Morris, *American Catholic: The Saints and Sinners Who Built America's Most Powerful Church* (New York: New York Times Books/Random House, 1997), p. 173.

6. Player '57, age 62, int. 6.11.98.

7. The signal missives enshrining Thomism and denouncing modernism were Pope Leo XIII's *Aeterni Patris* (1879) and *Testem Benevolentiae* (1899) and Pope Pius X's *Pascendi Dominici Gregis* (1907). For details of these developments, see Philip Gleason, *Contending with Modernity: Catholic Higher Education in the Twentieth Century* (New York: Oxford University Press, 1995), pp. 105–66. On postwar Catholic culture, see also William Halsey, *The Survival of Innocence: Catholicism in an Era of Disillusionment, 1920–1940* (Notre Dame, Ind.: University of Notre Dame Press, 1980).

8. Jay Dolan, *The American Catholic Experience: A History from Colonial Times to the Present* (Notre Dame, Ind.: University of Notre Dame Press, 1992), p. 352. From the 1940s, the Philadelphia school system used *Fr. McGuire's The New Baltimore Catechism and Mass* (New York: Benziger Brothers, 1941); see Morris, *American Catholic*, p. 454.

9. Bonner mentioned discipline, hard work, selflessness, and morality as benefits of sports in "The Value of Athletics to Boys," undated, Monsignor John Bonner Collection (MJBC) at the Philadelphia Archives and Historical Research Center, St. Charles Borromeo Seminary, Overbrook, Pennsylvania (PAHRC), box 1, folder 14, item 3, pp. 1–2. Bonner said "sound mind in a sound body" in dedication of Knute Rockne Memorial Hall at Sacred Heart in Allentown, Pa., untitled speech (September 20, 1942), MJBC, box 2, folder 7, item 6, p. 1. The encyclical quotation is from Pope Pius XI, "Christian Education of Youth," in *Four Great Encyclicals: Labor, Education, Marriage, the Social Order* (New York: Paulist, 1931), p. 62. In Philadelphia as elsewhere, this encyclical on pedagogy became programmatic for Catholic schools; its reminder not to neglect physical education, for example, was quoted in a history of Hallahan Catholic high school put together by alumnae: John W. Hallahan Girls' High School Alumnae Association, *Hallahan: The Story of Fifty Years of Free, Higher Education for Catholic Girls in Philadelphia* (Philadelphia: Campus/Zamsky Studios, 1951), p. 42, PAHRC. See Pius XII, "Sports and Gymnastics," in *Pope Pius XII and Catholic Education*, ed. Vincent A. Yzermans (St. Meinrad, Ind.: Grail, 1957), as well as excerpts from Pius XI, "Christian Education of Youth," and Pius XII, "Formative Value of Sports," "Influence of Athletics," and "Education and Modern Environment," in *The Popes on Youth: Principles for Forming and Guiding Youth from Popes Leo XIII to Pius XII*, ed. Raymond B. Fullam, S.J. (Buffalo: Canisius High School, 1956), pp. 53–64. Possible dangers to proper ends in physical education, Pius XII wrote in "Sports and Gymnastics," included "a certain nudism" and a "cult of the body" (pp. 59, 56, respectively).

10. I drew details of game reports from, respectively: Jeanmarie Dunn, "I.C. by Jeanmarie," *The Immaculatan* (TI) 14, no. 4 (February 27, 1947): 6; "Immaculata Stops Drexel, Penn, Marywood; Jayvees Roll Up Score in Penn Junior Game," TI 16, no. 5 (March 24, 1949): 6; "Mackies Down Cabrini College: Ursinus Hands I. C. First Defeat," TI 28, no. 5 (March 24, 1961): 4; "Hoopsters See 'Action' Season," TI 33, no. 4 (December 16, 1965): 4; "Mackies Conquer Cabrini," TI 33 (February 18, 1966): 4, in which student spectator Donna Manus also called the game a "good, fast one"; "I.C. Spotlights 'Mackie' Starting Team: Basketball Scorebooks Stand at 3–2–1," TI 24, no. 5 (March 25, 1957): 6; "Tid Bits," TI 17, no. 6 (April 27, 1950): 4; "Sports Shorts," TI 35, no. 7 (March 22, 1968): 4.

11. Steveda Chepko, "The Domestication of Basketball," in *A Century of Women's Basketball: From Frailty to Final Four*, ed. Joan S. Hult and Marianna Trekell (Reston, Va.: National Association for Girls and Women in Sport, 1991), pp. 112–13.

12. Chepko, "The Domestication," quoting *The Spalding Women's Basketball Guide 1917–18*, p. 115. Hult and Trekell date the first meeting of the DGWS rules committee in *A Century of Women's Basketball*, p. 427.

13. Pope Pius XII, "Address to Women of Catholic Action," October 21, 1945, in *The Pope Speaks: The Teachings of Pope Pius XII* (New York: Pantheon, 1957), p. 57; Player B '53, age 66, int. 5.11.98; MCM54, age 65, int. 6.23.98.

14. RDM46, age 73, int. 7.9.98. The quote beginning "in temperament" is from Pius XII, quoted in William B. Faherty, S.J., *The Destiny of Modern Woman, in the Light of Papal Teaching* (Westminster, Md.: Newman, 1950), p. 101. Certainly, Catholic teachings were not entirely separate from or immune to national trends in women's roles. During World War II, like women across the country, young Catholic women in Philadelphia joined the W.A.V.E.s, and their mothers worked outside the home in what Monsignor Bonner patriotically called wartime's "strange and necessary roles" (John Bonner, Chestnut Hill College commencement address, 1943, MJBC, box 1, folder 4, item 3). After the war, U.S. women, Catholics included, heard urgings to return to the home. On the postwar backlash against women's wartime roles, see Elaine Tyler May, "Explosive Issues: Sex, Women, and the Bomb," in *Recasting America: Culture and Politics in the Age of Cold War*, ed. Lary May (Chicago: University of Chicago Press, 1989), pp. 154–70. Throughout these years, Catholic women of the working and poor classes, of course, couldn't always afford to stop out-of-home work, even after having children. But women groomed at Catholic colleges for middle-class futures certainly got the message that they should stay at home and more often had the means to follow it. See Pope Pius XI, "On Christian Marriage (*Casti conubii*)," in *Four Great Encyclicals: Labor, Education, Marriage, the Social Order* (New York: Paulist, 1931), pp. 73–120; Pope Pius XII, *Dear Newlyweds: Pope Pius XII Speaks to Young Couples*, sel. and trans. James F. Murray Jr. and Bianca M. Murray (New York: Farrar, Straus, and Cudahy, 1961); Pope Pius XII, excerpts from "Address to Newlyweds," April 8, 1942, and "Address to Women of Catholic Action," October 26, 1941, in *The Pope Speaks: The Teachings of Pius XII* (New York: Pantheon, 1957), pp. 47–54.

15. Cheerleader '64, age 55, int. 7.20.98; MGD62, age 57, int. 7.21.98.

16. Sister M. Eucharius, I.H.M., *Esprit de Corps: The Immaculata Way* (Immaculata, Pa.: Immaculata College, 1945), ICGLA, pp. 11, 23–25, 47, 57–59, 7–8, and 69–70. The author wrote *Esprit de Corps* as a manual to orient freshmen to college traditions. The campus newspaper article quoted is "Visit Mary-Shrines!" TI 21, no. 4 (February 17, 1954): 2.

17. The Reverend F. X. Lasance, ed., *The Young Men's Guide: Counsels, Reflections, and Prayers for Catholic Young Men* (New York: Benziger Brothers, 1952), pp. viii–ix; and idem, *The Catholic Girls' Guide: Counsels and Devotions* (New York: Benziger Brothers, 1906), pp. 296–97, 14–15.

18. John Bonner, baccalaureate address to a women's college, untitled, undated, MJBC, box 1, folder 6, item 1, p. 7. There are textual hints that Bonner might have delivered this address during World War II at Immaculata, but that is not certain.

19. "The Marylike Standards of Modesty in Dress," pamphlet (Fresno, Ca.: Apostolate of Christian Action, 1956). I am grateful to Elizabeth Clark for providing me with a copy of this pamphlet.

20. John Bonner, sermon, untitled and undated, MJBC, box 4, folder 6, item 10. Successive editions of the I.H.M. constitutions affirmed the order's understanding that imitation of Mary, including her suffering, was an aspect of their community life, geared to participate in the "saving mission of the Church" (Sisters, Servants of the Immaculate Heart of Mary, *Faithful Witness: Constitutions* [Philadelphia: Sisters, Servants of the Immaculate Heart of Mary, 1997], pp. 46–48).

21. *Immaculata College Catalog, 1940–41*, p. 13; *Immaculata College Catalog, 1948–49*, p. 14; *Immaculata College Catalog, 1958–59*, p. 16–17, all ICGLA.

22. CLD70, age 49, int. 6.8.98. Players who said the college was overprotective or repressive included JV38, age 81, int. 7.20.98; EPC64, age 55, int. 6.11.98; and CLD70, age 49, int. 6.8.98. The stories of canceled mixers and hemline measuring come from my interview with a cheerleader, class of '64, although several repeated the stories. This cheerleader said she considered it an act of high treason when she posted a picture of Jackie Kennedy in her boots on a campus bulletin board (Cheerleader '64, age 55, int. 7.20.98).

23. Cheerleader '49, age 70, int. 7.23.98; Player B '53, age 66, int. 5.11.98.

24. JV38, age 81, int. 7.20.98; JD53, age 66, int. 6.8.98; Student, age 51, int. 7.12.98.

25. MFM50, age 69, int. 3.17.98. Of three hundred former Immaculata players whom I attempted to contact, two hundred and sixty-nine were married and thirty-one were single; of the single former players, six were nuns. I could not discern from my data who of the single and married women were divorced. Of sixty-five who responded to the survey, fifty-five were married and six were single, not including two religious and two divorced women. Of the fifty-five married respondents, all had children. A third had either three or four children; another full quarter had either five or six children.

26. "Wedding Bells Change Miss D. to Mrs. S.," TI 28, no. 4 (February 24, 1961): 4; "Are These Future Tommy Golas or Bob Schaffers?" TI 21, no. 6 (April 30, 1954): 4; "Hockey Fullback Margy McCormick," TI 14, no. 3 (December 14, 1946): 6. Many articles included in the *Spalding Guides* "sought to associate the participation of women in basketball with motherhood and morality" as a means of bridging the gap "between a sport that was suspiciously masculine and public approval of women's right to play," Chepko wrote ("The Domestication," p. 115). In contrast, no Immaculata interviewee voluntarily made a connection between basketball and motherhood. Those to whom I specifically addressed the question were puzzled by it or said the two had nothing to do with each other, such as MFM50, age 69, int. 3.17.98. See also "Immaculata Coach Rings Wedding Bells," TI 13, no. 7 (May 31, 1946): 8; "Captain Dolores Cofer Cedes Title To Junior Star," TI 22, no. 6 (April 17, 1955): 4; and "Wedding Bells Ring Out for All-Star Mary Frank," TI 22, no. 7 (May 29, 1955): 4.

27. "Barbara Flannigan [*sic*] Wins Runner-Up in '66 Philadelphia Sportsmen Show," TI 33, no. 6 (February 18, 1966): 1; Donna Anderson, "Feminine Approach to Basketball Conquers Again," TI 39 (March 29, 1973): 4.

28. For "ex-Mackie Mommies," see "Mackies Capture Two Games As Basketball Season Opens," TI 25, no. 4 (February 17, 1958): 4.

29. Player '57, age 62, int. 6.11.98; MOR66, age 53, int. 6.26.98 FFT50, age 70, ques. 18 and 6, 7.1.98. Several other players said basketball was an "outlet" for them, including Player A '48, age 71, ques. 16, 7.10.98; PCE57, age 62, int. 7.23.98; and MLMN65, age 54, int. 6.22.98. Mary Lou McCahon Noone '65 said basketball "balanced" her life (MLMN65, age 54, int. 6.22.98).

30. MLMN65, age 54, int. 6.22.98; HFD56, age 63, int. 7.23.98. The quotation about the fun of practice comes from MGD62, age 57, int. 7.21.98. For practice schedules, I drew on Player A '53, age 66, ques. 20, 5.8.98, and JYE74, age 45, int. 8.8.98, as well as media stories: "Cathy Rush's Formula: Defense and Diapers," *Philadelphia Inquirer*, April 1, 1973; and Joan Nobolt, "Q-town Girl Athlete Takes Pride in Sports, Work," *Free Press* (Quakertown, Pa.), June 27, 1974, both on microfilm, "I.C. in print," roll 11, ICGLA.

31. MBA51, age 68, int. 7.22.98; MMH63, age 57, corr. 11.22.99; MMKK58, age 62, ques. 21, 7.9.98; HFD56, age 63, int. 7.23.98; Player C '52, age 68, ques. 25, 6.20.98; Player A '45, age 73, ques. 21, 5.18.98; SFO72, age 48, ques. 21, 6.24.98. The quotation "happy-but-exhausted" comes from MKD62, age 57, ques. 23, 7.28.98.

32. MDK+, age 70, int. 1.9.98; ILH70, age 49, ques. 25, 5.8.98. Pauline Callahan Earl '57 talked about the "need to be active" (PCE57, age 62, int. 7.23.98).

33. JD53, age 66, int. 6.8.98; HFD56, age 63, int. 7.23.98. On Immaculata members of the Teamsterettes team, see Herm Rogul, "Immaculata's Champs Take Their Hoops Seriously," *Evening Bulletin* (Philadelphia), February 20, 1973, sec. G, p. 45. A class of '57 player said she "needed a sport for that season" (Player '57, age 62, int. 6.11.98). Maureen Mooney '73 was one of several who said she played other sports to keep in shape for basketball (MM73, age 46, ques. 9, 9.3.98). More than six out of ten survey respondents said they played other sports besides basketball. Field hockey was the only other varsity sport at Immaculata for most of these years, and the vast majority who played another sport played hockey. Volleyball became a varsity sport in the late sixties, and the tennis team added interscholastic competition in the early seventies.

34. DCC55, age 65, int. 6.26.98; JS, age 66, int. 8.25.99. Helen Frank Dunigan '56 described the Catholic game as "faster" and "give-and-go" (HFD56, age 63, int. 7.23.98). On Cathy Rush's use of men's strategies, see Frank Fitzpatrick, "Where It All Began," *Philadelphia Inquirer Magazine*, March 26, 2000, p. 6. Often Catholic girls also had more experience than their competitors, partly because they had fewer opportunities to try other sports that would shift attention from basketball, as Helen Frank Dunigan '56 and others pointed out (HFD56, age 63, int. 7.23.98). For these reasons, public schools often could not physically keep up with Immaculata. See Sarah Pileggi, "New Era for Delta Dawns," *Sports Illustrated*, March 31, 1975, p. 67; and Herm Rogul, "UD's Marianne Knew Where Playground Was," *News of Delaware County* (Upper Darby, Pa.), February 13, 1975, microfilm, "I.C. in print," roll 11, ICGLA.

35. Lucille Kyvallos, "Queens College—Success With No Frills," in *A Century of Women's Basketball*, ed. Hult and Trekell, p. 361.

36. LGF78, age 41, int. 7.23.98.

37. *The Gleaner 1938*, p. 48, ICGLA.

38. MJRL64, age 58, ques. 11 and 18, 8.4.98; FFT50, age 70, ques. 21, 7.1.98; Cheerleader '64, age 55, int. 7.20.98. On the street game setting the tone, I drew from GRS64, age 55, int. 8.5.98, among other interviews.

39. HFD56, age 63, int. 7.23.98; MCM54, age 65, int. 6.23.98; JYE74, age 45, int. 8.8.98.

40. MS77, age 42, int. 10.16.97; Mary Boardman, "Like a Family," *Main Line Times*, March 20, 1975, microfilm "I.C. in print," roll 11, ICGLA; EAHQ73, age 46, int. 7.2.98; Player '57, age 62, int. 6.11.98; MJRL64, age 58, ques. 18, 8.4.98; MOR66, age 53, int. 6.26.98, who also said basketball "probably" displaced sexual energy. Mary Jane Renshaw Lewandowski '64 also wrote of venting frustrations (MJRL64, age 58, ques. 18, 8.4.98). Evie Adams Atkinson '46 described herself and teammates as "competitive, very competitive" (EAA46, age 72, int. 6.17.98). Others who said specifically they enjoyed or benefited from competition included Player A '48, age 71, ques. 11, 7.10.98; Player A '52, age 66, ques. 11, 5.4.98; AML53, age 67, ques. 11, 5.22.98; MMH63, age 57, ques. 11, 6.10.98; AFC67, age 52, ques. 11, 5.10.98; JYE74, age 45, ques. 11, 8.8.98; GRS64, age 55, int. 8.5.98. The phrase "winning all the time" comes from ACC51, age 68, ques. 25, 5.10.98. Players who said specifically that they enjoyed winning or that their happiest moment in basketball was winning included Player A '52, age 66, ques. 21, 5.4.98; DCC55, age 65, ques. 23, 6.27.98; Player '57, age 62, ques. 23, 6.17.98; ADL57, age 62, ques. 21, 7.20.98; MMH63, age 57, ques. 11 and 25, 6.10.98; SFO72, age 48, ques. 25, 6.24.98; Player '75, age 45, ques. 21, 5.10.98; and MDK+, age 71, int. 1.9.98. If some players considered basketball a displacement of sexual tension, Catholic leaders expressed this sexual "steam valve" theory of sports only with regard to boys, as when Bonner said that sports gave a boy a "necessary outlet for his excess energies" and kept him occupied with "wholesome activities." It did not seem to occur to them that girls might need such an outlet as well. Probably this was because they idealized male sexuality as active and female sexuality as passive. For them, as I shall suggest later in the chapter, it was bodily display not physical exertion that flagged the sport's sexual dimensions for girls.

41. BND66, age 54, ques. 20, 6.1.98. Boarders who said they changed in their rooms included EAA46, age 72, ques. 20, 6.15.98; MCB63, age 56, ques. 20, 5.23.98; Player A '52, age 66, ques. 20, 5.4.98; MRL52, age 68, ques. 20, 5.20.98; and Player '57, age 62, ques. 20, 6.17.98. A player who graduated in 1944 said she changed in the lavatories (Player '44, age 74, ques. 20, 7.22.98). A player from the class of '45 said she changed in the coaches' or campus Athletic Association office (Player B '45, age 74, ques. 20, 6.27.98). In later years, there was a hall for the commuters' lockers—book lockers not gym lockers—where Christine Lammer DiCiocchio '70 said she changed (CLD70, age 49, int. 6.8.98). On changing in visitors' locker rooms, I drew on JYE74, age 45, ques. 20, 8.8.98, among others.

42. MFM50, age 69, int. 3.17.98.

43. On wearing T-shirts in practice, I drew on MLMN65, age 54, int. 6.22.98, although this was a concession allowed only sometime after 1950. Mary Jane Renshaw Lewandowski '64 said some teammates "loved the limelight" (MJRL64, age 58, ques. 18, 8.4.98).

44. Player '57, age 62, int. 6.11.98; ACC51, age 68, ques. 21, 5.10.98; MCM54, age 65, int. 6.23.98; MMS62, age 57, ques. 18, 5.24.98. Ann McSorley Lukens '53 described fellow players as "energetic" and "healthy" (AML53, age 67, ques. 21, 5.22.98). Players who said teammates were "strong" included JDT54, age 65, ques. 22, 5.28.98, and Player '56, age 63,

ques. 18, 5.4.98. Helen Frank Dunigan '56 said a teammate was "fast as the wind" (HFD56, age 63, int. 7.23.98).

45. MJRL64, age 58, ques. 18, 8.4.98; Player '56, age 63, ques. 19, 5.4.98.

46. MGD62, age 57, int. 7.21.98. Theories of the "gaze" exploring the pleasures of watching and being watched were inaugurated with Laura Mulvey's 1975 article "Visual Pleasure and Narrative Cinema," originally published in *Screen*, also available in *Film Theory and Criticism: Introductory Readings*, 4th ed., ed. Gerald Mast, Marshall Cohen, and Leo Braudy (New York: Oxford University Press, 1992), pp. 746–57. Mulvey's analysis of how traditional films, like patriarchal culture in general, narratively and cinematically position the viewer as a voyeuristic male opened the way for feminist work suggesting the potential subversiveness of women watching men—and other women.

47. DCC55, age 65, int. 6.26.98; MCB63, age 56, ques. 17, 5.23.98; MJRL64, age 58, ques. 8, 8.4.98; Ruth Sadler, "College Strictly Academic to Scharff," *Courier-Post* (Camden, N.J.), January 23, 1976, microfilm, "I.C. in print," roll 4, ICGLA.

48. LM78, age 42, ques. 21, 5.26.98. Sister Marian William Hoben '44 told of arriving in town and seeing Immaculata's name billed at Madison Square Garden (MWH+44, age 74, int. 10.16.97). The box office sold out—13,000 tickets—and 11,969 officially saw the game. See Lena Williams, "Women's Basketball Draws 11,969," *New York Times*, February 23, 1975; Dave Hirshey, "Gals Have Their Day in Court—Weaving Baskets in Garden," *Philadelphia Daily News*, February 22, 1975; "A Garden of Well-Versed Women," *Sports Illustrated*, March 3, 1975; Bill Verigan, "For Women Cagers, Equal Play But Not Equal Pay," *Sunday News* (Philadelphia), February 23, 1975; and Bill Verigan, "These Girls Take Basketball to College," *St. Paul Dispatch*, April 4, 1975, all on microfilm, "I.C. in print," roll 11, ICGLA. On the televised game, see Carol Towarnicky, "The Macs Are Treated Like One of the Boys," *Philadelphia Daily News*, January 27, 1975, microfilm, "I.C. in print," roll 11, ICGLA.

49. MCB63, age 56, ques. 18, 5.23.98. Mary Scharff '77 said that the idea of being ladies was not to "act like guys" (MS77, age 42, int. 10.16.97).

50. Mildred Barnes, "Coaching and Game Reflections, 1940s to 1980s," in *A Century of Women's Basketball*, ed. Hult and Trekell, pp. 340–41; ILH70, age 49, ques. 18, 5.8.98. Other players, coaches, and nuns who described the Immaculata gender ethos of "ladies" included EPC64, age 55, int. 6.11.98; KBL37, age 82, ques. 18, 5.9.98; FFT50, age 70, ques. 21, 7.1.98; TMM63, age 56, ques. 18, 5.25.98; MS77, age 42, int. 10.16.97; HFD56, age 63, int. 7.23.98; MFM50, age 69, int. 3.17.98; MSM, age 75, mem. 7.13.98; and MWH+44, age 74, int. 10.16.97.

51. FFT50, age 70, ques. 21, 7.1.98; MMKK58, age 62, ques. 18, 7.9.98; MS77, age 42, int. 10.16.97.

52. MMS62, age 57, ques. 18, 5.24.98; CLD70, age 49, int. 6.8.98; TMM63, age 56, ques. 11, 5.25.98. Twenty out of sixty-five respondents said their teammates were "very feminine" or "somewhat feminine." A few who described themselves or teammates as "jocks" included Player '59, age 61, ques. 18, 6.20.98; JD53, age 66, int. 6.8.98; and Cheerleader '57, age 62, ques. 18, 5.15.98.

53. DCC55, age 65, int. 6.26.98. Marcella Rominger Lusby '52 suggested there was a line past which players were too "masculine or tomboyish" (MRL52, age 68, ques. 18, 5.20.98). Those who attributed teammates' masculinity to hanging out with brothers included ADL57, age 62, ques. 18, 7.20.98, and EPC64, age 55, int. 6.11.98.

54. GRS64, age 55, int. 8.5.98; MRL52, age 68, ques. 18, 5.20.98; MDK+, age 71, int. 1.9.98.

55. ADL57, age 62, ques. 18, 7.20.98; MOR66, age 53, ques. 18, 6.27.98; Player '56, age 63, ques. 18, 5.4.98; MCEW+62, age 57, ques. 18, 6.2.98; Player B '45, age 74, ques. 18, 6.27.98. Four other survey respondents wrote notes, in addition to marking question 18, to the effect that their teammates were a mix of gender types. Others who said they really didn't think about players' gender one way or the other included RMW60, age 60, ques. 18, 5.23.98; Cheerleader '64, age 55, int. 7.20.98; and MKD62, age 57, ques. 18, 7.28.98. Others who declined to put gender descriptors on teammates included FFT50, age 70, ques. 18, 7.1.98, and JDT54, age 65, ques. 18, 5.28.98. The criticism of question 18 came from Player A '52, age 66, ques. 18, 5.4.98.

56. MFM50, age 69, int. 3.17.98; TMM63, age 56, ques. 18, 5.25.98; Player B '53, age 66, int. 5.11.98; MM73, age 46, ques. 18, 9.3.98; MCM54, age 65, int. 6.23.98.

57. The quotation came from Cheerleader '63, age 57, ques. 25, 5.18.98, who, like the overwhelming majority of basketball players, said the Immaculata administration supported basketball.

58. HFD56, age 63, int. 7.23.98. For dates of rules changes, see Hult and Trekell, *A Century of Women's Basketball*, pp. 427–30. The five-player full-court game was introduced on an experimental basis in 1969, as Hult recounts in "The Saga of Competition: Basketball Battles and Governance War," in *A Century of Women's Basketball*, p. 234. Jenepher Shillingford coached the Mackies during the transition. "Let's try it for a year . . . see if women drop on the ground, 'flush their heart[s],'" she said. "Whoever thought . . . up [the rover] was clever because they were the precursors to going full court. And they realized they couldn't go from two courts to full court without something, some transition. And so they came up with this little gem. It was really quite comical" (JS, age 66, int. 8.25.99).

59. Player B '45, age 74, int. 7.24.98; RMW60, age 60, ques. 21, 5.23.98; GRS64, age 55, int. 8.5.98; JYE74, age 45, int. 8.8.98.

60. GRS64, age 55, int. 8.5.98; RDM46, age 73, int. 7.9.98; MCM54, age 65, int. 6.23.98; EPC64, age 55, int. 6.11.98. Others said they didn't resent women's rules at the time they played but later coached or watched basketball and longed for the freer, full-court experience. "I would have loved to play that way," said Helen Frank Dunigan '56, who coached when the roving player scheme was introduced (HFD56, age 63, int. 7.23.98). Another former Immaculata player, Jean Doris '53, coached girls' gradeschool ball at St. Leonard's Academy in Philadelphia when leaders of the mixed Catholic-public Academic League met to discuss the new rover rules allowing one player to run full court. "I can remember this one woman saying, 'Oh, my girls couldn't do that'; I thought, 'My girls could,'" she recalled (JD53, age 66, int. 6.8.98).

61. EAHQ73, age 46, int. 7.2.98; Larry Eldridge, "Theresa Shank: New Queen of Women's Basketball," *Christian Science Monitor*, May 22, 1974, microfilm, "I.C. in print," roll 11, ICGLA; DCC55, age 65, int. 6.26.98. Jenepher Shillingford said that standing still when the ball wasn't in your half of the court, you felt "like a telephone pole" (JS, age 66, int. 8.25.99).

62. GRS64, age 55, int. 8.5.98. Gloria Rook Schmidt '64, among others, also said Immaculata teams ran full court at practice before the rule changes. The "run-and-gun" expression and the story of demotion come from Mary Jane Renshaw Lewandowski '64

(MJRL64, age 58, int. 8.4.98). The "by the numbers" comment comes from Player '57, age 62. int. 6.11.98.

63. MDK+, age 70, int. 1.9.98; HFD56, age 63, int. 7.23.98.

64. MJRL64, age 58, int. 8.4.98. By the seventies, coach Cathy Rush still benched her players for purposeful aggression but not for normal game contact. In fact, according to a 1950s player who traveled with other alumnae to watch the championship teams play, Rush found her Catholic charges "too polite" and told them if they knocked someone down, they should let her get up by herself (Player '57, age 62, int. 6.11.98).

65. JV38, age 81, int. 7.20.98; ADL57, age 62, ques. 20, 7.20.98. Some years, players dressed in the morning for the game, wore their jerseys to classes on game days, and did not change in a locker room at all, according to Mary Murphy Schmelzer '62 (MMS62, age 57, ques. 20, 5.24.98).

66. MMS62, age 57, ques. 20, 5.24.98; ADL57, age 62, ques. 20, 7.20.98. Izanne Leonard Haak '70 said they used visitor locker rooms "just to use the restrooms" (ILH70, age 49, ques. 20, 5.8.98). Janet Young Eline used the word "aghast" about opposing teams' locker room nakedness on the survey and told me the rest of the story when I interviewed her (JYE74, age 45, ques. 20, 8.8.98; int. 8.8.98). Betty Ann Hoffman Quinn '73 gave a similar account of her team's discomfort with "gang showers" (EAHQ73, age 46, int. 7.2.98).

67. MFM50, age 69, int. 3.17.98.

68. Player B '53, age 66, int. 5.11.98. From 1949 to 1967, Gorman's course "The Family" remained a graduation requirement: *Immaculata College Catalog, 1949–50*, p. 68, and *Immaculata College Catalog, 1965–66, 1966–67*, pp. 82–83, both ICGLA. For Dougherty's campaign against sex education, see Thomas J. Donaghy, F.S.C., *Philadelphia's Finest: A History of Education in the Catholic Archdiocese, 1692–1970* (Philadelphia: American Catholic Historical Society, 1972), p. 222. Catholic leaders could consider affection among girls and even same-sex "crushes" normal, as in the chapter "Gladys Has a Crush on Sister," in Reverend Joseph G. Kempf's *Helping Youth to Grow* (Milwaukee: Bruce, 1941), pp. 132–42, available to sisters in the Immaculata library. The warnings not to befriend older members of the same sex came from George A. Kelly, *The Catholic Youth's Guide to Life and Love* (Random House: New York, 1960), p. x, available in the collection of the Philadelphia archdiocese seminary library, at St. Charles Borromeo Seminary, Overbrook, Pennsylvania. The Pius XII quotation is in Fullam, *The Popes*, p. 147, from the missive "Psychotherapy and Religion." Most manuals settled for explaining that sexual activity "outside marriage is wrong, whether it be directed toward solitary enjoyment, or toward another person," as Mary Lewis Coakley put it in *Our Child—God's Child* (Milwaukee: Bruce, 1953), p. 113, also in the Immaculata College Gabriele Library regular collection. Sociology classes might have used books such as John L. Thomas, S.J., *The Catholic Viewpoint on Marriage and the Family* (Garden City, N.Y.: Hanover House, 1958), also in the Immaculata library collection. Thomas mentioned homosexuality only to recall that chastity prohibits "voluntary self-stimulation or . . . stimulation with one of the same sex or between an unmarried couple" (p. 108).

69. MM, age 44, int. 5.8.98; GFB57, age 62, int. 6.14.98; MJRL64, age 58, int. 8.4.98; Player B '53, age 66, int. 5.11.98.

70. MJRL64, age 58, int. 8.4.98; Player B '53, age 66, int. 5.11.98; DVA78, age 42, int. 7.9.99.

71. Player 1950s; JYE74, age, int. 8.8.98. Other players who defended teammates from the suggestion of homosexuality on surveys included MMP46, age 74, ques. 18, 5.6.98 and EAA46, age 72, ques. 18, 6.15.98. The phrase "right to be their own individual" comes from DVA78, age 42, int. 7.9.99. A player from the class of '53 said no one on her teams ever came out and said "I am" (Player B '53, age 66, int. 5.11.98). As I interviewed, there could have been many reasons why no gay players claimed gay identity. First, no question on the survey addressed homosexuality directly, and neither did I bring it up first in interviews. Second, not all those with same-sex attractions identify as gay or homosexual. Third, gay players could have not wanted former classmates or teachers to know. Fourth, they could have not felt comfortable with me or wanted me to know.

72. Pius XI's warning about the danger of display came from "Christian Education of Youth," p. 59. For Pius XII's remarks, see "Pope Counsels Girl Crusaders: Pontiff Warns Against Immodesty in Fashion, Sport, Amusement," *Catholic Standard and Times*, May 30, 1941, Archbishop Furey Scrapbook, ICGLA. These exhortations constituted part of a years-long papal campaign aimed at women's modesty, thought to be intimately related to sexual purity (Faherty, *Destiny of Modern Woman*, 93).

73. Player '56, age 63, ques. 20, 5.4.98; DCC55, age 65, int. 6.26.98; RMW60, age 60, ques. 20, 5.23.98; MSS66, age 53, ques. 20, 6.17.98. Dozens of players described the same outfit and lamented the black tights. Maureen Callahan Bigham '63 said the tights were "hot"; cheerleader Bernadette Ellis McBeth '56 described the "million runs"; Margaret Klopfle Devinney '62 said the runs "drew even more attention" (MCB63, age 56, ques. 21, 5.23.98; BEM56, age 63, ques. 12, 10.6.98; MKD62, age 57, ques. 12, 7.28.98).

74. MSM, age 75, mem. 7.13.98; ACC51, age 68, ques. 21, 5.10.98; Jeanmarie Dunn, "I.C. by Jeanmarie," TI 13, no. 5 (March 25, 1946): 5; ADL57, age 62, ques. 18, 7.20.98.

75. For comparisons of uniforms, I referred to photographs of teams and players in Hult and Trekell, *A Century of Women's Basketball*, pp. 189 and 336, and also in Pamela Grundy, "From Amazons to Glamazons: The Rise and Fall of North Carolina Women's Basketball, 1920–1960," *Journal of American History* 87, no. 1 (June 2000): 120, 145. For the 1948–49 season, the Wayland Baptist Flying Queens, an AAU team associated with Wayland Baptist College in Plainview, Texas, wore satin uniforms, donated by their first corporate sponsor, the Harvest Queen Mill. See Sylvia Faye Nadler, "A Developmental History of the Wayland Hutcherson Flying Queens from 1910–1979" (Ph.D. diss., East Texas State University, 1980), p. 29. Pictures of Immaculata playing teams around Philadelphia through the midsixties show I.C. and the other team in skirts. Jill Hutchison reported that for the first AIAW national collegiate invitational tournament at West Chester State in 1969, "approximately half the teams were clad in hockey tunics while others wore double knit polyester shorts" ("Women's Intercollegiate Basketball: AIAW/NCAA," in *A Century of Women's Basketball*, ed. Hult and Trekell, p. 311). A *Gleaner* photograph shows Immaculata playing a team that also wore stockings in 1951. Rosemont, Chestnut Hill, and Drexel are all possible candidates since they were the Catholic teams Immaculata played that year (*The Gleaner 1951*, p. 75, ICGLA). In the same year, *The Immaculatan* published an action shot of the Rosemont game in which both teams wore tights, captioned "On the Ball at Rosemont" (TI 18, no. 4 [February 26, 1951]: 6). In the 1959 *Gleaner*, however, there is an unpaginated photo of Immaculata versus Chestnut Hill in which opposing players are barelegged (ICGLA). On that evidence, it seems

probable that some other Catholic schools required tights, but for a shorter span of years than Immaculata. On basketball uniforms, see Pamela Grundy, "Bloomers and Beyond: North Carolina Women's Basketball Uniforms, 1901–1997," *Southern Cultures* 3, no. 3 (1997): 52–67.

76. MKD62, age 57, ques. 12, 7.28.98, who also described the uniforms as "Victorian"; MFM50, age 69, int. 3.17.98; ADL57, age 62, ques. 23, 7.20.98; EPC64, age 55, int. 6.11.98; MCB63, age 56, ques. 21, 5.23.98. Players who used the word "modesty" to explain uniform regulations included JCF53, age 66, ques. 12, 7.27.98; Player B '53, age 66, int. 5.11.98; JDT54, age 65, ques. 12, 5.28.98; and MKD62, age 57, ques. 12, 7.28.98.

77. For team photos, see *The Gleaner 1963*, p. 72, and *The Gleaner 1964*, p. 84, both ICGLA. On the warm-up slacks, see "Athletics Follow Fashion Trends," TI 33, no. 1 (September 23, 1965): 4. *The Gleaner 1968* featured a photograph of women wearing shorts at practice (p. 73, ICGLA). The story about opposing players offering to burn Immaculata uniforms came from Lynn Nicoletti, "'The Way We Were,'" TI 41, no. 7 (March 22, 1974): 4. The account of the booster club formation came from Player '57, age 62, int. 6.11.98.

78. MS77, age 42, int. 10.16.97. *The Gleaner 1968* featured a photograph of women wearing shorts at practice (p. 73); *The Gleaner 1974*, in an unpaginated basketball section, showed the team in skirts; in *The Gleaner 1975*, the team wore skirts for the preseason team photo but shorts for that year's games (pp. 32–34; all in ICGLA).

79. MWH+44, age 74, int. 10.16.97; JS, int. 8.25.99; JYE74, age 45, int. 8.8.98. All but one of the 1972 championship team members wore their hair long, while pictures of other women's teams at the same time show much more openness to short haircuts. See photographs in Hult and Trekell of the Immaculata College 1972 team (*A Century of Women's Basketball*, p. 291), in which all players except one posed with long hair draped over their shoulders, and of the West Chester State 1969 team (p. 308), in which all players except one posed with their hair short or pulled back.

80. PFM53, age 66, ques. 21, 5.15.98, who further observed, in her response to ques. 26, that she was never "a good player"; MBD58, age 61, ques. 26, 9.22.98; MABF46, age 73, int. 7.24.98; AFC67, age 52, ques. 21, 5.10.98. A player from the class of '56 said it was difficult to be less "talented" (Player '56, age 63, ques. 26, 5.4.98). At least eight others said they were not good players, and several said they were too short.

81. DCC55, age 65, int. 6.26.98. The list of injuries comes from, respectively, ACC51, age 68, ques. 26, 5.10.98; Player '51, age 69, ques. 26, 5.20.98; Player C '52, age 68, ques. 26, 6.20.98; and Player A '53, age 66, ques. 26, 5.8.98, who also said it was difficult "not being able to play." Dee Cofer Cull '55 remembered that when she hurt her knee, it was painful seeing "limited action" (DCC55, age 65, ques. 26, 6.27.98). Sue Forsyth O'Grady '72 reported it was hard to miss a particular big game when she had the flu (SFO72, age 48, ques. 24, 6.24.98). Another player, class of '56, said she played sick, "hoping you wouldn't be substituted for" (Player '56, age 63, ques. 20, 5.4.98).

82. MCB63, age 56, ques. 26, 5.23.98; MFM50, age 69, int. 3.17.98. On Immaculata alumnae who played for postcollege teams, see, on Peggy Bissinger, "Coaching and Teaching Highlight Sports Career of '49 Alumna," TI 21, no. 3 (December 17, 1953): 6; on Carol Leighton, "'53 Sports Queen Coaches West Catholic Basketeers," TI 21, no. 5 (March 22, 1954): 4; and, on Mary Frank, "Wedding Bells Ring Out for All-Star Mary Frank," TI 22, no. 7 (March 29, 1955): 4.

83. MDK+, age 71, int. 1.9.98; Player '57, age 62, int. 6.11.98; DCC55, age 65, int. 6.26.98; MCM54, age 65, int. 6.23.98. Although handfuls of players throughout the years received invitations to try out for semiprofessional and (in the seventies) professional teams, to my knowledge, only Mary Scharff '77 and Sue Martin '78 accepted. Mary went to California to try out for the new women's pro league, the Women's Basketball League, in 1978, while Sue played several seasons for the New Jersey Gems. See Leroy Samuels, "'Jerry West' Scharff Would Like Pro Career," *Courier-Post* (Camden, N.J.), January 23, 1975, microfilm, "I.C. in print," roll 11, ICGLA.

4. Praying for the Team

1. "Once More in '74," *The Immaculatan* (TI) 41 (March 22, 1974): 1.

2. MWH+44, age 74, int. 10.16.97. Several players recounted the Ash Wednesday story as well as Sister Marian William Hoben, who remembered Theresa Shank's promise to the fans.

3. LHO66, age 52, ques. 12, 6.23.98 (Lynn said she was the team "orange girl," whose job was to cut and serve oranges to both teams' players at half-time); JM42, age 77, int. 7.20.98. A 1956 graduate used the phrase "spiritual bond" (Player '56, age 63, ques. 14, 5.4.98). Meg Kenny Kean '58 suggested that team life would have felt incomplete without religious markers (MMKK58, age 62, ques. 12, 7.9.98). Margaret Monahan Hogan '63 wrote that praying with the team was "fun" (MMH63, age 57, ques. 22, 6.10.98), while a 1951 graduate said religious team rituals made her "feel good" (Player '51, age 69, ques. 12, 5.20.98).

4. Margaret Klopfle Devinney '62 said "it was *all* Catholic" (MKD62, age 57, ques. 14, 7.28.98).

5. Charles R. Morris, *American Catholic: The Saints and Sinners Who Built America's Most Powerful Church* (New York: New York Times Books/Random House, 1997), p. 175. For religious participation—and Irish conformism—see ibid., pp. 173–78 and 181–83, as well as Hugh J. Nolan, "The Native Son," in *The History of the Archdiocese of Philadelphia*, ed. James F. Connelly (Wynnewood, Pa.: Unigraphics Incorporated, 1976), pp. 410–11.

6. On Philadelphia devotion to the Miraculous Medal and the St. Vincent services, see Nolan, "Native Son," p. 410. For information on the Miraculous Medal, I drew on a pamphlet about the Miraculous Medal: "The Medal, A Sign, A Message . . ." (Paris: Chapel of Our Lady of the Miraculous Medal, undated). I am grateful to Immaculata's Gabriele Library archivist, Sister Loretta Maria Tenbusch, I.H.M., for providing me with this pamphlet.

7. On women's roles in Catholic devotional cultures, see Robert Orsi, *The Madonna of 115th Street: Faith and Community in Italian Harlem, 1880–1950* (New Haven: Yale University Press, 1985); and idem, *Thank You, St. Jude: Women's Devotion to the Patron Saint of Hopeless Causes* (New Haven: Yale University Press, 1996).

8. Philip Gleason described the "ideological" function of "Catholic culture" that attempted to make neo-Thomism a veritable "way of life," in *Contending with Modernity: Catholic Higher Education in the Twentieth Century* (New York: Oxford University Press, 1995), pp. 139, 141, and 146, respectively. The Phelan quote is from ibid., p. 146. I drew information on credits from Immaculata College catalogs for 1930–31, pp. 54–58; 1941–42,

p. 31; and 1948–49, pp. 61–63, all in the Gabriele Library Archives of Immaculata College, Immaculata, Pa. (ICGLA). For comparison, at Villanova in 1933, the bachelor of arts degree required eight semesters of philosophy, plus, for Catholic students, eight semesters of religion.

9. GFB57, age 62, int. 6.14.98. The archdiocesan newspaper noted Immaculata's new course on Vatican II themes in "Immaculata Plans Course on Second Vatican Council," *Catholic Standard and Times*, December 3, 1965, microfilm, "I.C. in print," roll 2, ICGLA. In "College Presidents Look at Campus Unrest," in the *Daily Local News* (West Chester, Pa.), Sister Mary of Lourdes McDevitt '36 said Immaculata's students were not following the nationally restless mood (September 29, 1970, microfilm, "I.C. in print," roll 2, ICGLA). For the Seeger and McGovern visits, see *The Gleaner 1968*, pp. 70–71, ICGLA. For a lecture on ecumenism, see "Father Wiegel Lectures on Ecumenical Movement," TI 27, no. 1 (October 30, 1959): 4; and, on the environment, see "Udall Is Guest Speaker at Immaculata 'Earth Day,'" *Suburban Advertiser* (Wayne, Pa.), April 16, 1970, microfilm, "I.C. in print," roll 2, ICGLA. For an editorial supporting the work of Daniel Berrigan, see Elaine Rendler, "A Symbol of Concern," TI 34 (March 21, 1967): 2. Sister Marian William Hoben '44 and Betty Ann Hoffman Quinn '73 narrated the dress code protest (MWH+44, age 74, int. 10.16.97; EAHQ73, age 46, int. 7.2.98). Many lectures, events, and editorials during these years reflected changing times on Immaculata's campus, but former players said it was very possible to attend the school in the sixties and remain sheltered from and even unaware of civil rights protests, Vietnam war demonstrations, and Vatican II changes, among them, Student, age 51, int. 7.12.98; Cheerleader '64, age 55, int. 7.20.98; EPC64, age 55, int. 6.11.98; CLD70, age 49, int. 6.8.98.

10. FGC45, age 74, int. 5.12.98; MS77, age 42, int. 10.16.97. A 1951 graduate described herself as "religious" while at Immaculata (Player '51, age 69, ques. 14, 5.20.98). Players who volunteered that they attended daily Mass at Immaculata included Rosemary Duddy McFadden '46 (RDM46, age 73, int. 7.9.98) and Fruff Fauerbach Timby '50 (FFT50, age 70, ques. 15, 7.1.98).

11. FFT50, age 70, ques. 12, 7.1.98.

12. ACC51, age 68, ques. 12, 5.10.98; MS77, age 42, int. 10.16.97.

13. MMH63, age 57, ques. 14, 6.10.98; DCC55, age 65, int. 6.26.98. Dee Cofer Cull '55 said the team prayed "that no one got injured" (DCC55, age 65, ques. 22, 6.27.98). Mary Scharff '77 said they prayed for safe return (MS77, age 42, int. 10.16.97). Others who said they prayed to win included ADL57, age 62, ques. 14, 7.20.98, and MOR66, age 53, ques. 14, 6.27.98.

14. DCC55, age 65, ques. 12, 6.27.98; MMKK58, age 62, ques. 14, 7.9.98; ADL57, age 62, ques. 12, 7.20.98; MCM54, age 65, int. 6.23.98.

15. SFO72, age 48, ques. 12, 6.24.98; MJRL64, age 58, ques. 14, 8.4.98; JBV74, age 45, ques. 12, 6.5.98; MM73, age 46, ques. 12, 9.3.98; MS77, age 42, int. 10.16.97. Lorrie Gable Finelli '78 was one of several who mentioned this "pre-game ritual" (LGF78, age 41, ques. 20, 5.15.98), which "pumped up" the team, wrote Laureen Mann '78 (LM78, age 42, ques. 20, 5.26.98). Cathy Rush told me the story of "Mr. Christopher" (CR, age 53, int. 8.20.02). Journalist Maralyn Lois Polak wrote the Macs' success was "faintly miraculous" in "Six Stormy Years That Made History in Girls' Basketball," *Philadelphia Inquirer Magazine*, April 25, 1976, p. 10.

16. MM73, age 46, ques. 22, 9.3.98; DCC55, age 65, int. 6.26.98. A player from the class of 1952 said she prayed "to make the team" (Player C '52, age 68, ques. 19, 6.20.98). Cheerleader Joan Davis Tynen '54 said she would "plead" in prayer for players on the court (JDT54, age 65, ques. 12, 5.28.98). Sister Marita David Kirsch said she attended her home parish's weekday masses before big games (MDK+, age 71, int. 1.9.98). A cheerleader from the class of 1963 remembered praying the rosary aloud on the bus (Cheerleader '63, age 57, ques. 23, 5.18.98). Jean Doris '53 remembered those who would walk in silence as a sacrifice for the good of the game (JD53, age 66, int. 6.8.98).

17. Sue Forsyth O'Grady '72 said she "prayed like crazy" from the bench (SFO72, age 48, ques. 14, 6.24.98). Marian Collins Mullahy '54 said her mother told her she prayed at church for a crucial game (MCM54, age 65, int. 6.23.98). Twenty-five of sixty-five survey respondents said basketball devotions included "private prayer"; forty-five marked "collective prayer"; three mentioned making the sign of the cross before foul shots; many interviewees mentioned some or all of these practices. The song "Rise and shine and give God your glory . . ." was included on a mimeograph of Mighty Macs cheers and songs, microfilm, "I.C. in print," roll 4, ICGLA.

18. RDM46, age 73, int. 7.9.98. Mary Scharff '77 remembered "Mass the next day" after big victories (MS77, age 42, int. 10.16.97). Sister Marian William Hoben '44 said campus priests would deliver a "fitting homily" before or after games (MWH+44, age 74, int. 10.16.97). Though a campus chaplain often said Mass for the team, the Mackies never had a "team chaplain," a fixture on the benches of Catholic men's teams such as St. Joe's and Villanova. The mass program was in the Immaculata archives: "I want to be in that number . . . When the MACS come marching in: A Eucharistic Celebration to Honor the 'MACS'—National Champions," photocopied mass program, undated, probably March or April 1974, ICGLA.

19. Player '56, age 63, ques. 19, 5.4.98.

20. MFM50, age 69, int. 3.17.98; MDK+, age 71, int. 1.9.98.

21. JYE74, age 45, int. 8.8.98. Players who mentioned the Miraculous Medals included TMM63, age 56, ques. 12, 5.25.98; SFO72, age 48, ques. 12, 6.24.98; LM78, age 42, ques. 12, 5.26.98; MS77, age 42, int. 10.16.97; MDK+, age 71, int. 1.9.98; and CLD70, age 49, int. 6.8.98. Janet Young Eline '74 and Sister Loretta Maria Tenbusch described the blue enamel pins (JYE74, age 45, int. 8.8.98; LMT+, age 79, int. 10.17.97). Other private intercessory devotions abounded. A columnist for *The Immaculatan* reported during the 1946 season that a senior guard had been clutching at her chest during a hotly contested Temple game, making sure that her "Sacred Heart badge hadn't been lost" (Jeanmarie Dunn, "I.C. by Jeanmarie," TI 13, no. 5 [March 25, 1946]: 5).

22. MWH+44, age 74, int. 10.16.97; MLM+36, age 83, int. 6.30.98.

23. Student '47, age 72, ques. 13, 5.20.98; HFD56, age 63, int. 7.23.98.

24. MS77, age 42, int. 10.16.97. Janet Young Eline '74 said she had the impression sisters intimidated opposing schools (JYE74, age 45, int. 8.8.98). Jeanmarie Dunn mentioned the "rosary-rooters" in "I.C. by Jeanmarie," TI 14, no. 5 (March 24, 1947): 6.

25. For "prayer power," I drew on "Reminiscences," unpaginated in Immaculata College Public Relations, "Remember the Glory Days!" booklet commemorating twentieth anniversary of the first national championship, April 1992, ICGLA.

26. MWH44+, age 74, int. 10.16.97.

27. LGF78, age 41, ques. 22, 5.15.98; MS77, age 42, int. 10.16.97.

28. PFM53, age 66, ques. 12, 5.15.98; Player '56, age 63, ques. 14, 5.4.98; JDT54, age 65, ques. 22, 5.28.98; Player C '52, age 68, ques. 22, 6.20.98; DCC55, age 65, ques. 22, 6.27.98; MMH63, age 57, ques. 22, 6.10.98.

29. MMKK58, age 62, ques. 12, 7.9.98; LGF78, age 41, ques. 12, 5.15.98; ADL57, age 62, ques. 12, 7.20.98; AML53, age 67, ques. 12, 5.22.98. Dee Cofer Cull '55 said the team prayed because prayers "worked" (DCC55, age 65, ques. 12, 6.27.98). Still others said praying was a "centering activity" (MMH63, age 57, ques. 12, 6.10.98) that aided "discipline, concentration, uniformity" (JYE74, age 45, ques. 12, 8.8.98) or helped "keep you focused" (MDK+, age 71, int. 1.9.98).

30. Player C '52, age 68, ques. 12, 6.20.98; MDK+, age 71, int. 1.9.98; EAA46, age 72, ques. 12, 6.15.98; LGF78, age 41, ques. 12, 5.15.98; Player '51, age 69, ques. 12, 5.20.98. Cheerleader Joan Davis Tynen '54 said she enjoyed the "spiritual" aspects of the sport (JDT54, age 65, ques. 12, 5.28.98).

31. JS, age 66, int. 8.25.99; MCB63, age 56, ques. 22, 5.23.98.

32. MWH+44, age 74, int. 10.16.97; MS77, age 42, int. 10.16.97. Sister Mary of Lourdes McDevitt '36 said Jenepher Shillingford brought Cathy Rush on board (MLM+36, age 83, int. 6.30.98). Mary Scharff recalled Rush "never said anything" against the college faith (MS77, age 42, int. 10.16.97). Rush's comment after the first championship was recorded by Don Lehnhoff in "Takes a Lot of Prayer To Win, Says Coach," *Daily Pantagraph* (Bloomington-Normal, Ill.), March 20, 1972, sec. B, p. 1. Don McKee recorded Rush's joke about rosary beads in "Scribes Topple to 'Lib,'" *Courier-Post* (Camden, N.J.), February 5, 1974, microfilm, "I.C. in print," roll 11, ICGLA.

33. Player A '53, age 66, ques. 12, 5.8.98; DGP56, age 62, ques. 12, 6.5.98; PFM53, age 66, ques. 12, 5.15.98; Cheerleader '57, age 62, ques. 12, 5.15.98.

34. *Immaculata College Catalog, 1948–49*, p. 28, ICGLA.

35. MCEW+62, age 57, ques. 6.2.98; LMT+, age 79, int. 10.17.97. Players who used Thomistic-sounding language of "diverse activities" in an "integrated" and "whole" life included Player A '53, age 66, ques. 6, 5.8.98 and MCEW+62, age 57, ques. 13, 6.2.98. Sports at Immaculata were "part of being a whole person," recalled Sister Marita David Kirsch (MDK+, age 71, int. 1.9.98), while Barbara Flanigan '68 said she gleaned from the sisters "the recognition that sports are an important part of education" (BF68, age 51, ques. 14, 8.17.98). A graduate of 1952 also reported that basketball "was integrated into the curriculum" (Player C '52, age 68, ques. 13, 6.20.98). Joan Clements Fromm '53 said basketball was Catholic because Catholicism is "always with you all your life" (JCF53, age 66, ques. 12, 7.27.98). Sister Marian William Hoben '44 also said sports were always understood at Immaculata as "part of an education" (MWH+44, age 74, int. 10.16.97).

36. JD53, age 66, ques. 13, 5.10.98; MCM54, age 65, int. 6.23.98. Mary Scharff '77 said the sisters did not "push" Catholicism (MS77, age 42, int. 10.16.97).

37. MCEW+62, age 57, ques. 12, 6.2.98; MS77, age 42, int. 10.16.97.

38. RDM46, age 73, int. 7.9.98.

39. MJRL64, age 58, int. 8.4.98.

40. MS77, age 42, int. 10.16.97. See also Chris Morkides, "Basketball Embodies Life Itself for Scharff," *Philadelphia Inquirer*, February 1, 1996, sec. E, p. 8.

41. PCE57, age 62, int. 7.23.98.

42. JDT54, age 65, ques. 20, 5.28.98; MCB63, age 56, ques. 12, 5.23.98. Many former players said something spiritual attracted them to Immaculata in general and on the surveys listed learning "teamwork" or "team effort" as a benefit of playing basketball. But only two of all the surveys and interviews mentioned "team spirit": MMP46, age 74, ques. 11, 5.6.98 ("team play and spirit") and PFM53, age 66, ques. 12, 5.15.98 ("Praying together helped a team spirit and camaraderie"). Three players mentioned "school spirit."

43. MWH+44, age 74, int. 10.16.97. Denise Conway Crawford spoke to Frank Fitzpatrick for "Where It All Began," *Philadelphia Inquirer Magazine*, March 26, 2000, p. 6.

44. MS77, age 42, int. 10.16.97.

45. Ibid.

46. Sister Marian William Hoben '44, I.H.M., "Athletics and Academic Achievement," speech, Middle States Association meeting (undated, probably mideighties), p. 4, ICGLA.

47. MRB+57, age 61, int. 10.16.97; MLM+36, age 83, int. 6.30.98; MMH63, age 57, ques. 12, 6.10.98. Sister Mary of Lourdes told reporter Nancy B. Clarke that she thought "prayer really did it," in "'I Can't Believe We Won the Whole Thing,'" *Sunday Bulletin*, March 26, 1972, sec. 4, p. 3.

48. Player '57, age 62, int. 6.11.98; Cheerleader '49, age 70, int. 7.23.98; MOR66, age 53, ques. 12, 6.27.98; LGF78, age 41, ques. 13, 5.15.98.

49. Player '57, age 62, int. 6.11.98; JD53, age 66, int. 6.8.98; MMP46, age 74, ques. 14, 5.6.98; FFT50, age 70, ques, 14, 7.1.98; TMM63, age 56, ques. 14, 5.25.98.

50. FFT50, age 70, ques. 12, 7.1.98.

51. PCE57, age 62, int. 7.23.98. Rosemary Duddy McFadden '46 said Catholicism was "intertwined" with everything in life (RDM46, age 73, int. 7.9.98).

52. DGP56, age 62, ques. 14, 6.5.98. Out of sixty-five respondents, fifty-five checked at least one devotion surrounding basketball. But eleven respondents used the word "nothing" to describe the connection between Catholicism and basketball.

53. MKD62, age 57, ques. 14, 7.28.98; Player '57, age 62, ques. 12, 6.17.98; PCE57, age 62, int. 7.23.98.

54. JD53, age 66, int. 6.8.98; CLD70, age 49, int. 6.8.98; SFO72, age 48, ques. 13, 6.24.98.

55. Player, 1960s; Player, 1970s.

5. Ladies of the Court

1. JV38, age 81, int. 7.20.98.

2. I gleaned details of the trip to Kansas from a sheet of instructions in the Immaculata College Gabriele Library Archives (ICGLA): The Bus Committee, "Victory Trip to Kansas State U.," mimeographed instruction sheet for basketball team's bus departure, undated, 1975. Lorrie Gable Finelli '78 said road trips meant "fun unrivaled" (LGF78, age 41, int. 7.23.98). In Kansas for the first time, manager Jean Brashears Vause '74 remembered seeing tumbleweeds (JBV74, age 45, ques. 23, 6.5.98).

3. For critical consideration of boundary crossing in U.S. sports history, see Elliot J. Gorn and Warren Goldstein, *A Brief History of American Sports* (New York: Hill and Wang, 1993), pp. 153–221. For anthropology of ritual, see Victor W. Turner, *The Ritual Process: Structure and Anti-Structure* (Chicago: Aldine, 1969); and John Eade and Michael

E. Sallnow, eds., *Contesting the Sacred: The Anthropology of Christian Pilgrimage* (London: Routledge, 1991). For general consideration of cross-cultural contact and its effects, see Edward W. Said, *Orientalism* (New York: Vintage, 1979). For scholarship on travel, see James Clifford, *Routes: Travel and Translation in the Late Twentieth Century* (Cambridge: Harvard University Press, 1997); Susan Morgan, *Place Matters: Gendered Geography in Victorian Women's Travel Books About Southeast Asia* (New Brunswick, N.J.: Rutgers University Press, 1996); Mary Louise Pratt, *Imperial Eyes: Travel Writing and Transculturation* (London: Routledge, 1992); and Caren Caplan, *Questions of Travel: Postmodern Discourses of Displacement* (Durham: Duke University Press, 1996).

4. TMD+53, age 66, int. 7.2.98 and 8.6.98. Fruff Fauerbach Timby '50 recalled the expense of a taxi to Immaculata when she missed her bus (FFT50, age 70, ques. 10, 7.1.98).

5. AFB+47, age 71, ques. 7, 6.18.98. For hitchhiking prohibitions, see Student Association of Immaculata College, *Hand Book, 1954*, p. 35, ICGLA. Another player, class of 1952, also remembered hitchhiking to town with teammates (Player A '52, age 66, ques. 10, 5.4.98).

6. Players who recalled riding with friends with cars included Fruff Fauerbach Timby '50 (FFT50, age 70, ques. 10, 7.1.98) and Maureen Callahan Bigham '63 (MCB63, age 56, ques. 10, 5.23.98). Other campus organizations offered occasional travel, evident in "Temperance Society Meets: College Sends Delegates," *The Immaculatan* (TI) 9, no. 5 (March 19, 1942): 3; "Eighteen Students Permitted to Teach Camden Negro Children" and "Girls Visit Blind Students at St. Mary's, Lansdale," TI 8, no. 2 (November 20, 1940): 4. The field hockey team traveled regularly to non-Catholic schools but over the years competed with fewer programs in a smaller geographic region than the basketball team did.

7. Player '57, age 62, int. 6.11.98. The *Villa Maria College Catalog, 1921–22* makes clear that non-Catholics were admitted to the new college (p. 10, ICGLA). According to a survey filled out by college personnel around 1935, non-Catholics constituted 5 percent of the student body (National Catholic Welfare Conference Special Questionnaire RE: Universities and Colleges of the United States, undated, ca. 1935, ICGLA). Players who mentioned anti-Catholic job discrimination, press coverage, or name-calling included Cheerleader '49, age 70, int. 7.23.98; JV38, age 81, int. 7.20.98; EPC64, age 55, int. 6.11.98; and CLD70, age 49, int. 6.8.98.

8. Charles Morris, *American Catholic: The Saints and Sinners Who Built America's Most Powerful Church* (New York: New York Times Books/Random House, 1997), p. 181.

9. For information on college ethnic makeup, I drew on articles such as "El Club Español Enacts Old Spanish Legend," TI 8, no. 5 (March 18, 1941): 6; "Puerto Ricans Have Gayety and Charm," TI 6, no. 2 (November 21, 1938): 4; and "Freshman Represent Nine States, Puerto Rico, Philippine Islands, and Peru," TI 11, no. 1 (October 26, 1943): 1. An exchange of letters between the college president and a mission priest indicated a student from China was offered a full scholarship to Immaculata in the spring of 1950 (the Reverend Vincent L. Burns, letter to the Reverend John B. Kao, O.F.M., November 29, 1949; and the Reverend John B. Kao, O.F.M., letter from director of China Catholic Central Bureau School Department to Immaculata president Reverend Vincent L. Burns, November 14, 1949, ICGLA). A player who graduated in 1953 mentioned resentment of South American girls' privilege (Player B '53, age 66, int. 5.11.98). Epiphany Pantaleo Collins '64 remembered "snide remarks" about South Philly (EPC64, age 55, int. 6.11.98).

10. MM, age 44, int. 5.8.98. A team member from the class of 1957 said mixed neighborhoods were also "absolutely all white" (Player '57, age 62, int. 6.11.98). On immigrant American claims to whiteness, see Noel Ignatiev, *How the Irish Became White* (New York: Routledge, 1995), a study of nineteenth-century Philadelphia, as well as David Roediger, *The Wages of Whiteness: Race and the Making of the American Working Class* (London: Verso, 1991), and Matthew Frye Jacobsen, *Whiteness of a Different Color: European Immigrants and the Alchemy of Race* (Cambridge: Harvard University Press, 1998).

11. For relations between blacks and whites in the archdiocese, see Hugh Nolan, "The Native Son," in *The History of the Archdiocese of Philadelphia*, ed. James F. Connelly (Wynnewood, Pa.: Unigraphics Incorporated, 1976), p. 368; Daniel Carroll, "The O'Hara Years," in *The History of the Archdiocese*, p. 472; and Morris, *American Catholic*, pp. 181–83. Monsignor Cunnie established the Philadelphia chapter of John LaFarge's Catholic Interracial Council and moderated it for twenty years. Mother Drexel founded the Sisters of the Blessed Sacrament, devoted to work in Native American and African American communities. She was canonized a saint in 2000. On other Philadelphia Catholic interracial work, see John McGreevy, *Parish Boundaries: The Catholic Encounter with Race in the Twentieth-Century Urban North* (Chicago: University of Chicago Press, 1996).

12. On Philadelphia Catholic harassment of black neighbors, see McGreevy, *Parish Boundaries*, pp. 91–92.

13. For Interracial Club activity, see "Shall We Be Color-Blind?" TI 4, no. 2 (November 19, 1936): 2; "Dear Girls," TI 7, no. 4 (February 20, 1940): 2; "Bishop Eustace Visits Interracial Club's Seven Rosary Centers in Camden," TI 8, no. 3 (December 17, 1940): 3; "Lay Apostles Teach Children in Homes," TI 26, no. 7 (May 29, 1959): 7; "The Voice of NF: The Problem of Racism," TI 29, no. 2 (November 17, 1961): 2; and "What Is Your Opinion of the 'Ole Miss' Crisis?" TI 30, no. 1 (October 25, 1962): 2. On prominent African Americans' visits to campus, see "Author Discusses Function of Novel in America," *Daily Local News* (West Chester, Pa.), April 2, 1969, microfilm, "I.C. in print," roll 2, ICGLA; "Writer Haley Probes His African Past," *Daily Local News* (West Chester, Pa.), March 22, 1973, microfilm, "I.C. in print," roll 3, ICGLA; and "Romare Bearden," photograph, TI 37, no. 4 (December 12, 1969): 4. The black theater group was Voices, announced in "Voices, Inc. Plans Artistic Performances Depicting Many Aspects of Negro Culture," TI 38, no. 10 (March 4, 1971): 1. A local paper announced the black history conference: "Immaculata Plans Session on Black History," *Suburban and Wayne Times* (Wayne, Pa.), October 16, 1969, microfilm, "I.C. in print," roll 2, ICGLA.

14. MCM54, age 65, int. 6.23.98. For information on institutional efforts to recruit black women, I drew on interviews with Sister Mary of Lourdes and Sister Virginia Assumpta (MLM+36, age 83, int. 6.30.98; VAM+, age 65, int. 6.25.98). The first apparent picture of a black student at Immaculata appears in *The Gleaner 1952*, p. 69, ICGLA; she is not identified by name and does not appear in subsequent senior pictures. The school kept no demographic data before the seventies, so to estimate the population of black students at Immaculata, I counted yearbook pictures, with the caveat that visual cues do not necessarily disclose so-called race. I counted approximately twenty-eight black women in yearbook pictures between 1952 and 1973. Out of approximately 2,829 in graduating classes from 1952–73, twenty-eight black women constituted an average of about 1 percent of the student body.

15. Player B '53, age 66, int. 5.11.98; MCM54, age 65, int. 6.23.98. Others who said there was little to no racial tension included MFM50, age 69, int. 3.17.98; Player '57, age 62, int. 6.11.98; and MS77, age 42, int. 10.16.97.

16. Different players recalled precollege contact with white or black Protestants as well as Jewish people: EAHQ73, age 46, int. 7.2.98; PCE57, age 62, int. 7.23.98; EAA46, age 72, int. 6.17.98; Player '57, age 62, int. 6.11.98; and JYE74, age 45, int. 8.8.98.

17. PCE57, age 62, int. 7.23.98; MMS62, age 57, ques. 14, 5.24.98; Player '57, age 62, int. 6.11.98; HFD56, age 63, int. 7.23.98.

18. HFD56, age 63, int. 7.23.98.

19. JYE74, age 45, int. 8.8.98.

20. Maureen Mooney '73 said the fun was "getting there and back" (MM73, age 46, ques. 23, 9.3.98). One busdriver friend was Connie Sweeney, featured in "Connie's Back From Erin," TI 15, no. 5 (March 19, 1948): 4. Margaret Klopfle Devinney '62 described the difficulty of fitting equipment on the bus (MKD62, age 57, ques. 23, 7.28.98). Patricia Furey McDonnell '53 remembered the bus ride as a "wonderful time" (PFM53, age 66, ques. 23, 5.15.98).

21. MMS62, age 57, ques. 16, 5.24.98; ILH70, age 49, ques. 23, 5.8.98; JBS53, age 67, ques. 23, 6.13.98; Player '57, age 62, ques. 23, 6.17.98. Rosemary McNichol Walsh '60 said she remembered a "general sense of fun" on bus trips (RMW60, age 60, ques. 23, 5.23.98). At least eight other respondents mentioned the "fun" of travel in particular. At least eight other players mentioned singing on the bus. A cheerleader from the class of 1963 said the team prayed together on the bus (Cheerleader '63, age 57, ques. 23, 5.18.98). The quote "cards or charades" comes from Mary Scharff '77, as reported in Herm Rogul, "Mary Scharff Likes Smaller Role," *Evening Bulletin*, December 13, 1975, microfilm, "I.C. in print," roll 4, ICGLA. Several players and cheerleaders said they drove to games with friends: Player B '45, age 74, ques. 23, 6.27.98; Cheerleader '49, age 70, int. 7.23.98; BF68, age 51, ques. 23, 8.17.98; LGF78, age 41, ques. 23, 5.15.98. A championship-era player said at that time carpooling vehicles were divided into smoking and nonsmoking cars (Player '75, age 45, ques. 23, 5.10.98). Several players recalled travel drama involving blizzards or ice storms: Player '51, age 69, ques. 23, 5.20.98; JD53, age 66, ques. 23, 5.10.98; and PFM53, age 66, ques. 23, 5.15.98.

22. JYE74, age 45, int. 8.8.98.

23. MMH63, age 57, ques. 21, 6.10.98; EAA46, age 72, int. 6.17.98. Information about the duties of the "orange girl" comes from LHO66, age 52, ques. 1, 6.23.98. Several players said I.C.'s signature treat was root beer floats, including Mary Murphy Schmelzer '62 (MMS62, age 57, ques. 21, 5.24.98).

24. LGF78, age 41, int. 7.23.98 and ques. 23, 5.15.98; VAM+, age 65, int. 6.25.98. Fan and volunteer team physician Frank Breen remembered being served catfish in Mississippi: Frank Breen, M.D., "Reflections in a Stethoscope: The Delta Syndrome," TI 43 (March 3, 1976): 4.

25. MCEW+62, age 57, ques. 23, 6.2.98; FFT50, age 70, ques. 7, 7.1.98; Cheerleader '49, age 70, int. 7.23.98. Maureen Callahan Bigham '63 said the dining room often closed before players returned from games (MCB63, age 56, ques. 16 and 23, 5.23.98).

26. RDM46, age 73, int. 7.9.98; Player A '53, age 66, ques. 23, 5.8.98.

27. LGF78, age 41, ques. 11, 5.15.98, and int. 7.23.98; MS77, age 42, int. 10.16.97.

28. EAA46, age 72, ques. 23, 6.15.98; DCC55, age 65, ques. 23, 6.27.98. Immaculatans who used the word "camaraderie" to describe the fun of road trips included JDT54, age 65, ques. 23, 5.28.98; MMKK58, age 62, ques. 23, 7.9.98; and JYE74, age 45, int. 8.8.98. Patricia Furey McDonnell '53 said she enjoyed the "conviviality" of road trips (PFM53, age 66, ques. 23, 5.15.98).

29. LGF78, age 41, int. 7.23.98.

30. Player A '52, age 66, ques. 23, 5.4.98.

31. EAA46, age 72, int. 6.17.98; DCC55, age 65, ques. 11, 6.27.98; MMS62, age 57, ques. 21, 5.24.98; JM42, age 77, int. 7.20.98; DGP56, age 62, ques. 11, 6.5.98.

32. MCM54, age 65, int. 6.23.98.

33. MOR66, age 53, int. 6.26.98. A cheerleader who graduated in 1949 said Rosemont was "too expensive" (Cheerleader '49, age 70, int. 7.23.98).

34. MOR66, age 53, int. 6.26.98; HFD56, age 63, int. 7.23.98; MGD62, age 57, int. 7.21.98.

35. A *Gleaner* photograph shows Immaculata playing another school in stockings in 1951 (*The Gleaner 1951*, p. 75, ICGLA). Rosemont, Chestnut Hill, and Drexel were the Catholic teams that played Immaculata that year.

36. TMM63, age 56, ques. 21, 5.25.98; MMKK58, age 62, ques. 25, 7.9.98. Margaret Guinan Delaney '62 said competition was "nebulous" with Chestnut Hill but sharp with Rosemont because Rosemont was "snootier" (MGD62, age 57, int. 7.21.98).

37. GRS64, age 55, int. 8.5.98.

38. On the Immaculata-Rosemont rivalry, see "Mackies Defeat Rosemont 36–25," TI 27, no. 5 (March 29, 1960): 4; "Hoopsters Tear Down Tea Town," TI 32, no. 7 (April 7, 1965): 6; "Mackies Trounce 'T-Town,'" TI 33, no. 8 (April 19, 1966): 4; and Gerry Coletta, "8–2 Record Closes Basketball Season," TI 38, no. 11 (March 18, 1971): 4. On the teabag corsages, I drew on my interview with Sister Cecile Marie Phelan (CMP+50, age 69, int. 6.25.98, int. 8.6.98).

39. EAA46, age 72, int. 6.17.98; JYE74, age 45, int. 8.8.98.

40. MOR66, age 53, int. 6.26.98; JS, age 66, int. 8.25.99, who also told me about her Friday postgame meal.

41. Player C '52, age 68, ques. 14, 6.20.98; MMS62, age 57, ques. 13, 5.24.98. Pauline Callahan Earl '57 said Immaculata was "always the best" (PCE57, age 62, int. 7.23.98).

42. MGD62, age 57, int. 7.21.98. Others who said they experienced no Catholic-Protestant tension playing non-Catholic teams included MDK+, age 71, int. 1.9.98, and MFM50, age 69, int. 3.17.98.

43. HFD56, age 63, int. 7.23.98; ACC51, age 68, ques. 14, 5.10.98; DCC55, age 65, int. 6.26.98.

44. GRS64, age 55, int. 8.5.98; JYE74, age 45, int. 8.8.98; AML53, age 67, ques. 14, 5.22.98; MS77, age 42, int. 10.16.97.

45. Player B '45, age 74, ques. 24, 6.27.98; Student '47, age 72, ques. 24, 5.20.98.

46. CLD70, age 49, int. 6.8.98; GRS64, age 55, int. 8.5.98. Maureen Callahan Bigham '63 said West Chester players were "big rivals" (MCB63, age 56, ques. 24, 5.23.98). Terri Murphy McNally '63 said "beating" physical education schools was satisfying (TMM63, age 56, ques. 25, 5.25.98). Marianne Specht Siecko '66 said "losing" to those schools was her unhappiest memory (MSS66, age 53, ques. 26, 6.17.98).

47. A 1945 graduate remembered that some physical education–minded classmates of Immaculata athletes transferred out of Immaculata to pursue their degrees (Player B '45, age 74, ques. 28, 6.27.98). These included Margaret Conroy, an Immaculata coach (1959–61) who as an undergrad had transferred out of I.C. to Temple ("New Coach Names Team Co-Captains," TI 27, no. 3 [December 15, 1959]: 4).

48. EAHQ73, age 46, int. 7.2.98.

49. Cheerleader '63, age 57, ques. 24, 5.18.98; MGD62, age 57, int. 7.21.98. Christine Lammer DiCiocchio '70 joked about opposing players who "major[ed] in basketball" (CLD70, age 49, int. 6.8.98).

50. HFD56, age 63, int. 7.23.98.

51. TMM63, age 56, ques. 25, 5.25.98; GRS64, age 55, int. 8.5.98.

52. Player A '53, age 66, ques. 18, 5.8.98; GRS64, age 55, int. 8.5.98; MCB63, age 56, ques. 18, 5.23.98; MS77, age 42, int. 10.16.97.

53. *Immaculatan* writers described players from physical education schools as "fizz-eds" in "Macs Impress in Initial Wins," TI 14, no. 4 (February 27, 1947): 6; and "East Stroudsburg, Ursinus, Bow to I.C.," TI 15, no. 4 (February 26, 1948): 6. Janet Young Eline '74 said an opposing player was "gigantic" and listed other teams' majors (JYE74, age 45, int. 8.8.98). The quotation from Cathy Rush is in John Waldeyer, "Bucket, Bugle Debate Bugs 'Bugs' Brachwitz," *Suburban and Wayne Times*, March 27, 1975, p. 15.

54. Helen Frank Dunigan '56, for example, said the competition with physical education schools definitely involved opponents' majors, not their religion (HFD56, age 63, int. 7.23.98).

55. Bunny Naughton DeArmond '66 said physical education opponents "heightened" the competition (BND66, age 54, ques. 21, 6.1.98).

56. In comparison to the Immaculata team's fall 1974 date of integration, a photograph in *The Immaculatan* ("Blocking Temple!" photograph, TI 26, no. 5 [March 24, 1959]: 4) shows a black player on Temple's team in 1959. Team photographs in Joan S. Hult and Marianna Trekell, eds., *A Century of Women's Basketball: From Frailty to Final Four* (Reston, Va.: National Association for Girls and Women in Sport, 1991), show a 1969 West Chester State team with two black women out of thirteen players (p. 308) and a 1974 Queens College team with five black women out of thirteen players (p. 361).

57. Regarding the racialization of basketball during the seventies, players said they barely noticed the roiling controversy over "street" and "strategic" styles. As far as Immaculata teams were concerned, "people on the outside made all the noise" about race, said Mary Scharff '77. "It wasn't the people that were involved in the sport" (MS77, age 42, int. 10.16.97). On the NBA-ABA story, see David Leviatin, "The Evolution and Commodification of Black Basketball Styles," *Radical History Review* 55 (winter 1993): 154–64.

58. MS77, age 42, int. 10.16.97; EAHQ73, age 46, int. 7.2.98. Lorrie Gable Finelli '78 said trips to all-black venues were "eye-awakening" (LGF78, age 41, int. 7.23.98).

59. DCC55, age 65, int. 6.26.98; MS77, age 42, int. 10.16.97.

60. For accounts of racial incidents in Philadelphia during these years, see McGreevy, *Parish Boundaries*, pp. 91–92, 175, 184, and 239.

61. On Catholic interracialism, see David W. Southern, *John LaFarge and the Limits of Catholic Interracialism, 1911–1963* (Baton Rouge: Louisiana State University Press, 1996).

On whiteness and U.S. culture, see Toni Morrison, *Playing in the Dark: Whiteness and the American Literary Imagination* (New York: Vintage, 1992).

62. Player, 1970s. I sent surveys to at least four black players, who played seasons from 1974–77, but none responded. With a 21 percent response rate to three hundred surveys, this was not statistically unusual. My attempts to call these players for personal interviews were also unsuccessful, because I could not locate them or they did not return calls. This, also, was not unusual in the course of the interviewing process. Still, because their perspectives are missing, I would stress that I drew my observations from white players', not black players', accounts.

63. Player, 1930s. A player from the 1940s said she and teammates feared for their safety when traveling to Temple.

64. Mary K. Doherty, "Mighty Macs Smash All Contenders; Second National Title Appears Likely," TI 39 (March 29, 1973): 4; Players, 1970s. A sister-fan talked about "mashed" bones.

65. Player, 1970s.

66. Player, 1970s. A sister-fan relayed that black players heard accusations of being "Uncle Toms." Dick Weiss reported that Sue Martin was questioned by opposing players as to why she was playing with "whitey" ("Martin Gives Macs a Fresh Look," *Philadelphia Daily News* [March 10, 1975], microfilm, "I.C. in print," roll 11, ICGLA).

67. JS, age 66, int. 8.25.99; George Minot Jr., "Triumphant Pantherettes Reflect Stockard Style," *Washington Post*, February 14, 1975, sec. D, p. 1. Skip Myslenski described the letter incident in "The Immaculata Mystique," *Today (Philadelphia Inquirer)*, May 4, 1975, p. 25.

68. Players, 1970s.

69. I quoted Gloria Rook Schmidt '64 in the first sentence (GRS64, age 55, int. 8.5.98). Cheerleader Joan Davis Tynen '54 said she liked going "N, S, E & W" as well as coming home (JDT54, age 65, ques. 23, 5.28.98).

6. Championships and Community

1. The sources for this reconstruction are Sister Marian William Hoben '44, Sister Virginia Assumpta McNabb, and Jenepher Shillingford (MWH+44, age 74, int. 10.16.97; VAM+, age 65, int. 6.25.98; JS, age 66, int. 8.25.99).

2. Kate Smith mentioned morning practices in "Hoops Heritage: Women's Basketball Traces Its Roots to Philadelphia," in *NCAA Division I Women's Final Four 2000 Program* (Lexington, Ky.: NCAA and Host Communications, 2000), p. 8. Cathy Rush's salary was reported in Frank Fitzpatrick, "Where It All Began," *Philadelphia Inquirer Magazine*, March 26, 2000, p. 30.

3. Sister Mary of Lourdes McDevitt '36 said she asked the trustees to sponsor players' travel (MLM+36, age 83, 6.30.98). Sister Marian William Hoben '44 said she solicited funds from businesses (MWH+44, age 74, int. 10.16.97). The Immaculata Office of Public Relations kept a box of toothbrushes like those players sold to fund their trip to Normal. When I saw them, they were labeled as mementos for a basketball team reunion in April 1992 (Office of Public Relations, Villa Maria Hall, Immaculata College, Immaculata, Pa.).

4. MWH+44, age 74, int. 10.16.97.

5. I reconstructed Sister Mary of Lourdes' phone call from interviews (MLM+36, age 83, 6.30.98; MWH+44, age 74, int. 10.16.97).

6. Smith cited Rush's career record in "Hoops Heritage," p. 8. George Heaslip coined the nickname "Mighty Macs" in "Immaculata Girls Win National Cage Title," *Daily Local News* (West Chester, Pa.), March 20, 1972, pp. 10–11.

7. On Cathy Rush's women's game innovations, see Fitzpatrick, "Where It All Began," p. 30. Jane Gross called Theresa Shank the best center in the nation in "She's the Center of Attention," *Sports Illustrated*, April 19, 1973, pp. 30–31. The next year, another top player in her position, point guard Marianne Crawford Stanley '76, enrolled at Immaculata; see Dan Lauck, "Can Marianne Dribble? Guys in Philly Know," *Daily Capital Sports* (Washington, D.C.), March 21, 1974, p. 23.

8. LGF78, age 41, int. 7.23.98; Rene Muth Portland '75 was quoted in Sharon O'Neal, "Immaculata Team Recalls the Winning Years," *Philadelphia Inquirer*, April 16, 1992, sec. DC, p. 22. Sister Mary of Lourdes McDevitt '36, not given to piety for piety's sake, said ultimately the victories were God's doing (MLM+36, age 83, 6.30.98).

9. I assume in this chapter that the Immaculata team was part of communities of college, religion, city, and gender, from within which they had, for a time, privileged positions to relate and change. In turn, this assumes that communities are as much a matter of "imagination" as material reality, that they are transient and permeable rather than stable and coherent. On the construction of communities, see Benedict Anderson, *Imagined Communities: Reflections on the Origin and Spread of Nationalism* (London: Verso, 1991); and Eric Hobsbawm and Terence Ranger, eds., *The Invention of Tradition* (Cambridge: Cambridge University Press, 1983).

10. Pope Paul VI, *Humanae vitae*, trans. Robert Bogan, in Peter Harris, Adrian Hastings, et al., *On Human Life: An Examination of* Humanae vitae (London: Burns and Oates, 1968), pp. 106–61. William B. Faherty, S.J., discussed the "true feminism"—opposed to liberal feminism—offered by the church in *The Destiny of Modern Woman, in the Light of Papal Teaching* (Westminster, Md.: Newman, 1950), pp. 81–83. For a discussion of Catholic women, feminism, birth control, and *Humanae vitae*, see Andrew M. Greeley, *The Catholic Myth: The Behaviors and Beliefs of American Catholics* (New York: Collier/Macmillan, 1990), pp. 226–42.

11. Player, 1960s. On post–Vatican II changes in the Philadelphia archdiocese, see Daniel Carroll, "The O'Hara Years," in *The History of the Archdiocese of Philadelphia*, ed. James F. Connelly (Wynnewood, Pa.: Unigraphics Incorporated, 1976), pp. 457–69, as well as Tim McCarthy and Jim McManus, "The Philly House That Krol Built Rests on Pre-Vatican II Foundation," *National Catholic Reporter* 22, no. 1 (October 25, 1985): 1ff. Mother Claudia wrote an article titled "I.H.M. Nuns' Head Cautions Against Secularist Renewal," *Catholic Standard and Times* (January 17, 1974): 10.

12. Sheila Konczweski, "Grumblings of Mutiny," TI 36, no. 11 (May 16, 1969): 2; VAM+, age 65, int. 6.25.98; MOR66, age 53, int. 6.26.98. On 1960s changes at Immaculata, I drew on my interview with Sister Mary of Lourdes McDevitt '36 (MLM+36, age 83, 6.30.98). For Native American events, see "SAIC and Cultural Affairs Co-Sponsor Special Events," *The Immaculatan* (TI) 39 (February 16, 1973): 4. Poet and mystic Kahlil Gibran visited campus (Jerry Boyle, "Kahlil Gibran Leaves Impressions," TI 38, no. 3 [November

19, 1970]: 2). On the witchcraft talk, see photograph of druid lecturer, *The Gleaner 1973*, unpaginated, Gabriele Library Archives of Immaculata College, Immaculata, Pa. (ICGLA). On feminist activities, see "Immaculata Lecture on Feminism," *Today's Post*, November 1, 1973, microfilm, "I.C. in print," roll 4, ICGLA. For the *Option*, see its mention in a letter to the editor, Letters (editor's note), TI 36, no. 6 (January 24, 1969): 4. For *The Soapbox*, I am grateful to the 1968 graduate who edited the paper and supplied me with copies.

13. CLD70, age 49, int. 6.8.98; LGF78, age 41, int. 7.23.98. Sister Mary of Lourdes characterized the campus tenor in "College Presidents Look at Campus Unrest," *Daily Local News* (West Chester), September 29, 1970, microfilm, "I.C. in print," roll 2, ICGLA. Others who said they left Immaculata unaware of social change in the outside world included Student, age 51, int. 7.12.98; MGD62, age 57, int. 7.21.98; and EPC64, age 55, int. 6.11.98.

14. Estimates of the number of airport greeters from the following sources ranged between five and seven hundred, so I estimated six hundred: MM73, age 46, ques. 24, 9.3.98; Skip Myslenski, "The Immaculata Mystique," *Today/Philadelphia Inquirer*, May 4, 1975, p. 22.

15. JYE74, age 45, int. 8.8.98. On the fire at Theresa Shank Grentz '74's family home, see Gregg Mazzola, "I to I: College Basketball's First Woman Superstar," interview with Theresa Shank Grentz, *Coach and Athletic Director*, March 1999, p. 44.

16. JYE74, age 45, int. 8.8.98. For the Immaculatans' tournament seed and Denise Conway Crawford's quotation, see Rich Hofmann, "Macs Still Mighty: Pioneer Story of Women's Basketball Holds Up Over Time," *Philadelphia Daily News*, March 30, 2000, sec. W, p. 4. Janet Young Eline '74 said she asked Rush if the opening ceremonies were going to be "like the Olympics" (JYE74, age 45, int. 8.8.98). For tournament details and average field goal percentage, I drew on Heaslip, "Immaculata Girls," plus a *Main Line Times* editorial and team father Leo Mooney's memoir: "Immaculata Is NCAA Champ," *Main Line Times*, March 23, 1972, p. 33, and LM, mem. 9.3.98.

17. LM, mem. 9.3.98; LGF78, age 41, ques. 21, 5.15.98. Nancy B. Clarke quoted the reporter who said he didn't know the women's game had gone full court in her article "'I Can't Believe We Won the Whole Thing,'" *Sunday Bulletin*, March 26, 1972, sec. 4, p. 3.

18. MWH+44, age 74, int. 10.16.97. The Immaculata College Office of Public Relations retained old Mighty Mac bumper stickers. Former Mackie Pauline Callahan Earl '57 said she remembered buying Mighty Mac T-shirts (PCE57, age 62, int. 7.23.98).

19. Donna Anderson, "Feminine Approach to Basketball Conquers Again," TI 39 (March 29, 1973): 4. Mel Greenberg was quoted saying the Macs played basketball "the way we remembered it" in Frank Fitzpatrick, "How He Became Mr. Women's Basketball," *Philadelphia Inquirer Magazine*, March 23, 2000, p. 9. Writer Wanda McGlinchey-Ryan '57 included the quotation from fan Rolf Brachwitz in "Mighty Macs Quotes" (copyright Wanda L. McGlinchey-Ryan, 1997).

20. MWH+44, age 74, int. 10.16.97; Myslenski, "Immaculata Mystique," p. 24. Mary Boardman described the team ethos as "warm" and "sisterly" in "Like a Family," *Main Line Times* (Philadelphia), March 20, 1975, p. 23.

21. EAHQ, age 46, int. 7.2.98; VAM+, age 65, int. 6.25.98. On the increased recruitment of women athletes in the seventies, see Neil Amdur, "Recruiters Stepping Up Drive

for Women Athletes," *New York Times*, March 15, 1974, microfilm, "I.C. in print," roll 11, ICGLA; and Gail Bronson, "Women, Long Ignored as College Athletes, Move into 'Big Time,'" *Wall Street Journal*, June 4, 1975, microfilm, "I.C. in print," roll 3, ICGLA.

22. Gross dubbed Shank the "the Bill Walton of the women's game" in "She's the Center of Attention," p. 30. For details of the Southern Conn game, see "Is UCLA the Immaculata College of the West?" *Catholic Standard and Times*, March 22, 1973, p. 42; and "Theresa Saves Mackies," *Evening Bulletin*, March 25, 1973, microfilm, "I.C. in print," roll 11, ICGLA.

23. Jim Barniak, "Immaculata Glitters to Win 30th: But There's No Gold—Let Alone Scholarships—in Mighty Macs' Paltry Budget," *Sunday Bulletin*, February 3, 1974, sec. 3, p. 3. For the chronology of rule changes, see Joan S. Hult and Marianna Trekell, eds., *A Century of Women's Basketball: From Frailty to Final Four* (Reston, Va.: National Association for Girls and Women in Sport, 1991), p. 429.

24. MS77, age 42, int. 10.16.97. Rolf Brachwitz was quoted in John Waldeyer, "Bucket, Bugle Debate Bugs 'Bugs' Brachwitz," *Suburban and Wayne Times*, March 27, 1975, p. 15.

25. VAM+, age 65, int. 6.25.98. Leo Mooney said the championships had an "electrifying effect" on the campus (LM, mem. 9.3.98). Bill Verigan quoted a fan saying basketball "pulls us together" in "These Girls Take Basketball to College," *St. Paul Dispatch*, April 4, 1975, microfilm, "I.C. in print," roll 11, ICGLA.

26. Barniak, "Immaculata Glitters," sec. 3, p. 3; LMT+, age 79, int. 10.17.97. Sister Marian William Hoben '44 was the probable or definite author of reworked lyrics on several songsheets in the archives: "Tune: SWEET VIOLETS," mimeographed Mighty Macs song sheet, undated, ca. 1973–74; "Rise and Shine and Give God Your Glory," mimeographed Mighty Macs song sheet, microfilm, "I.C. in print," roll 4; "Tune: Get Me to the Church on Time," mimeographed Mighty Macs song sheet, undated, ca. 1973–75, microfilm, "I.C. in print," roll 4; "Tune: Hey, Mom, I Want to Go Home," mimeographed Mighty Macs song sheet, undated, ca. 1974, microfilm, "I.C. in print," roll 11, all ICGLA.

27. LMT+, age 79, int. 10.17.97; MAK+51, age 68, int. 1.1.98, int. 8.6.98. Janet Young Eline '74 suggested sisters liked the attention basketball brought Immaculata (JYE74, age 45, int. 8.8.98). Sister Marie Roseanne Bonfini '57 said team members were "women of deep faith" (MRB+57, age 61, int. 10.16.97).

28. GRS64, age 55, int. 8.5.98; MGD62, age 57, int. 7.21.98; JD53, age 66, int. 6.8.98; Player '57, age 62, int. 6.11.98. Marie Olivieri Russell '66 said watching games in championship years made her "proud" (MOR66, age 53, int. 6.26.98). Mary Jane Renshaw Lewandowski '64 said she and teammates "lit the flame" (MJRL64, age 58, ques. 24, 8.4.98).

29. Verigan, "These Girls." A "President's Holiday" was declared for a 1974 regionals game at Rutgers ("IC Captures Regionals!" TI 41, no. 7 [March 22, 1974]: 4.) On the pins for the St. Patrick's Day game, see "Once More In '74," TI 41, no. 7 (March 22, 1974): 1. For details of the Rotunda pep rally, I drew on interviews with Sister Marian William Hoben '44 and Sister Marie Roseanne Bonfini '57, as well as a survey returned by manager Jean Brashears Vause '74 (MWH+44, age 74, int. 10.16.97; MRB+57, age 61, int. 10.16.97; JBV74, age 45, ques. 25, 6.5.98).

30. Ashley McGeachy wrote of Rene Muth's parents' cheerleading initiative in "Coach Gives Care to Her No. 1 Fan," *Philadelphia Inquirer*, March 19, 2000, sec. C, p. 17. For the

account of the hundred-strong bucket brigade, see "IC Captures Regionals!" TI 41, no. 7 (March 22, 1974): 4. Myslenski described the fracas surrounding the ban on buckets in "The Immaculata Mystique," p. 26.

31. VAM+, age 65, int. 6.25.98; JS, age 66, int. 8.25.99; MLM+36, age 83, int. 6.30.98. Lynn Nicoletti quoted Denise Conway in "The Way We Were," TI 47, no. 7 (March 22, 1974): 4. Theresa Shank Grentz '74 told Lorraine McKee she thumbed her way to Immaculata for McKee's article, "Mighty Macs," *St. Louis Post-Dispatch*, March 22, 1997, sec. 5, p. 21. Sister Marian William Hoben '44 said cheerleaders bought their own costumes: MWH+44, age 74, int. 10.16.97.

32. MS77, age 42, int. 10.16.97. Wanda McGlinchey-Ryan quoted a player saying the team tried to repay the hours fans spent following them ("Mighty Mac Joy," copyright Wanda McGlinchey-Ryan, 1998). Vince Curran noted fans' monetary support of the team in "Girls from Immaculata Won 'Whole Thing,'" *Catholic Standard and Times*, March 23, 1972, p. 34. Sister Marian William Hoben '44 told the story of the players cheering nuns from the court (MWH+44, age 74, int. 10.16.97).

33. LM, mem. 9.3.98.

34. JYE74, age 45, int. 8.8.98; MS77, age 42, int. 10.16.97. For the profile of tournament teams, I drew on Leo Mooney's memoir (LM, mem. 9.3.98).

35. MM, age 44, int. 5.8.98.

36. "Is UCLA," p. 42; MS77, age 42, int. 10.16.97. Mary Scharff '77 also said opposing teams saw there was "something" about Catholicism. For the Southern Connecticut story, see players' reminiscences in a commemorative program: Immaculata College Public Relations, "Remember the Glory Days!" booklet commemorating 25th anniversary of the first national championship, April 26, 1997, p. 12, ICGLA.

37. Sister Marian William Hoben '44 said the sister-fans raised few eyebrows in Philadelphia (MWH+44, age 74, int. 10.16.97). For the story of the program misprint "Immaculate State College," see Immaculata College Public Relations, "Remember the Glory Days!" p. 4. Sister Marian William also told me the sisters answered questions as to whether players were postulants (MWH+44, age 74, int. 10.16.97). For photographs of nuns in the stands, see Associated Press, "Little Sisters of the Floor," photograph, March 15, 1976; and Associated Press, "Heavenly Help," photograph, March 27, 1976, both on microfilm, "I.C. in print," roll 11, ICGLA.

38. The photograph illustrated Herm Rogul, "How Many Men Are on Philadelphia's Best Basketball Team? None," *Sports Philadelphia*, Winter 1974, pp. 18–20ff. I am grateful to Elizabeth McAlister for pointing out Sister Regina's maternal manner of holding the ball.

39. MWH+44, age 74, int. 10.16.97.

40. Randy Shantz was quoted in Immaculata College Public Relations, "Remember the Glory Days!" pp. 7–8; MS77, age 42, int. 10.16.97; LGF78, age 41, int. 7.23.98.

41. Jeanine Driscoll was quoted in Wanda L. McGlinchey-Ryan, "Mighty Macs Quotes"; Rolf Brachwitz was quoted in Wanda McGlinchey-Ryan, "Mighty Mac Joy"; JS, age 66, int. 8.25.99.

42. Player '57, age 62, int. 6.11.98; JYE74, age 45, int. 8.8.98; LGF78, age 41, int. 7.23.98.

43. Gene Gomolka noted that Rush was "blonde" and "pretty" in "'It's Woman's Year,' Figures Cathy Rush," *Delaware County Daily Times* (Chester, Pa.), April 10, 1974. The cap-

tion "They Bounce Better Than the Guys Do" appeared in *Sunday News*, March 25, 1973. Don McKee quoted the "motivated" honoree in "Scribes Topple to 'Lib,'" *Courier-Post* (Camden, N.J.), February 5, 1974. All on microfilm, "I.C. in print," roll 11, ICGLA.

44. Philadelphia area sportscaster Bill Campbell said he liked watching the Macs in part because the hometown Sixers were so awful in those years (Wanda McGlinchey-Ryan, "Mighty Mac Joy"). I drew comments from Dennis Daylor, Art Douglas, and Frank Farley from Wanda L. McGlinchey-Ryan, "Mighty Macs Quotes."

45. Mel Greenberg recounted the beginnings of the poll to Wanda L. McGlinchey-Ryan, "Mighty Macs Quotes." He told Frank Fitzpatrick the prepoll women's game was "in the dark ages" for the article "How He Became Mr. Women's Basketball," p. 9. Greenberg said to Wanda L. McGlinchey-Ryan that "Immaculata was responsible for the polls" ("Mighty Macs Quotes"). Smith quoted Greenberg's comment about being a "Jewish guy" who "found inspiration" at a Catholic school in "Hoops Heritage," p. 10.

46. Robert Lipsyte, "Helping Others Before Helping Herself: The Mother of Modern Sport Now Champions Health and Youth Issues," *New York Times*, July 12, 1998, sec. P, p. 11.

47. BGM71, age 48, int. 7.30.98.

48. LGF78, age 41, int. 7.23.98. On West Chester coaches' activism for tournament play, see Hofmann, "Mighty Macs Still Mighty," p. W-4.

49. Randy Shantz, "Platoon System Works in Immaculata's Victory," *Daily Local News*, February 2, 1976, microfilm, "I.C. in print," roll 4, ICGLA. Smith quoted Theresa Shank Grentz '74 in "Hoops Heritage," p. 8.

50. JS, age 66, int. 8.25.99. Smith described Rush's practices and research in "Hoops Heritage," p. 8.

51. On the Maryland game, see Kathleen Maxa, "TV Network Fades Out on Immaculata Romp," *Washington Star-News*, February 27, 1975, microfilm, "I.C. in print," roll 11, ICGLA.

52. Bronson, "Women, Long Ignored"; Dave Hirshey, "Gals Have Their Day in Court—Weaving Baskets in Garden," *Daily News* (New York City), February 22, 1975, microfilm, "I.C. in print," roll 11, ICGLA. For Rush's exhortation to the team to play better, see Carol Towarnicky, "The Macs Are Treated Like One of the Boys," *Philadelphia Daily News*, January 27, 1975, microfilm, "I.C. in print," roll 11, ICGLA. The Madison Square Garden game was featured in Bronson, "Women, Long Ignored"; and Lena Williams, "11,969 Watch Immaculata Win Women's Basketball at Garden," *New York Times*, February 23, 1975, sec. 5, p. 1. Bella Azbug was an outspoken New York City female politician, born in 1920. Bill Verigan was among reporters who raised questions about proceeds paid respectively to the men's and women's teams; see his "For Women Cagers, Equal Play But Not Equal Pay," *Sunday News*, February 23, 1975, p. 89.

53. The Macs were honored in Robert W. Creamer, "Scorecard," *Sports Illustrated*, December 1975, microfilm, "I.C. in print," roll 4, ICGLA. Marie Liguori '77 was quoted in Boardman, "Like a Family," p. 23.

54. MS77, age 42, int. 10.16.97. The quotations from Jeanine Driscoll and Brian McGlinchey come from Wanda L. McGlinchey-Ryan, "Mighty Macs Quotes."

55. LGF78, age 41, int. 7.23.98. Sister Marian William relayed the story of two students worried about Immaculata becoming a "jock college" (MWH+44, age 74, int. 10.16.97).

56. Player, 1970s. Immaculata professor and former student Kathy Clark '70 said sisters were anguished at the school's inability to send the whole team (KC70, age 49, int. 6.10.98). Lorrie Gable Finelli '78 said the sisters drew back from the program (LGF78, age 41, int. 7.23.98) and that many were "cautious and unfamiliar" (LGF78, age 41, ques. 6, 5.15.98).

57. JYE74, age 45, ques. 21, 8.8.98, who also said, in int. 8.8.98, that players put schoolwork first; Sister Marian William Hoben, I.H.M., "Athletics and Academic Achievement," speech, Middle States Association meeting (undated, probably mideighties), p. 4, ICGLA.

58. LGF78, age 41, int. 7.23.98. Wanda McGlinchey-Ryan gave the figure for Cathy Rush's highest salary in "Mighty Mac Joy," which Rush confirmed (CR, age age 53, int. 8.20.02). Rush remarked to reporter Barniak that Immaculata received valuable exposure through basketball ("Immaculata Glitters," sec. 3, p. 3). On athletic department politics, I drew on my interview with Jenepher Shillingford (JS, age 66, int. 8.25.99).

59. LGF78, age 41, int. 7.23.98.

60. DVA78, age 42, int. 7.9.99; JYE74, age 45, int. 8.8.98.

61. Dolly VanBuskirk Anderson '78 said she got the "hairy eyeball" (DVA78, age 42, int. 7.9.99). Marianne Crawford Stanley '76 was listed as a Kodak All-American in Kip Wolfe, "Crawford Selected an All-American," *Today's Post*, March 25, 1975, microfilm, "I.C. in print," roll 11, ICGLA. On her delivery before the 1976 season, see Ann Killion, "Her Days in Court," *San Jose Mercury News West*, November 24, 1996, p. 19.

62. JS, age 69, int. 8.20.02; MLM+36, age 83, int. 6.30.98. For details of the events surrounding Marianne's pregnancy, including a fellow player who was "stunned," see Killion, "Her Days," p. 19. Immaculata professor and former student Kathy Clark '70 described some in the community as "shocked" (KC70, age 49, int. 6.10.98).

63. Cathy Rush provided more details on the pregnancy and its aftermath (CR, age 53, int. 8.20.02).

64. MLM+36, age 83, 6.30.98. Marianne told reporter Linda DiMeglio she felt "a little weak" at the beginning of the season for "Marianne Crawford Stanley: The Best," *Delaware County Daily Times*, November 21, 1975, microfilm, "I.C. in print," roll 11, ICGLA.

65. JYE74, age 45, int. 8.8.98.

66. Steve Cady, "It's a Long Way from Bloomers and Blushes," *New York Times*, March 25, 1973, microfilm, "I.C. in print," roll 11, ICGLA. For "Amazons," see Religious News Service, "Immaculata, Girls' College Team 'Rates' with the Celtics and Knicks," March 30, 1973, Office of Public Relations Office, Villa Maria Hall, Immaculata College, Pa. Theresa Shank Grentz '74 commented that reporters used to be "surprised we combed our hair" to Tom Cushman, "Women Don't Want to be Considered 'Different,'" *Philadelphia Daily News*, May 9, 1975, microfilm, "I.C. in print," roll 11, ICGLA.

67. Editors for the *Main Line Times* joked about early questions about dress styles in "The 'Mighty Macs,'" editorial, *Main Line Times* (Ardmore, Pa.), March 28, 1974. Dick Weiss reported Rush's caustic replies to the question of whether male reporters could enter her team's locker room: "Don't 'Rush' that Locker-Room," *Philadelphia Daily News*, January 25, 1975. Both on microfilm, "I.C. in print," roll 11, ICGLA.

68. Mary Scharff '77 said the Immaculata championship teams were "pioneers" (MS77, age 42, int. 10.16.97). Marianne Crawford '76, quoted in Boardman, "Like a Family," said she was not the "women's lib-type" (p. 23). Theresa Shank Grentz '75 said she

and teammates "set our hair" in Herm Rogul, "People in Sports," *Evening Bulletin*, no date legible, microfilm, "I.C. in print," roll 11, ICGLA.

69. JS, age 66, int. 8.25.99. On Rush's early desire to be a boy, as well as the portable crib, see Maralyn Lois Polak, "Six Stormy Years That Made History in Girls' Basketball," *Philadelphia Inquirer Magazine*, April 25, 1976, p. 10. Rush said basketball came second to her family in Alan Pergament, "Women's Sports Advances Don't Help Top Cage Coach," *Buffalo Evening News*, October 11, 1974, microfilm, "I.C. in print," roll 11, ICGLA.

70. The headlines quoted are for "Immaculata's Formula: Defense and Diapers," *Philadelphia Inquirer*, April 1, 1973; and Larry Dill, "Great Expectations: Pregnant Coach Leads Team to Championship," *Twin Circle* (city unidentified), September 20, 1974, p. 6, both on microfilm, "I.C. in print," roll 11, ICGLA. For one of many media comparisons with Wooden, see Skip Myslenski, "What Could UCLA Offer That Cathy Doesn't Have?" *Philadelphia Inquirer*, February 23, 1975, microfilm, "I.C. in print," roll 11, ICGLA. On Rush's NBA-ref husband, see "Immaculata's Formula," in which Rush is initially described as "a 25-year-old housewife whose husband Ed is an NBA ref." Gene Gomolka, "'Knock It Off, Libbers!' Pleads Cathy Rush," *Delaware County Daily Times*, April 11, 1974, microfilm, "I.C. in print," roll 11, ICGLA.

71. Boardman, "Like a Family," p. 23.

72. Kip Wolfe reported the "ugly" comment in "Wayland Insults Fired Macs' 'Ugly' Temper," *Today's Spirit* (Hatboro, Pa.), March 21, 1975. Myslenski reported tension and interaction between Wayland and Immaculata in "The Immaculata Mystique," pp. 25–26. The makeover is discussed in Elaine Tait, "The Uglies Become the Swans," *Philadelphia Inquirer*, April 6, 1975. For one example of dozens of reprints, see Associated Press, "Immaculata Cage Uglies Dolled Up for Victory," *Times-Advocate* (Escondito, Ca.), April 7, 1975. All on microfilm, "I.C. in print," roll 11, ICGLA.

73. DVA78, age 42, int. 7.9.99. Theresa Shank Grentz '74 was quoted in Jean Lindquist, "Theresa Shank Plays Basketball Just 'Like One of the Boys,'" *Today's Post*, October 3, 1973, p. 15. Marianne Crawford Stanley '76 was quoted in the *Washington Post*, "Top U.S. Woman Cager Got Early Basketball Savvy," reprinted in *Telegram* (Elmira, N.Y.), January 26, 1975, microfilm, "I.C. in print," roll 11, ICGLA. Boardman quoted Marie Liguori '77 in "Like a Family," p. 23.

74. The *Main Line Times* editors compared Gloria Steinem's and the Macs' accomplishments in "The 'Mighty Macs,'" *Main Line Times* (Ardmore, Pa.), March 28, 1974, microfilm, "I.C. in print," roll 11, ICGLA.

Postscript: Immaculata Basketball and U.S. Religious History

1. With money, the women's game occasionally struggled with the same issues of regulation and recruitment, academic qualification and student accountability, as the men's game. But these problems went with the territory. Less expected was the decrease in percentages of women working in NCAA basketball after Title IX. A study by R. Vivian Acosta and Linda Jean Carpenter indicates that in 1972 more than 90 percent of women's college programs were headed by female administrators, whereas in 1998 only 19 percent were led by women. Also in 1972 more than 90 percent of women's programs were coached by women, but in 1998 less than half of women's teams had female coaches (R.

Vivian Acosta and Linda Jean Carpenter, "Women in Intercollegiate Sport: A Longitudinal Study—Twenty-One Year Update, 1977–1998," [Brooklyn, N.Y.: Department of Physical Education and Exercise Science, 1998]). On the NCAA in general, see Arthur A. Fleisher, *The National Collegiate Athletic Association: A Study in Cartel Behavior* (Chicago: University of Chicago Press, 1992).

2. In recent years, television networks covering the NCAA Women's Final Four have broadcast half-time features about the Mighty Macs, and media articles on the history of the women's game often mention Immaculata. The Naismith Basketball Hall of Fame in Springfield, Massachusetts, honors the team, and Cathy Rush and several team members have been inducted into the Women's Basketball Hall of Fame in Knoxville, Tennessee. During the 2000 NCAA Women's Final Four in Philadelphia, the First Union Center lobby featured an extensive display on the Mighty Macs' contribution to the women's game.

3. Robin D. G. Kelley, *Race Rebels: Culture, Politics, and the Black Working Class* (New York: Free/Macmillan, 1994), p. 1.

4. MLM+36, age 83, int. 6.30.98.

5. DCC55, age 65, int. 6.26.98. A player from the class of '57 remembered the future captain as a "tiny thing" (Player '57, age 62, int. 6.11.98).

6. SFO72, age 48, ques. 20, 6.24.98.

REFERENCES

Anderson, Benedict. *Imagined Communities: Reflections on the Origin and Spread of Nationalism.* London: Verso, 1991.

Axthelm, Pete. *The City Game: Basketball in New York from the World Champion Knicks to the World of the Playgrounds.* New York: Harper's Magazine Press, 1970.

Bell, Catherine. *Ritual Theory, Ritual Practice.* New York: Oxford University Press, 1992.

Beran, Janice A. *From Six-on-Six to Full-Court Press: A Century of Iowa Girls' Basketball.* Ames: Iowa State University Press, 1993.

Birrell, Susan and Cheryl L. Cole, eds. *Women, Sport, and Culture.* Champaign, Ill.: Human Kinetics, 1994.

Bishop, Elva and Katherine Fulton. "Shooting Stars: The Heyday of Industrial Women's Basketball." *Southern Exposure* 7, no. 3 (1979): 50–56.

Brown, Karen McCarthy. *Mama Lola: A Voudou Priestess in Brooklyn.* Berkeley: University of California Press, 1991.

Bourdieu, Pierre. *The Logic of Practice.* Trans. Richard Nice. Stanford: Stanford University Press, 1990.

Butler, Judith. *The Psychic Life of Power: Theories in Subjection.* Stanford: Stanford University Press, 1997.

Byrne, Donald E., Jr. "Folklore and the Study of American Religion." In *Encyclopedia of the American Religious Experience: Studies of Traditions and Movements,* ed. Charles H. Lippy and Peter W. Williams, 1:85–100. New York: Scribner's, 1988.

Cahn, Susan K. *Coming on Strong: Gender and Sexuality in Twentieth-Century Women's Sport.* New York: Free/Macmillan, 1994.

Caplan, Caren. *Questions of Travel: Postmodern Discourses of Displacement.* Durham: Duke University Press, 1996.

Clark, Dennis. *The Irish in Philadelphia: Ten Generations of Urban Experience.* Philadelphia: Temple University Press, 1973.

Clifford, James. *Routes: Travel and Translation in the Late Twentieth Century*. Cambridge: Harvard University Press, 1997.

Coakley, Mary Lewis. *Our Child—God's Child*. Milwaukee: Bruce, 1953.

Cohalan, Florence D. *A Popular History of the Archdiocese of New York*. Yonkers, N.Y.: United States Catholic Historical Society, 1983.

Comaroff, Jean and John Comaroff. *Of Revelation and Revolution: Christianity, Colonialism, and Consciousness in South Africa*. Vol. 1. Chicago: University of Chicago Press, 1991.

Connelly, James F., ed. *The History of the Archdiocese of Philadelphia*. Wynnewood, Pa.: Unigraphics Incorporated, 1976.

Deleuze, Gilles and Félix Guattari. *Anti-Oedipus: Capitalism and Schizophrenia*. Trans. Robert Hurley, Mark Seem, and Helen R. Lane. Minneapolis: University of Minnesota Press, 1983.

——. *A Thousand Plateaus: Capitalism and Schizophrenia*. Trans. Brian Massumi. Minneapolis: University of Minnesota Press, 1987.

Dolan, Jay P. *The American Catholic Experience: A History from Colonial Times to the Present*. Notre Dame, Ind.: University of Notre Dame Press, 1992.

Donaghy, Thomas J., F.S.C. *Philadelphia's Finest: A History of Education in the Catholic Archdiocese, 1692–1970*. Philadelphia: American Catholic Historical Society, 1972.

Eade, John and Michael E. Sallnow, eds. *Contesting the Sacred: The Anthropology of Christian Pilgrimage*. London: Routledge, 1991.

Faherty, William B., S.J. *The Destiny of Modern Woman, in the Light of Papal Teaching*. Westminster, Md.: Newman, 1950.

Ferraro, Thomas J., ed. *Catholic Lives, Contemporary America*. Durham: Duke University Press, 1997.

Fields, Karen E. *Revival and Rebellion in Colonial Central Africa*. Princeton: Princeton University Press, 1985.

Fleisher, Arthur A. *The National Collegiate Athletic Association: A Study in Cartel Behavior*. Chicago: University of Chicago Press, 1992.

Foucault, Michel. *Discipline and Punish: The Birth of the Prison*. Trans. Alan Sheridan. New York: Vintage/Random House, 1979.

Fr. McGuire's The New Baltimore Catechism and Mass. New York: Benziger Brothers, 1941.

Franchot, Jenny. "Invisible Domain: Religion and American Literary Studies." *American Literature* 67, no. 4 (December 1995): 833–42.

Fullam, Raymond B., S.J., ed. *The Popes on Youth: Principles for Forming and Guiding Youth from Popes Leo XIII to Pius XII*. Buffalo: Canisius High School, 1956.

Gems, Gerald R. "Sport, Religion and Americanization: Bishop Sheil and the Catholic Youth Organization." *International Journal of the History of Sport* 10, no. 2 (1993): 233–41.

Gleason, Philip. *Contending with Modernity: Catholic Higher Education in the Twentieth Century*. New York: Oxford University Press, 1995.

Gorn, Elliot J. and Warren Goldstein. *A Brief History of American Sports*. New York: Hill and Wang, 1993.

Greeley, Andrew M. *The Catholic Myth: The Behaviors and Beliefs of American Catholics*. New York: Collier/Macmillan, 1990.

Grundy, Pamela. "Bloomers and Beyond: North Carolina Women's Basketball Uniforms, 1901–1997." *Southern Cultures* 3, no. 3 (1997): 52–67.

——. "From Amazons to Glamazons: The Rise and Fall of North Carolina Women's Basketball, 1920–1960." *Journal of American History* 87, no. 1 (June 2000): 112–46.

Guha, Ranajit. *Elementary Aspects of Peasant Insurgence in Colonial India.* Delhi: Oxford University Press, 1983.

Hall, David D., ed. *Lived Religion in America: Toward a History of Practice.* Princeton: Princeton University Press, 1997.

Halsey, William. *The Survival of Innocence: Catholicism in an Era of Disillusionment, 1920–1940.* Notre Dame, Ind.: University of Notre Dame Press, 1980.

Hardiman, David. *Feeding the Baniya: Peasants and Usurers in Western India.* Delhi: Oxford University Press, 1996.

Harris, Peter, Adrian Hastings, et al. *On Human Life: An Examination of* Humanae vitae. London: Burns and Oates, 1968.

Hebdige, Dick. *Subculture: The Meaning of Style.* London: Methuen, 1979.

Higgenbotham, Evelyn Brooks. *Righteous Discontent: The Women's Movement in the Black Baptist Church, 1880–1920.* Cambridge: Harvard University Press, 1993.

Hobsbawm, Eric and Terence Ranger, eds. *The Invention of Tradition.* Cambridge: Cambridge University Press, 1983.

Hunter, Tera. *To 'Joy My Freedom: Southern Black Women's Lives and Labors After the Civil War.* Cambridge: Harvard University Press, 1997.

Hult, Joan S. and Marianna Trekell, eds. *A Century of Women's Basketball: From Frailty to Final Four.* Reston, Va.: National Association for Girls and Women in Sport, 1991.

Ignatiev, Noel. *How the Irish Became White.* New York: Routledge, 1995.

Jacobsen, Matthew Frye. *Whiteness of a Different Color: European Immigrants and the Alchemy of Race.* Cambridge: Harvard University Press, 1998.

James, C. L. R. *Beyond a Boundary.* Durham: Duke University Press, 1993.

Kane, Paula M. *Separatism and Subculture: Boston Catholicism, 1900–1920.* Chapel Hill: University of North Carolina Press, 1994.

Kaplan, Janice. *Women and Sports.* New York: Viking, 1979.

Kelley, Robin D. G. *Race Rebels: Culture, Politics, and the Black Working Class.* New York: Free/Macmillan, 1994.

Kelly, George A. *The Catholic Youth's Guide to Life and Love.* New York: Random House, 1960.

Kempf, Reverend Joseph G. *Helping Youth to Grow.* Milwaukee: Bruce, 1941.

Lancaster, Roger N. *Thanks to God and the Revolution: Popular Religion and Class Consciousness in the New Nicaragua.* New York: Columbia University Press, 1988.

Lannin, Joanne. *A History of Basketball for Girls and Women.* Minneapolis: Lerner, 2000.

Lasance, Reverend F. X., ed. *The Catholic Girl's Guide: Counsels and Devotions.* New York: Benziger Brothers, 1906.

——, ed. *The Young Man's Guide: Counsels, Reflections, and Prayers for Catholic Young Men.* New York: Benziger Brothers, 1952.

Lefebvre, Henri. *The Production of Space.* Trans. Donald Nicholson-Smith. Oxford: Blackwell, 1991.

Leviatin, David. "The Evolution and Commodification of Black Basketball Styles." *Radical History Review* 55 (winter 1993): 154–64.

Light, Dale B. *Rome and the New Republic: Conflict and Community in Philadelphia Catholicism Between the Revolution and the Civil War.* Notre Dame, Ind.: University of Notre Dame Press, 1996.

Lord, Robert H., John E. Sexton, and Edward T. Harrington. *History of the Archdiocese of Boston in the Various Stages of Its Development, 1604–1943.* Vol. 3. Boston: Pilot Publishing, 1945.

McDannell, Colleen. *Material Christianity: Religion and Popular Culture in America.* New Haven: Yale University Press, 1995.

McGreevy, John T. *Parish Boundaries: The Catholic Encounter with Race in the Twentieth-Century Urban North.* Chicago: University of Chicago Press, 1996.

——. "Thinking on One's Own: Catholicism in the American Intellectual Imagination." *Journal of American History* 84, no. 1 (June 1997): 97–131.

Mast, Gerald, Marshall Cohen, and Leo Braudy, eds. *Film Theory and Criticism: Introductory Readings.* 4th ed. New York: Oxford University Press, 1992.

May, Lary, ed. *Recasting America: Culture and Politics in the Age of Cold War.* Chicago: University of Chicago Press, 1989.

Morgan, Susan. *Place Matters: Gendered Geography in Victorian Women's Travel Books About Southeast Asia.* New Brunswick, N.J.: Rutgers University Press, 1996.

Morris, Charles. *American Catholic: The Saints and Sinners Who Built America's Most Powerful Church.* New York: New York Times Books/Random House, 1997.

Morrison, Toni. *Playing in the Dark: Whiteness and the American Literary Imagination.* New York: Vintage, 1992.

Nadler, Sylvia Faye. "A Developmental History of the Wayland Hutcherson Flying Queens from 1910–1979." Ph.D. diss., East Texas State University, 1980.

Orsi, Robert A. *The Madonna of 115th Street: Faith and Community in Italian Harlem, 1880–1950.* New Haven: Yale University Press, 1985.

——. " 'Mildred, Is It Fun to Be a Cripple?' The Culture of Suffering in Mid-Twentieth-Century American Catholicism." *South Atlantic Quarterly* 93, no. 3 (summer 1994): 547–90.

——. *Thank You, St. Jude: Women's Devotion to the Patron Saint of Hopeless Causes.* New Haven: Yale University Press, 1996.

Painter, Nell Irvin. *Sojourner Truth: A Life, a Symbol.* New York: Norton, 1996.

Pius XI, Pope. *Four Great Encyclicals: Labor, Education, Marriage, the Social Order.* New York: Paulist, 1931.

Pius XII, Pope. *Dear Newlyweds: Pope Pius XII Speaks to Young Couples.* Sel. and trans. James F. Murray Jr. and Bianca M. Murray. New York: Farrar, Straus, and Cudahy, 1961.

——. *The Pope Speaks: The Teachings of Pius XII.* Ed. Michael Chinigo. New York: Pantheon, 1957.

Pratt, Mary Louise. *Imperial Eyes: Travel Writing and Transculturation.* London: Routledge, 1992.

Price, Richard. *Alabi's World.* Baltimore: Johns Hopkins University Press, 1990.

Raboteau, Albert J. *Slave Religion: The "Invisible Institution" in the Antebellum South.* Oxford: Oxford University Press, 1978.

Reiss, Steven A. *City Games: The Evolution of American Urban Society and the Rise of Sports*. Urbana: University of Illinois Press, 1989.

Roediger, David. *The Wages of Whiteness: Race and the Making of the American Working Class*. London: Verso, 1991.

Ryan, Francis J. "Monsignor John Bonner and Progressive Education in the Archdiocese of Philadelphia, 1925–1945." *Records of the American Catholic Historical Society of Philadelphia* 102, nos. 1–2 (spring 1991): 17–43.

Said, Edward W. *Orientalism*. New York: Vintage, 1979.

Schrodt, Barbara. "Vancouver's Dynastic Domination of Canadian Senior Women's Basketball, 1942–1967." *Canadian Journal of History of Sport* 26, no. 2 (1995): 19–32.

Scott, James C. *Domination and the Arts of Resistance: Hidden Transcripts*. New Haven: Yale University Press, 1990.

Sisters, Servants of the Immaculate Heart of Mary. *Faithful Witness: Constitutions*. Philadelphia: Sisters, Servants of the Immaculate Heart of Mary, 1997.

Smith, Jonathan Z. *To Take Place: Toward Theory in Ritual*. Chicago: University of Chicago Press, 1987.

Southern, David W. *John LaFarge and the Limits of Catholic Interracialism, 1911–1963*. Baton Rouge: Louisiana State University Press, 1996.

Tentler, Leslie Woodcock. "On the Margins: The State of American Catholic History." *American Quarterly* 45, no. 1 (March 1993): 104–27.

Thomas, John L., S.J. *The Catholic Viewpoint on Marriage and the Family*. Garden City, N.Y.: Hanover House, 1958.

Tuan, Yi-fu. *Space and Place: The Perspective of Experience*. Minneapolis: University of Minnesota Press, 1977.

Turner, Victor W. *The Ritual Process: Structure and Anti-Structure*. Chicago: Aldine, 1969.

Tweed, Thomas A. *Our Lady of the Exile: Diasporic Religion at a Cuban Catholic Shrine in Miami*. New York: Oxford, 1997.

———, ed. *Retelling U.S. Religious History*. Berkeley: University of California Press, 1997.

Welch, Paula D. and Harold A. Lerch. *History of American Physical Education and Sport*. Springfield, Ill.: C. C. Thomas, 1981.

Wideman, John Edgar. *Hoop Roots: Love, Race, and Basketball*. Boston: Houghton Mifflin, 2001.

Yzermans, Vincent A., ed. *Pope Pius XII and Catholic Education*. St. Meinrad, Ind.: Grail, 1957.

INDEX

of, 84–85; intercession for basketball, 124–25; Mary of the Miraculous Medal, 116, 125, 128, 254n.6, 256n.21

Wall Street Journal, 195
Walsh, Francis (Father), 154
Walsh, Rosemary McNichol, 100, 106, 243n.33
Washington Mystics, 40
Washington State, 165
Watson, Ross, Jr., 189, 190
Wayland Baptist College, 25
Wayland Baptist Flying Queens, 25, 165, 204, 252n.75
WCOJ, 126, 192
Weese, Dean, 204
Weiss, Dick, 264n.66
West Catholic high school, 18–19
West Chester State University, 21, 22, 94, 161, 162, 163, 194, 262n.46; national championships and, 174, 181, 183, 194–95
white liberals, 168
Wideman, John Edgar, 77
William Penn College, 183

WMAL-Channel 7, 195
WNBA (Women's National Basketball Association), 40
women, as fans, 49–51
Women's Basketball Hall of Fame, 272n.2
Women's Basketball League, 254n.83
women's liberation, 177, 193, 201–5
Women's National Basketball Association (WNBA), 40
women's rules, 18–19, 21–22, 25, 47, 53, 81–82, 91, 99–101, 230–31n.36, 250nn.58, 60
Wooden, John, 203
Woodward, Elisabeth. *See* Woodward, Sister M. Charles Edward
Woodward, Sister M. Charles Edward, 98, 131, 132, 154
World Games, 150
World War II, 45, 51, 60, 245n.14

YMCA (Young Men's Christian Association), 16, 151
Young Man's Guide, The, 84
youth manuals, 84

DATE DUE

GAYLORD   #3523PI   Printed in USA